International Political Economy Series

Series Editor
Timothy M. Shaw
Visiting Professor
University of Massachusetts Boston
Boston, MA, USA

Emeritus Professor
University of London
London, UK

The global political economy is in flux as a series of cumulative crises impacts its organization and governance. The IPE series has tracked its development in both analysis and structure over the last three decades. It has always had a concentration on the global South. Now the South increasingly challenges the North as the centre of development, also reflected in a growing number of submissions and publications on indebted Eurozone economies in Southern Europe. An indispensable resource for scholars and researchers, the series examines a variety of capitalisms and connections by focusing on emerging economies, companies and sectors, debates and policies. It informs diverse policy communities as the established trans-Atlantic North declines and 'the rest', especially the BRICS, rise.

More information about this series at
http://www.palgrave.com/gp/series/13996

Emel Parlar Dal
Editor

Turkey's Political Economy in the 21st Century

palgrave
macmillan

Editor
Emel Parlar Dal
Faculty of Political Science
Marmara University
Istanbul, Turkey

ISSN 2662-2483   ISSN 2662-2491   (electronic)
International Political Economy Series
ISBN 978-3-030-27631-7   ISBN 978-3-030-27632-4   (eBook)
https://doi.org/10.1007/978-3-030-27632-4

© The Editor(s) (if applicable) and The Author(s) 2020
This work is subject to copyright. All rights are solely and exclusively licensed by the Publisher, whether the whole or part of the material is concerned, specifically the rights of translation, reprinting, reuse of illustrations, recitation, broadcasting, reproduction on microfilms or in any other physical way, and transmission or information storage and retrieval, electronic adaptation, computer software, or by similar or dissimilar methodology now known or hereafter developed.
The use of general descriptive names, registered names, trademarks, service marks, etc. in this publication does not imply, even in the absence of a specific statement, that such names are exempt from the relevant protective laws and regulations and therefore free for general use.
The publisher, the authors and the editors are safe to assume that the advice and information in this book are believed to be true and accurate at the date of publication. Neither the publisher nor the authors or the editors give a warranty, expressed or implied, with respect to the material contained herein or for any errors or omissions that may have been made. The publisher remains neutral with regard to jurisdictional claims in published maps and institutional affiliations.

Cover credit: © Rob Friedman/iStockphoto.com

This Palgrave Macmillan imprint is published by the registered company Springer Nature Switzerland AG
The registered company address is: Gewerbestrasse 11, 6330 Cham, Switzerland

I would like to dedicate this edited volume to my husband, Prof. Burçkin Dal and my two kids Berkin and Dilara…

ACKNOWLEDGEMENTS

The author would like to thank Samiratou Dipama, Nilay Tuysuz, Ahmet Tuzgen and Hakan Mehmetcik for their technical help.

CONTENTS

1 The Changing Landscape and Dynamics of Turkey's
Political Economy in the Twenty-First Century:
An Introduction   1
Emel Parlar Dal

Part I Domestic Diversification of Turkey's
Political Economy

2 The Political Economy of Turkey's Economic
Miracles and Crisis   31
Turan Subasat

3 Income Inequality in Turkey: 2003–2015   63
Alpay Filiztekin

4 Turkish Labor Market: Complex Dynamics
and Challenges   85
Seyfettin Gürsel, Gökçe Uysal and Tuba Toru Delibaşı

5 Syrian Entrepreneurs in Turkey: Emerging
Economic Actors and Agents of Social Cohesion   115
Omar Kadkoy

X CONTENTS

Part II   Instrumental Diversification of Turkey's Political Economy

6   **The Political Economy of Turkish Foreign Aid**   133
Abdurrahman Korkmaz and Hüseyin Zengin

7   **Emerging Middle Powers (MIKTA) in Global Political Economy: Preferences, Capabilities, and Their Limitations**   163
Gonca Oğuz Gök and Radiye Funda Karadeniz

8   **The Determinants of Turkish Foreign Aid: An Empirical Analysis**   195
Hakan Mehmetcik and Sercan Pekel

Part III   Geographical Diversification of Turkey's Political Economy

9   **The Political Economy of Turkey's Integration into the MENA Economy**   217
Imad El-Anis

10   **Assessing the Turkish "Trading State" in Sub-Saharan Africa**   239
Emel Parlar Dal and Samiratou Dipama

11   **The Political Economy of Turkey's Relations with the Asia-Pacific**   271
Altay Atlı

Index   297

Notes on Contributors

Altay Atlı is a lecturer at the Department of International Relations, Koç University, and a partner at Reanda Turkey, a member firm of Reanda International, which is one of the twenty largest business advisory networks in the world. His areas of study include international political economy, Asian comparative political economy and Asian international relations, the economics of Turkey's foreign policy and Turkey's relations with Asia. Having graduated from the German High School in Istanbul, Dr. Atlı obtained a B.A. degree in Economics from Boğaziçi University in Istanbul, Turkey, a M.A. degree in International Business from Deakin University in Melbourne, Australia, and a Ph.D. degree in Political Sciences and International Relations from Boğaziçi University. He was affiliated with Boğaziçi University's Asian Studies Center as well as Sabancı University Istanbul Policy Center, and Shanghai University's Center for Global Studies. Dr. Atlı also worked as research coordinator at Turkey's Foreign Economic Relations Board (DEİK), is an expert member at the China Network of Turkish Industry and Business Association (TÜSİAD), and a columnist at the Hong Kong-based international news and opinion portal Asia Times. Dr. Atlı regularly appears on programs in channels like Bloomberg, BBC World, Turkish Radio Television (TRT), TvNet, CCTV, CGTN, Channel News Asia, China Radio International, commenting on developments in the global economy and Turkey's relations with Asian countries, and more information about his work can be found in his personal Web site www.altayatli.com.

Samiratou Dipama holds a Ph.D. in EU Politics and International Relations from the European Union Institute of Marmara University. She published various articles on Political Conditionality, Democracy Promotion and Development Aid in *Indexed* journals and edited books.

Dr. Imad El-Anis is Senior Lecturer in International Relations at Nottingham Trent University, UK. He holds a B.A. (Hons.) in International Relations, an M.A. in International Political Economy, and a Ph.D. in International Political Economy. Dr. El-Anis has authored several books, including *Jordan and the United States: The Political Economy of Trade and Economic Reform in the Middle East* (2011), *A New A–Z of International Relations Theory* (2015), and *International Political Economy in the 21st Century: Contemporary Issues and Analyses* (2017). He has also authored several articles on various aspects of the political economy of the Middle East and North Africa, including work on economic integration and political cooperation, freshwater scarcity, energy security and nuclear energy proliferation.

Alpay Filiztekin is a professor of economics at Sabanci University, Istanbul, Turkey. He received his B.A. degree in economics from Bogazici University, Istanbul, Turkey, in 1989 and earned his Ph.D. also in economics from Boston College, Massachusetts, USA, in 1994. He worked as an assistant professor at Koc University, Istanbul, between 1994 and 2000 and then joined Sabanci University where he has been awarded full professorship in 2011 and served as Vice Dean of Faculty of Arts and Sciences between 2013 and 2016. He spent three years between 2016 and 2019 as a professor of economics and as the Dean of Business Faculty at Özyeğin University. His research interest is mostly in empirical studies of within and between regional disparities in economic development, labor market frictions, returns to education. His recent interest is on inequalities in Turkey. He has also conducted research about price dynamics and productivity. He has published several articles in scholarly journals and co-edited a book on *Turkish Economy*.

Seyfettin Gürsel Professor of Economics, Bahcesehir University. After completing his undergraduate studies in economics and political sciences, Professor Gürsel obtained his Ph.D. in economics at the University of Nanterre (Paris X). He started his academic carrier in The Faculty of Economics, University of Istanbul in 1980, he resigned in 1983 and became editor in chief of the Encyclopedia of Turkish Republic, published by İletişim Editions. Then he held multiple managerial positions in the private sector. He returned to academic career in 1994 in Galatasaray University (Istanbul) where he was also the Head of the Economics department from 1996 to 2007. After joining Bahcesehir University (Istanbul) in 2007, he founded a research center. Since 2008, he is the director of the Center for Economic and Social Research of the University of Bahcesehir. Professor Gürsel published books, articles and research in Turkish economic history (in particular "L'empire ottoman face au capitalisme", Harmattan), in labor economics, Turkish economy and electoral systems.

Omar Kadkoy is a policy analyst at the Economic Policy Research Foundation of Turkey (TEPAV). He works on migration, especially on the socioeconomic dynamics of the forcibly displaced populations. His research focuses on the labor market integration of Syrian refugees in Turkey, Syrian entrepreneurship in Turkey as well as the Turkish policy framework regarding refugees and the evaluation of subsequent legal adjustments.

Radiye Funda Karadeniz is assistant professor of International Relations at Gaziantep University, İslahiye Faculty of Economics and Administrative Sciences. After graduating from Marmara University Political Science and International Relations Department in 2003, she received her M.A. degree in International Politics from Warwick University in the UK as a scholar of Turkish Education Foundation— TEV and Chevening Scholarship of British Council. She received her Ph.D. from Marmara University, Social Sciences Institute with the thesis titled *'Outside Turks' in Turkish Foreign Policy: A Comparative Theoretical Analysis* in 2011 which has been awarded honorable mention for Ph.D. Dissertation Category of 2015 Young Social Scientist Awards by Turkish Social Sciences Association. In 2007, she was a Fulbright Scholar of Study of US Institutes. Her research area and published works focus on Turkish Foreign Policy, 'Outside Turks' and Turkish-American Relations.

Abdurrahman Korkmaz is an associate professor of economics at İzmir Kâtıp Çelebi University. He received a Ph.D. degree in Economics from Karadeniz Technical University. His main research interests are the propagation of financial crises and the open economy macroeconomics.

Hakan Mehmetcik is an assistant professor at the Department of International Relations, Marmara University, Turkey. He has two master

xiv   NOTES ON CONTRIBUTORS

degrees in Economics and Eurasian Studies from Dalarna and Uppsala Universities in Sweden respectively. He finished his Ph.D. in 2017 in International Relations from Yildiz Technical University in Turkey and his research interests lie in the area of International Political Economy, Regionalism, Globalization and broader international relations. He has several major publications on *Middle Powers, Rising Powers*, and *Turkish Foreign Policy*. His recent article has appeared in *International Politics* and *Third World Quarterly*. He teaches several thematic and theoretical courses including "Globalization and Regionalism," "Theories of International Relations," "Theories of International Political Economy and Coercive Diplomacy."

Gonca Oğuz Gök is associate professor of International Relations at Marmara University, Faculty of Political Science. Her research focuses on International Politics, Global governance, the UN and Turkish Foreign Policy. She has various publications on these topics. Her most recent book chapter is Oğuz Gök, Gonca and Radiye Funda Karadeniz (2018) *Analyzing 'I' in MIKTA: Turkey's Changing Middle Power Role in the United Nations* in Emel Parlar DAL (eds.) *Middle Powers in Global Governance*, Palgrave Macmillan.

Emel Parlar Dal is associate professor at Marmara University's Department of International Relations. She received her B.A. from Galatasaray University in 2001, her M.A. degrees respectively from Paris 1 Panthéon-Sorbonne University (2002) and Paris 3 Nouvelle Sorbonne Universities (2003). She received her Ph.D. degree on International Relations from Paris 3 Sorbonne Nouvelle University (2009). She conducted research at the Graduate Institute of International and Development Studies in Geneva during the 2010–2011 academic year thanks to Swiss Government scholarship. In 2013, she was an academic visitor at St. Anthony's College Middle East Centre, Oxford University. During 2015–2016, she worked as the coordinator of a TUBITAK-SOBAG research project on the contribution of Turkey and the BRICS to global governance. Her recent publications have appeared in *Third World Quarterly* (SSCI), *Global Policy* (SSCI), *Contemporary Politics, International Politics* (SSCI), *Turkish Studies* (SSCI), *International Journal: Canada's Journal of Global Policy Analysis* (SSCI), and *Perceptions*. Her most recent works are *Middle Powers in Global Governance: The Rise of Turkey* (ed.), Palgrave, 2018; Rising powers in international conflict management, Special Issue (guest editor), Third World Quarterly, 2019 and *Status Competition and Rising Powers, Special Issue* (guest editor), *Contemporary Politics*, 2019, *Russia in the Changing International System* (ed. With Emre Erşen), Palgrave, 2019.

Sercan Pekel is a Ph.D. candidate in Marmara University International Relations Program and works as a research assistant in the same department. His main research interests are Forecasting Conflict/Cooperation, Quantitative Analysis in International Relations as well as European Union and its Security/Defence Policies on which he completed his M.A. thesis.

Turan Subasat is a professor at the University of Mugla. He received his B.Sc. from the University of Istanbul, his M.Sc. (Birkbeck College) and Ph.D. (SOAS) from the University of London, UK. He previously taught development studies at the University of London (SOAS), economics at the University of Bath, UK and economics at the Izmir University of Economics, Turkey. His research focuses on development, international and political economics. He has published in political economy journals including the *Review of Radical Political Economics* and *Journal of Balkan and Eastern Studies*. He edited a book titled *The Great Financial Meltdown: Systemic, Conjunctural or Policy-Created?* published by the Edward Elgar in 2016.

Tuba Toru Delibaşı received her B.Sc. degree in Economics from Middle East Technical University in 2004. She obtained a M.Sc. degree in Mathematical Economics and Econometrics, and M.Phil. degree in Quantitative Economics from Toulouse School of Economics (TSE), in 2006 and 2007, respectively. She has received her Ph.D. degree in Economics with highest distinction from Ecole des Hautes Etudes en Sciences Sociales and Toulouse School of Economics in 2013. She has been a researcher at the European Organisation for the Safety of Air Navigation and the French National Civil Aviation University from 2007 to 2011. In 2011, she worked as a junior lecturer at Toulouse 1 Capitole University. She has been a Ph.D. researcher at the University of Bristol in 2012. Since 2013, she is an assistant professor in the Department of Economics. Dr. Tuba Toru Delibaşı has worked on the industrial organization of aviation industry during her graduate studies. Her research interests are main topics in industrial economics, in particular, transportation economics, two-sided markets, aviation industry, competition and structural modeling.

Gökçe Uysal is currently an associate professor of economics at Bahcesehir University and the deputy director at Bahcesehir University Center for Economic and Social Research (Betam). She received her B.A. from Galatasaray University and her M.A. and Ph.D. from University of Rochester in 2006. She works on labor markets, economics of gender, economics of education and household savings. Her articles have appeared in *Journal of Economic Growth, Social Indicators Research* and the *International Journal of Educational Development.*

Hüseyin Zengin is a Ph.D. student in Political Science Department at the University of Pittsburgh, with research interests in emerging powers, foreign aid, and authoritarianism. His recent articles have been published in *Social Science Information* and *New Perspectives on Turkey.*

ABBREVIATIONS

AFAD	Disaster and Emergency Management Authority
AKP	Justice and Development Party, Adalet ve Kalkınma Partisi
ASEAN	Association of Southeast Asian Nations
BIST	Stock Market Istanbul
BJC	Beijing Consensus
BRI	Belt and Road Initiative
BRIC	Brazil, Russia, India, China
BRICS	Brasil, Russia, India, China, South Africa
BRSA	Banking Regulation and Supervision Agency
CAD	Current Account Deficit
CBRT	Central Bank of the Republic of Turkey
CELAC	Community of Latin American and Caribbean States
CMEC	China Machinery Engineering Corporation Council of Turkey
CPMIEC	China Precision Machinery Export-Import Corporation
CSO	Civilian Society Organisation
DAC	Development Assistance Committee
DEIK	Foreign Economic Relations Board
DFS	Daily Food Supply
DGMM	Directorate General of Migration Management
DMA	Defense and Military Agreements
EAC	East African Community
EBRD	European Bank for Reconstruction and Development
ECB	European Central Bank
ECOWAS	Economic Community of West African States
EIB	European Investment Bank
EIF	European Investment Fund

xviii   ABBREVIATIONS

EOT	Existence of Office
EU	European Union
EXP	The Level of Export
FDI	Foreign Direct Investment
FED	Federal Reserve Bank of the USA
FETO	Fethullahist Terrorist Organisation
FTA	Free Trade Agreement
G20	A Group of Finance Ministers and Central Bank Governors from 20 Economies
G7	Group of Seven (Germany, USA, UK, France, Italy, Japan, Canada)
GATT	General Agreement on Tariffs and Trade
GCC	Gulf Cooperation Country
GDP	Gross Domestic Product
GESF	Global Expenditure Support Fund
GMM	Generalized Method of Moments
GNI	Gross National Income
HBES	Household Budget and Expenditure Surveys
HDI	High-Pressure Direct İnjection
IGAD	Intergovernmental Authority on Development Partners Forum
IHH	The Foundation for Human Rights and Freedoms and Humanitarian Relief
IMF	International Monetary Fund
IPE	International Political Economy
ISO	Istanbul Chamber of Commerce
JDP	Justice and Development Party
JICA	Japan International Cooperation Agency
KYC	Know Your Customer
LDC	Least Developed Country
LDCs	Least Developed Countries
LE	Life Expectancy
LFIP	Law on Foreigners and International Protection
LFPR	Labor Force Participation Rates List of Acronyms
LSDV	Least Square Dummy Variables
MENA	Middle East and North Africa
MHP	Nationalist Movement Party, Milliyetçi Hareket Partisi
MIKTA	Emerging Middle Powers (an Informal Partnership Between Mexico, Indonesia, South Korea, Turkey and Australia)
MKEK	Mechanical and Chemical Industry Corporation
MNCs	Multinational Cooperation
MTP	Medium-Term Programs

MTV	Motor Vehicle Tax
MUSIAD	Independent Industrialists' and Businessmen's Association
NAFTA	North American Free Trade Agreement
NATO	North Atlantic Treaty Organization
NEET	Neither in School nor in Employment
NGDP	National Graduate Development Programme
NGOs	Non-Governmental Organisations
NOA	Number of Agreement
Non-DAC	Non-Development Actor
NOV	Number of Visit
ODA	Official Development Assistance
OECD	Organisation for Economic Cooperation and Development
OLS	Ordinary Least Squares Estimator
OT	Ottoman Territory Regional Identification
PKK	The Kurdistan Workers Party, Partiya Karkeren Kurdistane
POM	Percentage of Recipient Population
PPP	Purchasing Power Parity
PWC	Post-Washington Consensus
R&D	Research and Development
REG	Regional Identification
RERI	Real Exchange Rate Index
RGDP	Real Gross Domestic Product
RSD	Real Social Dynamics Nation
SA	Seasonally Adjusted
SILC	Survey of Income and Living Conditions
SME	Small and Medium-Sized Enterprise
SNPTC	State Nuclear Power Technology Corporation
SSA	Sub-Saharan Africa
STATA	Software for Statistic and Data Science
TEPAV	Economic Policy Research Foundation of Turkey
TIKA	Turkish Cooperation and Coordination Agency
TOBB	Turkish Union of Chambers and Commodity Exchanges
TR	Turkish Origin
TSEP	Transition to the Strong Economy
TTA	Technology Transfer Accelerator Turkey
TTIP	Translate Trade and Investment Partnership
TUBITAK	Scientific and Technological Research Council of Turkey
TURKSTAT	Turkish Statistical Institute
TUSIAD	Turkish Industry and Business Association
UAE	United Arab Emirates
UN	United Nation

xx ABBREVIATIONS

UNHCR	United Nations High Commissioner for Refugees
US	United States
USA	United States of America
USAID	United States Agency for Development
USD	United States Dollars
VAT	Value and Tax
WB	World Bank
WC	Washington Consensus
WIT	World Informatics Technology
WTO	World Trade Organization
YTB	Presidency for Turks Abroad and Related Communities
ZPN	Zero Problem with Neighbours

LIST OF FIGURES

Fig. 2.1	Nominal GDP, gross fixed capital formation and gross domestic savings (new series as a percentage of old series) (*Note* The source for this and subsequent figures and tables is the World Development Indicators database)	35
Fig. 2.2	Relationships between economic performance and selected variables	38
Fig. 2.3	Turkey's relative RGDP growth performance	39
Fig. 2.4	GDP (PPP) deflator (indexed to 1990)	44
Fig. 2.5	Alternative NGDP (PPP) calculations	45
Fig. 2.6	NGDP and GDP (ADJ)	46
Fig. 2.7	GDP (ADJ) per capita, GDP per capita (PPP) and their ratio	47
Fig. 2.8	Per capita GDP percent rank of Turkey with alternative measures (*Note* The number of countries used in calculations is in brackets)	48
Fig. 2.9	Percent rank of Turkey in terms of key macroeconomic indicators (*Note* The number of countries used in calculations is in brackets)	50
Fig. 2.10	Cumulative current account deficit to GDP ratio (*Note* Higher numbers indicate higher cumulative current account deficits since 1990)	54
Fig. 2.11	Percent rank of Turkey in terms of real interest rates and current account deficits (*Note* For figures B and C higher numbers indicate higher rank based on higher current account deficits)	54
Fig. 3.1	Trend in inequality	71

xxii LIST OF FIGURES

Fig. 3.2	Trends in percentile ratios	73
Fig. 3.3	Share of public transfers	78
Fig. 3.4	Inequality before and after public transfers	79
Fig. 3.5	Public transfers by bottom, middle and top 10 percentile	80
Fig. 4.1	Labor force, employment and unemployment: 2016–2017 (Seasonally adjusted)	96
Fig. 4.2	Shares of woman in services and manufacturing: 2005–2017	98
Fig. 4.3	Labor force participation by gender (*Source* Authors' calculations using TurkStat HLFS data)	99
Fig. 4.4	Female LFPR by education (*Source* Authors' calculations using TurkStat HLFS data)	102
Fig. 4.5	Unemployment rates by gender	103
Fig. 4.6	The youth unemployment rate, 2005–2017 (*Source* OECD Database)	105
Fig. 5.1	Turkey exports to Syria and number of companies partnered by Syrians (*Source* Turkish Statistical Institute and Union of Chambers and Commodity Exchanges of Turkey)	122
Fig. 5.2	Provincial exports to Syria, million US dollars (*Source* Turkish Statistical Institute and Union of Chambers and Commodity Exchanges of Turkey)	123
Fig. 6.1	Turkish official development assistance, million US$	140
Fig. 6.2	Top 10 Turkish aid receivers in 2016, million US$	141
Fig. 6.3	Top 10 Turkish aid receivers in 2016, excluding Syria, million US$	141
Fig. 6.4	Amount of aid disbursed by Turkish NGOs, 2005–2016, million US$	143
Fig. 6.5	Turkish multilateral aid, 2002–2016, million US$	145
Fig. 6.6	Turkish bilateral-multilateral aid, 2002–2016, million US$	145
Fig. 9.1	Turkey's trade balance with MENA Partners, 2016 (US$billions) (*Source* World Bank 2018)	229
Fig. 9.2	Turkey's total trade with the MENA, 1996–2017 (US$billions) (*Source* Turkstat [www.turkstat.gov.tr] 2018)	230
Fig. 9.3	Turkey's FDI flows with the MENA 2005–2017 (US$millions) (*Source* Central Bank of the Republic of Turkey [CBRT]: Statistical Data [EVDS] 2018)	231
Fig. 11.1	Turkey's Bilateral Trade with the Regions of the World (*Source* TUIK)	275

Fig. 11.2	Turkey's Bilateral Trade with the Asia-Pacific (selected countries) ($ million) (*Source* Calculated by the author using TUIK data)	276
Fig. 11.3	Turkey's Exports to and Imports from the Asia-Pacific in 2018 (selected countries) ($ million) (*Source* Calculated by the author using TUIK data)	277
Fig. 11.4	Regional sources of FDI into the Turkish economy as of 2017 ($ million) (*Source* Turkish Central Bank [TCMB, n.d.])	283

LIST OF TABLES

Table 2.1	Percent rank of Turkey in terms of per capita RGDP growth rates	41
Table 2.2	Percent rank of Turkey in terms of per capita real exports growth rates	42
Table 3.1	Summary statistics on income and inequality	72
Table 3.2	Static subgroup decomposition: between inequality (%)	73
Table 3.3	Dynamic subgroup decomposition	74
Table 3.4	The contribution of income sources to inequality	76
Table 3.5	Contribution of factor income to changes in overall inequality	78
Table 3.6	Shares of population subgroups	82
Table 3.7	Relative incomes (μ_k/μ)	83
Table 4.1	Labor market outlook, Turkey, 2005–2017	88
Table 4.2	Unemployment, employment and NEET	104
Table 4.3	Unemployment rates concerning educational status of youth in 2017 (%)	107
Table 6.1	Descriptive statistics	150
Table 6.2	Estimation results	154
Table 7.1	Comparative economic outlook of MIKTA countries (2000–2017)	167
Table 7.2	Comparative economic outlook of MIKTA countries as of % change (2000–2017)	168
Table 7.3	Mexico's economic outlook (2000–2017)	170
Table 7.4	Indonesia's economic outlook (2000–2017)	173
Table 7.5	South Korea's economic outlook (2000–2017)	176
Table 7.6	Turkey's economic outlook (2000–2017)	181

xxvi   LIST OF TABLES

Table 7.7	Australia's economic outlook (2000–2017)	184
Table 7.8	MIKTA countries trade statistics	186
Table 8.1	The determinants of Turkish foreign aid	206
Table 8.2	Top Turkish foreign aid total flows by country (2004–2013)	209
Table 9.1	Turkey's trade with leading partners, 2016 (US$billions)	224
Table 9.2	Turkey's trade with MENA partners, 2016 (US$billions)	226
Table 9.3	Turkey's total trade with the MENA, 1996–2017 (US$billions)	228
Table 9.4	Turkey's total FDI flows with MENA states, 1990–2016 (US$millions)	233
Table 10.1	2005–2016 exports of Turkey by regions (billion USD)	245
Table 10.2	2005–2016 imports of Turkey by Regions (in Billion USD)	246
Table 10.3	Share of Turkey's exports, imports, and total trade by regional groupings	249
Table 10.4	List of business councils created in the bottom of DEIK between Turkey and SSA countries	257
Table 10.5	Trading partners of Turkey in SSA, in 2018	258
Table 10.6	Share of products imports and exports by turkey with SSA in 2016	259
Table 10.7	SSA's trade with Turkey and the world	259
Table 10.8	Change in Turkey's trade with SSA countries between 2005 and 2018	261
Table 10.9	Turkey's trade with Nigeria, Ethiopia, and South Africa (in USD)	263
Table 10.10	Rankings of Import Partners of sub-Saharan Africa	265
Table 10.11	Rankings of export partners of sub-Saharan Africa	265
Table 10.12	Number of official foreign military bases in SSA by owner	266
Table 11.1	Japanese and Korean companies in Istanbul Chamber of Commerce 500 rankings	287

CHAPTER 1

The Changing Landscape and Dynamics of Turkey's Political Economy in the Twenty-First Century: An Introduction

Emel Parlar Dal

INTRODUCTION

Turkey's political economy in the 2000s has shown a remarkable diversification in its *international* political economy landscape, its *domestic* political economy framework, *instrumental* alternatives and *geographic* outreach, despite intensifying internal and external challenges. Regardless of the degree of success of the major economic reforms in the 2000s, it is possible to argue that change and diversification in the *international, domestic, instrumental* and *geographic* domains of Turkey's political economy have provided it with a variety of foreign policy options and tools. In this regard, the interplay between Turkey's *domestic, instrumental* and *geographic* political economy diversification and its changing foreign policy preferences in the 2000s constitutes the main scope of this book project.

E. Parlar Dal (✉)
Faculty of Political Science, Marmara University, Istanbul, Turkey

© The Author(s) 2020
E. Parlar Dal (ed.), *Turkey's Political Economy in the 21st Century*, International Political Economy Series,
https://doi.org/10.1007/978-3-030-27632-4_1

1

Why is there a need for such an edited book? First, the increasing complexity of Turkey's regional and global political economy in a rapidly expanding and challenging internal political environment makes it difficult to assess Turkey's current political economy without a comprehensive and embedded research focus. This cluster's integrationist approach helps the audience delve into the general contours of Turkey's political economy direction since post-Washington Consensus (PWC) era which also witnessed the twin crises of 2000 and 2001 in the country. The new trends and tools of Turkey's political economy create new regional networks that may also be linked to its global outreach. This collection also focuses on multiple regions such as the Middle East and North Africa (MENA), sub-Saharan Africa (SSA) and Asia-Pacific while engaging in understanding Turkey's evolving political-economical motivations, strategies and orientations. On the other hand, the twenty-first century has witnessed the use of a grand variety of new political economy tools by Turkey's decision-makers such as foreign aid, development aid, membership to informal groupings such as MIKTA, new free trade agreements and increasing voting weight in global financial organizations. These interconnected aspects of contemporary Turkish foreign policy are addressed in this volume with the aim of providing the international and Turkish reader with a complete picture of Turkey's diversified political economy in terms of domestic politics, tools and varying geographies.

A bird's eye view of the literature on emerging countries' political economy in general and Turkey's political economy in particular reveals an urgent need for an updated collection that focuses on Turkey's political economy in the 2000s from a broader and comprehensive perspective. This book therefore aims to contribute to the existing literature on three levels. First, despite the various studies on the changing dynamics of emerging powers' political economies such as China, India, Brazil and others, there is still lack of comprehensive and comparative works locating the political-economic transformations of countries having in-between characteristics between the West and East and the North and South such as Turkey. In this regard, this book attempts to fill this research gap by analyzing Turkey's political economy in the 2000s with a specific focus on its in-between role and its new orientations in the changing global economy of the 2000s. Therefore, by incorporating Turkey into the ongoing debates on the role of emerging powers in global economy, this book attempts to contribute to the literature by providing a selected collection of works about Turkey's motives, roles, strategies, capabilities and limits in the changing global economy in the 2000s. Second, the domestic and external challenges Turkey has faced and their repercussions, particularly after 2010, have not been analyzed together with Turkey's changing political-economic actorness. Multiple crises including increasing domestic polarization, ongoing criticisms about its democratic credentials, the impact of the recent coup attempt, effects of the Arab Spring and the Syrian Civil War and deepening rifts with European capitals have not yet been integrated into the studies on Turkey's political economy from a broader perspective. This book thus aims at contributing to the literature by looking at how an emerging economy like Turkey copes with domestic and external challenges with an eye to understanding the question of how substantial Turkey's recent rise in global politics really is. In that sense, this book contributes to the literature on Turkey as a rising power by also bringing critical insights into the topic. Third, although international political economy as a discipline has started to become more institutionalized in Turkey with recently opened graduate programs on IPE in Turkish universities, there is a growing need for reference works more than ever for educational purposes to support these programs.

Based on this, this volume aims at bringing together some of the best research essays on the most debated and important topics on contemporary Turkish political economy. Necessarily selective, this collection focuses on a limited number of chapters specifically covering both the diversification-expansion and transformation in Turkish political economy since the 2000s. As mentioned above, the volume begins with the domestic diversification of Turkish political economy (Part I), including a general article dealing with the recent dynamics of Turkey's political economy and radical political transformation and three other articles dealing with respectively income inequality in Turkey: 2003–2015, dynamics and challenges of Turkey's labor market, the Syrian entrepreneurs in Turkey as new economic actors. Part II moves on to contributions on the instrumental diversification of Turkey's political economy and covers topics such as Turkey's new donor role among established and emerging donors, emerging middle powers (MIKTA) in the changing global political economy, determinants of Turkey's foreign aid as a new political economy tool and appeal to changing global governance structure. Part III seeks to illustrate the rapid evolution of Turkey's political economy with regard to its geographic outreach in an era of multiple and complex changes in the country's domestic, regional and international environment with a special focus on the following topics: the Political Economy of Turkey's Integration into the MENA Economy, the Turkish "Trading State" in the SSA and the Political Economy of Turkey's Relations with the Asia-Pacific.

In order to draw the above-explained three interconnected rationales together, this present project addresses the following research questions:

- In which ways and through which instruments has Turkey's contemporary political economy transformed since the 2000s?
- What are the main driving factors, motives and strategies behind the diversification of contemporary Turkey's political economy?
- To what extent have domestic and foreign policy shifts in Turkey's political landscape contributed to the diversification of its political economy in the 2000s?
- Which new geographies have been added to Turkey's landscape of political-economic engagement in the 2000s?
- How has Turkey redressed the balance between its traditional political-economic engagements with its Western partners and its new political-economic relations with its emerging partners in the Global South in the 2000s?
- What are the illusions and realities about Turkey's political-economic achievements in the 2000s? Is it really a success story or backlash?
- To what extent have domestic, regional and global crises affected Turkey's political economy?
- Does Turkey's current political-economic landscape resemble its Western partners more than other emerging powers in the Global South?
- What are the opportunities and challenges of contemporary Turkish political economy?

Based on these research questions, the overall framework of this book seeks to make a comprehensive analysis of Turkey's political economy in the twenty-first century and to grasp how it has diversified in the *domestic, instrumental* and *geographic* domains. To this end, this introductory chapter will first rethink Turkey's political economy with an eye to explaining Turkey's economic growth and political transformation in line with the changes occurring in world economics from the Washington Consensus (WC) era to the current "mix" or "hybrid" era encompassing both the characteristics of post-Washington and Beijing Consensus

(BJC) era. In sum, the overarching aim of this book project is twofold: to scrutinize the transformation experienced in Turkey's political economy in the 2000s and to link this transformation with the changing preferences in Turkish foreign policy.

International and Structural Change of Turkey's Political Economy from PWC to the Mix-Consensus Era

The PWC refers to the period following the WC era, particularly the early 2000s.[1] Developed in the 1980s and 1990s, the WC underlined three core principles (trade liberalization, privatization and deregulation) to be implemented by the developing world to push economic growth (Serra and Stiglitz 2008). Increasing evidence that the WC failed to spur the desired development outcomes in the developing world in the 1990s resulted in the development of a new complementary model of development, the so-called PWC. Although the PWC did not totally reject all of the WC' core tenets such as liberalization of inward FDI and free trade policies, it nevertheless introduced the regulatory functions of the state, especially in the financial and banking systems, and paid more attention to the institutional and democratic landscape of developing countries.

In this context, the world's leading economic and financial institutions, namely the IMF and WB, included the implementation of the post-Washington principles. However, the financial crisis that hit the USA and Europe in 2007–2008 resulted in an increasing challenge to the PWC' status as a model of sustainable development. This has given rise to what is called the BJC, considered as an alternative model of development based on the Chinese's successful development experience. The Beijing model rejects the one-size-fits-all model of the WC, which required homogeneous reforms, and instead called for flexibility in development reforms and for them to be constantly adapted to each nation's unique challenges. The BJC is based on three core tenets: innovation, developmentalist-oriented policies and self-determination. This section will briefly analyze Turkey's political-economic policies in the post-Washington and BJC era in order to highlight the strengths and weaknesses of its policies (Serra and Stiglitz 2008; Hibben 2016).

---

[1] The Washington Consensus developed in the 1980s and 1990s underlined three core principles—trade liberalization, privatization and deregulation—that needed to be implemented by the developing world to push economic growth.

Turkey's Political Economy in Post-Washington Consensus Era

Turkey began following the logic of the WC policies of free trade liberalization, deregulation of the financial system, liberalized inward FDI, and limited state interventions and social policy in the 1980s and 1990s under the leadership of Turgut Ozal. The two economic crises that hit Turkey in 2000 and 2001 combined with increasing evidence of the failure of the Washington model of economic development resulted in the progressive implementation of the PWC in Turkey under the "Transition to the Strong Economy" program (TSEP) adopted in May 2001. TESP suggested strong regulatory institutions, especially in the banking and financial sectors. Ziya Onis, Turkish scholar specialized on Turkish political economy, rightly underlined that Turkey's post-2001's political economy reflected its "encounter with the emerging post-Washington consensus" (Öniş 2010).

Although the progressive implementation of the IMF program signed in December 1999 started under the coalition government of Kemal Dervis, Turkey began to strengthen its commitment to the implementation of the IMF's reform programs between 2002 and 2007 following the coming to power of the AK Party in November 2002, thus succeeding in legitimizing the IMF reform program in Turkey. The official acceptance of Turkey as an EU candidate in December 1999, which was accompanied by profound economic and political reforms, gave further impetus to the successful implementation of the post-Washington neoliberal reforms in the early years of the 2000s. In this vein, "these dual external anchors resulted in a firm commitment to rebuilding the Turkish state's economic arm on grounds of macroeconomic stability and enhanced regulatory capacity" (Güven 2016, 189).

The reform program based on the post-Washington model encompassed deep reforms in banking, financial and social policies, among others. The AK Party pushed hard in the early years of its rule for the strengthening of the state's regulatory functions in the financial and banking systems, increased economic growth and sustainable public debt, and the reduction of inflation rate to one digit (Yagci 2017, 90). Major reforms included the declaration of the Central Bank of the Republic of Turkey (CBRT) as the sole institution responsible for monetary policies and granting it full legal independence in April 2001 (Official Gazette, April 25, 2001), the creation of the Banking Regulation and Supervision

Agency (BRSA) to be responsible for banking regulation and supervision, and the Turkish Treasury, which is responsible for debt management and sovereign borrowing (Yagci 2017, 90).

Other reforms included the creation of the Law on the Regulation of Public Finance and Debt Management (No. 4749), enacted in March 2002, to unify the borrowing framework for all state and quasi-state organizations and set strict limits to total borrowing, "based on the projected incomes and expenditures in the annual Budget Law" (Güven 2008, 11). Under AKP rule, Turkey also initiated a social security reform establishing a unique social security system with equal health coverage for all citizens and a social assistance scheme in 2006 (Yagci 2017, 90).

During the first decade of the 2000s, Turkey was relatively successful in increasing the value of the Turkish lira, implementing the privatization program and increasing foreign direct investment. Revenue generated by private companies quadrupled since 2002 until today (from 9.5 billion USD to 34 billion USD) and FDI increased from 5 billion USD in 2004 to 20 billion USD in 2007 (Bank and Karadag 2012). In terms of economic growth, "Turkey enjoyed a relatively steady growth during the AKP's rule, with a 5.2% average annual real GDP growth rate for the period between 2002 and 2012" (Tekin and Tekin 2015, 25). Thanks to the IMF reforms, Turkish financial institutions were able to survive the 2008 financial crisis and the "economic turmoil in the Euro zone without going into bankruptcy" (Tekin and Tekin 2015, 25).

The first decade of the 2000s also witnessed an era in which Turkey managed to pacify its relations with its Middle Eastern and Eurasian neighbors and establish itself as a strong regional political and economic actor. This move led some scholars to qualify Turkey as a trading state (Kirişçi 2009), which denotes the prevalence of economic considerations in the formulation and implementation of Turkey's foreign policy. Yet, as exposed by Emel Parlar Dal's article in this edited volume, recent developments in the Middle East, most particularly the ongoing Syrian crisis, have significantly deteriorated Turkey's trading state status, certainly leading to the gradual return of political and ideological considerations in the making of Turkey's foreign policy. Despite these achievements, Turkey experienced various challenges from regional instabilities such as the Arab upheavals and the Syrian Civil War in the second decade of the 2000s. These challenges, combined with the recent economic crisis in Turkey, have negatively affected the country's economy through an increasing account deficit, the depreciation of the lira and a high unemployment rate. As a result, a series of domestic and external factors have pushed Turkey to increasingly include some developmentalist features in its political economy in the beginning of 2011.

Once following the logic of WC policies of free trade liberalization, deregulation of financial system, liberalized inward FDI, and limited state interventions and social policy in the 1980s and 1990s under the leadership of Turgut Ozal, two economic crises that hit Turkey in 2000 and 2001 combined with the increasing evidence of failure of the Washington model of economic development, resulted in the progressive implementation of the PWC in Turkey in late 2001 under the "Transition to the Strong Economy" program (TSEP) adopted in May 2001, which suggested strong regulatory institutions, especially in the banking and financial sectors. Ziya Onis rightly underlined in this line that the post-2001's political economy of Turkey reflected "Turkey's encounter with the emerging post-Washington consensus."

Although the progressive implementation of the IMF program signed in December 1999 started under the coalition government with the leadership of Kemal Dervis, Turkey started to give greater commitment to the implementation of the IMF's reform programs between the period 2002 and 2007, following the coming to power of the AKP in November 2002, which succeeded to legitimize the IMF reform program in Turkey. The official acceptance of Turkey as an EU candidate in December 1999, which was accompanied by profound economic and political reforms, gave further impetus to the successful implementation of the post-Washington neoliberal reforms in the early years of 2000s. In this line, "these dual external anchors resulted in a firm commitment to rebuilding the Turkish state's economic arm on grounds of macroeconomic stability and enhanced regulatory capacity."

The reform program, based on the post-Washington model, encompassed deep reforms in the banking, financial and social policies, among others. The AK Party pushed hard in the early years of ruling for the strengthening of the regulatory functions of the state in the financial and banking systems especially as well as for the increasing of economic growth and sustainable public debt, and the reduction of inflation rate to one digit (Yagci 2017, 90). Major reforms include the declaration of the CBRT as solely responsible for monetary policies, which gained its legal full independence under the Law No. 4651 amended the original Central Bank Law No. 1211 of April 2001 (Official Gazette, 25 April 2001), the creation of the BRSA, which is solely responsible for banking regulation and supervision, and the Turkish Treasury, which is responsible for debt management and sovereign borrowing (Yagci 2017, 90).

Other reforms include the new Law on the Regulation of Public Finance and Debt Management (No. 4749), enacted in March 2002, which mainly unified the borrowing framework for all state and quasi-state organizations and set strict limits to total borrowing, "based on the projected incomes and expenditures in the annual Budget Law" (Güven 2008, 89). Turkey under AKP rule also initiated in 2006 a social security reform, which established a unique social security system with equal health coverage system for every citizen and a social assistance scheme (Yagci 2017).

During the last decade of the 2000s, Turkey has also been relatively successful in increasing the value of the Turkish lira, in the implementation of the privatization program, with the increasing number of private companies, and in the increase of foreign direct investment. Some argue that the revenue generated by private companies mostly quadrupled since 2002 (from 9.5 billion USD to 34 billion USD) and that FDI increased from 5 billion USD in 2004 to 20 billion USD in 2007 (Bank and Karadag 2012). In terms of economic growth, "Turkey enjoyed a relatively steady growth during the AKP's rule, with a 5.2% average annual real GDP growth rate for the period between 2002 and 2012" (Tekin and Tekin 2015, 25). Thanks to the IMF reforms, Turkish financial institutions resisted without going onto bankruptcy to the 2007 global crisis and the "economic turmoil in the Euro zone" (Tekin and Tekin 2015, 27).

The first decade of the 2000s also witnessed an era where Turkey also managed to pacify its relations with its Middle Eastern and Eurasian neighbors to establish itself as a strong regional political and economic actor. This move led some scholars to qualify Turkey as a trading state (Kirişçi 2009), which denotes the prevalence of economic considerations in the formulation and implementation of Turkey's foreign policy.

TURKISH POLITICAL ECONOMY IN THE MIX-CONSENSUS ERA (2010 ONWARD) AND THE LIMITS OF THE TURKISH DEVELOPMENTALIST STATE

The current structure of the international political economy is considered as a mix or a dual form consisting of both PWC and BJC characteristics. Turkey also seems to be affected by this evolution and as a result has recently begun implementing some developmentalist policies in line with BJC principles. Many factors such as the current economic crisis, which has significantly slowed Turkey's economic growth, the increasing account deficit resulting from low export-oriented industrialization, increasing trade deficit, the depreciation of the lira, the high unemployment rate and an increasing inflation rate have pushed the current government to adopt a developmentalist state discourse, yet not without some limits.

In this context, the hard criticisms directed against the central bank policies and resulting high interest rates by the AKP (Güven 2016, 194); the establishment of a sovereign wealth fund; the priority given to national and local production in the defense and automobile industry thanks to domestic technology development; the enactment of a "long-term industrial strategy plan"; the facilitation of establishment procedures for foreign investors in Turkey; President Erdoğan's emphasis on employment mobilization; the launch of public bank-funded mega projects; and the declaration of several subsidy schemes for the private sector are all clear manifestations of the AK Party's increasing developmentalist (Yagci 2017, 104).

In order to overcome trade deficit-related challenges deriving from weak industrialization of manufactured goods, in 2011 Turkey adopted the Turkish Industrial Strategy Document (toward EU Membership) which sets as its long-term goal the positioning of Turkey as "the production base of Eurasia in medium- and high-tech products" (Kutlay 2015, 7). The strategy aims to do so by encouraging investments in the production of intermediate goods and technological innovation and by strengthening capacity-building. Institutionally and following the BJC logic of associating sciences and technology in the industrialization process, the Ministry of Industry was restructured and renamed the Ministry of Science, Industry and Technology. The creation of the Ministry of Development to coordinate Turkey's economic development policies is another evidence of the increasing importance attached to the development aspect of Turkey's political-economic policies (Kutlay 2015, 7).

The main challenges facing Turkey include the low level of industrialization in manufacturing goods and the resultant trade and account deficit, the lack of export-oriented industrialization, the slowing development of the innovation and technology sectors, and energy dependence. The share of manufacturing within the GDP decreased from 20% in 2002 to nearly 17% in 2015 and the share of high-technology exports within manufactured exports increased minimally from 18% in 2002 to 21% in 2015 (Yagci 2017, 96). The slow development of the industry sector is mainly attributed to the policies of the current government, which in recent years prioritized conservative business groups affiliated to the party which concentrated on construction and retail sectors at the expense of the high-tech manufacturing sector. Indeed, the new urban development law adopted in 2012 provided a legal framework for exponential growth in housing investments at the expense of manufacturing investments. According to official data, "between 2005 and 2016, the share of manufacturing in investments declined from 27.6% to 18.1% while the share of housing increased by 9.5%" (Oyvat 2018, 5).

More specifically, innovation and technology is still very weak in Turkey and needs to be strengthened. For this to be achieved, Turkey should seek to improve its domestic technology capabilities in different sectors by facilitating technology transfer from foreign investments. Such moves would oblige political authorities to find ways to transfer technology to local companies. In addition, like China, Turkey needs to strengthen the industrialization of its infrastructure sector (Oyvat 2018, 106).

Turkey's heavy energy dependence is another critical issue which increases its account deficit and relatedly limits its potentials as a developmentalist state. Indeed, it is noted that "Turkey imports more than 90 percent of the energy it consumes" (Kutlay 2015, 6) and as such Turkey's economy is heavily dependent on the fluctuations of energy prices on global market. In order to overcome this challenge, Turkey has adopted a recent strategy document for 2015–2019 aimed at diversifying its energy suppliers, partners and routes, increasing the share of renewables and achieving the inclusion of nuclear energy. Other recent developments include the 2015 launch of a project constructing the first nuclear power plant in Akkuyu, located in the southern province of Mersin (Kutlay 2015, 6).

Finally, Turkey pursues an embedded economic policy informed by both post-Washington and BJC principles. Turkey's recent economic problems seem to have pushed its ruling elites to return to the neoliberal post-Washington policies of low-interest rates with limited fiscal and monetary regulatory policies in order to save the Turkish lira on one hand and to adopt a series of "new/new generation developmentalist state" policies slightly inspired from state capitalist economy policies on the other hand. Despite having adopted a developmentalist state discourse in recent years with limited actions on the ground, Turkey still does not fulfill all the requirements for being a real development state. As the existing literature on developmentalist/post-developmentalist state suggests, one of the key preconditions for becoming a developmental state is to have a high level of industrialization, an efficient coordination between private and public sectors (Onis 1991, 109–126), and an all-inclusive and long-term strategy with the participation of multiple sectors including private, public, real, and financial sectors, NGOs and universities.

MULTIPLE LAYERS OF DIVERSIFICATION OF TURKEY'S POLITICAL ECONOMY

Domestic Diversification

The successive AKP governments in Turkey since 2002 have facilitated a notable transformation in Turkey's domestic political economy, reflected in both the institutional structure and the ideology and background of the dominant actors of the political-economic domain. As the AKP government consolidated its power inside the country, Turkish capital and capital markets became dominated by more conservative circles in place of the secular or Western political-economic elites of the past. Indeed, one of the AKP's main aims has been to change the domestic political-economic balance inside the country in favor of the new conservative elites supporting the party.

Herein, Chapter 2 by Turan Subaşat entitled "*The Political Economy of Turkey's Economic Miracle(s) and Crisis*" looks at this radical political-economic transformation, arguing that the government has created an illusion of an economic miracle to sustain itself. For the author, the first economic miracle created by the current Turkish government was fictional because Turkey's nominal GDP tripped but it was largely due to the exchange rate movements, and when it is adjusted with the real GDP, Turkey's performance was not extraordinary and he also added that the country experienced large account deficits and external debt during the first term of the AKP government. The second miracle just started after the global financial crisis and the author claims that although the first miracle was studied extensively in the literature, there is not enough research for the second one. Between 2010 and 2017, Turkey experienced a fast RGDP growth rate as well as investment and saving rates improved significantly. Turkey's growth rate with over 7% RGDP in 2017 was one of the highest in the world; however, as the author asserts, this was mainly due to revisions of the Turkish Statistical Institute (TURKSTAT) in 2016. Also, the election-oriented stimulation of the economy affected the rates which were not sustainable. Similar to the first miracle, he argues that Turkey continued to experience account deficits and accumulated external debt which has deep linkages with the currency crisis.

According to the author, Turkish lira faced similar pressures in 2015 and 2016 and survived because the CBRT used its reserves and raised interest rates. However, in 2018, the CBRT had fewer reserves compared to previous years to stabilize the exchange rates and raising the interest rates is not seem to be a permanent solution while the rates were already high. The author concludes by questioning the sustainability of the current state of Turkish economy. With the current external debt and the prevailing consumption-based economy approach, the author argues that this development model could not continue for long and was prone to a painful adjustment. In short, this first chapter challenges the widespread idea that Turkey has been transformed domestically into a solid economic power.

The chapter entitled "Income Inequality in Turkey: 2003–2015" by Alpay Filiztekin, investigates the characteristics of the income distribution in Turkey during the JDP era by using data from Household Budget and Expenditure Surveys with mixed econometric methods and aims to describe the level and changes in the trend of inequality as well as the possible determinants and sections of society that are affected. In his chapter, the author reminds that before IMF and WB imposed structural reforms the weaknesses of the banking system alongside with the deficits of the budget ended up with the 2001 crisis. After several reforms been made and the new government took power, Turkey experienced a rapid growth period. However, starting in 2008, the growth slowed significantly and productivity growth stagnated. According to the author, a parallel process can be observed in inequality in both absolute and percentage terms.

This chapter argues that Turkey's income inequality is one of the highest within the OECD countries, and despite a decline in the Gini coefficient in the early years of the millennium, the gains have stalled. For the author, whatever the reasons for this reversal are, both macroeconomic growth and gains in inequality slowed down if not stopped. He also asserts that current trends are also not promising and inequality seems in a rise again. He deduces from the evidence that the early improvement in inequality was mostly due to the strengthening of the position of middle classes; however, increasing share of university graduates with high earnings worsened the distribution after 2007. In addition to education, the author claims that the proletarianization of the labor force caused changes in inequality through both allocation and income effect.

In his final analysis, Filiztekin questioned the future of the inequality with a special focus on the influence of macroeconomic policies on the shaping of the income distribution. He emphasizes that the Turkish population's reliance on the public transfers has recently increased. However, as the author implies, this situation cannot be sustained in the long term, thus inequality expected to rise in the absence or decline in the amount of the transfers.

The fourth chapter by Seyfettin Gürsel, Gökçe Uysal, Tuba Toru Delibaşı on *Turkish Labor Market: Complex Dynamics and Challenges* scrutinizes the transformation in the labor market and attempts to evaluate the recent changes in labor productivity by evaluating the new issues with regard to gender and youth. The authors argued that in the aftermath of the disastrous crisis in 2001 a new era has begun regarding the economic regime and politics for Turkey where not only decisive institutional reforms such as the independence of the central bank policy, the restructuring of the banking system and transparency in public finances were implemented, but also a comprehensive stabilization program started under the aegis of the IMF. As the authors suggest, the most striking economic characteristic of this period is the impressive GDP growth performance. From 2005 to 2017, the chained volume index of

GDP doubled, including the contraction of 2009 caused by The Great Recession. Given such a success in economic growth, one would have expected that the rather high unemployment, inherited from the lost decade of the 1990s, could have been significantly diminished. In hindsight, disappointment in this matter abounds. During the period after 2005, as underlined by the authors excluding the contraction year of 2009, the overall unemployment rate varied between 8.4 and 10.9% and the non-farm rate between 10.3 and 13.7%.

Given this, the authors suggest that the complex dynamics characterizing Turkish Labor Market during this period are the culprits, which ensues from the high variance of labor supply (i.e., the evolution of the labor force) on one side and a remarkable shift in the growth-employment elasticity causing sizable variation in the labor demand on the other. According to the labor force dynamics coupled with varying job creation capacity and the size of the GDP growth, they distinguished five sub-periods (2005–2007, 2008–2009, 2010–2012, 2013–2015 and 2016–2017) during which they observed ups and downs in unemployment, due to either labor force increases that are stronger than those in employment or weak employment increases in spite of relatively high growth rates.

In their study, the authors pointed out that the sustained increases in the labor force are primarily caused by increases in the female labor force participation rates that rose from 25.9% in 2010 to 33.6% in 2017. They also indicated that during this period, the education levels of women soared as the share without a high school degree fell and the share with a college degree increased. Furthermore, the labor force participation rates of women increased for each education category, particularly for women who do not have college degrees. Unfortunately, the authors also reminded that this period is also marked by an unswerving widening of the gender gap in unemployment rates after the Global Recession.

Finally, in a similar vein, the authors touched upon the youth unemployment rate which has risen substantially since 2008, following the worldwide financial crisis. He underlined that the rate of unemployment was twice as high as the average of OECD countries (i.e., 20.9 and 11%, respectively), although the number of young people in education has increased in Turkey. Also, they suggested that the higher education graduates are more likely to be unemployed than the lower education level indicating the problems in the efficiency of the education system, school-to-work transitions and mismatches between the skill set of the youth labor force and the skill demands of the employers.

In the fifth and last chapter of the first part of this edited volume, Omar Kadkoy discussed the process and challenges on the integration of the labor market and entrepreneurship of Syrian refugees in Turkey. In his study, the author departs from the fact that Turkey has become the largest refugees hosting country in the world where 3.6 million Syrians live together with 368,400 persons of concern namely from Afghanistan, Iraq, Iran and Somalia in the aftermath of the Syrian Civil War. Acknowledging that 89% of forcibly displaced people around the world are hosted in developing countries, the author underlines the uniqueness of the Turkey's case which is a G20 middle-income country with a fairly globalized economy.

According to the author, rooted out of their home countries, resettlement choices of forcibly displaced people are very narrow as they usually seek safety in neighboring countries and consequently, they find themselves in environments they are entirely unfamiliar with and unprepared for. This is why they seek to accomplish two things over all else which are blending in with the hosting new environment and making ends meet. He claims that the refugees see entrepreneurship as a way to serve both ends; however, in contrast to refugees, entrepreneurs who emigrate for economic reasons are likely to have prepared themselves for their relocation. He argues that the element of choice means that they are better prepared for the language and culture, bureaucratic procedures and market conditions of their destination and this group often does not see their business as a vehicle for integration the way refugees do. The chapter continues with the argument of the potential impact of Syrian refugees on the Turkish economy, and the business environment through entrepreneurial activities has so far been largely overlooked.

For the author, understanding the challenges faced by Syrian firms in Turkey has the potential to contribute to a private sector-driven sustainable integration process in at least four aspects. First, he points out that such an initiative would naturally yield a bottom-up assessment of the investment climate and business practices for Syrian entrepreneurs and businesspeople in Turkey. In turn, this will allow for the identification of gaps, bottlenecks and inefficient practices, paving the way for competitiveness-raising and capacity-building interventions from the public and private actors. Second, anecdotal evidence indicates Syrian business owners are more likely to employ other Syrians, leading to additional employment opportunities for the refugee population. Third, having a comprehensive understanding on the challenges faced by Syrian entrepreneurs starting from the business idea stage to establishing the business would enable designing and implementing interventions to the entrepreneurship ecosystem to make it more startup-friendly for refugees. And finally, Kadkoy suggests that such initiatives may also help transform host communities' perceptions of Syrians as productive members of local communities by raising awareness of the opportunities created by refugee-driven businesses.

Instrumental Diversification

Following this general survey of the domestic diversification of Turkey's political economy, the second part of this edited volume analyzes how Turkey has instrumentalized this domestic political-economic consolidation as a foreign policy tool in its regional and global engagements. Indeed, starting in the 2000s, Turkey has drawn upon its domestic political-economic stability in order to become more active in regional and global affairs. In this regard, Turkish policy makers have relied on the relatively stable political-economic environment inside the country to instrumentalize the accumulated resources in various areas in its foreign policy options.

Another important aspect of Turkey's instrumental diversification is the fact that it has attempted to find itself a place in the donor world by increasing aid to different geographies around the world. To analyze this, in the sixth chapter entitled "The Political Economy of Turkish Foreign Aid," Hüseyin Zengin and Abdurrahman Korkmaz attempt to locate Turkey in the donor world by comparing it with emerging and established donors. To this end, they analyze foreign aid behavior of Turkey and adopt a multicentric world politics approach where non-state actors have decisive power over state policies.

To build a political economy framework for the analysis, they form a framework to evaluate state-society-business interconnectedness, for which concepts like controlled neopopulism by Ziya Öniş and non-state stakeholders by Gürol Baba were utilized. For the authors, these two concepts are important because the former captures the state's populist motivations by focusing on redistribution policies and neoliberal regulatory economic strategies while the latter examines conservative capital owners and their cooperative, complementary and substitutive relations with the related state apparatuses. They argue that foreign aid is a political-economic tool enabling the government to pursue a benevolent image while entrenching the presence of conservative capitalists in the Turkish economy.

In order to enrich the analysis and fill the quantitative gap in Turkish foreign policy studies, Zengin and Korkmaz design an econometric model—generalized method of moments. The results of this model suggest that Turkey gave more aid to the countries that imported goods from Turkish firms; the countries formerly governed by Ottoman rule also received more Turkish aid, which was parallel to the established donor behavior, and Turkey attributed more importance to the common language when determining the amounts of aid to give and to whom, in comparison with the established donors.

The chapter thus concludes by discussing the future challenges ahead for sustaining a generous foreign aid policy in the context of the recent economic difficulties in Turkey. The authors distinguish two main challenges. First, they express that the depreciation of Turkish lira against other international currencies might end up with a drop in the total amount of Turkish aid, and second, the recipient countries' senses on historical/ethnic bonds might not fully overlap with the one with Turkey's.

The seventh chapter by Gonca Oguz Gök and R. Funda Karadeniz on "Emerging Middle Powers (MIKTA) in Global Political Economy: Preferences, Capabilities and Their Limitations" aims to locate the emerging middle powers in MIKTA in the changing international political economy. Drawing on the emerging middle power concept, this study attempts to analyze MIKTA states' capabilities and preferences in order to find out whether there is enough evidence that makes it possible to talk about an enhanced cooperation under MIKTA initiative. What are the material capabilities of MIKTA countries in current global economic order? Do they share same or similar ideational preferences and historical attachments toward neoliberal institutions? How do they define their roles in changing norms of global governance from PWC toward BJC? Are there any common "niche areas" in political economy that can push for a common constructive MIKTA identity? Is there an "increasing" or "decreasing" willingness among its members to push for an enhanced role of "MIKTA"? In order to answer those questions, the paper will compare and contrast the (1) material capabilities, (2) behavioral initiatives, and (3) ideational preferences of each MIKTA countries between 2010 and 2018 in a time of clashing norms of global political economy.

The paper concludes that although G20 provided the rationale for MIKTA's emergence, the UN is likely to provide a more relevant framework for future MIKTA action. Among others, so far, "sustainable development" issues have played a relatively prominent role in MIKTA's general rhetoric. The fact that democratic governance characterizes all of its members is what makes MIKTA a unique emerging powers' initiative in global political economy. Therefore, their domestic developments supported by the "willingness" in forming effective, coalition-buildings around MIKTA platform will determine these states' capacity to turn this new initiative to a "role model" of a more constructive multilateral emerging middle power collaboration.

The eighth chapter by Hakan Mehmetçik and Sercan Pekel entitled *"The Determinants of Turkish Foreign Aid: An Empirical Analysis"* analyzes the political economy of Turkish foreign aid program and interests/motivations in the formulation and implementation of Turkish foreign aid policies by conducting an empirical analysis on data derived from a volume of aid flows from Turkey to 143 countries and five sets of determinants drawing upon 19 different variables of both interval and nominal types. The Turkish case is important and worth to analyze for several reasons. Turkey is now the largest donor of humanitarian and development aid in terms of GDP per capita and the largest non-Western and non-DAC donor. Studying Turkey would also inform us about many cross-national trends among emerging donors and fast-changing foreign aid regimes. Therefore, Turkey's rapidly increasing humanitarian and development assistance merits further study. As a rising power, Turkey has been clearly seeking to use foreign aid in expanding its influence and power. Turkey provides humanitarian and development aid to expand its "humanitarian/virtuous power" brand. Turkey's contributions to development aid is also a form of ethical criticism to the international order. There are studies indicating that domestic politics has had a large impact on Turkey's priorities in giving aid. Given the lack of empirical evidence, this highly confusing set of explanations needs to be interpreted by empirical research. Based on a statistical analysis derived from a number of empirical data, this study seeks to assess the motivations behind Turkey's foreign aid policies focusing on its political economy. In this sense, the chapter fundamentally tries to understand economic, humanitarian, political, cultural/religious grounds and regional sensitivity of Turkish humanitarian and development assistance. A panel data has been compiled based on the variables and analyzed in R with a linear regression model.

The authors acknowledge that Turkish foreign aid allocation depends on a multi-track approach embodying distinct interests and motivations. The economic potential of the recipient country for Turkey seems to be an important factor to extend Turkey's economic interests. That is an expected outcome when the literature on foreign aid also puts forward similar findings. The institutional capacity-building of aid management via TIKA offices in recipient countries and the number of official high-level visits are also important variables determining Turkish foreign aid. The effects of the existence of free trade agreements as well as defense and military agreements on Turkey's foreign aid distribution also need to be evaluated. The altruistic side of Turkish foreign aid scheme is not undermined as aid flows more to countries with lower life expectancy despite the lack of sufficient aid toward countries with critical food shortage in distant regions. The religious similarity and regional positioning are the last significant determinants of Turkish foreign aid according to the authors' framework.

Geographic Diversification

Turkey expanded its geographical outreach in extra-regional zones such as Africa, Latin America and Asia-Pacific in the 2000s as a consequence of its proactive and multi-regional foreign policy. This geographic diversification of Turkey's foreign policy has indeed been accompanied by a series of political economy-related objectives in the field of trade, energy, tourism and development cooperation. Yet, this new geographical orientation and its political and economic repercussions have not yet been presented from an integrative and comprehensive perspective. The third section of this project seeks to accomplish this aim by surveying the old and new geographies in which Turkey has engaged political-economic relations since the 2000s. In this regard, the ninth chapter of this book written by Imad El-Anis on "*The Political Economy of Turkey's Integration into the MENA Economy*" addresses Turkey's rediscovery of the MENA as an economic partner in the 2000s. However, the chapter takes the argument a step further and explains that Turkey not only increased its economic engagements with the Middle Eastern countries in the 2000s but rather became more integrated with this geography in terms of economic relations. In this study, the author assessed Turkey's increasing integration with the MENA region with regard to trade, foreign direct investment (FDI) and cooperations. The author claims that through the twentieth century Turkey had looked westward and had limited relations with its eastern and southern neighbors, however, especially after 2002 Turkey has rediscovered the MENA region and developed political, economic and sociocultural relation linkages. By doing so, Turkey has not only reengaged with MENA, but also integrated with the region.

According to the author, three sets of structures have had an impact on the reintegration of Turkey with the MENA. These structures are material interests which were focused on economic relations, multiple dialogue channels which did not only consist of formal but also cover informal relations and finally the perceptions of other MENA actors about Turkey. El-Anis underlines that Turkey's increasing involvement with MENA is closely related to the country's global governance aspirations. In this way, Turkey has diversified its trading partners, increased its trade volume and overcome the effects of the 2008 financial crisis, and, however, experienced vulnerabilities from the instabilities that began with the Arab Spring.

In Turkey's relations with MENA, the author first analyzes the data of the World Bank on the trade volume and balance. He points out that Turkey has a trade surplus with all MENA countries and has over $32 billion total trade with Iraq, Iran, Saudi Arabia and the UAE. The over $20 billion trade surplus with MENA becomes more important for Turkey when it is taken into account that the country has a deficit with 11 of the top 20 trade partners. Trade with MENA consists of 26% of Turkey's total exports, and although it is inconsistent after the Arab upheavals, the trade volume increased ninefold when it is compared with the pre-2002 era.

Turkey has also an investment surplus in regard to the total FDI of MENA countries. However, when it is compared with trade, the character of FDI is irregular in the 2000s. Also, while Turkey has a trade surplus with all MENA countries, the case on FDI has differed from country to country. Turkey has FDI deficits with countries such as Iraq and Egypt, but has FDI surpluses with petrol-rich GCC states. The author also emphasized that cooperations have a significant role in integration and Turkish cooperations have important business relations especially on the construction and infrastructure sectors. They have also helped to connect political decision-makers together through both formal and informal channels.

In the final analysis, the author concludes that economic integration with the MENA has potential spill-over effects into political, security and sociocultural relationships, yet there are structural limitations to further integration. Turkey has become a more central component of the MENA system when it is compared with any time in the post-World War I era. He argues that this situation contributes to the achieving of Turkey's global governance aspirations. Increased trade will promote political cooperation between Turkey and other MENA states over time but is unlikely to lead to the type of economic interdependence that promotes regional security. For this to happen, greater FDI flows as well as an increased role for Turkish MNCs will be needed.

The tenth chapter by Emel Parlar Dal and Samiratou Dipama entitled "Assessing the Turkish "Trading State" in the Sub-Saharan Africa" deals with Turkey's trade policy toward the SSA as a part of its political-economic engagements with this region where Turkey has begun to pursue an active foreign policy since the mid-2000s as a part of its Africa opening strategy. In their study, the authors apply the trading state concept of Rosecrance to the case of Turkey's foreign policy toward SSA to assess the role of economic factors in Turkey's Africa opening. While applying the concept of trading state borrowed from Rosecrance, the authors also put this concept in the context of Turkey's multiple motivations in increasing its cooperation with the SSA countries. Whether trade occupies a significant place in Turkey's African engagements constitutes the central preoccupation of this study. In the first part of this study, the authors tent to reassess Rosecrance's trading state versus military/conquest state and investigate whether Rosecrance's trading state has now been witnessing a decline in face of the military state. In the second part, the authors delve in the assessment of Turkish trading state since the 1990s and try to understand the differences between Turkey's past and current trade strategies. In the third part of the study, Parlar Dal and Dipama attempt to compare Turkey's trading state with the other countries pursuing active trade relations with the region. In doing so, they also focus on the instruments, geographical focus and sectors of the Turkish trading state in the SSA since the 2000s. In the last part of their study, the authors question whether Turkey acts as a real trading state in the SSA by analyzing the strengths and weaknesses of its trading state strategy toward this region.

In the final analysis, the authors conclude that economic factors are the main motivation behind Turkey's engagement with SSA.

They underline that the total trade volume of Turkey with SSA has reached 19.5 billion USD in 2015 while it was 810 million USD in 2002, and despite this sharp increase in Turkey's trade volume with the SSA in the last decade, Turkey has still a weak trading state status in this region which needs to be further reinforced by overcoming some challenges and limitations such as the asymmetries in trade relations and the small share of Turkey's trade with SSA compared to the country's total external trade.

The eleventh chapter by Altay Atlı on "The Political Economy of Turkey's Relations with the Asia-Pacific" moves on to the emerging Asia-Pacific aspects of Turkey's political economy with a special focus on developing trade and diplomatic relations with countries of the region, most specifically Japan and China. The chapter looks both descriptively and empirically at the political and economic strategies Turkey turns toward in this region. The author also gives a specific place to China's Belt and Road Initiative (BRI) and its possible impacts on Turkey's political economy. As the author argues, recent years have indeed witnessed a significant increase in the dialogue between Turkey and Asian countries at both the governmental and the non-state levels; however, with respect to economic relations, the Asia-Pacific as a region still remains a major source of Turkey's deficit, and the gap is widening. In 2017, Turkey's overall trade deficit amounted to $58.9 billion, while in the same period Turkey's trade deficit with the countries of the Asia-Pacific was $45.9 billion—figures clearly showing how trade with the Asia-Pacific contributes negatively to the chronic current deficit problem of the Turkish economy.

Despite this adverse situation, Turkey has a strong motivation for improving its economic relations with the Asia-Pacific. For one thing, while imports from this region—and particularly from the People's Republic of China, which is Turkey's largest source of imports—are contributing to an ever-widening deficit and to a deterioration in terms of the nation's balance of payments, a remarkable portion of these imports consists of intermediary products and components that are vitally needed by the Turkish economy and sourced from these countries in high quality and at relatively low cost.

Atli argues that Asia-Pacific's rising importance for Turkey's economy, however, goes beyond the benefits created by imports. Turkey is currently making efforts to upgrade its economy, by increasing its technological capabilities, improving self-sufficiency in energy and developing its physical infrastructure. In this sense, working with the economic powerhouses of the Asia-Pacific and drawing in more investment from them can be a useful instrument to achieve the objectives. While the inflow of financial capital from Asia-Pacific into Turkey is certainly desirable, a more crucial objective from the Turkish perspective is to generate added value for the economy by sourcing technology and know-how from Asian partners through foreign direct investment.

For the author, Turkey's position within China's BRI can be understood within this context. Turkish policy makers have repeatedly expressed their intention to be a part of this project, and the main motivation here is that cooperating with China and undertaking large-scale projects together can help Turkey's efforts to close its deficits in areas such as infrastructure and energy. BRI is new; however, Turkey's collaboration with Asia countries in this manner is not. Starting with the 1980s, Turkey has managed to attach significant amounts of Japanese investment, mainly in the automotive sector. While Japanese capital was seeking to reduce labor costs and have access to sizable markets in Turkey, the Middle East and also Europe, benefiting from Turkey's customs union with the European Union, Turkey has benefited from incoming foreign capital in terms of improved industrial capacity, increased employment generation, rise in exports and exchange of know-how.

Finally, the author contends that while today Turkey's relations with Asia are gaining significance, they take place in an increasingly interconnected and interdependent world, meaning that economic relations with the Asia-Pacific are not meant—as some pundits suggest—to replace those with Turkey's more established partners such as Europe, Middle East and the former Soviet Union; rather, they are complementing them into a global network of trade and investment ties.

In Guise of Conclusion

Turkey's current political international landscape has been witnessing significant changes during the last decade as a result of a series of changes occurring in the international, regional and domestic politics. As the chapters in this edited volume suggest, Turkey's changing international political environment has led to the diversification and extension of this academic field opening up new avenues for further research. Turkey's increasing politic-economic relations with multiple geographies such as Africa, Latin America and Asia-Pacific, its new politic-economic instruments and the outweighing importance of domestic politics on the country's political economy are among the numerous rationales for further research on this subfield of International Politics.

The various chapters herein demonstrate the enriching content of Turkish political economy and how the interplay of economic, political, institutional, geopolitical and social factors impact its enduring transformation at the structural, regional and national levels. Furthermore, the chapters also portray the complexity of Turkish politics and its fragilities and limitations at the political economy level. In sum, the book approaches the topic from the duality of opportunities and challenges that Turkey has faced since the 2000s.

This edited volume also has its limitations due to the lack of studies on energy, climate change politics of Turkey, the role of business associations and civil society organizations in the shaping of Turkey's current political economy landscape, and the impact of Turkey's domestic developments and its regime type change on the future of Turkey's political economy policies. However, it provides a wide range of topics covering the current challenges of Turkey's economics, its multiple politic-economic tools and its new roles in the emerging donor world and in the informal groupings such as MIKTA and its expanding regional and global outreach.

Acknowledgements The author would like to thank Samiratou Dipama, Nilay Tuysuz, Ahmet Tuzgen and Hakan Mehmetcik for their technical help.

References

Arestis, P., & Saad-Filho, A. (Eds.). (2007). *Political Economy of Brazil: Recent Economic Performance*. New York: Palgrave Macmillan.

Arrighi, G., & Zhang, L. (2011). Beyond the Washington Consensus: A New Bandung? In J. Shefner & P. Fernández-Kelly (Eds.), *Globalization and Beyond: New Examinations of Global Power and Its Alternatives* (pp. 25–57). University Park, PA: Penn State University Press.

Bank, A., & Karadag, R. (2012). *The Political Economy of Regional Power: Turkey Under the AKP* (GIGA Working Papers No. 204).

Breslin, S. (2013). *China and the Global Political Economy*. Basingstoke, UK: Palgrave.

Casanova, L., & Kassum, J. (2014). *The Political Economy of an Emerging Global Power: In Search of the Brazil Dream*. IPE Series. Basingstoke, UK: Palgrave.

Falola, T., & Achberger, J. (2013). *The Political Economy of Development and Underdevelopment in Africa*. New York: Routledge.

Gu, J., Shakland, A., & Chenoy, A. (2016). *The BRICS in International Development*. IPE Series. Basingstoke, UK: Palgrave.

Güven, A. B. (2008). *Post-Washington Consensus in Action: Lessons from Turkey, Draft Version*. Paper presented at the Annual Meeting of the Canadian Association of Political Science University of British Columbia, Vancouver, BC, June 4.

Güven, A. B. (2016). The Political Economy of Turkish Democracy. In C. Erişen & P. Kubicek (Eds.), *Democratic Consolidation in Turkey* (pp. 184–203). London: Routledge.

Hibben, M. (2016). *Poor States, Power and the Politics of IMF Reform Drivers of Change in the Post-Washington Consensus*. IPE Series. Basingstoke, UK: Palgrave.

Kar, S., & Sen, K. (2016). *The Political Economy of India's Growth Episodes*. SPREI. London, UK: Palgrave Macmillan.

Kirişçi, K. (2009). The Transformation of Turkish Foreign Policy: The Rise of the Trading State. *New Perspectives on Turkey, 40*, 29–56.

Kutlay, M. (2015). *Turkish Economy at a Crossroads: Unpacking Turkey's Current Account Challenge*. Global Turkey in Europe III: Democracy, Trade, and the Kurdish Question in Turkey-EU Relations, 19, 219.

Li, J., & Wang, L. (2014). *China's Economic Dynamics a Beijing Consensus in the making?* New York: Routledge.

Lin, Y. M. (2017). *Dancing with the Devil the Political Economy of Privatization in China*. New York: Oxford University Press.

Nagaraj, R., & Moritam, S. (2017). *Political Economy of Contemporary India*. Cambridge, UK: Cambridge University Press.

Parlar Dal, E. (2014). On Turkey's Trail as a "Rising Middle Power" in the Network of Global Governance: Preferences, Capabilities, and Strategies. *Perception, 19*(4), 107.

Parlar Dal, E., & Gök, G. O. (2014). Locating Turkey as a 'RisingPower' in the Changing International Order: An Introduction. *Perceptions, 19*(4), 1–19.

Sandal, N. A. (2014). Middle Powerhood as a Legitimation Strategy in the Developing World: The Cases of Brazil and Turkey. *International Politics, 51*(6), 693–708.

Serra, N., & Stiglitz, J. E. (2008). The Washington Consensus Reconsider Towards a New Global Governance. Oxford and New York: Oxford University Press.

Tekin, B. Ç., & Tekin, B. R. (2015). *The Limits, Dilemmas and Paradoxes of Turkish Foreign Policy: A Political Economy Perspective*. London: LSEE-Research on South Eastern Europe.

Oyvat, C. (2018). *The End of Boom and the Political Economy of Turkey's Crisis*.

Oniş, Z. (1991). The Logic of the Developmental State. *Comparative Politics,* *24*(1), 109–126.

Öniş, Z. (2010). Crises and Transformations in Turkish Political Economy. *Turkish Policy Quarterly, 9*(3), 45–61.

Yagci, M. (2016). A Beijing Consensus in the Making: The Rise of Chinese Initiatives in the International Political Economy and Implications for Developing Countries. *Perceptions, 21*(2), 29–56.

Yagci, M. (2017). The Political Economy of AK Party Rule in Turkey: From a Regulatory to a Developmental State? *Insight Turkey, 19*(2), 89–113.

Yang, D. L. (2012). *The Global Recession and China's Political Economy.* New York: Palgrave.

PART I

Domestic Diversification of Turkey's Political Economy

CHAPTER 2

The Political Economy of Turkey's Economic Miracles and Crisis

Turan Subasat

INTRODUCTION

Turkey is facing one of the most severe currency crises in its history. The government maintains that the crisis is caused solely by political factors. In this view, Turkey has a sound economy with low public deficit and debt, a strong banking sector, high saving and investment rates. The crisis, therefore, is a part of a big conspiracy by the *enemies* of Turkey who are envious of Turkey's economic *success*. The *enemies* include a wide array of states and interest groups, and the leading enemies often change based on the conjunctural factors. The USA is the leading country behind the current crisis.

This paper argues, however, that Turkey's economy suffers from structural problems, and the key to understand the crisis is the nature of the two economic *miracles* that Turkey experienced since 2002. The first *miracle* occurred between 2002 and 2008 when the country's nominal GDP in current US dollars (NGDP) tripled. This *miracle* was fictional since the increase in NGDP was largely due to the exchange

---

T. Subasat (✉)
Muğla Sıtkı Koçman University, Mugla, Turkey
e-mail: turansubasat@mu.edu.tr

© The Author(s) 2020
E. Parlar Dal (ed.), *Turkey's Political Economy in the 21st Century*, International Political Economy Series,
https://doi.org/10.1007/978-3-030-27632-4_2

31

rate movements and the real GDP in current US dollars (RGDP) performance was unimpressive. Subasat (2014) analyzed the first *miracle* extensively and concluded that there was neither a miracle nor even a mild success story. During the first *miracle* period, however, Turkey experienced large current account deficits and accumulated large external debt, which are at the heart of the current crisis.

The second *miracle* started after 2009 when Turkey suffered the impacts of the global financial crisis. Between 2010 and 2017, Turkey experienced one of the fastest RGDP growth rates in the world. The investment and saving rates also improved significantly. While the NGDP progressively declined since 2013, RGDP and nominal GDP in purchasing power parity (NGDP [PPP]) have increased rapidly. In 2017, Turkey achieved an astonishing 7.42% RGDP growth rate, which was one of the highest in the world. The second *miracle* was also fictional, promoted by the notorious 2016 revision of the Turkish Statistical Institute (TURKSTAT), as well as the election-oriented stimulation of the economy, which was unsustainable. In this period, Turkey continued to experience large current account deficits and the external debt has become large enough to threaten the economy. The deterioration of the global environment and drying up the global liquidity marked the end of the second *miracle* and created the conditions for a painful adjustment. As the recent economic history shows, once the underlying causes of a crisis were formed, all that was needed was a trigger which, in this case, was the bizarre conflict with the USA over a pastor.

This paper argues that Turkey's two economic *miracles* and the current crisis are dialectically linked and the crisis cannot be comprehended without a proper grasp of how the *miracles* were manufactured. The paper starts by analyzing the *miracles* but focuses mainly on the second *miracle* since the first *miracle* has been extensively analyzed in the literature. It then focuses on the link between the *miracles* and the crisis.

The Miracles

Turkey adopted capital account liberalization in the 1980s, which led to financial and economic instabilities allied with irregular capital flows. After the crisis in 2001, Turkey entered into the first *miracle* phase with the election of the Islamist-oriented Justice and Development Party (AKP) in November 2002. Inflation and public debt declined while NGDP and nominal exports increased threefold between 2002 and

2008. The government proclaimed that Turkey was marching decisively toward becoming the 10th largest economy in the world by 2023. Turkey's economic growth was particularly admirable in the face of the 2008 crisis. The large current account deficits and the accumulation of external debt during this period were played down as a minor hurdle.

Despite the above success story, the first *miracle* was largely an illusion (Subasat 2014). The depreciation of the US dollar against most currencies (including the Turkish lira) artificially boosted their NGDP. While this was not unique to Turkey (all countries experienced similar growth patterns), Turkey's growth was amplified further since the Turkish lira also appreciated against most major currencies. In this period, the average RGDP growth rates remained modest compared to the pre-AKP period. Turkey's average growth was higher than that of high-income countries (that experienced one of the worst crises in their history) during the period but was slower than the low- and middle-income countries. Turkey's export performance lagged behind that of all income groups. Marked by the large and stubborn current account deficits, external financing was the main source of economic growth. Although Turkey attracted substantial external resources (by offering very high real interest rates), they were largely directed into consumption rather than investment. The investment and saving rates declined substantially. Turkey's first *miracle* signified an unsustainable bubble economy. The large current account deficits and the accumulation of external debt during this period were proven more than a minor hurdle and are at the heart of the current crisis.

The second *miracle* was even more *impressive*. Excluding 2009 (when the RGDP contracted by 4.8%), the average RGDP growth rate between 2010 and 2016 was 6.76% and the gross fixed capital formation growth rate was 11.3%. Gross domestic savings increased from 22 to 25.3% of the NGDP. Out of 170 countries, Turkey was ranked at 55th in terms of per capita GDP (PPP) in 2010 and moved up to the 49th place in 2016 (6 places up in 6 years).

The second *miracle* is more curious because most political and economic indicators, which had improved earlier, started deteriorating and Turkey experienced internal and external setbacks. Turkey had accomplished considerable political and social progress between 2002 and 2011 (Subasat 2017). The press, religious and ethnic freedoms improved; the relationships with the neighboring countries were promoted under the "zero problems policy" and significant progress with the EU membership negotiations was achieved. The key aspects of democratic and legal life enriched. There was widespread optimism about the future of Turkey's democracy and economy.

These all changed rapidly since 2011 when the AKP won the general election with almost 50% of the votes. Democratic and legal life has deteriorated and political chaos has replaced relative stability. Turkey's position in the World Press Freedom Index worsened rapidly from the 99th in 2008 to the 157th in 2018. Increased authoritarianism instigated the Gezi Park protests in May 2013. The coalitions within the AKP collapsed and led to the corruption allegations in 2013 and the coup attempt in 2016. The *zero-problem policy* turned into *zero friends policy* and the relations with the EU deteriorated (Zalewski 2013). The "democratic initiative process" crumbled abruptly in 2015, the war with the PKK intensified and Turkey endured a vicious circle of violence. The state of emergency was declared after the failed coup, which targeted a wide segment of the political opposition.

The economy started experiencing an array of economic troubles since 2013: the stubbornly large trade and current account deficits (despite the sliding currency), high external debt, smaller foreign exchange reserves, high reliance on short-term capital inflows, high budget deficit, high inflation, high interest rates (real and nominal), high unemployment rates, high corporate exposure to foreign exchange risk and oversupply in the housing market. The widespread optimism is now replaced with widespread pessimism. These are not the prevailing conditions under which an economic miracle could thrive. TURKSTAT's 2016 national income revision, which will be investigated in the next section, is the key to understand Turkey's mysterious second *miracle*.

TURKSTAT'S 2016 REVISION

An assessment of the recent performance of the Turkish economy is no longer a simple task due to the 2016 national income revision of TURKSTAT, which disproportionately affected the most important macroeconomic variables. While the revision, taken at face value, boosted Turkey's economy, it has been widely criticized for its inaccuracies. The timing of the revision is particularly noteworthy, which boosted the popularity of the government in the face of the ailing economy and contributed to the recent election victory.

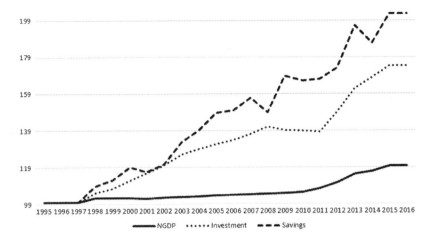

Fig. 2.1 Nominal GDP, gross fixed capital formation and gross domestic savings (new series as a percentage of old series) (*Note* The source for this and subsequent figures and tables is the World Development Indicators database)

The revision went far beyond Eurostat's proposals (Boratav 2017), bringing extraordinary changes in the national income series and pointing to a major departure from similar experiences of other countries (Aydogus 2018). Figure 2.1 shows the impact of the revision on GDP, investment and saving rates. The divergence between the old and new series is due to methodological changes and statistical improvements. The methodological changes are instigated by a move from ESA 1995 to ESA 2010. The most important components are R&D and purchases of weapons systems, which are now considered as a fixed investment rather than consumption expenditure.

The statistical improvements are mainly caused by a move to official records of economic activity and mainly influenced the investment in the construction sector. While the data was updated back to 1998 for the methodological changes, it was updated back to 2009 for the statistical improvements. The series are identical until 1998 but they start diverging from each other due to the introduction of methodological changes. The impact of the methodological changes on GDP is minimal but significantly large for investment and savings. For GDP, the difference between the new and old series becomes larger after 2009 due to the introduction of statistical improvements. Since the statistical improvements account for over 90% of the overall GDP changes, a major inconsistency has been introduced and this made an accurate assessment of Turkey's pre- and post-2009 relative GDP performance near impossible (Aydogus 2018). In 2016, the GDP is 20% higher with the new series. The same figures are 74% for investment and 103% for savings. These are extraordinarily high figures compared to the similar revisions in the OECD. The statistical improvements, for example, accounted only for 18% of the average overall changes, and the revisions caused only 3.8% (on average) increase in NGDP in the OECD countries (Aydogus 2018).

The inaccuracies of the revision are obvious given that the usual correlations between the revised variables and the others (not altered by the revision) have been significantly weakened. With the new series, for example, per capita RGDP increased by 6.75% in 2013 whereas per capita CO_2 emissions (in metric tons) declined by 3.04%, which is a major inconsistency. Yükseler (2017) argues that the rapid increase in construction investments between 2013 and 2015 is incompatible with the decline in the relevant indicators such as the employment index, number of hours worked, building use permits and domestic cement sales. Similarly, Aydogus (2017) reveals the inconsistencies between value-added, production, employment and labor productivity in the construction sector during the same period. Construction investment is the main determinant of gross fixed capital formation, which is the main determinant of GDP. Since construction investment growth is exaggerated, so is GDP growth.

In a series of excellent blog articles, Meyersson revealed the inconsistencies of the revision. Firstly, by using cross-sectional data, Meyersson (2017a) estimated a simple regression model between RGDP per capita growth rates (by using the data for both before and after the revision) and a number of standard growth variables[1] to comprehend how much of Turkey's growth can be explained. He estimated this model for the two periods (2004–2009 and 2010–2015) and for a selection of 73 countries.[2] The model predicted the growth performance of all

---

[1] These are the current account balance, inflation rate, investment rate, government debt, unemployment rate, labor force participation rate, domestic credit to the private sector, age-dependency ratio, urbanization rate and the net international investment position.

[2] Mayersson excluded the poorest, smallest (in terms of both population and land areas) and the main oil and gas exporter countries.

countries (including Turkey) quite well for the 2004–2009 period. The results for the 2010–2015 period, however, portrayed a different picture for Turkey. Turkey's residuals, for both the revised and unrevised data, are by far the largest in absolute terms. In this period, Turkey became an outlier compared to the rest of the countries, which implied that the selected indicators failed to explain Turkey's rapid growth. This is noteworthy because Turkey was an outlier in this period even with the old series. Turkey's data was already problematical and the revision aggravated the problem. Meyersson, therefore, concluded, "if Turkey's growth model before the revision was from Mars, it is now from Mercury." Meyersson, then, estimated what the growth rates would have been based on the predictors and found that Turkey must have grown by 1.6% (rather than 6%) with the new series and only by 0.3% with the old series. In this light, the accuracy of TURKSTAT's 2008 revision, which introduced a 38% increase in national income, could also be questioned.

Meyersson (2017b) took a more direct approach by employing time-series data. He identified a number of variables that were directly linked with overall economic activity but not influenced by the revision such as primary energy consumption, electricity generation, carbon dioxide emissions, total bank loans and construction permits. He first compares the growth rates of GDP (with new and old series) and the above variables for the 2004–2009 and 2010–2015 periods. Although both revised and unrevised GDP growth rates radically increased in the 2010–2015 period, the growth rates of the other variables declined, revealing a major inconsistency.

He then estimates three regressions between GDP growth and growth rates of a selection of the above variables during the 1981–2009 period. As the independent variables, the first regression includes only the energy variables (primary energy consumption and electricity generation), the second adds bank loans and the third adds construction permits. He then uses the results of these models to predict Turkey's GDP growth rates for the 2004–2009 and 2010–2015 periods. The models predict the GDP growth rate well in the first period, which proves their accuracy. In the second period, however, they predict much lower growth rates than the official growth rates (with the new and old series). Interestingly, the third model, which includes all the variables, predicts a close to zero growth rate for the 2010–2015 period.

Finally, Meyersson (2017c) argues that although the revised GDP grew faster during the 2010–2015 period, the Turkish stock market grew

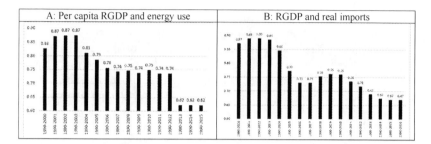

Fig. 2.2 Relationships between economic performance and selected variables

much faster during the 2004–2009 period. An investor, for example, would have made a 153% real return by investing funds into BIST100 equity index of the Borsa Istanbul in the first period but would have made an 8.1% loss in the second period. If the stocks are adjusted for risk using the (refined) Sharpe ratio, the real returns are 17% and −42.2%, respectively. This is an inconsistency if one takes the profitable stock markets as an indication of a healthy economy.

An examination of the link between GDP and variables that are expected to be highly correlated with it through time would also be very informative regarding the structural breaks that the revisions introduced. Figure 2.2A indicates the changes in the strength of relationship (measured by R^2) between per capita RGDP and per capita energy use (kg of oil equivalent) through the 1990 and 2016 period by using their logarithmic growth rates. The higher the R^2, the stronger the relationships between the variables. The first correlation covers the 1990 and 2000 period and the subsequent correlations were calculated to see the impact of each additional year on the relationship. If the relationship starts strong but grows weaker with the revision, this would provide extra evidence for the inaccuracy of the revision. As Fig. 2.2A indicates, the correlation between per capita RGDP and per capita energy use is very strong (R^2 is as high as 87%) before the AKP years. With the inclusion of 2004 in the regression, R^2 declines to around 75% and declines further to 62% with the inclusion of 2013. The two-stage decline is notable because the 2016 revision mostly affected the years after 2013 and the 2008 revision mostly affected the years after 2004. Similar trends are observed between RGDP and real imports (Fig. 2.2B), which confirms Meyersson's analogy. If Turkey's growth model after the 2016 revision was from Mercury, the growth model after the 2008 revision was from Mars.

Growth Analysis

In this section, we first compare Turkey's RGDP growth against four income groups (high, upper-middle, lower-middle and low-income countries) since 2003 in order to assess Turkey's relative economic performance. This is a useful exercise because success is a relative concept and the conjunctural conditions that affect many countries must be taken into consideration. Because the lower-middle-income group includes India and the upper-middle-income group includes China, the figures for these income groups will also be calculated without these large countries since they disproportionately influence the overall performance of their groups. Growth comparisons require the use of the variables to be measured in constant prices (Subasat and Uysal 2018).

Figure 2.3 shows Turkey's relative RGDP growth performance by means of the difference between the growth rate of Turkey and the income groups. Turkey, for example, grew by 2.26% on average during the 1980–2002 period, high-income countries grew by 2.08% and the difference between the growth rates was 0.18%. During the 2003–2016 period, the difference increased to 2.11% with the old series and to 3.17% with the new series. Turkey's relative growth performance compared to high-income countries, therefore, was much better during the 2003–2016 period. The figures for the other income groups, however, indicate that Turkey's relative success was not because of its superior

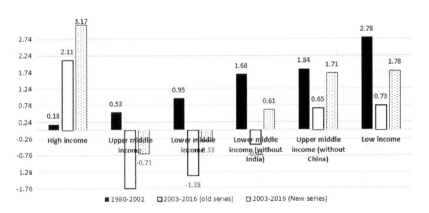

Fig. 2.3 Turkey's relative RGDP growth performance

performance but because of the inferior performance of high-income countries (due largely to the 2008 crisis). The relative performance of Turkey compared to the other income groups was much better during the 1980–2002 period than the 2003–2016 period, with both the new and old series. During the 1980–2002 period, Turkey grew faster than all the income groups. During the 2003–2016 period, however, Turkey grew slower than the upper-middle-income, lower-middle-income and lower-middle-income without India groups with the old series, and slower than the upper-middle-income and lower-middle-income groups with the new series. Even when Turkey grew faster, the relative performance of Turkey was much better in the 1980–2002 period. In the case of low-income countries, for example, Turkey grew by 2.78% faster in the 1980–2002 period whereas in the 2003–2016 period grew by 0.73% faster with the old series and by 1.78% faster with the new series.

Comparing Turkey's growth rates with the above income groups is indicative but has limitations since each income group includes a wide variety of countries. Excluding large countries such as India and China helps but comparing Turkey's performance against individual countries would be more informative. Table 2.1 shows percent rank of Turkey's growth performance with the old and new series through four periods: 1980–2003 (pre-AKP period), 2003–2010 (first *miracle* period), 2010–2016 (second *miracle* period) and 2003–2016 (entire AKP period).

With the old series, Turkey's RGDP growth performance was better than 70.7% of all countries during the 1980–2003 period. During the first *miracle* period, it declined to 65.9% but went up to 72.1% in the second *miracle* period. It was at 71.4% during the entire AKP period which is marginally (by 0.7%) higher than the pre-AKP period. International comparisons often require the elimination of structurally different countries from the sample to achieve more meaningful results. The exclusion of small-, low- and high-income countries could improve the results, as Turkey is a large upper-middle-income country. The exclusion of the 25 small countries (with a population less than one million) produces a flimsy picture for Turkey in both *miracle* periods. Turkey is now ranked at 74.5% in the pre-AKP period, 63.9% in the first *miracle* period, 59.8% in the second *miracle* period and 61.4% in the entire AKP period. This picture gets progressively flimsier when Turkey is compared with the middle-income countries and with the

Table 2.1 Percent rank of Turkey in terms of per capita RGDP growth rates

	Old series				New series			
	All (149)	All w/o small (124)	MI (75)	MI w/o small (65)	All (149)	All w/o small (124)	MI (75)	MI w/o small (65)
1980–2003	70.7	74.5	71.2	74.6	71.4	75.4	72.6	76.1
2003–2010	65.9	63.9	56.1	49.2	70	68	61.6	55.5
2010–2016	72.1	59.8	49.3	42.8	91.8	91.8	89	87.3
2003–2016	71.4	61.4	52	44.4	82.9	83.6	78	74.6
Difference	0.7	−13.1	−19.2	−30.2	11.5	8.2	5.4	−1.5

All: All countries with available data
All w/o small: All countries without small countries with a population less than one million
MI: Only middle-income countries are included
MI w/o small: Middle-income countries without small countries
Difference: The difference between 2003–2016 and 1980–2003 periods. A positive number implies a higher growth rate in the 2003–2016 period
The number of countries used in the calculations is in parentheses

middle-income countries excluding the small countries.[3] In the latter case, Turkey was ranked at 74.6% in the pre-AKP period, which declines to 44.4% during the AKP period indicating an astonishing 30.2% decline.

Figures with the new series indicate a significantly superior performance for Turkey, particularly in the second *miracle* period. Turkey's RGDP growth performance was better than 71.4% of all countries in the pre-AKP period. During the first *miracle* period, Turkey's percent rank decreased to 70%, which means (even with the new series) there was, in fact, no miracle. In the second *miracle* period, however, Turkey performed better than 91.8% of all countries. During the entire AKP period, Turkey grew faster than 82.9% of the countries, which is substantially (by 11.5%) higher than the pre-AKP period. Excluding the small countries from the full sample and comparing Turkey only with the middle-income countries still produce results that favor the AKP periods. When the small countries are excluded from the middle-income countries, however, Turkey's rank is higher in the pre-AKP period than the AKP period by 1.5%.

[3] The focus on the middle-income countries is justified because the middle-income countries are structurally different from the low- and high-income countries and the high-income countries have experienced the worst economic crisis in their history since 2008. The middle-income countries are the most crowded group, which include 110 countries out of 218 countries in the world.

42   T. SUBASAT

Table 2.2 Percent rank of Turkey in terms of per capita real exports growth rates

	Old series				New series			
	All (113)	All w/o small (107)	MI (59)	MI w/o small (56)	All (113)	All w/o small (107)	MI (59)	MI w/o small (56)
1987–2003	81.0	80.9	78.9	79.6	82.8	82.8	82.4	83.3
2003–2010	48.6	47.6	45.6	44.4	50.4	49.5	49.1	48.1
2010–2016	63.0	62.8	70.1	70.3	79.2	79.0	82.4	81.4
2003–2016	48.6	47.6	52.6	51.8	64.8	64.7	70.1	70.3
Difference	−32.4	−33.3	−26.3	−27.8	−18.0	−18.1	−12.3	−13.0

All: All countries with available data
All w/o small: All countries without small countries with a population less than one million
MI: Only middle-income countries are included
MI w/o small: Middle-income countries without small countries
Difference: The difference between 2003–2016 and 1980–2003 periods. A positive number implies a higher growth rate in the 2003–2016 period
The number of countries used in the calculations is in parentheses

A similar exercise indicates a bleak picture for per capita exports (Table 2.2). With the old and new series, Turkey's export performance was much better in the pre-AKP period than both the *miracle* periods. Given that exports are considered as an important determinant of economic growth, such a remarkable RGDP growth (particularly during the second *miracle* period) with such a poor exports performance appears to be a major inconsistency.

The growth analysis above, therefore, provides no support for a success story for the AKP period even with the revised series.

RANK ANALYSIS

Turkey's relative performance can also be assessed by using the absolute values of selected indicators. For this purpose, three alternative GDP measures (all suffer from various problems) could be used. A brief discussion of these problems is necessary to interpret the analysis below and justify the alternative measure that will be introduced.

Strengths and Weaknesses of Alternative Measures of GDP

While RGDP is the best measure for growth analysis, it is unreliable for rank analysis since it is highly sensitive to the selection of the base year (of the GDP deflator), which can produce inconsistent results in international rankings (Subasat and Uysal 2018).

NGDP is the most commonly used measure to rank countries, which is heavily influenced by exchange rate movements. International comparisons based on this measure, therefore, do not always yield accurate results. The overvaluation (undervaluation) of the exchange rate artificially expands (contracts) NGDP and makes an economy appear to be more successful (unsuccessful) than it actually is. For this reason, the international ranking of countries, where exchange rates are excessively volatile, may show significant variations that will not reflect real developments in the economy. For example, the depreciation of the US dollar and the appreciation of the Turkish lira against other currencies artificially tripled Turkey's NGDP between 2002 and 2007, resulting in an illusion of rising prosperity (Subasat 2014).

GDP at purchasing power parity (PPP) exchange rates, by definition, eliminates the impact of the changes in the market exchange rate on GDP but it has its own weaknesses. GDP (PPP) data is available only from 1990, which provides a limited number of observations to analyze long-term trends. More importantly, GDP (PPP) suffers from a methodological bias. As the benchmark country, NGDP and NGDP (PPP) must be the same for the USA. Likewise, RGDP and RGDP (PPP) must also be the same. NGDP and RGDP are linked via the GDP price deflator (P^G), which reflects price changes (inflation or deflation). NGDP (PPP) and RGDP (PPP) are also linked via the GDP (PPP) price deflator (P^P).

$$P^G = \text{NGDP} \div \text{RGDP}$$

$$P^P = \text{NGDP (PPP)} \div \text{RGDP (PPP)}$$

The P^G and P^P must be the same for the USA. While P^G indicates the domestic price changes and varies from country to country, P^P indicates the price changes in the USA and must be identical for all countries.[4] This is true for many but unfortunately not for all countries.

---

[4] In other words, if there was no inflation in the USA, the NGDP (PPP) and RGDP (PPP) would give the same results for all countries.

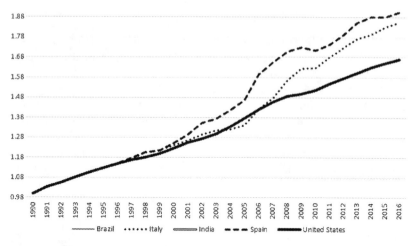

Fig. 2.4 GDP (PPP) deflator (indexed to 1990)

Figure 2.4 shows the P^P's for five countries: Brazil, Italy, India, Spain and the USA.[5] Although there are figures for five countries, only three lines are visible. This is because Brazil's P^P and India's P^P are the same as the USA's P^P, whereas Italy's P^P and Spain's P^P differ. It is interesting to note that Italy's P^P and Spain's P^P were the same as the USA's P^P until the late 1990s. This implies a methodological change in the calculation of P^P after the mid-1990s for Italy, Spain and similar (mostly) high-income countries, which marks a major methodological inconsistency.

NGDP (PPP) is calculated by multiplying RGDP (PPP) with P^P.

$$\text{NGDP (PPP)} = \text{RGDP (PPP)} \times P^P$$

If for some countries NGDP (PPP) is calculated by multiplying RGDP (PPP) with USA's P^P but not for the other countries, a major methodical bias is introduced. Countries that have the same P^P (of the USA) will be comparable but countries that have different P^P's will have modified

---

[5] While the original data is indexed to 2011 (i.e., takes the value of one in 2011), here it is indexed to the beginning year 1990 for better visibility.

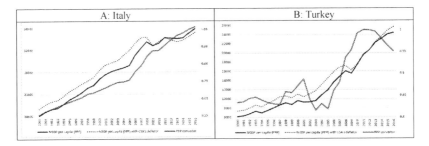

Fig. 2.5 Alternative NGDP (PPP) calculations

NGDP (PPP) and become incomparable through time.[6] For Italy's NGDP (PPP) to be comparable with Brazil, Italy's RGDP (PPP) should be converted into NGDP (PPP) by multiplying it with the USA's P^p, which produces significantly different results (Fig. 2.5A). Clearly, NGDP (PPP) with the USA's P^p indicates a slower increase between 1990 and 2016.

Likewise, Turkey's NGDP (PPP) would indicate a slower growth rate if it was calculated by using the USA's P^p. Figure 2.5B shows that Turkey's P^p fluctuated around 0.84 until 2005 and then increased rapidly to 1.00 until 2011 and started declining again. The pattern of Turkey's P^p indicates that it is not entirely immune to the bubble economy experienced during the 2000s. The rapid increase in Turkey's P^p is particularly important as Turkey's typical competitors (middle-income countries) tend to use the USA's P^p. Turkey, therefore, experienced an artificially faster increase in its NGDP (PPP) compared to its main competitors.[7]

The problems associated with the above GDP measures led Subasat and Uysal (2018) to introduce a new measure, which is named the "adjusted GDP" (GDP [ADJ]). The GDP (ADJ) is calculated by

---

[6] Imagine two countries with the identical RGDP (PPP) figures. If one country's NGDP (PPP) is calculated by using the USA's P^p but the other country's NGDP (PPP) is calculated by using a different P^p, the second country will have higher or lower NGDP (PPP), which will not be comparable with the first country.

[7] In fact, countries that with a separate P^p experienced faster increases than the USA's P^p, which implies that they have systematically higher NGDP (PPP) than the others.

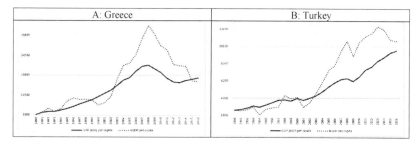

Fig. 2.6 NGDP and GDP (ADJ)

dividing the NGDP by an index, which is named the real exchange rate index (RERI). RERI is calculated by dividing each country's GDP price deflator (P^G) by the GDP deflator of the USA and indexing it to one for the starting year of the series. An increase in RERI implies that prices rise in the country faster than the USA and (holding everything else constant) the country becomes less competitive. Therefore, it is a real exchange rate index. GDP (ADJ) aims to eliminate the impacts of real exchange rate changes and produce a more stable GDP measure, which can be seen in Fig. 2.6. For Greece (Fig. 2.6A), NGDP per capita fluctuates around GDP (ADJ) until 2002. It then increases faster than GDP (ADJ) until the 2008 crisis when Greece's real exchange rate appreciates. Since 2008, the real exchange rate depreciates and NGDP per capita declines faster than GDP (ADJ) and two indicators converge. Similar trends are observed for Turkey (Fig. 2.6B).

GDP (ADJ), therefore, eliminates the real exchange rate effects on NGDP and establishes a more stable GDP measure that can be used more reliably for international comparisons. Note that GDP (ADJ) has the same trends as the GDP (PPP) for the countries that use USA's P^P, such as Brazil and India (Fig. 2.7A and B). Both variables for these countries, therefore, could be used to rank countries over time. While the ranking of countries would vary depending on the measure used, the change in ranking over time would produce similar trends. For the countries that use different P^Ps, such as Italy and Spain, however, GDP (ADJ) and GDP (PPP) would produce different trends after the late 1990s. Figure 2.7C and D indicate that GDP (PPP) to GDP (ADJ) ratio starts increasing noticeably after 2005. This is the reason why GDP (ADJ) is a more reliable indicator.

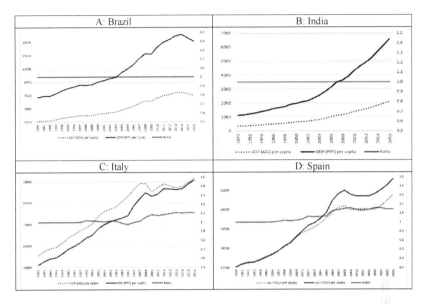

Fig. 2.7 GDP (ADJ) per capita, GDP per capita (PPP) and their ratio

Rank Analysis

After a comprehensive discussion of alternative measures of per capita GDP, we can begin our rank analysis. While GDP (ADJ) is the best measure, we also present the results of NGDP and GDP (PPP) for comparison. Before considering the following figures, it is important to bear in mind that the 1990s was the most difficult time period for Turkey, with three (1994, 1997 and 2001) crises and a massive earthquake in 1999.

The NGDP trends in Fig. 2.8A indicate that while there were severe fluctuations in the 1980–2003 period, Turkey's ranking increased considerably. Turkey was ranked at 48.7% on average between 1980 and 1988, then had a major leap forward and increased its ranking to 60.1% in 1990. While there were extreme fluctuations between 1990 and 2003 (due to the economic crises and earthquake), Turkey maintained its place until 2003 when it was ranked at 60.7% with the old series and at 62.3% with the new series. While Turkey's position fluctuated less between 2003 and 2016, it declined with the old series to 58.4%. With the new

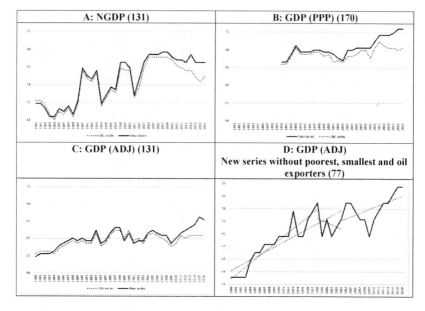

Fig. 2.8 Per capita GDP percent rank of Turkey with alternative measures (*Note* The number of countries used in calculations is in brackets)

series, it first increased to 64.6% in 2004 and eventually declined back to 62.3% in 2016. It is clear therefore that Turkey's ranking improved between 1980 and 2003 but deteriorated with the old series and remained the same with the new series. The NGDP analysis, therefore, provides no support for an economic miracle during the AKP period.

Per capita GDP (PPP) trends provide a supportive view of the AKP period (Fig. 2.8B). With the new series, Turkey was ranked at 62.5% in 1990, which went up to 67.2% in 1993 before declining to 63% in 2003. It then increased to 66.6% in 2006, to 70.2% in 2011 and to 72% in 2016. The old series followed a similar pattern to the new series until 2008. The first major difference occurred in 2009 when Turkey's ranking declined from 66% to 63.6% with the old series whereas remained the same with the new series. This is important because while many countries experienced the impacts of the global crisis in 2008, Turkey experienced it in 2009. The lack of decline in Turkey's ranking with the new series is rather peculiar, which signals its inaccuracy. The second difference occurred after 2011, when Turkey's rank improved rapidly with the new series, whereas declined with the old series, which is also rather peculiar. As will be discussed below, the old series is more consistent with the other developments in Turkey's economy. It is also important to remember the above-discussed limitations of GDP (PPP). Not only GDP (PPP) series start from 1990, a period in which the economy suffered from various shocks, but it also suffers from a methodological problem, which favors Turkey particularly against middle-income countries it competes with. Furthermore, bear in mind that the 2016 revision updated the statistical improvements back to 2009, which created the structural break that the new series exhibit. If the data had been revised for earlier years, the structural break would either disappear or lessen. The limitations of the GDP (PPP) and the revision created the illusion that Turkey experienced a second *miracle* between 2010 and 2016.

The GDP (ADJ) figures with the old series fluctuated around an increasing trend between 1990 and 1997, declined between 1998 and 2002 and fluctuated around a flat trend between 2003 and 2016 (Fig. 2.8C). The old series, therefore, indicates no miracle during the AKP periods. The GDP (ADJ) figures with the new series had a similar trend to the old series until 2009 and increased rapidly since then. Turkey's rank increased from 54.6 to 61.5% between 2009 and 2016, which reflects a significant success. To explore this success, Fig. 2.8D presents the GDP (ADJ) with the new series. Note that it excludes the poorest, smallest and the main oil and gas exporter countries and adds trend lines into 4 periods (1980–1997, 1980–2003, 1997–2002 and 2003–2016) for easy assessment.

The trend lines indicate that the increase in Turkey's ranking is faster in the pre-AKP period (1980–2003) than the AKP period (2003–2016). This is particularly true if the 1997–2002 period (one of the worst periods in Turkey's history due to the crises and earthquake) is excluded from the pre-AKP period. The magnifier impact of the 2016 revision also needs to be taken into consideration here.

None of the above figures indicates a miracle for the 2003–2009 period. The second *miracle* is supported, taken at face value, by the above figures but was facilitated by the 2016 revision. The second *miracle* was flimsier because in this period the economy lost its vitality and began to show the strains of the bubble economy created since 2003. The observation of the change in Turkey's ranking in major economic indicators supports this view (Fig. 2.9).

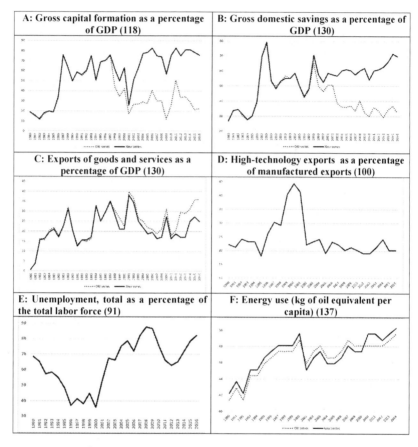

Fig. 2.9 Percent rank of Turkey in terms of key macroeconomic indicators (*Note* The number of countries used in calculations is in brackets)

The gross capital formation and gross domestic savings are the most heavily revised indicators (Fig. 2.9A and B). For both indicators, Turkey's rank improved significantly during the 1980s and early 1990s and deteriorated in the 1997–2001 period. The new series indicate a recovery after 2002 but the old series indicate further deterioration. While the revised investment and saving rates are consistent with the revised GDP figures, they are inconsistent with the other key economic indicators and former discourses and policies of the government.

The government officials themselves often complained about the very low saving rates and adopted policies to rectify this problem. The compulsory Personal Pension System, for example, was specifically designed to address low savings. If the saving rates were so high, Akcay (2016) rightly asks, why is it still compulsory?

Exports are expected to be highly correlated with GDP performance. Turkey's rank in terms of exports to GDP ratio improved significantly between 1980 and 2001 and deteriorated subsequently (Fig. 2.9C). While it remained low during the AKP period, it started improving with the old series since 2010. With the new series, however, it remained low because the new series increased NGDP but the nominal exports remained unaffected. Likewise, Turkey's rank regarding high-technology exports as a percentage of manufactured exports increased sharply between 1995 and 2000, and declined back to where it was before (Fig. 2.9D). Even these figures overstate the actual export performance because Turkey experienced one of the fastest increases in import dependency of exports during the 2000s, which implies that the domestic value-added in Turkey's exports declined considerably (Terzioglu and Subasat 2018).

Regarding unemployment, Turkey's rank declined significantly between 1990 and 1996 and remained static until 2000 (Fig. 2.9D). It increased rapidly between 2000 and 2002 due to the economic crisis and continued to increase until 2008. In 2008, Turkey had a higher unemployment rate than 87.6% of the countries in the sample. The first *miracle*, therefore, is associated with high relative unemployment, which is, therefore, called "jobless growth" (Voyvoda and Yeldan 2005). Although Turkey's rank declined until 2012, probably because of the 2012 crisis that influenced many other countries, it started increasing again afterward, which is inconsistent with the second *miracle*.

Similarly, Turkey's rank in terms of energy use increased rapidly between 1980 and 2000 and declined rapidly afterward due to the 2001 crisis. Since 2001 (with the new and old series), it fluctuated around an increasing trend but this was not at a level that could be considered consistent with the increase in GDP and investment rates.[8]

The above analysis shows that there were no economic miracles in Turkey. What emerged as the first *miracle* was due to exchange rate

---

[8]Although the new and old series move close to each other, it is interesting that the revision influenced this measure.

changes and the second *miracle* was facilitated by the 2016 revision. While there were no miracles, Turkey was rapidly accumulating external debt and resources were used mostly to support consumption and investment in the construction sector. This development model could not continue for long and was prone to a painful adjustment.

The Crisis

The long-expected currency crisis arrived unexpectedly and unfolded rapidly. The snap general elections in June 2018 had signaled the imminent crisis but not many expected it to begin before the upcoming local elections. As discussed extensively by Subasat (2014), the substantial current account deficits and the accumulation of external debt have been the main weaknesses of the Turkish economy since 2002. Such large and persistent current account deficits could not be sustained indefinitely and a painful adjustment was inevitable.

For a long time, however, the government's supporters argued that the current account deficits in Turkey were unproblematic for a number of reasons. First, they allowed the country to invest more than it saved, which in turn promoted economic growth and facilitated debt service without major problems (Yasar 2013). Second, current account deficits are a by-product of a rapid economic growth, particularly in energy importing countries (Yildirim 2013). Third, the current account problems are global (i.e., not specific to Turkey) and public debt to GDP ratio in Turkey is low.

These arguments were misleading since external resources could be used to lower savings rather than stimulating investment. This was the case in Turkey until the 2016 revision, which artificially pushed up domestic savings and investments. External resources could be invested in productive areas that do not generate foreign currency, which will be problematical as the debt will have to be serviced in foreign currency. Indeed, the large portion of the domestic investment in Turkey has gone into the construction sector, which fails to generate (but consumes) foreign currency. Moreover, Turkey's current account deficit was not caused by the rapid expansion of imports but by declining real export growth, resulting from the overvalued currency (Subasat 2014). Countries with large current account surpluses such as China and Germany attest that neither rapid GDP growth nor energy dependency needs to cause current account deficits. While current account imbalances are indeed a global phenomenon, Fig. 2.11B and C verify that Turkey is one of the leading countries in terms of the increase in the current account deficits. The global liquidity during the 2000s (caused by conjectural factors) allowed many countries (including Turkey) to have large current account deficits and accumulate large external debts (Subasat 2016).

Turkey also turned the 2008 crisis into a short-term opportunity through policies for Turkish companies to facilitate their foreign borrowing. Turkey managed to attract large capital inflows that were fleeing from the crisis countries. While this policy helped the economy, it increased the future cost of adjustment by increasing the debt burden. The good fortune in the short-run has become a misfortune for Turkey in the long-run.

Financing a current account deficit for a considerable period is possible provided that the creditors are willing to transfer resources. Ultimately, however, a correction is inevitable and the damage will be positively linked with the length of the delay.

Such a flawed development strategy, which heavily relies on external funds, will inevitably face problems once external funds dry up. The Federal Reserve's announcement in June 2013 regarding its intentions to reduce bond purchases signaled that difficult times were ahead of the countries that took a ride of ample global liquidity and borrowed heavily. Since then, many countries experienced stock market loses, currency devaluations and interest rate rises, which could be considered as a rehearsal of what is likely to happen when external conditions worsen, and Turkey is no longer able to attract adequate external resources.

Figure 2.10 compares Turkey's cumulative current account deficit to GDP ratio (net external debt stock) in 2016 with selected countries that experienced a financial crisis in 2008. Both with the old and new series, the risk in Turkey is close to or exceeds the risks in these countries.

Historical experiences confirm that excessive foreign borrowing and a housing bubble often experienced concomitantly, which creates conditions for a corrective crisis. The housing bubble in Istanbul has now exceeded the bubbles in New York and London before these countries experienced their corrective crises in 2008 (Subasat 2017).

Turkey is in a structural crisis conjuncture since 2013 (Akcay 2019). The impressive growth rate in 2017 was designed to secure a victory in the 2018 elections. It was achieved through stimulation via tax reductions, credit guarantee fund, large spending on infrastructure, a series of incentives (such as exemptions from customs duty and VAT) to unrelated

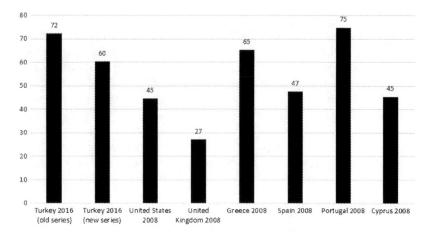

Fig. 2.10 Cumulative current account deficit to GDP ratio (*Note* Higher numbers indicate higher cumulative current account deficits since 1990)

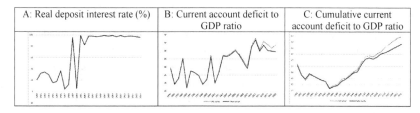

Fig. 2.11 Percent rank of Turkey in terms of real interest rates and current account deficits (*Note* For figures B and C higher numbers indicate higher rank based on higher current account deficits)

"strategic" projects and sectors, and the encouragement of the state banks to cut mortgage rates below their deposit rates to boost lending to real estate. These policies resulted in the worsening of the budget deficit and were unsustainable in the long-run.

Turkish lira experienced similar pressures in 2015, 2016 and in May 2018 (before the elections) and survived because the Central Bank of the Republic of Turkey (CBRT) used its reserves and (despite the president's rhetoric) interest rates were increased sufficiently. The collapse of the currency could not have been tolerated because of upcoming elections. The capital inflows from unidentified sources (measured by "net errors and omissions" in the balance of payments), which increase rapidly whenever Turkey faced economic challenges, also helped to stabilize the exchange rates.[9]

After the June 2018 elections, the government had fewer options to halt the inevitable currency crisis. The CBRT had very little real reserves to stabilize the exchange rates. Raising the interest rates could have postponed the rapid capital outflows but interest rates were already high and whether further increase could help the economy without pushing it into recession was doubtful. President Erdogan's well-known attitude over interest rates also played a part which will be considered below.

The government maintains that the economic fundamentals are solid and blames the USA for adopting policies to undermine the Turkish economy for political reasons. In this view, the currency crisis is caused by a premeditated speculative attack. In our view, however, the conflict with the USA over the arrest of Pastor Brunson may have acted as a catalyst but it was not the root cause of the crisis. A good understanding of any crisis requires the separation of the triggers from the underlying causes. Once the conditions for an adjustive crisis are imminent, the triggers only start the process. Speculative attacks are in the nature of currency crisis and blaming speculation and considering it as a conspiracy is pointless.

Some analysts also questioned whether the political crisis with the USA was deliberately provoked in order to scapegoat the USA for the mismanagement of the economy and impending economic meltdown (Zaman 2018). As O'Brien (2018) writes

> This might be the dumbest crisis ever. Turkey has hurt itself with bad policies, tried to blame foreigners for this fact, but then, unbelievably, seen Trump seem to vindicate their scapegoating by trying to bring their economy down in retaliation for them bringing it down themselves. It's a comedy of errors that couldn't be less funny for the Turkish people.

[9]The cumulative unaccounted net capital inflows into Turkey since 2002 add up to 48 billion dollars. In the first half of 2018 alone, Turkey received 8.3 billion dollars of unidentified capital, which is likely to hit a record by the end of the year. Subasat (2017) argued that the net error and omission figures significantly underestimate the real unaccounted capital inflows.

The Turkish government insisted that the Brunson case was a legal process that the government could not intervene. This argument is unconvincing for two reasons. First, Erdogan is probably the most pragmatic leader in Turkey's history, who is well known for his extreme U-turns as reactions to the changing political environment (Subasat 2017). Letting the court case of a Pastor to ruin the economy is inconceivable. Second, judicial independence has deteriorated significantly in Turkey since 2011 and political interference has become widespread. The commitment to the judicial independence is often no more than lip service. For example, the German-Turkish journalist Deniz Yücel, who had been jailed for alleged espionage, was released after extensive German diplomatic efforts.

Erdogan's insistence on lower interest rate during a massive currency crisis is odd and deserves a separate discussion.

The Interest Rate Debate

One of the most peculiar debates in Turkey has been about President Erdogan's insistence on low interest rates. Erdogan has long been pressurizing the *independent* CBRT to lower (or not to rise) interest rates, which has caused conflicts even within the cabinet members. Erdogan blames the CBRT for embracing conservative monetarist policies, which have failed to control inflation and promote growth.

While some believe that Erdogan has religious motives, he (or his advisers on his behalf) makes two theoretical and one practical argument for lower interest rates. First, lower interest rates would facilitate more investment, rapid growth, lower unemployment rates and eventually lower inflation rates (Unay 2015). Second, neo-Fisherism, according to Erdogan, implies that reducing inflation requires lowering the nominal interest rates rather than increasing them (Ertem 2018). The famous Fisher Effect states that the nominal interest rate equals the real interest rate plus the expected inflation rate. Increase in inflation, therefore, must either reduce real interest rates or increase nominal interest rates, or a combination of both. Neo-Fisherism emerged in the post-crisis USA when inflation failed to rise despite interest rates were slashed. It argued that there is a positive correlation between nominal interest rates and inflation, and inflation could be increased by rising nominal interest rates, rather than by cutting them, as orthodox economics would suggest. In the same vein, Erdogan argues, inflation could be reduced by reducing nominal interest rates. This makes sense, in his view, since high interest rates are a major cost of production, which causes high prices. Third, Erdogan wants lower interest rates to boost the housing market, which has been the backbone of the economy since 2009. The housing and mortgage sales declined considerably in 2018 and Turkey has over 1.5 million unsold housing stock. As a temporary measure, the government pressurized the public banks to cut mortgage rates below their deposit rates. Since banks make losses, which cannot be sustained for long, only lower interest rates could resolve the problem.

Erdogan rightly criticizes mainstream economists' claims that the only way to lower interest rates is to reduce inflation and risk premium. He is essentially correct to argue for lower interest rates to promote higher investment and growth rates. However, he mistakenly focusses on the nominal interest rates and believes that this can be achieved by pressurizing the CBRT without supportive policies.

Most mainstream economists believe that macroeconomic instabilities result from irresponsible government policies. In this view, budget deficit, inflation and balance of payment problems are caused by excessive domestic demand, which should be brought under control by reducing government spending, controlling the money supply and devaluing the exchange rate. Very often, however, macroeconomic instabilities are caused by factors other than the government's irresponsibility. Many external and internal factors and the lack of growth itself could instigate macroeconomic instabilities. Macroeconomic instabilities are often a symptom (not a cause) of economic problems. The direction of causality, therefore, may run from a healthy economy to macroeconomic stability.

The East Asian Miracle countries, for example, adopted carefully design industrial policies to facilitate rapid growth and economic stability (Subasat 2004). In other words, these countries did not grow rapidly because they had macroeconomic stability but they had macroeconomic stability because they had a healthy economy facilitated by industrial policies. These countries are well known for their low real interest rates, high saving and high investment rates, which were achieved as part of broad industrial policies.

For this reason, the experience of East Asian Miracle countries rejects not only mainstream arguments but also Erdogan's arguments. Demanding low interest rates does not bring low interest rates unless they are part of a wider industrial policy. Moreover, it is the real (non-nominal) interest rates that are essential for high investment.

Even if the neo-Fisherism is taken seriously, its relevance to Turkey is highly questionable. The theory aims to explain and rectify low inflation in an advanced economy facing recession. Turkey, on the other hand, is a middle-income country with excessive foreign debt, current account deficits and high inflation. The implementation of neo-Fisherit model in Turkey proved to be a major blunder. The failure to increase interest rates promptly despite rising inflation made foreign investment in Turkey less attractive and greatly contributed to the currency crisis. CBRT's inability to act on time not only caused excessive exchange rate devaluation but also caused higher than needed interest rates, which still fails to reduce exchange rates. This was not the first time that Erdogan pressurized the CBRT to lower interest rates but rapid capital outflows caused interest rates to rise. Under Erdogan's pressure, the CBRT cut the interest rates by 0.5% in January 2015. Within a few weeks, the Turkish lira depreciated almost 10% and interest rates surged by more than 13%. Unuvar (2015) called this "an interest rate reduction that increased interest rates."

Pressurizing the CBRT will not bring lower interest rates since Turkey's economy has become dependent on large capital inflows to grow, and high real interest rates have been offered to attract them. Figure 2.11A shows that among 98 countries Turkey was ranked low in terms of real deposit interest rates during the 1990s, except for 1999 when Turkey had a devastating earthquake and for 2001 when Turkey had a financial crisis. Between 2003 and 2016, however, Turkey was never ranked below at 96.8% and on average Turkey had the highest real interest rates in the group.[10] There is an irony in offering high real interest rates to attract large capital inflows and blaming the *interest rate lobby* for causing it.

Low real interest rates cannot be achieved in an economy that depends heavily on external capital inflows. Figure 2.11B shows Turkey's rank in terms of current account deficit to GDP ratio and 11C shows in terms of cumulative current account deficit to GDP ratio (termed as "net external debt stock ratio" by Subasat 2014), which reveals the long-term risks better. While the indicators are slightly lower with the new series, they both indicate an increased risk during the AKP period. Turkey

---

[10] This figure also stands in contrast to Fig. 2.9A which shows a rapid increase in gross capital formation with the new series. If the new figures were correct, one would face a dilemma in explaining it in the face of high real interest rates.

needs well over $200 billion new capital inflows within a year to service its external debt and finance its current account deficit, which makes it impossible to lower real interest rates. In an open liberal economy, low interest rates can only be achieved by increasing domestic savings and reducing the need for foreign financial capital. Otherwise, a decline in interest rates encourages capital outflows and debt service becomes unviable.

CONCLUSION

This paper argued that Turkey experienced two manufactured economic *miracles* that require a corrective crisis. The first *miracle* was linked with the favorable global environment, which enabled Turkey to attract large capital inflows. Although Turkey grew rapidly in this period in terms of NGDP, this was largely due to the appreciation of the exchange rate. The RGDP performance was unimpressive. Turkey grew faster than high-income countries but lagged behind the low- and middle-income countries. Our rank analysis also lends no support for the miracle. During this period, however, Turkey offered very high real interest rates to attract capital inflows, which created large current account deficits, external debt and low investment rates. The first *miracle*, therefore, sowed the seeds of the current crisis.

The second *miracle* was even more curious since it was associated with the deterioration of many economic and political indicators. It was mainly manufactured by the TURKSTAT's 2016 revision, which increased the NGDP by 20%, investment by 74% and savings by 102%. The accuracy of the new figures is questionable because they display major inconsistencies with the unrevised variables. During this period, Turkey has received more capital inflows from countries experiencing crisis and witnessed a further deterioration of the current account and external debt, which have reached levels that started compromising the economy. The Federal Reserve's announcement in 2013 signaled the end of ample global liquidity and the beginning of a worrying period for over-borrowing countries. A debt-driven economy could not last very long and the 2018 currency crisis marked the beginning of the painful adjustment process.

While many consider the second *miracle* as a mirage, the first *miracle* is widely perceived as real even by many opponents. In this view, the AKP managed the economy well until the late 2000s. The increased authoritarianism since 2011, however, reduced investors' confidence and put the Turkish economy into trouble. These arguments fail to grasp the dialectical link between the two *miracles*, the regime change and the subsequent crisis. Why the government moved to authoritarianism and adopted unsustainable economic policies, which would inevitably backfire, cannot be understood unless Turkey's radical political transformation since 2002 is properly grasped.

Subasat (2017) argued that all the policies the AKP implemented have been designed to facilitate this transformation. The first *miracle* period was designed to consolidate the AKP's powers against many challenges. This was a defensive period in which the AKP needed the broadest political support to survive. In this process, economic policies played a decisive role. Vast segments of society have experienced improvements in their living standards through policies that boosted consumption, which created the illusion of an economic miracle. These policies were unsustainable in the long-run but needed in the short-run to support the AKP's electoral appeal.

Once a strong government was secured and the threats were lifted, the next phase of the regime change process could begin. The second *miracle* period was the transformation phase, which entailed authoritarianism since the fear of a regime change raged the opposition. The AKP was ready to face this challenge since almost all of the strategic positions of the state apparatus were under their control. The strongest challenge came from the internal struggles within the AKP, which ultimately developed into acute conflicts and led to a coup attempt in 2016. The AKP turned the coup into an *opportunity* and used the state of emergency to coerce a wide range of opponents.

Because economic success was built on weak fundamentals and was unsustainable, there was a time pressure on the AKP to accelerate the transformation. A crisis would undermine the AKP's hegemony and jeopardize its long-term goals. Only a more authoritarian regime could rescue the AKP and retain what had been achieved. For this reason, the AKP surged for a radical constitutional change to a "Turkish style presidential system" in 2017 and a snap general election in 2018, despite the state of emergency undermined their legitimacy. The AKP could take no chances with the ailing economy. The second *miracle* (via the statistical revision) alongside with the last attempt to boost the economy before a crisis (via expansionist policies) was essential to secure these crucial election victories.

In conclusion, both *miracles* were fake and used to create the conditions for a radical political transformation. Now that this objective has largely been achieved and unavoidable crisis started, the AKP blames everyone and everything except its own policies. It claims that the economy has strong fundamentals and the problems are caused by the enemies of Turkey, which should be perceived as political rhetoric and a sign of desperation.

REFERENCES

Akcay, U. (2016, December 19). Ya tuz kokarsa? *Gazete Duvar*. https://www. gazeteduvar.com.tr/yazarlar/2016/12/19/ya-tuz-kokarsa/.

Akcay, U. (2019). Stuck up in a Blind Alley. *1+1 Forum*. https://www.birartibir. org/international/328-stuck-up-in-a-blind-alley.

Aydogus, O. (2017). Sorunlu Milli Gelir Revizyonu ve Kuşkulu Büyüme, İktisat ve Toplum, No. 78.

Aydogus, O. (2018). Türkiye'de Milli Gelir Revizyonunun Sonuçları ve İnşaat Sektörü: OECD ve AB ile Bir Karşılaştırma. *Efil Journal, 1*(1), 10–20.

Boratav, K. (2017). Milli gelir revizyonu arızalıdır. *Birgün*. https://www.birgun. net/haber-detay/milli-gelir-revizyonu-arizalidir-153403.html.

Ertem, C. (2018, May 17). Enflasyon-faiz üzerine: Teorik bir giriş. *Milliyet*. http://www.milliyet.com.tr/yazarlar/cemil-ertem/ enflasyon-faiz-uzerine-teorik-bir-2670467/.

Meyersson, E. (2017a). *Is New Turkey's Growth Model from Outer Space?* https://erikmeyersson.com/2017/01/22/is-new-turkeys-growth-model-from-outer-space/.

Meyersson, E. (2017b). *Will the Real Real GDP in Turkey Please Stand Up?* https://erikmeyersson.com/2017/02/16/will-the-real-real-gdp-in-turkey-please-stand-up/.

Meyersson, E. (2017c). *Asset Prices and Turkey's Revised GDP Growth*. https:// erikmeyersson.com/2017/03/06/asset-prices-and-turkeys-revised-gdp-growth/.

O'Brien, M. (2018). Trump is Mad that Turkey's Economic Crisis has Made Their Currency Weaker, so Now He's Making It Even Weaker. *The Washington Post*. https://www.washingtonpost.com/business/2018/08/ 10/trump-is-madthat-turkeys-economic-crisis-has-made-their-currency-weaker-so-now-hes-making-it-even-weaker/?noredirect=on.

Subasat, T. (2004). Bretton Woods Kurumları Bağlamında Doğu Asya Mucizesi ve Kriz. In T. Subasat & S. Dedeoğlu (Eds.), *Kalkınma ve Küreselleşme*. İstanbul: Bağlam Yayıncılık.

Subasat, T. (2014). The Political Economy of Turkey's Economic Miracle. *Journal of Balkan and Near Eastern Studies, 16*(2), 137–160.

Subasat, T. (2016). Conjunctural and Policy Based Causes of the 2008 Crisis. In T. Subasat, *The Great Meltdown of 2008: Systemic, Conjunctural or Policy-Created?* London: Edward Elgar.

Subasat, T. (2017). Turkey at a Crossroads: The Political Economy of Turkey's Transformation. *Markets, Globalization Development Review, 2*(2), 1–32.

Subasat, T., & Uysal, S. (2018). Ülkelerin Ekonomik Gelişmişlik Düzeyi Karşılaştırmalarında Yeni Bir Ölçüt: Düzeltilmiş Gayri Safi Milli Hasıla. *Efil Ekonomi Araştırmaları Dergisi, 1*(2), 74–89.

Terzioglu, N., & Subasat, T. (2018). Import Dependency of Exports as a Cause of Current Account Deficit. *Central European Review of Economics & Finance, 25*(3), 37–49.

The World Bank. (2018). *World Development Indicators.* http://data.worldbank.org/data-catalog/world-development-indicators.

Unay, S. (2015). Erdoğan and the Interest Rates Debate. *Daily Sabah.* https://www.dailysabah.com/columns/sadik_unay/2015/02/07/erdogan-and-the-interest-rates-debate.

Voyvoda, E., & Yeldan, E. (2005). *Turkish Macroeconomics Under the IMF Program: Strangulation of the Twin-Targets, Lopsided Growth and Persistent Fragilities.* Mimeo. http://www.Bagimsizsosyalbilimciler.Org/Yazilar_Uye/Vydec05.pdf.

Yasar, S. (2013, October 15). Madem riskli o halde kim kullanıyor sıcak parayı? *Sabah Newspaper.*

Yildirim, A. (2013, April 2). Yüksek Büyümenin Bedelini Ödedik. *Haber Turk Newspaper.*

Yükseler, Z. (2017). 2017 yılı üçüncü çeyrek GSYH büyümesinin analizi (Yüksek Büyüme Niçin Hissedilmedi?). Technical Report, December 2017. https://www.researchgate.net/publication/322050314_2017_YILI_UCUNCU_CEYREK_GSYH_BUYUMESININ_ANALIZI_Yuksek_Buyume_Nicin_Hissedilmedi.

Zalewski, P. (2013). How Turkey Went From 'Zero Problems' to Zero Friends. *Foreign Policy.* Retrieved April 2017, from http://foreignpolicy.com/2013/08/22/how-turkey-went-from-zero-problems-to-zero-friends/.

Zaman, A. (2018). Erdogan Sneers at Trump as Turkey Lines up New Friends, Turkey Pulse. *Al-monitor*, 13 August 2018. https://www.al-monitor.com/pulse/originals/2018/08/erdogan-trump-war-twitter.html.

CHAPTER 3

Income Inequality in Turkey: 2003–2015

Alpay Filiztekin

Introduction

Turkey entered into the new millennium with a severe financial crisis. A long period of economic and political instability, persistent high inflation and erratic yet on average slow growth, unsustainable budget deficits and heavy reliance on foreign capital accompanied with a weak banking system led to a crisis in 2001. Significant structural changes imposed by the International Monetary Fund and the World Bank and implemented by a caretaker government in 2002 brought discipline on the budgetary process; creation of autonomous regulatory agencies improved efficiency of decision-making and introduced transparency in many corrupt government practices. Consequently, inflation was brought down to single digits and Turkey enjoyed very high economic growth reaching on average 7.1% per annum between 2002 and 2007, an historically unprecedented level. However, starting in 2008 the growth slowed significantly to an average of 4.8% and productivity growth stagnated.

There are a number of, not necessarily mutually exclusive, explanations for this sudden change. It has been argued that Turkey went into as a "stop-go cycle," a high growth followed by a decline in economic

A. Filiztekin (✉)
Sabanci University, Istanbul, Turkey
e-mail: alpay.filiztekin@sabanciuniv.edu

© The Author(s) 2020
E. Parlar Dal (ed.), *Turkey's Political Economy
in the 21st Century*, International Political Economy Series,
https://doi.org/10.1007/978-3-030-27632-4_3

63

64   A. FILIZTEKIN

activity, usually caused by ill-timed and incorrect interventions by the government. Starting in 2008, government spending has increased faster than the growth in GDP, signaling the end of impressive fiscal discipline. Others claim that Turkey was caught into a middle-income trap that it has lost its competitive advantage due to rising wages and declining attraction of foreign direct investment due to comparatively lower rates of return relative to their risk profile. Indeed, following the global crisis of 2008, real interest rate fell zero-to-negative range, savings declined and current account balance worsened. Without a change in investment level, these developments imply that foreign financial capital financed mostly consumption in the years after 2007.

Acemoglu and Ucer (2015), on the other hand, argue that the change is due to reversal in institutional mind-set and implementation of rule-based policies. Following the crisis, the newly formed Justice and Development Party (Adalet ve Kalkinma Partisi, AKP) came to power by a large popular support. It embraced new policies and institutions that the previous political establishment could not. What is more important is that the new government "broaden[ed] base of economic activity both geographically and socially" (Acemoglu and Ucer 2015). Starting with AKP's third term in 2011 (although it can be argued even earlier), the structural reforms stalled, the positive role of autonomous agencies were blocked (Atiyas 2012; Gurakar and Gunduz 2015) and broadening of economic activity decelerated.

Changes in inequality can be seen parallel to what has been described above. Turkey had the third highest income inequality among OECD countries after Chile and Mexico in mid-1990s. While its relative position has not changed since then, the decline in inequality in both absolute and percentage terms from mid-nineties to mid-2010s is not matched by any other country in the group. The decline in Gini coefficient was substantial, from 0.49 to 0.39 (a decline of 18.8%), compared to second best performer, Mexico, with a decline of four points (or 11.2%) (OECD 2011).[1] Major improvement in equality occurred between 2003 and 2007, and Gini coefficient dropped from 0.437 to 0.381. It came to a halt and stayed around the same level with some fluctuations afterward. While it is not possible to link specific policies and

---

[1] The figures are taken from OECD database and numbers for Turkey are from TurkStat, Turkish Statistical Institute, based on a different survey as described later in data section of this paper.

change in institutional environment with inequality given limited span of data, one may be able to identify groups that are potentially affected by them. The goal of this chapter is, then, to describe the level and changes in the trend of inequality in Turkey and discuss possible determinants and sections of society that are affected using data from Household Budget and Expenditure Surveys (HBES) for years 2003–2016.

Turkey is subject to significant socio-demographic changes since mid-twentieth century. While the dissolution of agriculture increased the speed of urbanization, a young population reached working age putting serious pressure on labor market. Average household size was in decline, education was rapidly expanding despite problems in quality, and employment choice of most individuals changed over time. All these factors in conjuncture with changes in nationwide policies are suspect to explain the trend in inequality and thus incorporated into the analysis through a set of subgroup decompositions, as well as a decomposition of income sources.

There are several studies that investigate income distribution in Turkey since early 1970s. Most studies on inequality in Turkey have been either static in nature, for example Bulutay et al. (1971) and Esmer et al. (1986), or provide comparison of two years, Silber and Özmucur (2000), Gürsel et al. (2000) and Başlevent and Dayıoğlu (2005), among others, with the exception of Filiztekin (2015). Following the latter paper, this study expands the time frame to 2016.

The next section describes the data and methodology. Section "Findings" provides general information about the income distribution in Turkey and an in-depth analysis of the structure of income distribution in terms of both subgroups and income sources. While the static analysis emphasizes the importance of several factors, the dynamic analysis allows to determine the influence of these factors on the trend of inequality. The last section provides a summary of major findings.

DATA AND METHODOLOGY

There are two different surveys to measure inequality in Turkey conducted by Turkish Statistical Institute (TurkStat). The first one is Survey of Income and Living Conditions (SILC) conducted since 2006. TurkStat announces inequality statistics based on this survey. The other one is HBES which is available since 2003. The aim of this chapter is to provide evidence starting right after the crisis and since the AKP took power

66 A. FILIZTEKIN

and therefore, relies on HBES as it covers years before 2007. The analysis stops at 2015 as Turkey faced a coup attempt in the following year and it is not possible to examine possible outcomes of this unfortunate event.

The 2003 sample of HBES covers more than 25,000 households with over 110,000 individuals. Starting in 2004, surveys cover approximately 8500–11,000 households and 35–42 thousand individuals annually. Surveys contain questions pertaining to the household (information about the type of dwelling, household size, etc.) and to individuals within the household (relation between members, age, gender, education and a set of labor market characteristics). Each individual's net income and source of income (labor income, transfers and other sources such as rents and capital) are also reported. The sum of incomes of all members in the household yields total net household income. The data set includes also imputed rents for owner-occupied houses which are considered as a part of capital income in the analysis. Using national price index, all monetary amounts are converted to real terms in 2008 Turkish liras, with a dollar exchange rate of 1.30 TL/$.

The unit of analysis is individual adjusted with "OECD-modified equivalence scale" (also adopted by EuroStat) to account for family composition. It assigns a value of 1 to the household head, of 0.5 to each additional adult member and of 0.3 to each child. The definition of income in this chapter is, then, annual per equivalent income. All statistics are weighted by an elevation factor provided in the data to represent population. When discussing family characteristics, the reference is to the householder (those who are called "reference person" in the surveys).

To measure inequality I am using several different measures. The most known one is the Gini coefficient, defined as $Gini = \frac{1}{2n^2\bar{y}} \sum_{i=1}^{n} \sum_{j=1}^{n} |y_i - y_j|$. While Gini coefficient is most popular inequality measure and enables comparability with other studies, it cannot be decomposed unless constituent groups are non-overlapping. Three indices of generalized entropy class ($GE(\alpha)$ or I_α) which satisfy all desirable axioms including decomposability are provided as well. These are,

$$I_0 = \frac{1}{n} \sum_{i=1}^{n} log\frac{\bar{y}}{y_i}, \text{ also known as mean log deviation,}$$

$$I_1 = \frac{1}{n} \sum_{i=1}^{n} \frac{y_i}{\bar{y}} log\frac{y_i}{\bar{y}}, \text{ sometimes referred as Theil-T index, and}$$

$$I_2 = \frac{1}{2n\bar{y}^2} \sum_{i=1}^{n} (y_i - \bar{y})^2, \text{ which is half of the square of the coefficient of}$$

variation.

The parameter α in the I_α class represents the weight given to distances between incomes at different parts of the income distribution and can take any real value. For lower values of α, I is more sensitive to changes in the lower tail of the distribution, and for higher values, I is more responsive to changes that affect the upper tail. A value of $\alpha = 0$ gives more weight to distances between incomes in the lower tail, $\alpha = 1$ applies equal weights across the distribution, while a value of $\alpha = 2$ gives proportionately more weight to gaps in the upper tail.

In the following sections I investigate the structure of inequality in Turkey in two different dimensions: by subgroups of households and by composition of the income source, in Jenkins' (1995) terminology "*income recipient*" and "*income package*" influences, respectively.

For the former I will consider age, gender and education of householder and household type. It should also be noted that partitioning of households by some characteristics could admittedly be arbitrary. The break points are chosen following previous literature and considering presumably more suitable cutoffs for the Turkish case. The age of household head is grouped, for example, into five categories: under age 30, ages between 30–39, 40–49, 50–64 and 65 and over. Gender is simply considering whether the householder is male or female. Education of the householder grouped into four categories based on the latest degree achieved, those who have no degree, those with a primary school diploma (8 years), with a high school (11 years) and with a university degree (15 years). The last household characteristic considered is household type and there are six categories, "single-adult," "single-adult with child(ren)," "couples without child(ren)," "couple with child(ren)," "three or more adults (extended) but no child(ren)" and "three or more adults with child(ren)."

A static decomposition by population subgroups divides total inequality I into between-group inequality, I^b, sometimes referred as explained component and within-group inequality, I^w, the unexplained component, such that $I = I^b + I^w$. Following Cowell and Jenkins (1995), the within component can be defined as

$$I_u^W = \sum_{k=1}^{K} v_k (\lambda_k)^\alpha I_\alpha^k \qquad \text{for } \alpha \neq 0, 1;$$

$$I_0^W = \sum_{k=1}^{K} v_k I_0^k;$$

$$I_1^W = \sum_{k=1}^{K} v_k(\lambda_k)I_1^k,$$

where v_k is the population share of subgroup k, λ_k is the mean income of subgroup k (μ_k) relative to the population mean (μ), and I_α^W is inequality within group k, $k = 1,\ldots,K$. Then between inequality measure is

$$I_\alpha^B = \frac{1}{\alpha^2 - \alpha}\left[\sum_{k=1}^{K} v_k(\lambda_k)^\alpha - 1\right] \qquad \text{for } \alpha \neq 0, 1;$$

$$I_0^B = \sum_{k=1}^{K} v_k \log\left(\frac{1}{\lambda_k}\right);$$

$$I_1^B = \sum_{k=1}^{K} v_k \lambda_k \log(\lambda_k)$$

Cowell and Jenkins (1995) then suggest a summary measure of explained inequality for a partition Π as

$$R^B(\Pi) = \frac{I^B(\Pi)}{I}$$

Comparing static decomposition of inequality over time could be indicative of the changing structure of the income distribution. However, it masks the contribution of changing composition of groups within partitions which may be non-negligible and a better approach would be using a dynamic decomposition suggested by Mookherjee and Shorrocks (1982). The dynamic decomposition of income inequality considers three different sources: change in subgroup inequality, change in relative variations in the subgroup mean incomes and shift in the subgroup population shares.

Although it is possible to dynamically decompose any generalized entropy index, using I_0 provides more information than the others, even it is an approximation, as it relates changes in inequality to changes in subgroup inequalities, shares and means rather than relative means and the approximation in practice turns out to be quite exact.

$$\Delta I_0 = \sum_{k=1}^{K} \bar{v}_k \Delta I_0^k + \sum_{k=1}^{K} \bar{I}_0^k \Delta v_k - \sum_{k=1}^{K} \left[\overline{\log(\lambda_k)}\right]\Delta v_k - \sum_{k=1}^{K} \bar{v}_k \Delta \log(\lambda_k)$$

$$\approx \sum\nolimits_{k=1}^{K} \bar{v}_k \Delta I_0^k + \sum\nolimits_{k=1}^{K} \bar{I}_0^k \Delta \lambda_k - \sum\nolimits_{k=1}^{K} \left[\lambda_k - \overline{\log(\lambda_k)} \right] \Delta v_k - \sum\nolimits_{k=1}^{K} \left(\bar{\theta}_k - \bar{v}_k \right) \Delta \log(\mu_k)$$

where v_k, λ_k, μ_k and I_0^k are as defined before; θ_k is group k's share of total population income, Δ stands for change between two time periods, and a bar over variables denotes average of base and current period values. The first term in the second line (term A) is the unexplained inequality or the pure inequality effect. The second and third terms (terms B and C) capture the allocation effects, holding inequality and relative mean incomes constant, respectively. The last term (term D) corresponds to the income effect, that is, changes in total inequality due to changes in relative incomes of different partitions.

A complementary analysis would be considering income sources. I consider six different sources of income: paid employment income, entrepreneurial income, asset income, agriculture income, retirement income and transfers. Entrepreneurial income includes income of both entrepreneurs that employ others and self-employed. While retirement income could be treated as transfer income, I prefer to include as a separate source since the retirement age and pension system has changed in 2000 to affect different cohorts in various ways.

Similar to subgroup decompositions, the effect of income sources can also be decomposed in both a static and a dynamic way. The methodology is first developed by Shorrocks (1982) for a single cross section and extended to a dynamic comparison by Jenkins (1995). Starting with the premise that total income is the sum of factor incomes, overall inequality can be decomposed as:

$$I = \sum\nolimits_f S_f \sum\nolimits_f s_f I = \sum\nolimits_f \rho_f \mu_f \sqrt{I_f} \sqrt{I}$$

where S_f depends on income source f and signifies the absolute contribution of the source to overall inequality. Factor source f has a disequalizing contribution when $S_f > 0$ and an equalizing contribution if $S_f < 0$. $s_f = \frac{S_f}{I}$ is the proportional factor contribution indicating the importance of f. The last equation is obtained by regressing income from source f on total income (Shorrocks 1982), and ρ_f is the correlation between total income and income from source f, μ_f is f's share in total and I_f is inequality for factor source f. While the choice of decomposition rule is independent of inequality measure, Shorrocks (1982) provides a convincing argument for using this particular rule which became a standard in the

70   A. FILIZTEKIN

literature. Provided that there are many income sources, it is important to use an index that can handle the regular incidence of zero values. Inequality index I_2 has this property and thus used in decompositions performed here.

To account changes in inequality, Jenkins (1995) proposes a dynamic decomposition based on proportionate inequality changes $\%\Delta I_2 \equiv \frac{\Delta I_2}{I_2} = \sum_f s_f \%\Delta S_f$ such that the change in aggregate inequality is decomposed into an exact sum of changes in the factor contributions.

FINDINGS

Figure 3.1 presents the trend in inequality measured by Gini coefficient and three generalized entropy indices over time. Gini coefficient exhibits a sharp decline from 2003 until 2007. The reversal in the pattern of inequality started in 2008, before the global crisis hit the Turkish economy. It is true that inequality reached its post-2001 peak in 2009, yet it stayed around that level or very slightly declined until 2013 and started increasing again in the last two years of the sample. The pattern is similar in all indices until 2009. While I_0 follows Gini closely, the other two indices show no sign of a decline after the global crisis. Yet all indices show an increase in the last two years.

The trend in inequality follows the changes in overall economy closely. Table 3.1 provides more information on levels of income and different inequality measures. Average per equivalent income grew around 4.5% per annum between 2003 and 2015. However, as for the entire population, the growth rate of individual income was much higher between 2003 and 2007 than between 2007 and 2015, 6.4% as opposed to 3.5%.

A more interesting picture emerges when one focuses on income levels of different percentiles. Median income increased slightly more (annual growth rate of 9.5%) than average income in the first subperiod, yet the growth slowed down to 2.5% in the second subperiod. In comparison with income of both the tenth and ninetieth percentile, the growth rate of the median income was higher earlier but lower in later years. Figure 3.2 shows the ratios of income of the 90th percentile to median and median to 10th percentile with a third-order polynomial fitted to the data. It is apparent that the pattern of aggregate inequality does not speak of changes in different parts of the distribution. In fact, there was a convergence of median to upper group and a slight

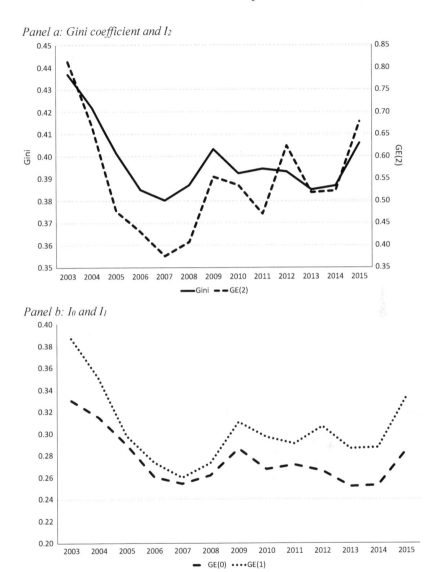

Fig. 3.1 Trend in inequality

Table 3.1 Summary statistics on income and inequality

	2003	2007	2015
Avg. income p.e.	6744	8727	11,572
10th percentile income	1899	2630	3578
Median income p.e.	4781	6999	8693
90th percentile income	12,259	15,896	20,921
Gini	0.437	0.380	0.406
GE(0)	0.330	0.254	0.285
GE(1)	0.387	0.260	0.333
GE(2)	0.813	0.375	0.678

divergence from the lower group between 2003 and 2007. However, there is a reversal of this pattern in the second half of the sample period. What was driving the decline in the first half of the sample was faster growth in the incomes of the middle groups in early years has slowed down more than the growth of incomes of other groups in later years.

Decomposing Inequality

This section explores the extent to which subgroup partitions and income sources described above contributed to income inequality in Turkey. I have chosen three years, the beginning and end years of the sample and the break in 2007. While static decompositions divide total inequality in the distribution into two components, inequality between groups in each partition and inequality within groups, dynamic decomposition allows to analyze whether the change over time is due to change in each of these components or due to a change in composition of groups.

Static Decomposition by Subgroups

Table 3.2 provides between inequality statistics using all three measures of inequality and in three years. The decomposition results are quite suggestive. Between inequality explains a smaller portion of overall inequality regardless of the partition used. As pointed out by Kanbur (2000), this fact does not necessarily imply that differences between groups are unimportant. The aim here is to discuss relative magnitudes of different partitions and how they have changed over time.

The age and gender of household head explain relatively very little of inequality in any of the years. The lack of evidence for the importance of gender of the householder is most likely a result of the way

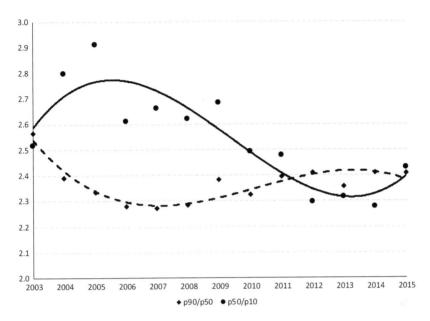

Fig. 3.2 Trends in percentile ratios

Table 3.2 Static subgroup decomposition: between inequality (%)

	I_0			I_1		
	2003	2007	2015	2003	2007	2015
Hh head age	0.54	0.86	1.63	0.45	0.84	1.38
Hh head gender	0.30	0.10	0.28	0.27	0.10	0.25
Hh head education	26.46	18.43	27.22	26.83	20.17	25.81
Hh type	7.08	7.76	11.62	6.16	7.51	10.01

Notes Partitions are as described in the text. Author's calculations using HBE Surveys in respective years

"householder" is defined. The women in Turkey have little power within the households and they do participate much less in economy relative to men albeit there is a change in their share in total households.[2]

---

[2] The shares of subgroups and their relative equivalent incomes are provided in the Appendix.

74   A. FILIZTEKIN

The low explanatory power of age structure implies the absence of life-cycle effects, yet it does not necessarily imply that earning profiles across ages is flat. This finding is possibly due to averaging out of life-cycle factors within the households.

The most important determinant of overall inequality is the educational attainment of household head which can be explained from 18 to 27% of overall inequality depending on the year and measure. It is not possible to make causal inferences from a statistical decomposition, as educational attainment, on the one hand, could be a cause of wealth and income accumulation across generations and hence may widen the difference between rich and poor, on the other hand, skill-biased change in the economy and increasing returns to schooling could also be responsible for the observed difference among educational groups. Nonetheless, it is clear that the importance of education in inequality is relatively less in 2007 when inequality was low and higher when inequality was higher.

Dynamic Decomposition by Subgroup

The results of dynamic decompositions are presented in Table 3.3. Most striking feature of the table is that between 2003 and 2007 decline in within component (term A) in all partitions played a major role. In other words, improvement in income distribution is mostly achieved by reducing inequality within groups in this subperiod. The only exception

Table 3.3   Dynamic subgroup decomposition

			% Change in agg. ineq. explained by			
Partitions		*% Change in agg. ineq.*	*Within ineq. (Term A)*	*Allocation effect (Term B)*	*Allocation effect (Term C)*	*Income effect (Term D)*
Age	2003–2007	−23.1	−23.1	0.1	0.0	0.0
	2007–2015	12.0	11.7	0.3	0.0	0.0
Gender	2003–2007	−23.1	−23.0	0.0	0.0	0.0
	2007–2015	12.0	12.1	−0.4	0.0	0.2
Education	2003–2007	−23.1	−10.7	0.0	0.2	−12.6
	2007–2015	12.0	−0.7	0.2	6.1	6.3
Hh type	2003–2007	−23.1	−21.9	−0.1	−0.1	−1.0
	2007–2015	12.0	5.6	1.2	1.9	3.5

Notes Partitions are as described in the text. Author's calculations using HBE Surveys in respective years

is education of the householder. The between component (term D) has contributed significantly to decrease in overall inequality. Indeed, neither the share of nor the equivalent income in households with a university graduate householder has increased during this subperiod.

In the second subperiod when inequality was rising, the only contribution from age and gender of householder came through within components as before. In this period, however, the contribution of within inequality component of education has fallen down to a negligible level. Instead, a rise in between inequality accompanied with allocation effect, mostly due to increasing share of university graduates who enjoy higher income levels, plays the major role. (The growth rate of incomes of less educated was significantly lower than the rise in more educated. Similarly, the share of households with a university graduate householder increased to 14.2% from a mere 8.3%.)

The changing household formation has also played an important role in this period. The shares of singles and 2-adult households with younger householders increased to unprecedented levels, particularly among middle-income groups. The changing social structure has increased inequality both within and between household types.

Decomposition by Income Source

An alternative and complementary analysis inequality can be obtained by considering the statistical structure of income inequality and how different income sources contribute to overall dispersion. Table 3.4 provides the results of this decomposition for six income sources defined above. The value of inequality (I_2) of each individual source is higher than aggregate inequality and varies across income sources. This is mostly due to the fact that many households do receive zero incomes from the relevant source. In 2003, for example, inequality within salary income is lowest whereas employers' income exhibits higher value. While 57.6% of households have paid employment income, only 22.0% have employer/self-employment income. The last three rows in the table show the share of population that receive positive amounts from each source, mean income and inequality within these groups. Measured in this way, inequality within each source declines significantly, more so for incomes that accrue to minority of households.

Earnings from paid employment account for the largest share of total household per equivalent incomes in Turkey and it has increased over time. The share of population with nonzero paid employment income

76 A. FILIZTEKIN

Table 3.4 The contribution of income sources to inequality

	Total inc.	Paid empl. inc.	Employer/ self-emp. income	Agr. inc.	Asset inc.	Pension inc.	Trans. inc.
			2003				
Mean	6744	2532	1372	572	1064	848	356
Rel. mean	1	0.376	0.203	0.085	0.158	0.126	0.053
I_2	0.813	1.642	8.423	5.440	5.707	2.489	5.286
Fac. contr.	0.813	0.206	0.339	0.012	0.206	0.040	0.009
Rel fac. contr.	1	0.253	0.417	0.015	0.254	0.050	0.011
Corr(Υ, Υ_f)	1	0.475	0.637	0.070	0.608	0.225	0.079
Pop share ($\Upsilon_f > 0$)	1	0.576	0.220	0.209	0.780	0.261	0.288
Mean ($\Upsilon_f > 0$)	6744	4393	6234	2737	1364	3251	1236
I_2 ($\Upsilon_f > 0$)	0.813	0.735	1.463	0.742	4.341	0.279	1.165
			2007				
Mean	8727	3760	1480	399	1360	1170	558
Rel. mean	1	0.431	0.170	0.046	0.156	0.134	0.064
I_2	0.375	0.849	6.456	7.370	1.407	2.071	3.241
Fac. contr.	0.375	0.115	0.160	0.002	0.060	0.031	0.006
Rel fac. contr.	1	0.306	0.427	0.005	0.160	0.084	0.017
Corr(Υ, Υ_f)	1	0.472	0.607	0.026	0.531	0.266	0.091
Pop share ($\Upsilon_f > 0$)	1	0.684	0.221	0.155	0.740	0.292	0.530
Mean ($\Upsilon_f > 0$)	8727	5495	6685	2583	1838	4014	1051
I_2 ($\Upsilon_f > 0$)	0.375	0.423	1.040	0.716	0.911	0.249	1.483
			2015				
Mean	11,572	5537	1572	508	1539	1448	968
Rel. mean	1	0.478	0.136	0.044	0.133	0.125	0.084
I_2	0.678	1.030	12.050	9.031	6.534	2.021	2.461
Fac. contr.	0.678	0.206	0.244	0.008	0.177	0.034	0.009
Rel fac. contr.	1	0.304	0.360	0.011	0.261	0.050	0.013
Corr(Υ, Υ_f)	1	0.516	0.629	0.072	0.632	0.232	0.080
Pop share ($\Upsilon_f > 0$)	1	0.746	0.211	0.153	0.639	0.292	0.504
Mean ($\Upsilon_f > 0$)	11,572	7423	7469	3326	2407	4955	1918
I_2 ($\Upsilon_f > 0$)	0.678	0.641	2.142	0.955	3.996	0.237	0.993

has also increased significantly, implying majority of Turkish population relies on this kind of income. In contrast, income from agriculture has also declined. This is partly due to rapid urbanization and worsening of relative prices of agricultural products which led to most complained increase in agricultural imports. Similarly, both the shares of employment and self-employment income and asset income have declined within the observed time period. The former decreased from over 20 to 13.5%, showing the demise of traditionally important small-scale self-employment businesses. The decline in asset income is possibly indicative of declining savings rate. Particularly after 2007, the share of asset income fell to 13.3%, asserting what has been observed at aggregate macroeconomic level.

Interestingly, during the whole period the share of transfer income increased drastically. The share of pension income which has been treated separately than other transfers increased from 12.6% in 2003 to 13.4% in 2007 and return to original level. The retirement policy prior to the 2000 allowed many individuals to retire at a very early age. Together with aging of the population, this policy has increased burden on state-governed pension funds. The change in the policy in 2000, increasing the retirement age to 60 from 45 for males and to 58 from 38 for females, seems to start showing its effect eventually. Inequality among pensioners is also the lowest among all income sources and declines over time, indicating an egalitarian retirement policy.

The share of population benefiting from other (public and private) transfers increased from less than 30% in 2003 to over 50% in 2015. Moreover, the correlation between total income and transfer income has also increased. As more people depend on (mostly public) transfers, the generosity of social security system is likely not sustainable.

Table 3.5 provides contribution of income sources to inequality dynamically. Between 2003 and 2007, the inequality measure (I_2) declined 54% and all income packages had positive contribution, though the major contributions were from employment/self-employment, asset and paid employment incomes. These income sources are also major culprits of increasing inequality after 2007. Once again, contrary to expectations, transfer income has also contributed to increasing inequality.

The Role of Social Transfers

The analysis above suggests that transfers play an important role in shaping income inequality. In this subsection, I provide some more information on public transfers.[3] Figure 3.3 provides information on shares of

---

[3] Private transfers are excluded as they are not direct policy tools, although policies may have indirect effect on private transfers.

Table 3.5 Contribution of factor income to changes in overall inequality

	Total inc.	Paid empl. inc.	Employer/ self-emp. income	Agr. inc.	Asset inc.	Pension inc.	Trans. inc.
2003–2007	−53.9	−11.2	−22.0	−1.3	−18.0	−1.1	−0.3
2007–2011	80.8	24.4	22.4	1.5	31.1	0.7	0.6

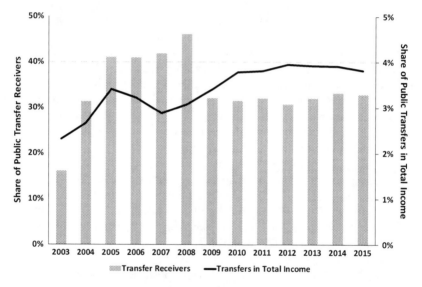

Fig. 3.3 Share of public transfers

people who receive public transfers and the share of public transfers in total household income. Starting in 2003, the share of population who enjoy public transfers increased from a little above 15 to 45%. Despite a decline in its share in total income in 2007, public transfers grew to reach almost 4% of total household income.

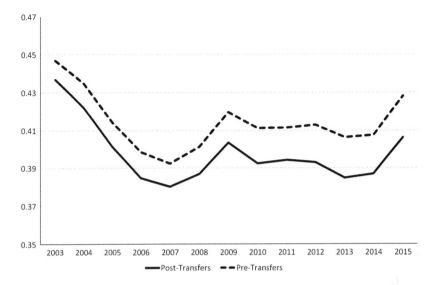

Fig. 3.4 Inequality before and after public transfers

The increasing share of public transfers helped to decrease inequality measured by Gini coefficient (Fig. 3.4) although the trend over time is very similar. While the share of people receiving transfer declined after 2008, its effect on inequality and its importance increased.

This is possible if transfers were directed to poor households. As shown in panels of Table 3.5, both the share of transfer receivers and share of transfers in total income of bottom 10% increased drastically. The share of poor receiving transfers increased from a mere 15% in 2003 to 70% at the end of the sample period, whereas the share of middle class and rich declined considerably after 2008 (Fig. 3.5).

Not only more poor people depend on public transfers, but a transfer also constitutes a significant share of their income, more than 11%. Despite a decline in share of receivers among middle classes, the share of transfers continued to increase but much a lesser extent than the poor. The change in transfer policy, then, explains partially the closing gap between incomes of bottom and middle 10%.

Panel a: Share of transfer receivers

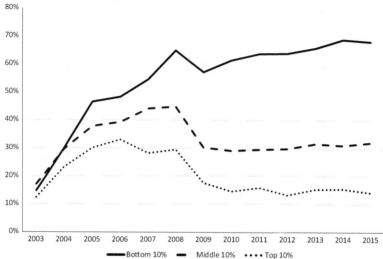

Panel b: Share of transfers in total income

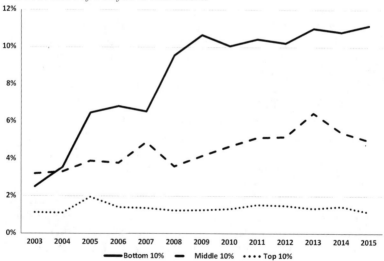

Fig. 3.5 Public transfers by bottom, middle and top 10 percentile

CONCLUSION

The crisis at the beginning of the millennium gave Turkey a chance for a new and fresh start and there were positive developments for a few years. However, starting in 2007 a number of things seem to have changed. Whatever the reasons for this reversal are, both macroeconomic growth and gains in inequality slowed down if not stopped. Current trends are also not promising. Inequality seems in a rise again.

The data used in this chapter shows that early improvement in inequality was mostly due to strengthening of the position of middle classes. A particularly important factor in shaping the income distribution is education. Between 2003 and 2007, there was a rapid convergence between education groups and income effect amounted more than half of the decline in inequality. However, after 2007 increasing share of university graduates with high earnings worsened the distribution. Any policies that will affect availability and access to education seem to improve or worsen income inequality.

Another important factor is changing social weave, aging population, postponement of marriage and childbearing and thus household formation all of which require deeper studies and understanding. The decomposition analysis hints that age and gender of the householder do not play a significant role in shaping the income distribution, though that observation should not lead to conclude that they are unimportant. Most probably, these effects are smoothed out within the households. In fact, the analysis shows that household types become an important source of inequality. It is very likely that social and economic developments manifest themselves in household formation. There are very few studies on family structure, how do they evolve over time and what causes changes. The paper by Yavuz (2004) provides some descriptive statistics but does not provide an in-depth analysis of the causes. Policies and institutions have to be thought in accordance with these changes.

There is also significant evidence that most household in Turkey now rely heavily on paid employment income: There is a secular downward trend in the share of self-employed and increasing trend in wage-earners, particularly workers. The proletarianization of the labor force contributed to changes in inequality through both allocation and income effect. This change is also evident in factor source decomposition. Not only main income source of most households is wages and salaries in later years, but the contribution of this income source to total inequality change becomes most important, requiring more research on wage inequality in Turkey. A number of macroeconomic policies have also affected the shape of income distribution. The importance of asset income declines in later years and within inequality is increasing. This finding supports the evidence of increasing debt within the Turkish population.

Relative stability of inequality after 2007 is coming from a convergence of the poor segments of the society to middle classes. Public transfers seem to play an important role. Turkish population's, especially the poor's, reliance on transfers is increasing and the generosity of the state cannot be sustained for long. In the absence or decline in the amount of transfers, inequality is expected to rise even faster.

It is clear that the analysis here does not provide direct causal links to inequality. Nonetheless, the findings are implicating a number of factors that have to be taken seriously.

Appendix

See Tables 3.6 and 3.7.

Table 3.6 Shares of population subgroups

	2003	2007	2015
Ages under 30	7.0	8.0	5.9
Ages 30–39	25.4	26.6	23.3
Ages 40–49	29.7	28.0	27.1
Ages 50–64	26.2	26.2	30.2
Ages 65+	11.7	11.1	13.4
Male	92.7	91.7	88.4
Female	7.3	8.3	11.7
No degree	65.7	65.1	56.2
5-year primary	11.0	10.1	13.0
8-year primary	15.1	16.4	16.6
High school	8.2	8.3	14.2
College	1.6	1.8	6.9
Single	1.6	1.8	6.9
Single w\ children	0.8	0.8	0.6
Couple	10.0	10.5	14.1
Couple w\ children	26.5	27.5	23.3
Extended	22.6	23.8	24.0
Extended w\ children	38.6	35.6	31.1

3 INCOME INEQUALITY IN TURKEY: 2003–2015   83

Table 3.7 Relative incomes (μ_k/μ)

	2003	2007	2015
Ages under 30	0.89	0.89	0.93
Ages 30–39	0.94	0.99	1.00
Ages 40–49	1.00	0.99	0.95
Ages 50–64	1.08	1.08	1.09
Ages 65+	1.02	0.93	0.91
No degree	1.00	1.00	0.99
5-year primary	1.05	1.03	1.05
8-year primary	0.74	0.81	0.72
High school	0.98	1.01	0.88
College	1.28	1.26	1.16
Male	2.59	2.00	2.03
Female	1.59	1.41	1.67
Single	1.59	1.41	1.67
Single w\ children	0.70	0.81	0.82
Couple	1.44	1.31	1.24
Couple w\ children	1.02	1.01	1.01
Extended	1.14	1.17	1.05
Extended w\ children	0.78	0.77	0.70

REFERENCES

Acemoglu, D., & Ucer, M. (2015). *The Ups and Downs of Turkish Economic Growth, 2002–2015: Political Dynamics, the European Union and the Institutional Slide* (NBER Working Paper No. 21608).

Atiyas, I. (2012). Economic Institutions and Institutional Change in Turkey During the Neoliberal Era. *New Perspectives on Turkey, 14,* 45–69.

Başlevent, C., & Dayıoğlu, M. (2005). A Household Level Examination of Regional Income Disparity in Turkey. *METU Studies in Development, 32,* 275–302.

Bulutay, T., Timur, S., & Ersel, H. (1971). *Türkiye Gelir Dağılımı 1968.* A.Ü. Siyasal Bilgiler Fakültesi yayını.

Cowell, F., & Jenkins, S. P. (1995). How Much Inequality Can We Explain? A Methodology and an Application to the United States. *The Economic Journal, 105*(429), 421–430.

Esmer, Y., Fişek, H., & Kalaycıoğlu, E. (1986). *Türkiye'de Sosyo-Ekonomik Öncelikler, Hane Gelirleri, Harcamaları ve Sosyo-Ekonomik İhtiyaçlar Üzerine Araştırma Dizisi,* Cilt II. Istanbul, Turkey: Turkish Industrialists' and Businessmen's Association (TUSIAD).

84   A. FILIZTEKIN

Filiztekin, A. (2015). Income Inequality Trends in Turkey. *Iktisat, Isletme Ve Finans, 350,* 63–92.

Gurakar, E. C., & Gunduz, U. (2015). *Europeanization and De-Europeanization of Public Procurement Policy in Turkey: Transparency Versus Clientelism (Reform and Transition in the Mediterranean).* US: Palgrave Pivot.

Gürsel, S., Levent, H., Selim, R., & Sarıca, Ö. (2000). *Individual Income Distribution in Turkey.* Istanbul, Turkey: Turkish Industrialists' and Businessmen's Association (TUSIAD).

Jenkins, S. (1995). Accounting for Inequality Trends: Decomposition Analyses for the UK, 1971–86. *Economica, 62,* 29–63.

Kanbur, R. (2000). Income Distribution and Development. In A. B. Atkinson & F. Bourguignon (Eds.), *Handbook of Income Distribution.* North Holland, Amsterdam: Elsevier.

Mookherjee, D., & Shorrocks, A. (1982). A Decomposition Analysis of the Trend in UK Income Inequality. *The Economic Journal, 92,* 886–902.

OECD. (2011). *Divided We Stand: Why Inequality Keeps Rising.* Paris: OECD Publishing.

Shorrocks, A. F. (1982). Inequality Decomposition by Factor Components. *Econometrica, 50,* 193–211.

Silber, J., & Özmucur, S. (2000). Decomposition of Income Inequality: Evidence from Turkey. *Topics in Middle Eastern and North African Economies, Electronic Journal, 2,* 1–17. http://meea.sites.luc.edu/volume2/meea2.htm.

Yavuz, S. (2004). Changing Household and Family Compositions in Turkey: A Demographic Evaluation for 1968–1998 Period. *Hacettepe University E-Journal of Sociological Research, 2,* 1–34.

CHAPTER 4

Turkish Labor Market: Complex Dynamics and Challenges

Seyfettin Gürsel, Gökçe Uysal and Tuba Toru Delibaşı

INTRODUCTION

The current incumbent Justice and Development Party (JDP) came to power as the winner of the general elections of November 2002[1] while Turkey was struggling to exit painfully from its worst-ever economic crisis that devastated its economy in 2001. The IMF standby program based on exchange rate targeting had gone out of order; the Turkish lira

[1] At that time, JDP won 35% of the vote, but as only two parties (JDP and Republican People's Party-CHP) were able to beat the very high electoral threshold of 10%, JDP won the majority of seats in Parliament and formed a single party government which had not happened since 1987. In the following elections, JDP increased its vote's shares and has been governing Turkey since.

S. Gürsel (✉) · G. Uysal (✉) · T. Toru Delibaşı (✉)
Bahcesehir University, Istanbul, Turkey
e-mail: seyfettin.gursel@eas.bau.edu.tr

G. Uysal
e-mail: gokce.uysal@eas.bau.edu.tr

T. Toru Delibaşı
e-mail: tuba.toru@eas.bau.edu.tr

© The Author(s) 2020
E. Parlar Dal (ed.), *Turkey's Political Economy in the 21st Century*, International Political Economy Series,
https://doi.org/10.1007/978-3-030-27632-4_4

had depreciated by 100%; inflation had reached triple digits; half of the banks had failed; and, finally, gross domestic product (GDP) had contracted by 4.8%.

The three-party coalition formed in the aftermath of April 1999 elections was so desperate that it nominated in extremis Kemal Derviş, the World Bank vice-president, as the minister of economy. A new macroeconomic setup based on floating exchange rates, central bank policy independency and a restructuring of banking system under strict regulatory rules was implemented, and then a comprehensive standby agreement with the IMF requiring a very strong fiscal discipline (primary surplus/GDP ratio targeted at 6.5%) was signed.

In a sense, arriving into power, JDP had found a clean ground propitious to high economic growth and adhered sufficiently well to this new macroeconomic setup. Abundance of capital inflows, reinforced by a surge of FDI in 2005, thanks to the start of membership negotiations with EU, coupled with fiscal discipline and rapid disinflation opened an era of high GDP growth; from 2003 to 2017, yearly average GDP growth reached 5.8% despite the contraction of 2009 due to the adverse effects of the Great Recession.

In the context of this high-growth performance, it would have been expected that high unemployment inherited from the 1990s, a period that suffered from three economic crises, could have been brought down sizably. In fact, the overall and the non-farm unemployment rates varied up and down during this period between 8.4–10.9 and 10.3–13.7%, respectively, excluding the overall and non-farm unemployment rates of 2009 at 13.1 and 16%. It is worth noting that the evolution of unemployment displays various cycles based on the ever-changing job creation capacity of GDP growth, the unstable evolution of agricultural employment as well as the strong increase in the labor force, in which female participation played a crucial role along with the increasing trend in working age population.

In this chapter, we first present broadly the evolution of the Turkish labor market during the last decade (2005–2017)[2] in order to shed light

---

[2] Turkish Statistical Institute (TurkStat) started the Household Labor Surveys (HLS) in 1989 publishing the figures twice a year and since it introduced time to time some changes in its sampling and methodology that caused breaks in the time serials. The first significant break occurred in 2005 with publishing monthly figures as three months moving averages. So, we restrict the analysis of Turkish labor market to 2005–2017 period. Another break

on the complex dynamics of the labor force, employment and unemployment coupled with the varying job creation capacity of economic growth. At a second stage, these complex dynamics will be further scrutinized in two particular dimensions: gender and youth. The strong increase of female labor force and employment accompanied by a wide gender gap in unemployment as well as the persistent high youth unemployment deserves close scrutiny.

The fight against unemployment was constituted in the aftermath of the Great Recession as one of the main concerns of the JDP government since in public opinion polls, unemployment is perceived to be one of the top concerns. So, different employment strategies and policies were included in official programs like the Medium-Term Programs (MTP) and National Employment Strategy. Various labor policies have been implemented in different phases of the period under study but their effectiveness is disputable. This policy aspect will be embedded in appropriate parts of the chapter.

THE UPS AND DOWNS OF THE TURKISH LABOR MARKET

During the last twelve years under the rule of JDP, Turkish economy went through five different phases in terms of economic growth performance and labor market dynamics where the latter is directly affected by the former. The first phase 2005–2007 might be characterized by three basic facts: High GDP growth, modest job creation and resilient unemployment. Then came the shock of the Great Recession (2008–2009) that caused a jump in unemployment shaking up the usual dynamics of the labor force and employment. The period of 2010–2012 is characterized by a strong economic revival beating world GDP growth records and a jump in job creation capacity resulting in a rapid and sizable decline in unemployment. Growth remained relatively high until 2016,

---

to be noted occurred in 2014 due to some methodological changes in the definition of unemployed (active job search in the last month in spite of three months) and to the use of renewed demographic estimations. TurkStat revised the statistics of the main indicators like labor force, employment and unemployment for the period of 2005–2013. Needless to say that in the first part of this chapter, we use these revised figures. However, since the figures of females were not revised by TurkStat for 2005–2013, they have been estimated by the authors. See section "The Ups and Downs of the Turkish Labor Market".

88 S. GÜRSEL ET AL.

Table 4.1 Labor market outlook, Turkey, 2005–2017

	Labor force	Employment	Unemployment rate (%)	Non-farm unemployment rate (%)
2005	21691	19633	9.5	12.0
2006	21913	19933	9.0	11.1
2007	22253	20209	9.2	11.2
2008	22899	20604	10.0	12.3
2009	23710	20615	13.1	16.0
2010	24594	21858	11.1	13.7
2011	25594	23266	9.1	11.3
2012	26141	23937	8.4	10.3
2013	27047	24601	9.0	10.9
2014	28786	25933	9.9	12.0
2015	29678	26621	10.3	12.4
2016	30535	27205	10.9	13.0
2017	31643	28189	10.9	13.0

Note Numbers of the sub-period 2005–2013 are revised by TurkStat

but a decline in job creation capacity, in other words an implied improvement in labor productivity, coupled with strong labor force increases is observed in the period of 2013–2015 during which an increase in unemployment is observed. The two last years, 2016 and 2017, although having the same unemployment rates (10.9 for overall and 13.0 for non-farm unemployment) (Table 4.1), this coincidence hides a great cycle in unemployment caused by opposite growth performances originated first from the trauma caused by the military coup attempt in July 2016 and then from the intense stimulation policies with the aim of winning the constitutional referendum in April 2017. This recent period deserves a deeper analysis using the monthly labor figures instead yearly statistics.

Before analyzing these particular periods, we would like to underline two common characteristics of the whole period under study: The working age population (15+), more specifically the non-institutional population that is at least 15 years old, increased from 48 million in 2005 to 60 million approximately in 2017 with a regular yearly addition of roughly 1 million people, and at the same time, labor force participation increased from 44.9 to 52.8% with a perceptible acceleration after 2007 thanks to number of working women (discussed in the following section). Finally, labor force reached 31 million 641 thousand in 2017 increasing by 46% comparing to 2005 (Table 4.1). This increase in labor force that will keep its strong trend in the years to come constitutes the basic challenge for Turkey regarding economic growth and unemployment.

High GDP Growth, Modest Job Creation and Resilient Unemployment (2005–2007)

As we noted in introduction, JPD government accepted the new macroeconomic setup as well as the stabilization program that worked quite well, producing a cumulative real GDP increase of 12.5% from 2005 to 2007 thanks to a virtuous cycle.[3] However, this impressive growth performance did not translate into a significant improvement in unemployment as the high economic growth was largely due to increases in labor productivity (Atiyas and Bakis 2014); hence, the increase in employment was rather modest. During these two years, total employment increased by 2.9% and net job creation was limited to 576 thousand. Unemployment rate decreased from 9.5% in 2005 to 9.2% in 2007 while non-farm unemployment rate receded back to 12.6% from 13.5%. In this period, cumulative GDP growth reached 12.4% implying a quite low growth-employment elasticity (0.23) overall. The highest elasticity coefficient (0.8) was calculated for the service sector as expected (Kaya and Küçükşahin 2018).

In fact, even this modest improvement in unemployment would have been missed had the labor force increase not remained also modest; the increase was limited to 562 thousand, an increase of 2.6%. Note that this slow dynamic of the labor force is exceptional in light of the following periods. Indeed, a slight decline in the labor force participation rate (LFPR) (from 44.9 to 44.3%) is observed during this period; part of the explanation may lie in the fact that female participation had not yet undertaken its acceleration.

[3] Fiscal discipline did not turn into an austerity since public expenditures have not been obliged to be cut. High primary surpluses have been realized thanks to increasing tax revenues originating from high growth and from improvements in tax collection. Indeed, the fiscal discipline increased the confidence among economic actors. Inflation fell below 10% in 2006, as did real interest rates. However, we have to note that the domestic-led growth accompanied by an appreciation of Turkish lira increased the current account deficit (CAD), but the deficit was easily financed by the abundance of international liquidity, as well as by a booming foreign direct investment following the start of the EU-Turkey membership negotiations in October 2005 (Gürsel 2013; Acemoglu and Ucer 2015).

90 S. GÜRSEL ET AL.

During this period, the JDP government was not particularly worried by the rather high unemployment level for a couple of reasons: First, it was decreasing albeit slowly. Second, per capita income in USD terms was rapidly increasing thanks not only to high GDP growth but also to the rapid appreciation of Turkish lira[4] caused by sizable capital inflows in portfolio investments as well as in FDI that made a real jump in 2005 as Turkey started the membership negotiations with the European Union. So, in the MTP of 2006 and 2007 the fight against unemployment is not mentioned at all among "primary objectives."

Jump in Unemployment During the Great Recession (2008–2009)

When the Great Recession struck, the growth in GDP was already decelerating from the second quarter of 2008 due to curtailing domestic demand, which had increased too rapidly during the preceding years. Turkish economy went into a deep recession in the last quarter of 2008 following the international financial crisis. The recession lasted for a year causing a rather strong contraction of Turkish economy (0.8% in 2008 and—4.7% in 2009) as the overall unemployment rate surged from 9.2 to 13.1% and non-farm rate from 11.2 to 16%.

This jump in unemployment cannot be solely explained by the expected negative effect of the economic crisis on employment. Indeed, various other effects intervened producing a complex dynamic process in the Turkish labor market during these difficult years. First, note that the labor force had increased tremendously from 2007 to 2009, by 1 million 457 thousand, while the increase of employment remained limited to 406 thousand. An employment increase during a recession is rather an unexpected phenomenon, but it must be noted that the increase in non-agricultural employment was limited to 200 thousand, the difference corresponding to an increase in the number of farmers in the agricultural sector.[5] Although rather limited, the increase in non-farm employment may still seem paradoxical. In fact, this increase has been

---

[4] The real exchange rate index (2003 = 100) computed by CBRT reached its pick at 130 in 2007 while per capita income being 7.384 USD in 2005, it reached 9.710 USD in 2007.

[5] Agricultural employment increased by 17.0% between 2007 and 2010, and its share in total employment increased by 1.7 percentage points. For possible reasons, see Gürsel and Imamoglu (2013).

the result of the "added worker effect," a well-known phenomenon in developing countries, occurring during economic crises. This phenomenon will be scrutinized in the next section. In summary, in spite of weak employment increases during the crisis period, exceptional labor force increases pushed the unemployment up rapidly and strongly as noted above.

As the crisis was unfolding, the PJD government began to worry about unemployment rate. In the MTP of 2010–2012 published in September 2009,[6] flexibility was the main focus: "To increase employment and reduce informal economy, flexible working models will be encouraged and expanded in the framework of flexicurity." Turkish labor market, being relatively rigid with labor taxes and the severance pay regime compared to the OECD countries, the first measure taken in May 2008 was a 5-percentage point diminution in the social security premiums paid by the employers.[7] The package also included the progressive subsidies to employers' share of social security taxes for new hires of women and youth (see section "The Ups and Downs of the Turkish Labor Market" for further information).

As for the severance pay regime, Turkey is still ranked on the top of OECD countries[8] as the severance pay is not only paid at retirement but also in case of involuntary job loss. A reform agenda to redesign the severance pay system is being included in all MTPs as the JDP tirelessly insists. Nevertheless, the trade unions are harshly opposing the change by threatening with a general strike.

The striking point regarding the government's policy approach to unemployment is that the MTV published in the middle of a crisis was totally unable to predict the evolution of Turkish economy in the three years that followed. Indeed, the policymakers were planning a smooth

---

[6]The MTPs are available at the Web site of the Ministry of Development.

[7]High labor taxes and severance payment system are considered as the main rigidities. In 2008, the share of labor taxes was standing at 42.7% before 5 points cut while OECD average was at 37.5%; Turkish labor cost became close to OECD average but continued to be ranked above East European countries.

[8]The severance pay regime has been implemented in 1970s on the pretext of unemployment indemnity absence. In case of retirement or firing one month gross salary for each year of work is paid by the employer. In 2003, unemployment indemnity has been introduced albeit quite limited in regards of selection rules, recovery ratio and duration. A new regime has been debated extensively among public and private institution as well as economists. See Betam's "Kıdem Tazminatı Reiformu: Sorunlar ve Çözümler," July 2012.

exit from the crisis, keeping the main macroeconomic balances under control given that the GDP growth targets for the 2010–2012 period were 3.5, 4 and 5%, respectively. In accordance with these growth rate targets, and a slightly decreasing LFPR target from 47.6 to 47.3%, general unemployment rate was predicted to decrease by 1.6 percentage points. All these targets were missed by far, but fortunately, the numbers were on the right track.

Strong Economic Revival, Decrease in Unemployment (2010–2012)

The exit from the recession was impressive: GDP grew by 8.5 in 2010 and then by 11.1% in 2011. A conjunction of factors is behind this unexpected successful recovery. First, we have to note that being frightened by international financial crisis, firms preferred to reduce their production and to tap into stocks for sales. Indeed, half of the violent contraction of GDP in 2009 is explained by the reduction in stocks. However, firms did overcome this shock rapidly, mainly for three reasons: (1) Turkish banks remained clear of the Western financial mess thanks to a close monitoring of risks since the 2001 restructuring, and they could easily increase the volume of their loans supported by the abundance of international liquidity, (2) Turkish Central Bank (CBRT) seized the opportunity presented by the global recession in reducing interest rates further without increasing the inflation risk; real interest rates paid on Treasury Bonds declined around 1%, further encouraging investment, and (3) low public debt ratio (under 40%) gave room for public finance maneuvers, rendering possible a slight increase in public expenditures (Gürsel 2013, 2015; Akat and Gürsel 2016).

Nevertheless, this high-growth performance reached its limits rather quickly since it was based exclusively on domestic demand. The current account deficit (CAD) reached its historical peak at 10% by 2011. Admittedly, this was not a sustainable state of affairs, also given the fact that the Turkish lira was appreciating dangerously under the pressure of excessive capital inflows. So, Ali Babacan, the vice prime minister in charge of the economy, was quite wise in deciding upon a cooling down operation called, "the rebalancing of the economy." The corrective measures worked rather well; since the Turkish lira retracted part of its overvaluation, the CAD started to decrease rapidly and the price of rebalancing in terms of GDP growth was quite acceptable as it went down to 4.8% in 2012.

As one would expect, the very high cumulative GDP growth attaining 26.3% pushed overall employment sharply up by 16.1% and non-farm employment by 17.5%. More than 2 million 770 thousand net jobs were created in non-agricultural sectors within 3 years. This success in generating employment cannot be explained only by the striking economic growth performance since growth started also to create more jobs as implied by the growth-employment elasticity of 0.67 during this period.

A strong increase in the labor force was also observed, largely due to the pull effect of the labor demand. Over three years, non-farm labor force increased by 1 million 900 hundred thousand. In parallel to the increases in the working age population, thanks in particular to the growing appetite of women for work, a strong increase was observed in the participation rate from 45.7 to 47.6%. Finally, given the high-growth-high-job creation, the overall unemployment rate decreased from 13.1% in 2009 to 8.4% in 2012 and the non-farm unemployment rate from 16.0 to 10.3%.

Increase in Unemployment Despite High Growth (2013–2015)

This period of three years constitutes one of the amazing episodes in Turkish labor market. The rebalancing strategy was abandoned step by step after 2012. In the global context of quantitative easing policies carried out by the Federal Reserve Bank of the United States (FED) and the European Central Bank (ECB), the banking system in Turkey used the abundant international financial flows to open up credit lines to Turkish firms and households. The investment (particularly in housing) and consumer durables appetite were so vast that the yearly increase in credits peaked at 40% during this period. Hence, the GDP growth rate jumped to 8.5% in 2013 and then slowed down to some extent, but the 3-year cumulative rise of the GDP attained 21%.

Given this successful growth and keeping in mind its employment creation capacity observed during the previous period, one might expect the decreasing tendency in unemployment to continue during this period. Indeed, the MTP of the period 2013–2015 published in October 2012 was targeting 4–5% GDP growth and a quite low yearly increase in employment of 2%, assuming a rather high labor productivity performance. Assuming a poor improvement in the labor force participation at 0.6 percentage points, a consistent but quite modest decrease in the unemployment rate by 0.3 percentage points was forecasted.

Once again, the MTP was out of touch with the reality. It turned out that the government was incapable of managing the macroeconomic dynamics. In fact, unemployment started a noticeable and steady rise from 2013. The overall unemployment rate increased from 8.4% in 2012 to 10.3% in 2015 and the non-farm rate from 10.3 to 12.4%. How could this unexpected increase in unemployment be explained? At a first glance, we have to look at the employment dynamics. From 2012 to 2015, overall employment increased by all most 2 million 700 thousand (11.2%) and by 2.5 million in non-farm sector (13.4%). Two notes should be made: First, the additional amount of workers during the two consecutive three-year periods (2010–2012 and 2013–2015) is rather close to each other: 2.7 and 2.5 million; a difference of 200 thousand may be easily explained by a smoothly lower growth rate in the second period all the more since, and this the second remark, the growth-employment elasticity of non-farm sector is almost equivalent in the two periods: 0.67 (17.5/26.3) and 0.64 (13.4/21.0).

Obviously, we have to focus on the labor force dynamics to identify the basic reason behind rising unemployment. Within three years, non-farm labor force increased by 3 million 350 thousand. To clarify, the labor force increase during the previous three years had been 1 million 900 hundred thousand. The yearly average increase almost doubled from 635 thousand to 1 million 117 thousand. Working age population increases were 3 million 126 thousand and 2 million 893 thousand respectively during the two consecutive periods. Needless to say, this explosion in the labor force originated from the acceleration of the participation rates which rose from 47.6 to 51.3%, implying a 3.7 percentage point increase, which in turn is considerably higher compared to the 1.9 percentage point increase of the previous period. As noted above, the MTV had forecasted 0.6 percentage points. This labor supply shock still constitutes a puzzle as research has not explored this issue further yet. Meanwhile, in the next section, the role played by a rush into the labor market by women is explored further. Indeed, female LFPR increase, which was 1.7 points cumulatively in the 2010–2012 period, jumped to 3.9 points in the 2013–2015 period.

Ups and Downs in Unemployment Driven by Opposing Growth Performances (2016–2017)

The last two years, 2016–2017, are characterized by immensely varying GDP growth: The trauma provoked by the failed military coup in 15th of July 2016 caused a contraction in the third quarter while a slowdown in economic growth was already perceptible in the second quarter. So, the yearly growth rate decreased to 3.2% in 2016 provoking a strong increase of unemployment that reached its peak in December 2016. In the meantime, securing the support of the Nationalist Movement Party (MHP), the PJD government had decided upon a constitutional referendum to be held in April 2017, with the aim of establishing a new presidential regime. So, a wide package of incentives and subsidies was implemented rapidly[9] that stimulated domestic demand, pushing GDP growth rate to 7.4% in 2017, and as expected, unemployment started a substantial decline from January 2017 onwards.

As already noted, the yearly unemployment rates stood at the same level, by pure coincidence of course, at 10.9 and at 13.0% in 2016 and 2017 (Table 4.1). So, in order to describe the great cycle that occurred in Turkish labor market during this period, the seasonally adjusted (SA) monthly figures of the non-farm sectors are used.

Along with the high economic growth in 2015 (6.1%), the non-farm unemployment had started a decline in the fall of 2015 and went down to 11.8% in March 2016 (Fig. 4.1). However, because of the slowdown observed in economic growth, unemployment began a moderate incline in April but the increase accelerated in the third quarter due to the contraction of the GDP. First a slowdown, then a decline in non-farm employment can be easily observed from March to September; the number of workers in non-farm sectors was slightly below the March number: 21,930,000 versus 21,939,000 (Fig. 4.1). The rapid economic recovery in the 4th quarter of 2016 allowed employment to recover, but it was not sufficient to compensate the labor force increase; the peak of unemployment at 14.3% was reached in December. Needless to note that the labor force kept its strong upward trend: Within 9 months, it

---

[9]Two main incentives were the distribution of an amount of 235 billion Turkish lira (67 billion USD at 2017 average exchange rate) to small size enterprises with Treasury guarantee and consumption tax reductions for durables goods. Another incentive was the tax and social security premium subsidy to additional employment. See footnote 8 for a brief discussion.

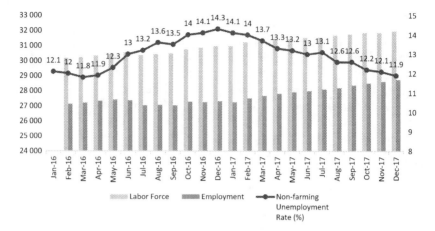

Fig. 4.1 Labor force, employment and unemployment: 2016–2017 (Seasonally adjusted)

increased by 722 thousand and the number of unemployed people jumped from 2 million 935 thousand to 3 million 660 thousand.

As the strong revival took the growth rate back up to 7.4% in 2017, the robust job creation came back, causing an increase in non-farm employment by 1 million 368 thousand, a growth rate of 6.2% and a high employment-growth elasticity at 0.84.[10] On the other hand, the non-farm labor force increase attained 856 thousand in 2017 and the number of unemployed decreased by 512 thousand, bringing down the unemployment rate to 11.9% (Fig. 4.1).

The labor force dynamics in Turkish labor market remain an underexplored field, but its strong increase will undoubtedly continue in the next decade given the increase in the working age population (albeit at a diminishing rate), rising duration of average working period (or late retirement) and growing female participation. These fundamental factors determine a minimal threshold for economic growth in order to keep unemployment at its current level at least. We will discuss this issue further in the concluding section.

---

[10]This employment-growth elasticity slightly higher than the average might be attributed partially to the "additional workers" subsidy implemented in February 2017 and consisting in the payment of social security premiums and income taxes to companies for each worker hired as additional to the number of workers as of 31st of December 2016 until the end of 2017.

SUSTAINED INCREASE IN FEMALE LABOR FORCE PARTICIPATION

The female LFPRs have been historically low in Turkey. OECD statistics show that in 2017, Turkey ranked the last among a vast array of countries when it comes to female LFPR.[11] Among the 15- to 64-year-olds, the female LFPR was a mere 37.6% in Turkey. Turkey performs poorly not only compared to northern European countries such as Sweden (80.6%), but also compared to ex-Soviet countries such as the Czech Republic (68.7%) and Hungary (64.2%). Being on the Mediterranean, Turkey is frequently compared to the countries that border the Mediterranean, such as Italy and Greece. Yet the female LFPR is relatively higher in Greece (60.3%) and Italy (55.9%), where the rates are already lower than EU averages.

Furthermore, Turkey is lagging behind Latin American countries which have comparable development levels. Female LFPR was 60.3% in Brazil and 46.7% in Mexico. Under such circumstances, the low female LFPR is widely studied structural problem of the labor market in Turkey. The usual culprits are commonly cited in the literature, low education levels, high unemployment rates discouraging labor market entry and unfavorable working conditions.

Nevertheless, even controlling for educational differences fails to explain the gap between Turkey and other countries on the Mediterranean that have relatively lower female LFPRs, such as Greece and Italy. A simple decomposition exercise reveals that the educational differences across these countries can merely explain one-third of the difference between Turkey and the rest (Gürsel et al. 2011). The literature indicates that a large part of the remaining two-thirds of the difference stems from institutional factors such as lack of affordable and quality childcare facilities, absence of work-life reconciliation mechanisms as well as cultural factors such as traditional gender roles that are widely accepted and practiced (Guner and Uysal 2014; Paker and Uysal 2015; İlkkaracan 2012; Göksel 2013).

Is the Female LFPR Catching Up?

The U-shaped evolution of female labor force participation is observed in Turkey, although Turkey has only recently passed the trough.

---

[11] https://stats.oecd.org/Index.aspx?DataSetCode=LFS_SEXAGE_I_R#.

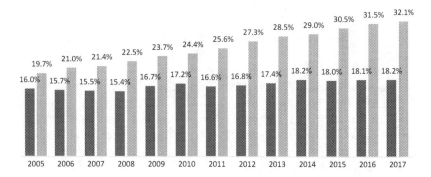

Fig. 4.2 Shares of woman in services and manufacturing: 2005–2017

The U-shaped trajectory of the female LFPR is characterized by a decline caused by the shift from agriculture to manufacturing and by an increase as production in the economy shifts toward services and education levels increase steadily (Goldin 1994). In Turkey, the overall female LFPR decreased from 36.1% in 1989 to 23.3% in 2004 as production shifted from agricultural to non-agricultural sectors. Parallel to increases in education levels and the growth of the service sector, female LFPR has been increasing since 2005 to reach 33.6% in 2017.

The share of women in manufacturing and in service sectors demonstrates the evident increase in services. The share of women in services increased from 19.7% in 2005 to 32.1% in 2017, indicating a rise of 12.4 points. During the same period, the share of women in manufacturing rose only by 2.2 points (from 16 to 18.2% (Fig. 4.2). On a different note, recent research by Kubota (2014) as well as Genc Ileri and Sengul (2017) finds that the current share of the service sector in total employment should imply a higher female LFPR in Turkey. Kubota (2014) shows that the rise in the share of services does explain the increase in female LFPR in France, Portugal, Spain and the UK, but fails to predict such low levels in Turkey. Kubota (2014) cites cultural factors; Genc Ileri and Sengul (2017) remain silent as to the reasons. Yet again, it is not difficult to imagine that not only the cultural but also the institutional factors may be determinative.

Note that the labor market series are shorter than usual and not exactly comparable across this time period as TurkStat has revised the household labor force statistics in 2014, causing a break in the time

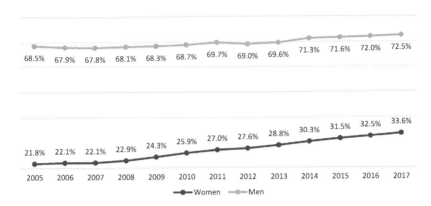

Fig. 4.3 Labor force participation by gender (*Source* Authors' calculations using TurkStat HLFS data)

series as explained above. Even though some key statistics have been revised back to 2005, gender series were not included. Therefore, we use a simple revision strategy to revise the labor market series for women and youth. To adjust the 2013 levels, we use the geometric average of the growth in the preceding three years and then use the growth rates in the old series to take them back to 2005.[12] The resulting data reveals the following LFPR (Fig. 4.3).

The data clearly shows that following a flat course between 2005 and 2007, the female LFPR starts to increase dramatically during the Global Recession when the non-farm unemployment rates soared from 2008 to 2009.[13] Household labor supply models demonstrate that labor supply of inactive household members may increase in case of employment loss and thus in periods of increasing unemployment risk, such as the Global Recession. In other words, when employed household members become unemployed or face higher risks of unemployment, previously inactive members may enter the labor market to counterbalance a possible

---

[12]TurkStat provides revised series for total working age population, total labor force, total employment and total unemployment. We compare the results of our revision for these series to those released by TurkStat. The differences are negligible for employment and for the working age population (i.e., less than 2%). However, the unemployment levels are more difficult to match, particularly for years before 2009.

[13]The revised series indicate a lower trough for female LFPR at 21.8%.

decrease in household income. This increase was named "added worker effect" by Ashenfelter (1980). The added worker effect can be particularly strong in labor markets with low participation rates like Turkey as established by Başlevent and Onaran (2003), Karaoglan and Okten (2015) as well as Degirmenci and İlkkaracan (2013) where the latter two papers concentrate on the period from 2004 to 2010.

Intriguingly, the increase in female LFPR is sustained over a longer period of time. The effects of the Global Recession on the labor market in Turkey are erased rather quickly by 2011.[14] In other words, the added worker effect should have been phased out. Yet the female LFPR has risen from 25.9% in 2010 to 33.6% in 2017. An increase of 7.7 percentage points over a 7-year window deserves closer scrutiny.

Increasing Female LFPR in All Education Levels

The educational distribution of the population changed drastically from 2005 to 2017 as the compulsory years of education were increased from 8 years to 12 years in 2012. Among women, the share without a high school degree declined from 80.9 to 71% during the 12 years under study. Meanwhile, the share of high school graduates almost stagnated with a negligible increase of 1.5 points. Interestingly, the share of university graduates rose from 5.4 to 13.7%. In other words, getting women through high school implied that they continued on to university. A 9.9-point decrease in the share of women without a high school degree was matched by an 8.4-point increase in the share of those with a university degree. The fact that the education levels of women soared during this period implies directly that the LFPR increase.[15]

However, the rise in the total female LFPR is not only due to a composition effect whereby the education levels increase and so does the average participation rate. Data indicates that the LFPRs have increased for all women, regardless of their education levels. Interestingly, the surges do not happen simultaneously. The added worker effect that is observed during the Global Recession seems to be driven by increases

---

[14]The non-farm unemployment rates increased from 12.3 to 16% in 2009 and are down to 11.3% by 2011.

[15]As wages are closely linked to education levels, individuals with higher education levels have higher labor force participation rates. Women who hold university degrees are more likely to participate than women who hold high school degrees.

in LFPR of women who have at most a high school degree. The LFPR of women who have less than a high school degree increases from 17% in 2007 to 21.6% in 2011. In other words, 4.6 percentage points of the total 7.6-point increase in LFPR of the lowest education category happened during the Global Recession. This finding is consistent with the policies enacted during this period. In May 2008, the government announced a stimulus package to boost the employment of women and youth. Uysal (2013) shows that the subsidies to employers' share of labor taxes that were a part of this package were more effective in generating employment for women with lower education levels and thus may have triggered a pull effect.

Even though the LFPR of women without high school degrees continued to increase after 2011, the rise is much less pronounced than that of high school graduates. The period from 2012 to 2017 is marked by a 5.4-point increase in the LFPR of high school graduates who observed the largest hike during 2005–2017 of 8.5 percentage points. The surge in the LFPR of high school graduates is in line with the increase in the share of the service sector during this period. Jobs in the service sector are thought to be "better jobs" compared to those in manufacturing, as the working conditions are considered to be more favorable.[16] The growth of employment in services and an increase in labor demand may have a pull effect thereby encouraging entry into the labor market.

The university graduate women also experienced a rise in LFPR albeit much less conspicuous. Their LFPR increased from 67 to 72.7% over the 2005–2017 period. Two increments, one of 2.4 points from 2009 to 2010 and another of 2.6 points from 2013 to 2014, are the reasons.

The increase in female LFPR can thus be decomposed into two components: one part stemming from the increase in education levels and the other from the increase in LFPR in each educational category. A simple exercise helps decompose the 11.8 percentage points (33.6–21.8%) whereby 4.3 points are due to higher education levels and 7.5 points are due to increased LFPR within each education category. The driving factors behind this increase in female LFPR remain to be investigated. Needless to say, increasing the female LFPR has been a policy priority since 2008 when the first incentives to female employment were introduced. Nevertheless, the AKP government has taken contradictory steps in addressing the issue.

---

[16]The mean wage in 2016 was 1477 TL in manufacturing and 2000 in services. Workers also frequently talk about better working environments in the service sector.

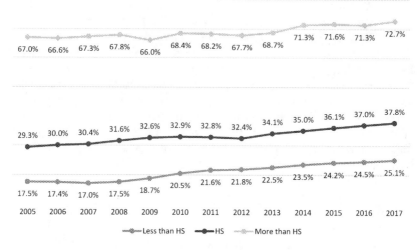

Fig. 4.4 Female LFPR by education (*Source* Authors' calculations using TurkStat HLFS data)

On the one hand, they have introduced and sustained incentives to female employment, a first in history in Turkey. On the other hand, they have followed a heavily gendered discourse, repeatedly accentuating the role of women as mothers and homemakers, insisting that women have three children to keep the demographic window of opportunity open, thereby discouraging female labor force participation (Fig. 4.4).

Widening of the Gender Gap in Unemployment Rates

Revising the unemployment rates back to 2005 also reveals a crucial gender divide in the labor market along another dimension: unemployment. The gender gap in unemployment rates was stagnant around 1 percentage point until the Global Recession during which it actually receded to 0.6 points. However, once the labor market started recovering from the effects of the Global Recession, the gender gap in unemployment rates started to increase, and it has not diminished since. On the contrary, the gender gap is widening at a steady pace and has reached 4.7 points by 2017 at which point the unemployment rates are 9.4% for men and 14.1% for women.

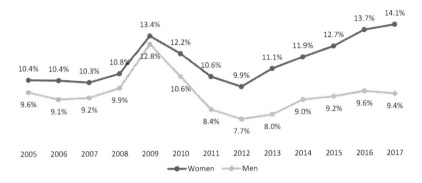

Fig. 4.5 Unemployment rates by gender

The gender gap in unemployment rates shrinks during the Global Recession as the manufacturing sector was hit hard. As GDP contracted, there were net employment losses for men in the manufacturing sector. Women, on the other hand, did not experience net losses in employment in this sector (Uysal 2013). Furthermore, they managed to increase their employment in services (Gürsel et al. 2014). Taken together, these two developments implied that the increase in women's unemployment was less than that of men, even when the added worker effect was strong. Uysal (2013) argues that the tax subsidies to female employment were particularly important in generating formal employment in the manufacturing sector during this period (Fig. 4.5).

To sum up, the female LFPR has been steadily increasing in Turkey since the Global Recession. Since 2012, the rise has accelerated to more than 1 percentage point a year. Furthermore, the contribution of the rising LFPRs by education levels, particularly that of high school graduates, is greater than that of rising education levels. The reasons remain to be investigated. Nevertheless, even if this accelerated trend continues, the female LFPR may stay below 50% in the next decade. Given that EU and other high-income countries are constantly implementing policies to increase the female LFPR and female employment rates further, convergence is not likely in the near future. Moreover, the widening of the gender gap in unemployment rates points to the existence of another problem in the labor market that of gender discrimination. Not only do high unemployment rates discourage individuals from labor market entry, gender discrimination will form a barrier that is difficult to surmount, particularly in a country like Turkey where gender roles are already laying high and thick walls to labor force participation (İlkkaracan 2012; Guner and Uysal 2014; Paker and Uysal 2015).

IMPLACABLE YOUTH UNEMPLOYMENT

The youth unemployment (15–24-year-olds) constitutes, as female unemployment, one of the main challenges Turkey is facing. During the period under study (2005–2017), it remained sizably higher than the overall as well as the non-farm unemployment. Indeed, youth unemployment to unemployment ratios fluctuated within a narrow band of 1.8 to 2.0. In other words, youth unemployment rate is almost the double of the overall rate (see Tables 4.1 and 4.2), evidencing the existence of chronicle problems.

Turkish Youth Unemployment Among the Highest Ones

On the other hand, as of 2017, Turkish youth unemployment stays well above the OECD average (respectively 20.6 and 11.9%) but also compared to the EU average of 16.9% (Fig. 4.6). Moreover, albeit Turkish youth unemployment rate appears less dramatic than Greek, Spanish,

Table 4.2 Unemployment, employment and NEET

	Unemployed (000)	Unemployment rate (%)	Employment rate (%)	NEET (%)
2005	881	19.1	30.2	39.5
2006	696	16.5	30.3	38.5
2007	729	17.3	30.2	39.2
2008	788	18.5	30.3	37
2009	982	22.9	28.9	34.9
2010	852	19.8	30	32.3
2011	742	16.7	32	29.6
2012	678	15.7	31.5	28.7
2013	760	17	32.2	25.5
2014	853	17.8	33.5	24.8
2015	912	18.5	34.1	23.9
2016	978	19.5	34.1	24
2017	1053	20.6	34.4	24.2

Source OECD and World Bank Database

4 TURKISH LABOR MARKET: COMPLEX DYNAMICS AND CHALLENGES   105

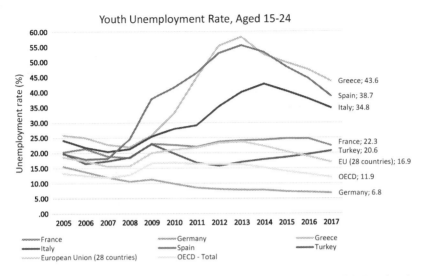

Fig. 4.6 The youth unemployment rate, 2005–2017 (*Source* OECD Database)

Italian and even French youth unemployment rates, countries that suffered harshly by the Great Recession effects, it is worthy to note that the turning down process that took place in EU is not observed in Turkey; the youth unemployment rate is on an upward trajectory since 2012 along with the general unemployment. To sum up, 1 million 53 thousand young people aged 15–24 were unemployed in 2017, an increase of 375 thousand over 2012, while the number of unemployed young people was decreasing in almost all European countries (see OECD 2018).

There exist successful countries in OECD, such as Germany, Switzerland, Norway, Austria and Australia, where youth unemployment rates are quite close to general unemployment rates, and range in average from 6 to 10% for the last 10 years. It may well be that the high youth unemployment is not unavoidable, but success requires specific policies that target structural problems. Together with the increase in the young labor force, youth employment rates have significantly increased in Turkey during the period 2005–2017. Over the past decade, it increased from about 30% in 2005 to 35% in 2017. It still remains significantly below the OECD average (41%).

Causes of Youth Unemployment

Youth unemployment rate has been increasing in Turkey since 2011. As Turkey has a relatively young population, youth unemployment is a serious issue that can have social and economic consequences such as driving young people toward low-skilled, low-paying and precarious work and leading to deprivation of young people's social position and solidarity within the social division of labor (Jin et al. 2016; Bell and Blanchflower 2010). Thus, understanding the trajectory and causes of youth unemployment in Turkey should be the main objective of labor policy. Bayırbağ et al. (2018) point out that youth unemployment and the overall unemployment should be considered together and further suggest the macroeconomic conditions of the country, including total demand for labor, young population, insufficient labor market and education policies and the minimum wage policy, are the main factors for the rise in youth unemployment in Turkey.

Bayırbağ et al. (2018) point out that youth unemployment and the overall unemployment should be considered together and further suggest the macroeconomic conditions of the country, including total demand for labor, the high relative size of young population, insufficient labor market and education policies and the minimum wage policy, are the main factors behind the rise in youth unemployment in Turkey.

There are many factors affecting the youth unemployment in Turkey. First, young workers are more exposed to the negative consequences of economic crises. Since hiring freezes and separations are more common during a recession, it is very likely that the rise of unemployment among the young population is faster than that among the adults. Bruno et al. (2017) state that the impact of financial crises on youth unemployment rate is larger compared to the overall unemployment rate, in both the short and long run. As employers make low investments for the young workforce, they have low firing costs, which make them more vulnerable to economic fluctuations (Murat and Şahin 2013). The large share of young people (15–24) in the population, approximately 16%, distorts the situation.

A second reason is that young people have difficulties during school-to-work transitions and mismatches, especially due to the fact that the educational curricula and the labor market requirements are not well aligned. Furthermore, school dropout, which is relatively more common in Turkey, implies that young people are not sufficiently prepared for the labor market. Cahuc et al. (2013) discuss the reasons why Germany

Table 4.3 Unemployment rates concerning educational status of youth in 2017 (%)

	Men	Women
Primary school	13.7	14.9
Junior high school	16.2	16.2
High school	21.5	29.2
Universities or other higher education institutions	25.4	41.2

Source TURKSTAT

tackles youth unemployment while France fails. They argue that the absence of national statutory minimum wage for young people under 18 together with the existence of a dual apprenticeship system constitute a strong asset allowing the youth in Germany to transit smoothly from school to work.[17]

Data in Table 4.3 shows that the youth unemployment rate rises as the education level increases both for young men and for young women. This indicates the difficulties in the school-to-work transition and skill mismatches in Turkey (Filiztekin 2011; Johansen and Gatelli 2012; Akgunduz et al. 2017). Since 2002, Turkey has successfully increased access to higher education. It is unfortunate, however, that this growth has not been accompanied with adequate labor supply planning and quality control. Erdem and Tugcu (2012) show that the increase of the level of education is one of the factors which raise the unemployment rate in Turkey and state that the higher education is used as a tool to solve the problems of the labor market in the short run which in return leads to higher unemployment rates in the long run. Note also that the gender gap in youth unemployment takes start at the high school level (7.7 percentage points) and makes a jump at the university level (5.8 percentage points) contributing significantly to the overall gap observed in unemployment (see Table 4.3 and section "The Ups and Downs of the Turkish Labor Market").

[17]There has been a national statutory minimum wage for all employees throughout Germany since 2015. Young people aged under 18 and apprentices are permanently exempted from minimum wage regulations. In addition, the minimum wage does not apply to people who do a compulsory internship or voluntary internship of up to three months during their education/training or studies. Neither does it apply to long-term unemployed people during the first six months of employment.

108   S. GÜRSEL ET AL.

Finally, labor market institutions and policies (e.g., minimum wages, employment protection legislation, etc.) are also behind the relatively high levels of youth unemployment. Taş and Bilen (2014) claim that the problem youth unemployment is aggravated due to high minimum wage policies and deficiencies in the quality of young labor force which in return decrease demand of employers for the youth.

Neither in School Nor in Employment

There are other sides to the youth unemployment problem. Table 4.2 also presents the Neither in School nor in Employment (NEET) ratio for 15–24 age group in Turkey. The proportion of young people who are not in employment, education or training (the NEET) to youth population in Turkey decreased from 38 to 24.2% from 2005 to 2017. Nevertheless, the NEET ratio gives disturbing signs of stabilization (Table 4.2)

Although Turkey experienced a large decline in the NEET youth rate, it still sits at the highest level in the OECD. Most of this improvement in the NEET arises from increasing school enrollment rates in the last decade. The length of compulsory education increased first in 1997 from 5 to 8 years and then in 2012 from 8 to 12 years. TurkStat (2013) indicates that the percentage of students in the inactive 15–24-year-olds rose from 39 to 60% between 2000 and 2012.

However, low public, social and educational spending in Turkey, especially on working age population, is indicating that further improvements in the NEET rate among the youth will be challenging for Turkey. High dropout (early school leaving) rates and low educational performance especially among young women remain an important challenge for Turkey (OECD 2018). The high NEET rate for women, at 46%, may reflect a traditional gender-related assignment of roles, which translates into low female participation in the labor market while women take on most of the unpaid domestic work and care for children and the elderly. In most countries, the NEET rates are similar between men (15%) and women (18%). However, women's risk of entering NEET is three times that of men (17%) in Turkey (OECD 2018). This reflects that the NEET problem in Turkey essentially boils down to the exclusion of young women both from education and labor market. Ensuring that young women can carry on their studies is essential to improve their opportunities and increase female labor market participation.

Policy Recommendations for the Youth Unemployment

The question of how youth unemployment can be alleviated has several dimensions. First of all, Turkey needs to stimulate demand and create jobs for youth through employment-friendly macroeconomic policies by investing in education and training to enhance employability and facilitate the school-to-work transitions. In the last twenty years, Turkey has increased spending and effort put into education, particularly to higher education; therefore, there is a noticeable growth in the number of higher education graduates. However, production processes still rely largely on traditional technologies that use a workforce with a relatively lower set of skills. The incompatibility between the labor market demand and the increasing number of higher education graduates is one of the main reasons for the high youth unemployment rates among higher education graduates.

Second, establishing an education system that not only provides the entire labor force with a fundamental education that is of high quality, but also directs the optimal number of young people to vocational high schools that teach necessary skills, should be a priority (Akgunduz et al. 2017; ILO 2013). According to a recent Turkish Employment Agency report (2016), some 21% of employers encounter difficulties in filling in positions with qualified employees and this number rises to 46% in manufacturing industry. Hence, the skills required for professions should be analyzed in detail, and skill provision in the education system needs to prioritize the skills that are in high demand.

Finally, labor market policies should build on an optimal balance between labor market flexibility for employers and job security for employees. As discussed in this chapter, Turkish labor market is characterized by low levels of female participation in economic activity, a large share of informal sector employment and insufficient levels and quality of human capital together with skill mismatches in the labor market. Hence, many of the necessary conditions for implementing flexibility and security explained by Auer (2007) are missing in Turkey.[18] Policymakers

---

[18] Flexibility in labor market refers to high mobility of workers through the ease with which firms can hire and fire staff and also the availability of options for these workers in a dynamic labor market. Moreover, the existence of a broad network of public institutions that provide care for children, older adults and the sick is vital to increase female labor participation rate in a country. The social security system should provide a high level of income protection for the unemployed together with active labor market policies on the retraining system for these workers.

should focus on enhancing the ability of the young labor force to adjust to external conditions that can vary widely through providing education and vocational training. In this way, they can increase the employability of the youth in Turkey while reducing youth employment in informal sectors.

CONCLUDING REMARKS

The basic challenge that Turkish labor market will be facing in the next decade and beyond is certainly the creation of enough employment in order to compensate, at least partially, the strong labor force increase that will persist for years to come. Indeed, on the one side, favorable demographics that sustain a window of opportunity as well as a persistent increase in female labor force participation pump hundreds of thousand individuals into labor market continuously. On the other side, the full use of an increasing labor force necessitates a quite high and employment-friendly economic growth that is sustainable as well, which constitutes another challenge in itself.

The aggregate data summarizing the development of the Turkish labor market in the last 12 years reveals the scope of this challenge. In the period of 2005–2017, the labor force increase attained roughly 10 million (from 21.7 to 31.6 million), a yearly average of 833 thousand. The two main drivers of this sizable increase have been, on the one side, the increase of working age population (15+) by 11.5 million individuals (from 48.4 to 59.9 million) and, on the other side, the rapid increase of labor participation rate that reached 52.8% from 44.9%. The major role played by women in this strong increase has been discussed in section "The Ups and Downs of the Turkish Labor Market". Furthermore, the composition effect due to the improvement in average education levels and the increases in each education level contribute separately. Meanwhile, the increase of employment stood at 8.6 million (from 19.6 to 28.2 million), adding to the stock of 2 million unemployed people another 1.4 million individuals and thus increasing the unemployment rate from 9.5% in 2005 to 10.9% in 2017 in spite of ups and downs.

What is remarkable in this rather mediocre performance is the fact that GDP yearly growth was rather high on average, at 5% (5.8% excluding Great Recession). Furthermore, this growth was generally employment-friendly since the average employment-growth elasticity stood around 0.7. This past experience does not describe an optimistic future.

Indeed, according to TurkStat's demographic projections, population growth will continue albeit at a diminishing rate, and the baseline scenario predicts that current population of 81 million will reach 100 million in 2040. Along with this demographic trend, the working age population (15–64) is projected to attain its peak at 64 million within two decades, adding approximately 9 million individuals into labor market. As the participation rate will continue its rise from the current low level (52.8%) thanks to rapid increase of female participation, the strong labor force increase has a long way to go despite its deceleration tendency.

While many countries are facing the challenge of aging population, this demographic trend certainly constitutes a positive factor in regard to economic development for Turkey but on the condition of a high and sustained GDP growth. The latter is far from guaranteed. First, we have to note that Turkish economy entered a recession in the second half of 2018. The midterm forecasts in the last MTP (October 2018) for GDP growth are not bright at all: 3.8% for 2018 and 2.3 and 3.5% for 2019 and 2020. These official forecasts could be revealed as optimistic since the OECD predicts a much more pessimistic performance: 3.2% for 2018 and a mere 0.5% for 2019 (OECD Interim Outlook, October 2018).

Almost certainly, the already high unemployment which already increasing since March 2018 will follow a rising trend in the near future. Then, can we hope for a new era of sustained and high economic growth? Given the doubts on the macroeconomic management capacity of the new presidential regime and evaluations of experts on the potential growth around 4.5% (Özbilgen 2017) due to a modest performance in productivity gains, the question remains open.

References

Acemoglu, D., & Ucer, M. (2015, October). *The Ups and Downs of Turkish Growth, 2002–2015: Political Dynamics, the European Union and the Institutional Slide* (NBER Working Paper No. 21608).

Akat, A. S., & Gürsel, S. (2016, Juin). La Turquie à la recherche d'une croissance équilibrée. *IRIS*.

Akgunduz, Y. E., Aldan, A., Bagir, Y. K., & Torun, H. (2017) *Turkiye'de Genc Issizligi: Tespit ve Oneriler*. CBT Research Notes in Economics, Research and Monetary Policy Department, Central Bank of the Republic of Turkey. https://EconPapers.repec.org/RePEc:tcb:econot:1714.

Ashenfelter, O. (1980). Unemployment as Disequilibrium in a Model of Aggregate Labor Supply. *Econometrica, 48*(3), 547–564.

Atiyas, I., & Bakis, O. (2014). Aggregate and Sectoral TFP Growth in Turkey: A Growth Accounting Exercice. *İktisat, İşletme ve Finans, 29*(341), 9–36.

Auer, P. (2007). *Security in Labour Markets: Combining Flexibility with Security for Decent Work.* Geneva: International Labour Office.

Başlevent, C., & Onaran, Ö. (2003). Are Married Women in Turkey More Likely to Become Added or Discouraged Workers? *Labour, 17,* 439–458.

Bayırbağ, M. K., Göksel, A., & Çelik, C. (2018). Child Poverty and Youth Unemployment in Turkey. *Poverty & Public Policy, 10,* 390–413. https://doi.org/10.1002/pop4.228.

Bell, D. N. F., & Blanchflower, D. G. (2010). *Youth Unemployment: Déjà Vu?* (IZA Discussion Papers, No. 4705).

Bruno, G. S. F., Choudhry Tanveer, M., Marelli, E., & Signorelli, M. (2017). The Short- and Long-Run Impacts of Financial Crises on Youth Unemployment in OECD Countries. *Applied Economics, 49*(34), 3372–3394.

Cahuc, P., Carcillo, S., Rinne, U., & Zimmermann, K. F. (2013). Youth Unemployment in Old Europe: The Polar Cases of France and Germany. *IZA Journal of European Labor Studies, 2,* 1–23.

Degirmenci, S., & İlkkaracan, İ. (2013). *Economic Crises and the Added Worker Effect in the Turkish Labor Market* (Working Paper, Levy Economics Institute, No. 774). Levy Economics Institute of Bard College.

Erdem, E., & Tugcu, C. T. (2012). Higher Education and Unemployment: A Cointegration and Causality Analysis of the Case of Turkey. *European Journal of Education, 47*(2), 299–309.

Filiztekin, A. (2011). *Education-Occupation Mismatch in Turkish Labor Market* (MPRA Paper No. 35123).

Genc Ileri, S., & Sengul, G. (2017). *The Rise of Services and Female Employment: Strength of the Relationship* (CBRT Working Paper Series No. w1702). Central Bank of the Republic of Turkey.

Goldin, C. (1994). *The U-Shaped Female Labor Force Function in Economic Development and Economic History* (NBER Working Paper Series No. w4707). National Bureau of Economic Research.

Göksel, İ. (2013). Female Labor Force Participation in Turkey: The Role of Conservatism. *Women's Studies International Forum,* Part 1, *41,* 45–54.

Guner, D., & Uysal, G. (2014). *Culture, Religiosity and Female Labor Supply* (IZA Discussion Paper No. 8132).

Gürsel, S. (2013). Turkey as a Regional Power: Unfounded Ambition or Future Reality? In R. Kastoryano (Ed.), *Turkey Between Nationalism and Globalization* (pp. 199–216). Oxon and New York: Routledge.

Gürsel, S. (2015). *The AKP Decade: An Economic Success Story?* Al-Jazzera.

4 TURKISH LABOR MARKET: COMPLEX DYNAMICS AND CHALLENGES   113

Gürsel, S., Acar, A., & Uysal, G. (2014). *Kadın işgücü piyasasında çarpıcı gelişmeler* (Betam Araştırma Notları 14/160).

Gürsel, S., & Imamoglu, Z. (2012, July). *Kıdem Tazminatı reformu: Sorunlar ve çözümler* [Severance Pay Reform: Problems and Solutions]. Betam's Report.

Gürsel, S., & Imamoglu, Z. (2013, April). *Why Is Agricultural Employment Increasing in Turkey* (Betam WD 004).

Gürsel, S., Uysal, G., & Acar, A. (2011). Women Face Institutional and Cultural Barriers to Participation in the Labor Market. *Betam Research Briefs, 115.* http://betam.bahcesehir.edu.tr/en/wp-content/uploads/2011/12/ResearchBrief115.pdf.

İlkkaracan, İ. (2012). Why So Few Women in the Labor Market in Turkey? *Feminist Economics, 18*(1), 1–37.

ILO. (2013). *Global Employment Trends for Youth: A Generation at Risk.* Geneva: International Labour Organization.

Jin, Y., Fukahori, R., & Morgavi, H. (2016). *Labour Market Transitions in Italy: Job Separation, Re-employment and Policy Implications* (OECD Economics Department Working Papers, 1291). https://doi.org/10.1787/18151973.

Johansen, J., & Gatelli, D. (2012). *Measuring Mismatch in ETF Partner Countries: A Methodological Note.* European Training Foundation.

Karaoglan, D., & Okten, C. (2015). Labor-Force Participation of Married Women in Turkey: A Study of the Added-Worker Effect and the Discouraged-Worker Effect. *Emerging Markets Finance and Trade, 51*(1), 274–290.

Kaya, H., ve Küçükşahin, Y. 2018. Türkiye'de büyüme ve istihdam ilişkisi: 2005–2016 dönemi, Bilimevi İktisat, Sayı 1, ss:1–12.

Kubota, S. (2014). *Culture and Labor Supply: Decline in Female Market Work in Turkey.* Retrieved at https://sites.google.com/site/gkubotaso/research. October 2019.

Murat, S., & Şahin, L. (2013). Gençlerin İstihdamı/İşsizliği Bakımından Türk Eğitim Sisteminin Değerlendirilmesi. *Çalışma Ve Toplum, 3*, 93–135.

Paker, H., & Uysal, G. (2015). *Türkiye'de lise ve üniversite mezunu kadınların işgücüne katılım kararlarının incelenmesi* (TÜBİTAK Project Report No. 113K365).

OECD. (2018). *Youth Unemployment Rate (Indicator).* https://doi.org/10.1787/c3634df7-en. Accessed 2 Oct 2018.

OECD Interim Outlook. (2018, October). https://www.oecd.org/eco/outlook/interim-economic-outlook-september-2018/. Accessed Oct 2019.

Özbilgen, M. H. (2017, July). *Forecasting the Growth Cycles of the Turkish Economy* (CBRT WP No. 17/15).

Taş, H. Y., & Bilen, M. (2014). Avrupa Birliği ve Türkiye'de Genç İşsizliği Sorunu ve Çözüm Önerileri. *HAK-İŞ Uluslararası Emek Ve Toplum Dergisi, 3*(6), 51–69.

Turkish Statistical Institute (TurkStat). 2013. *Labor Force Statistics* (Working Paper).

Uysal, G. (2013). *Incentives to Formal Female Employment* (Betam Research Brief No. 13/151).

CHAPTER 5

Syrian Entrepreneurs in Turkey: Emerging Economic Actors and Agents of Social Cohesion

Omar Kadkoy

INTRODUCTION

Globally, war, violence, or persecution uprooted an estimated 68.5 million people as either refugee (25.4 million), asylum seekers (3.1 million), or internally displaced people (40.0 million) (UNHCR Global Trends 2017). Among the uprooted are 5.65 million Syrians who are currently residing in the neighboring countries, with Turkey alone hosting 64% as a result of Ankara's open door policy between 2011 and 2016 that offered Syrians fleeing war safe heaven and a larger and a better space for prosperity.

Almost a decade after the influx to Turkey, Syrians have been weaving themselves into the fabric of the hosting communities. Nonetheless, the dwindling state of the Turkish economy, which in return fanned competition for jobs, has been fueling locals' unacceptance of Syrians. Little is publicly known, however, about Syrians'

O. Kadkoy (✉)
Economic Policy Research Foundation of Turkey, Ankara, Turkey
e-mail: omar.kadkoy@tepav.org.tr

© The Author(s) 2020
E. Parlar Dal (ed.), *Turkey's Political Economy in the 21st Century*, International Political Economy Series,
https://doi.org/10.1007/978-3-030-27632-4_5

115

contribution, especially about entrepreneurs' contribution who have been setting and running businesses all over Turkey. With regard, Syrian entrepreneurs established approximately 10,000 companies since 2010, creating, albeit on a small scale, inclusive employment opportunities and contributing to macroeconomy, especially at the sub-national level by undertaking export activities mainly in provinces adjacent to Syria.

GUESTS WHO TURNED FOREIGNERS UNDER TEMPORARY PROTECTION

The escalation of violence in the face of the Syrian uprisings initiated waves of forced displacement while the responsibility of hosting Syrians fell chiefly on the shoulders of neighboring countries. Turkey, in this regard, set a global example not only by taking in the largest number of forcibly displaced Syrians, but also with policy developments that followed. Ankara initially handled the influx of Syrians as a 'crisis' by assigning the Disaster and Emergency Management Presidency (AFAD) to the responsibility of addressing the urgent needs of Syrians through establishing camps next to the border. In addition, the government referred to Syrians as 'guests.' This pertains to Turkey maintaining the geographical limitation in the 1951 Convention relating to the status of refugees (UNHCR-State Parties to 1951 Geneva Convention). Meaning, Ankara is legally obliged to grant refugee status only to European citizens seeking asylum 'due to events occurring in Europe.' Ironically, the majority of asylum seekers in Turkey are either from the Middle East or from Africa (UNHCR-Turkey Key Facts and Figures 2018).

The continuous influx of Syrians, however, exceeded the accommodation capacity of the camps and Syrians started to settle in urban settings. Hence, the need to access the basic public services of health and education became necessary. The aforementioned symbolic status, however, was confusing the lower circles of bureaucracy. Hence, the need for a legal status snowballed. Ankara, therefore, took the first of its kind decision in the history of the Republic and enacted in 2013, the Law on Foreigners and International Protection (LFIP), which entered into force in October 2014 as the legal umbrella governing Syrians alongside international protection seekers and migrants in Turkey. Equally important was the establishment of the first civil institution to overlook the implementation of LFIP: the Directorate General of Migration Management (DGMM 2015).

The belated introduction of LFIP caused a level of legal instability for Syrians in Turkey. Plus, the overwhelming spillovers in the aftermath of the Arab Spring did not spare Europe as 1.01 million forcibly displaced people and economic migrants reached the old continent in 2015 alone. In this context, Turkey provided the principal gate to entering into Europe: 853,650 immigrants, of whom 56% were Syrians who rode the Aegean on rubber dinghies and beaten ships, docked in Greece, and moved inward to Western Europe (IOM 2016). Consequently, alarm bells deafened Brussels pushing it to halt the influx and voices called for 'securing' the continent's borders. Hence, the European Union elaborated a Statement on Irregular Migration in March 2016, otherwise known as the EU-Turkey Deal (see Box 5.1). Prior to the Deal, Ankara ended the open door policy in January 2016 by resurrecting the visa requirement for Syrians to enter Turkey (*Hurriyet Daily News* 2016). These developments effectively turned Turkey into a unique country of destination: a fairly globalized middle-income economy hosting the largest forcibly displaced population in the world.

When forcibly displaced, self-reliance becomes a priority as a necessity to fend for one's self and family. When the LFIP entered into force in October 2014, it overlooked a critical and politically sensitive subject: Foreigners under Temporary Protection access to the labor market. Accordingly, the regulation on work permits opened the door in January 2016 for Foreigners under Temporary Protection to formally enter the labor market. To channel down social friction and to protect the local labor force, the law on work permits introduced certain measures: The number of Syrians under Temporary Protection cannot exceed 10% of the total workforce at any workplace (Ministry of Labor and Social security 2016). The late introduction of the work permit regulation also meant Syrians who were making a living had been doing so informally, causing certain changes in the labor market.

The spillover of Syrians' forced displacement did not stop at the borders of the neighboring countries. It also reached Europe. At its peak in 2015, near one million immigrants of different nationality – mostly Syrian – crossed the Aegean Sea. Consequently Brussels called for cooperation with Ankara. In October 2015, the cooperation foundations metalized with the EU-Turkey Joint Action Plan, which then was activated in November 2015. The negotiations continued and chiefly targeted, among other critical topics, migration.

As a result, the two sides concluded in March 2016 with a framework that turned Turkey from a transit country of migration to a destination country.

The EU and Turkey agreed that:

1) All new irregular migrants crossing from Turkey to the Greek islands as of 20 March 2016 will be returned to Turkey;
2) For every Syrian being returned to Turkey from the Greek islands, another Syrian will be resettled to the EU;
3) Turkey will take any necessary measures to prevent new sea or land routes for irregular migration opening from Turkey to the EU;
4) Once irregular crossings between Turkey and the EU are ending or have been substantially reduced, a Voluntary Humanitarian Admission Scheme will be activated;
5) The fulfilment of the visa liberalization roadmap will be accelerated with a view to lifting the visa requirements for Turkish citizens at the latest by the end of June 2016. Turkey will take all the necessary steps to fulfil the remaining requirements;
6) The EU will, in close cooperation with Turkey, further speed up the disbursement of the initially allocated €3 billion under the Facility for Refugees in Turkey. Once these resources are about to be used in full, the EU will mobilize additional funding for the Facility up to an additional €3 billion to the end of 2018;
7) The EU and Turkey welcomed the ongoing work on the upgrading of the Customs Union.
8) The accession process will be re-energized, with Chapter 33 to be opened during the Dutch Presidency of the Council of the European Union and preparatory work on the opening of other chapters to continue at an accelerated pace;
9) The EU and Turkey will work to improve humanitarian conditions inside Syria.

Box 5.1 EU-Turkey statement on irregular migration (Council of the European Union 2016)

Syrians' Impact on Turkey's Labor Market and Trade

Syrians' integration into the Turkish labor market before 2016 is best described as integration by interaction: Employing Syrians was not subject to any criteria, and there was not a legal framework to protect their rights. In the four years leading to the regulation on work permits, and even afterward, the majority of Syrians have been filling labor-intensive jobs in the lower ranks of the labor market, namely in agriculture, construction, and textile in which reportedly around 650,000 Syrians work informally (Erdoğdu 2018). On the other hand, formal employment of Syrians remains marginal as only 27,930 work permits were issued between January 2016 and September 2018, representing 1% of the 2.1 million Syrians in working age (15–64) (T24). Pulse from the ground suggests fear of being cutoff financial aid once formally employed, unawareness of employment rights, and poor command of Turkish as reasons behind the low number of Syrians working formally. Additionally, lengthy bureaucratic process, unavailability of vocational certificates, and lack of legal documentation stand out as factors giving employers cold feet about applying for work permits for Syrian workers. The result, in return, is 'flexible labor': a term coined for instances where Syrians are exploited to work for wages lower than the minimum and forcing them to work for longer hours.

Syrians infiltration to the informal labor market, however, triggered a number of reactions. For starters, Syrians' influx caused a supply shock to the informal labor market, suggesting a displacement of natives of whom especially women and the less educated experienced net displacement. Nevertheless, there were increases in formal employment although only for men with lower than high school education (Del Caprio and Wagner 2015). The impact of Syrians on wages in the informal labor market, on the other hand, was negligible (Ceritoglu et al. 2017).

Appropriate to the purpose is looking at the impact of immigrants on hosting countries' foreign trade performance. Knowing market preferences, having familiarity with bureaucracy and regulations of the markets in the countries of origin, and combined with specific product demands of the new arrivals in the countries of destination allow foreign trade channels to expand. Indeed, there are a number of countries, with diverse levels of economic sophistication, whose trade performance gained from receiving immigrants. In North America, analysis of Canada's bilateral trade with 136 countries indicated that a 10% increase in immigrants is associated with a 1% increase in Canada's exports to those immigrants' country of origin and a 3% increase in its imports (Head and Ries 1998). From across the Atlantic, immigration had a positive, statistically strong, and robust effect on Sweden's foreign trade (Hatzigeorgiou 2010). It is worthwhile mentioning that the impact of immigration on trade in developed countries is more nuanced and is less profound in developing economies, most likely due to deficiencies in the economic structure in the latter. Nonetheless, there is a relatively positive example coming from Bolivia indicating that when immigrants arrive, even in less robust economies, they tend to capitalize on the opportunities in a way that boosts foreign trade of the host country (Bacarreza et al. 2006).

While the aforementioned examples are at the national level, the impact on the provincial trade further strengthens the argument on the positive effect of immigration on trade. In Spain, the elasticity of export in provinces with a high density of immigrants has been particularly large (Peri and Requena-Silvente 2010). A similar trend also exists in Canada where the effect of immigration on provincial trade has also been positive (Wagner et al. 2002). In Turkey, improvement in foreign trade balance materialized in a number of Turkish regions, mainly adjacent to the Syria border, after the arrival of Syrians (Bahcekapili and Cetin 2015). The attribution of these improvements could find place in the businesses established or partnered by Syrian entrepreneurs as they tend to be more export-oriented compared to their Turkish counterparts.

Syrian Entrepreneurs in Turkey: The New Export Engines

Indeed, Syrian entrepreneurs are gaining ground in the Turkish economy. With regard, the number of companies partnered by Syrians is a strong indicator: 9977 companies partnered by Syrians between 2010 and June 2018. The seed capital invested to establish these companies is 527 million dollars, and 46% operate in the wholesale and retail trade. This is trailed by companies operating in manufacturing (14%), construction (11%), real estate activities (9%), and administrative and support service activities (5%). Similar to the trend at the national level, wholesale and retail trade is also prevailing at the sub-national level for Syrian entrepreneurs: 43.6% in Istanbul, 50.0% in Gaziantep, 48.0% in Mersin, and 64.3% in Hatay (TOBB 2018).

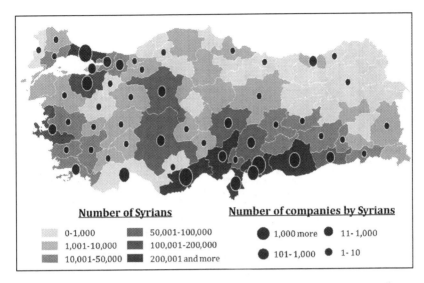

Map 5.1 Distribution of companies established by or partnered by Syrian entrepreneurs, 2010–June 2018 (*Source* TOBB data and DGMM)

Geographically speaking, these companies cluster in two regions: the northwest and the south-southeast of Turkey (see Map 5.1). In the northwest cluster, Istanbul is home to 4874 companies. The south-southeast cluster hosts one-third of all companies established by Syrians: 1331 companies in Gaziantep, 1251 companies in Mersin, and 827 companies in Hatay. The decision of Syrian entrepreneurs to operate in the aforementioned provinces is fueled by reasons such as proximity to Syria and presence of business networks dating back to pre-war period or personal preference. Needless to say, the five provinces collectively host 1.6 million (45%) of Syrians in Turkey (Directorate General of Migration Management 2018).

Looking at Turkey's exports to Syria, there is not a causal link between the revival of exports and the increase in the number of companies established by Syrians, but there is a correlation, being the strongest in 2013 and in 2014. Turkey's trade with Syria peaked in 2010 with $1.84 billion in exports. The spillover effect hit Turkey's trade with Syria. Consequently, Turkey's exports dwindled to a mere half a billion dollars in 2012. The following two years, Turkey's exports to Syria

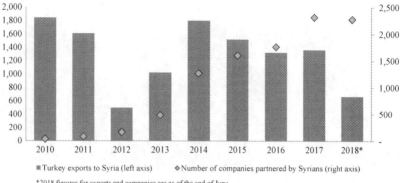

Fig. 5.1 Turkey exports to Syria and number of companies partnered by Syrians (*Source* Turkish Statistical Institute and Union of Chambers and Commodity Exchanges of Turkey)

rebounded to almost pre-war levels and reached $1.8 billion in 2014 (see Fig. 5.1). Thereafter, Turkey's exports declined and landed at $1.36 billion at the end of 2017. In the face of this decline, the number of Syrian companies has kept steadily increasing: from 36 companies in 2010 to a total of 7701 by the end of 2017. The disassociation could take root in different reasons. The export destinations of the companies partnered by Syrians in Turkey may have diversified and have started targeting countries other than Syria. On the other hand, Syrians establishment of companies might not be for business purposes. An obsolete law since the 1930s, after the annexation of Hatay, prohibits Syrians from owning property under their individual names (Kadkoy 2016). The law was amended only in 2012 allowing Syrians to own property only through a legal entity. Hence, setting some inactive companies to buy and register property under the companies' names.

The correlation, however, between the increase in the number of companies and exports is more nuanced at the sub-national. The border provinces are taking over as the new export engines to Syria (see Fig. 5.2).

Traditionally, Istanbul served as the hub of Turkey's exports to Syria. The megacity's share in Turkey's exports was 22% in the heyday of trade between the two countries. Henceforth, Istanbul's share in

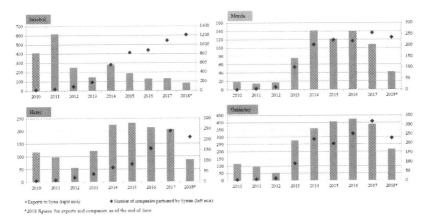

Fig. 5.2 Provincial exports to Syria, million US dollars (*Source* Turkish Statistical Institute and Union of Chambers and Commodity Exchanges of Turkey)

Turkey's exports decreased, representing only 10% in 2017. The decline in Istanbul's exports to Syria could be attributed to logistics costs due to geographic distance (Özpınar et al. 2015) or to targeting new export destination other than Syria. Interestingly enough, new export engines emerged and compensated for Istanbul's declining exports and those engines are none other than the three provinces mentioned earlier. Gaziantep emerges as the new export engine to Syria as Gaziantep's exports quadrupled in six years from $96 million to $393 million. In the same period, Hatay's exports more than doubled from $97 to $207 million. Lastly, Mersin's exports were as low as $17 million in 2011. In six years, however, Mersin's exports to Syria grew nine folds, reaching $107 million in 2017.

The inability to verify a causal link between the number of companies established by Syrians at the national level or at the sub-national level in abovementioned provinces, and the increase in exports to Syria has structural roots. For starters, data falls short of providing a detailed destination of the companies' exported products. Nonetheless, the above figures combined with the tendency of Syrian entrepreneurs to be more export-oriented (see section below) suggest a positive correlation between the number of companies established or partnered with Syrians and the rise of Turkey's exports to Syria.

Features of and Challenges Facing the Refugee-Driven Entrepreneurship in Turkey

The refugee-driven companies are growing in the economy of Turkey. Hence, these companies possess certain features that set them apart from their Turkish peers, but also face specific challenges as they operate in a new business environment (see "Annex"). A number of the findings indicate the following:

- Businesses established by Syrian entrepreneurs are more export-oriented compared to the Turkish counterparts. The findings show 55% of the surveyed Syrian companies are in the export business compared to 31% of the surveyed Turkish companies. This has two root causes. First, Syrian entrepreneurs transferred their business networks when they relocated to Turkey. Second, penetrating the domestic market remains difficult due to intense competition and Syrian entrepreneurs' low command of Turkish.
- Syrians business owners in Turkey are seasoned entrepreneurs, meaning they ran a business while in Syria. Indeed, findings indicate 75% of Syrian business owners have already operated a company before coming to Turkey. On the other hand, 25% of Syrian business owners established their first-ever businesses following their arrival in Turkey. These are actual refugee start-ups.
- Most Syrian companies are micro-sized. As a matter of fact, 66% of the refugee-driven companies employ an average of 7 people. In relation, with an average Syrian household size of 6 people, findings assert that approximately 250,000 Syrians are benefiting from the advantages of employment by these companies.
- 71% of businesses established by Syrian entrepreneurs operate in the service sector. This implies they are carrying on with the know-how they possessed in Syria.
- The business environment of Turkey was attractive for relatively larger companies operating in other neighboring countries. Before coming to Turkey, 11% of Syrian entrepreneurs had already established a company in another country, mostly in Egypt, Saudi Arabia, and UAE. Of those companies, which relocated to Turkey, 59% operate in the service sector. Surprisingly, 32% of relocated

companies are in the manufacturing sector for reasons relating to the flexibility of Turkey's business environment, the richness of the domestic market with raw materials, and proximity to export destinations.

- An overarching obstacle for companies partnered by Syrian entrepreneurs is the access to finance. Legally speaking, Syrians—whether business owners or not—have the ability to open bank accounts. Nonetheless, Syrians face hardships accessing financial services due to the respective Turkish bank's own internal policies. Reasons behind banks' decision relate to the international sanctions imposed on Syria or the inadequate legal status of Syrians in Turkey. For example, opening a commercial bank account is problematic for 28% of Syrian entrepreneurs. In addition, 27% of the Syrian companies face problems with domestic money transfers and 20% with opening a personal bank account.
- Syrian entrepreneurs are in Turkey for the long run as 72% of Syrian entrepreneurs do not want to return to Syria even after the war settles down. Different reasons stand behind Syrians entrepreneurs' choice of selecting Turkey over other countries. These are the geographic proximity to Syria and to the business networks they had with the local business owners since pre-war time. Indeed, 59% of Syrian business owners have a successful business in Turkey, and 48% of them think the Turkish business environment is better when compared to the one in pre-war Syria.

CONCLUSIONS

Turkey followed a generous refugee-hosting policy since the outbreak of the Syrian war by hosting millions of Syrians. This was followed by introducing a number of legal measures to assure Syrians to pursue a regular life while uprooted. Consequent to Ankara's open door policy, some Syrians found stability and a fertile business environment in Turkey where they opened businesses, which are growing and contributing to both local and national economy. Nevertheless, the companies possess the necessary merits to succeed yet run across a number of challenges. Amplifying the advantages of the refugee-driven companies and overcoming the obstacles they face requires undertaking further steps.

First, local qualities matter for Syrian business owners as they tend to be selective over the provinces in which they establish and run a business. So far, there is only a glimpse as to why Syrian entrepreneurs chose one city over another. Nonetheless, further efforts into detailing the reasons could unfold in two ways. Identify and support the pull factors in the selected provinces so businesses established by Syrians interbedded with the local economy. Pinpoint similar pull factors in other provinces where less or no Syrian entrepreneurs invested in establishing a business. Doing so has the potential of flushing new investments and reviving the economic dynamics there. Second, and complementary to detailing the local pull factors, is building the capacity of the local chambers and municipalities. At large, this should address overcoming the language barrier hindering Syrian entrepreneurs from acquiring necessary information about the available business support schemes. Doing so, in return, increases the involvement of the chambers and municipalities as the forefront players of not only integrating Syrian entrepreneurs but also supporting and executing inclusive socioeconomic policies. Third, relevant to enriching local institutions' involvement is awareness-raising campaigns, especially for banks. Although the latter pursue risk-averse practices for refugee-driven companies, the companies are bound to domestic laws and regulations. Hence, banks could apply trust-building measures with Syrians business owners. Know Your Customer (KYC) guidelines would be a tool for banks' evaluation process of customers. Last but not least, the involvement of Syrian entrepreneurs in wholesale and trade activities reflects the less sophisticated economy of Syria compared to the industry-based one in Turkey. The real potential, however, lies with Syrian manufacturers, who have the upper hand in contributing to Turkey's 2023 economic goals and in creating large-scale inclusive employment opportunities. Unraveling that capability, nevertheless, requires integrating Syrian manufacturers into the global supply chains. Hence, the need for international trade concessions for goods is produced by Syrians.

All in all, the potential of Syrians in Turkey as entrepreneurs is understudied. While the political scene in Syria remains unsettled, Syrians in Turkey seem to be settling in and preparing for what they hope to be a bright future. Uncovering the opportunities in the possession of Syrians is necessary for building economic inclusivity. This is only achievable through a bottom-up approach starting with multilayer dialogue at the local level where the first and foremost levels of interaction and integration occur. Appropriate to the purpose is bringing Syrian entrepreneurs' potential closer to the awareness of the public. Doing so would help deconstruct the biased perceptions, reduce the mounting social tension, and edge further toward coexistence.

ANNEX

'Syrian Entrepreneurship and Refugee Start-ups in Turkey: Leveraging the Turkish Experience' is a study based on a survey designed by European Bank for Reconstruction and Development (EBRD) and the Economic Policy Research Foundation of Turkey (TEPAV) to highlight the Syrian refugee-driven companies' features and identify the challenges they face.

The main method of analysis utilized in this study includes survey data analysis obtained from a tailor-made survey conducted with a total of 416 companies (207 Turkish and 209 refugee-driven companies) operating in 8 provinces along the Turkish-Syrian border: Gaziantep, Mersin, Hatay, Şanlıurfa, Kilis, Adana, Kahramanmaraş, and Mardin.

The sample of companies was selected based on stratified random sampling, and the list of refugee-driven and local micro-, small-, and medium-sized enterprises (MSMEs) was drawn from the Turkish Union of Chambers and Commodity Exchanges of Turkey (TOBB) database.

The topics covered in the survey ranged from infrastructure, trade, finance, regulations, taxes and business licensing to corruption, crime and informality, labor market integration, and perceptions on the obstacles on doing business. Additional methods utilized in the report include cross-sectional data analysis and desk research on previous studies carried out regarding Syrians under Temporary Protection (SuTPs) and legal and regulatory framework relating to SuTPs' status in Turkey.

REFERENCES

Bacarreza, C., Javier, G., & Ehrlich, L. (2006). *The Impact of Migration on Foreign Trade: A Developing Country Approach* (MPRA Paper 1090). Germany: University Library of Munich. https://ideas.repec.org/p/pra/mprapa/1090.html.

Bahcekapili, C., & Cetin, B. (2015). The Impacts of Forced Migration on Regional Economies: The Case of Syrian Refugees in Turkey. *International Business Research, 8*(9). https://doi.org/10.5539/ibr.v8n9p1.

128 O. KADKOY

Ceritoglu, E., Burcu Gurcihan Yunculer, H., Torun, H., & Tumen, S. (2017). The Impact of Syrian Refugees on Natives' Labor Market Outcomes in Turkey: Evidence from a Quasi-experimental Design. *IZA Journal of Labor Policy, 6*(5). https://doi.org/10.1186/s40173-017-0082-4.

Council of the European Union. (2016, March 18). EU-Turkey Statement. https://www.consilium.europa.eu/en/press/press-releases/2016/03/18/eu-turkey-statement/.

Del Caprio, X. V., & Wagner, M. (2015). *The Impact of Syrian Refugees on the Turkish Labor Market* (World Bank, Policy Research Working Paper 7402). http://documents.worldbank.org/curated/en/505471468194980180/pdf/WPS7402.pdf.

Directorate General of Migration Management. 2015. Law on Foreigners and International Protection. http://www.goc.gov.tr/icerik/law-on-foreigners-and-international-protection-lfip_913_975.

Directorate General of Migration Management. 2018. http://www.goc.gov.tr/icerik6/temporary-protection_915_1024_4748_icerik. Accessed 7 Oct 2018.

Economic Policy Research Foundation of Turkey. (2018, November). Syrian Entrepreneurship and Refugee Start-ups in Turkey: Leveraging the Turkish Experience.

Erdoğdu, S. (2018). Syrian Refugees in Turkey and Trade Unions Responses. *Globalizations, 15*(6), 838–853. https://doi.org/10.1080/14747731.2018.1474038.

Europe—Mixed Migration Flows to Europe, Yearly Overview. (2016). International Organization for Migration (IOM). http://migration.iom.int/datasets/europe-%E2%80%94-mixed-migration-flows-europe-yearly-overview-2015.

Global Trends. Forced Displacement in 2017. United Nations High Commissioner for Refugees. https://www.unhcr.org/globaltrends2017/.

Hatzigeorgiou, A. 2010. Does Immigration Stimulate Foreign Trade? Evidence from Sweden. *Journal of Economic Integration, 25*(2), 376–402. http://www.jstor.org/stable/23000981.

Head, K., & Ries, J. (1998). Immigration and Trade Creation: Econometric Evidence from Canada. *The Canadian Journal of Economics/Revue Canadienne D'Economique, 31*(1), 47–62. https://doi.org/10.2307/136376.

Hurriyet Daily News. (2016). *Turkey's New Visa Law for Syrians Enters into Force.* http://www.hurriyetdailynews.com/turkeys-new-visa-law-for-syrians-enters-into-force-93642.

Kadkoy, O. (2016). *'You Shall Not Buy': Syrians and Real Estate Ownership in Turkey.* The Economic Policy Research Foundation of Turkey. http://www.tepav.org.tr/en/blog/s/5746.

Key Facts and Figures. (2018). United Nations High Commissioner for Refugees (UNHCR), Turkey Office. https://www.unhcr.org/tr/en/unhcr-turkey-stats.

Ministry of Labor and Social Security, Republic of Turkey. (2016). *Geçici koruma sağlanan yabancilarin çalişma izinlerine dair uygulama rehberi* [Work Permits Guide for Foreigners Under Temporary Protection]. https://www.csgb.gov.tr/media/5893/gkkuygulamarehberi.pdf.

Özpınar, E., Başıhoş, S., & Kulaksız, A. (2015). *Trade Relations with Syria after the Refugee Influx*. The Economic Policy Research Foundation of Turkey. http://www.tepav.org.tr/upload/files/1460720443-3.Trade_Relations_with_Syria_after_the_Refugee_Influx.pdf.

Peri, G., & Requena-Silvente, F. (2010). The Trade Creation Effect of Immigrants: Evidence from the Remarkable Case of Spain. *The Canadian Journal of Economics/Revue Canadienne D'Economique, 43*(4), 1433–1459. http://www.jstor.org/stable/40925283.

States Parties to the 1951 Convention Relating to the Status of Refugees and the 1967 Protocol. United Nations High Commissioner for Refugees. https://www.unhcr.org/protection/basic/3b73b0d63/states-parties-1951-convention-its-1967-protocol.html.

T24. (2018). *CHP'li Adıgüzel: Son üç yılda 28 bin Suriyeli çalışma izni aldı* [28 Thousand Work Permits Issued to Syrians in the Last Three Years]. http://t24.com.tr/haber/chpli-adiguzel-son-uc-yilda-28-bin-suriyeli-calisma-izni-aldi,773713.

Union of Chambers and Commodity Exchanges of Turkey. 2018. Database Private. Accessed on September 2018.

Wagner, D., Head, K., & Reis, J. (2002). Immigration and the Trade of Provinces. *Scottish Journal of Political Economy, 49*(5). https://doi.org/10.1111/1467-9485.00245.

PART II

Instrumental Diversification of Turkey's Political Economy

CHAPTER 6

The Political Economy of Turkish Foreign Aid

Abdurrahman Korkmaz and Hüseyin Zengin

INTRODUCTION

'Turkey: the most generous country in the world' is the slogan adorning the last two Development Assistance Reports' cover sheets, which are published annually by the Turkish Cooperation and Coordination Agency (TIKA). The reports consider the ratio of humanitarian aid to the gross national income (GNI) as the main indicator of Turkey's international efforts to promote a humanitarian/benevolent narrative, through which Turkey deepens its relations with the least developed countries. In the case of development aid, Turkey ranks 4th with a ratio of 0.76% of GNI in 2016, just after Norway, Luxemburg, and Sweden who are Organisation for Economic Co-operation and Development/Development Assistance Committee (OECD–DAC)

A. Korkmaz (✉)
İzmir Katip Çelebi University, Izmir, Turkey
e-mail: abdurrahman.korkmaz@ikc.edu.tr

H. Zengin
University of Pittsburgh, Pittsburgh, PA, USA
e-mail: huseyin.zengin@pitt.edu

© The Author(s) 2020
E. Parlar Dal (ed.), *Turkey's Political Economy in the 21st Century*, International Political Economy Series,
https://doi.org/10.1007/978-3-030-27632-4_6

133

members. Also, in 2016, Turkey came in 2nd among all donors in terms of humanitarian aid disbursement and in 6th in terms of net ODA (official development assistance) spending.

As is the case in almost all the subfields of International Relations, literature, types, amounts, motivations, and impacts of foreign aid have also been (re-)shaped by the end of the Cold War. During the Cold War, hampering the spread of communism was the main coalition motivation among traditional donors. The dissolution of the Soviet Union led to a new quest to determine a reason to act multilaterally and in harmony. In parallel with the Millennium Development Goals declared by the United Nations, OECD/DAC, of which many of the established donors are members, is the target goal that economically advanced countries should spend 0.7% of their gross national income on the official development assistance to support the sustainable development and welfare in developing countries. In addition, it is widely accepted that enhancing democratic values like the freedom of press, the transparency in governmental bodies, and fair elections is a key condition for a recipient to receive donations from the established donors.

However, the heterogeneity among donors has prevented scholars of foreign aid to draw a clear line between and within donor countries. Because the aid disbursements and patterns of aid are determined by strategic and political interests of the donor countries (Alesina and Dollar 1998, 1) and each donor has its own sui generis strategic and political interests, it is not easy to suggest a monolithic aid policy for both emerging and established donors. Despite having been known as established donors, France and Norway, for instance, have considerable differences in their motivations. While Norway focuses on income levels, openness, and strong institutions, France does not seem to attribute importance to these criteria; instead, France prefers giving aid to its former colonies regardless of income level (Alesina and Dollar 1998, 1). Therefore, the differences within both emerging and established donor groups and similarities between the behaviour of emerging and established donors are the two warning signs that keep us from seeing emerging donors as having the same purposes, effects, and scopes.

Because of this chapter's exclusive focus on Turkey, we initially attempt to discuss why Turkey has surpassed other countries in disbursing foreign aid by borrowing notions of multi-stakeholder diplomacy and controlled neo-populism. Afterwards, we establish an empirical set-up to lay bare the similarities and the differences between economic, political, and cultural determinants of Turkish foreign aid behaviour and those of some traditional donor countries. From the extant aid literature, we already know that colony relations matter for donor–recipient relations (Alesina and Dollar 1998; Kavaklı 2018; Mascarenhas and Sandler 2006). Therefore, we consider France, Spain, and the UK as traditional donor countries for the following reasons: (i) they have strong historical ties with some of the aid recipients at hand, (ii) their languages are spoken beyond their territories, and (iii) they want to deepen their relations with far-away regions.

The rest of the chapter is organized as follows: the notions of multi-stakeholder diplomacy and neo-controlled populism are introduced and associated with the Justice and Development Party's (AKP) political economy in the following section. We deal with aid-benevolence-export triangle in section "Aid-Benevolence-Export Triangle". Section "A Brief Analysis on Path Dependency of Donors in a Historical Context" introduces hypotheses, data, estimation methodology, and results. Section "Future Challenges Ahead" presents a discussion related to future challenges ahead, and finally, section "Conclusion" concludes the paper with a general overview.

THE BACKGROUND OF FOREIGN AID: FOREIGN POLICY AND POLITICAL ECONOMY

Pro-activism in a Multi-stakeholder Diplomacy Era

Perhaps 'pro-activism' is the most encapsulating keyword which can be used to understand and conceptualize Turkish foreign policy in the AKP era. Especially after the concrete reflections of Davutoglu's foreign policy visions on Turkish state policy, the term has even been used in the titles of many academic papers (Keyman and Gümüşçü 2014; Dincer and Mehmet 2016; Ünay 2017). Pro-activism with AKP characteristics is not encapsulated within a strict and immediate geographical sphere; instead, pro-activism itself is featuring ambitious leaps forward in the international arena with a global agenda equipped with local discourses and values. Even though there is quite a continuousness through the transition from the statist Kemalist policies to the AKP era especially in terms of holding onto neoliberal economic policies dating back to the Özal era in the 1980s, it is undeniable that the AKP has created some ruptures through multi-stakeholder diplomacy both in the foreign policy and in the political economy of Turkey, which then urged scholars to label the AKP as a reformist actor.

Multi-stakeholder diplomacy presents a sphere where non-state actors are not only the units affected by state policies but also are the ones who are, to some extent, responsible for producing these policies (Hocking 2006; Baba 2018, 76). 'Official diplomatic practitioners... are more of facilitators and entrepreneurs' (Baba 2018, 77) where governments, NGOs, and businesses are the three key sectors which do not have absolute authority over agenda- and policy-setting. In this respect, the pro-activism of AKP governments is not solely a consequence of AKP elites' and state officials' motivations towards a more inclusionary global order, but also because of the fact that civil society has stakes in this kind of initiatives from governmental bodies. Therefore, when discussing Turkey's courageous opening to some regions, it is necessary to address the foreign aid issue in the context of political economy.

The openings to different regions which had no direct geographical borders with Turkey might be a clear indicator of Turkey's recent era activism in foreign policy. Latin America and sub-Saharan Africa are two salient regions where Turkey tries to be involved via NGOs, sub-state level agencies like TIKA, and business associations. In spite of existing drawbacks stemming from different languages, geographical distance, and cultural barriers, Turkey has embarked upon a versatile state policy including the complementary multi-stakeholder efforts of Turkish Airlines, Müsiad (Independent Industrialists and Businessmen's Association), and some faith-based NGOs like IHH (Humanitarian Relief Foundation) (Gonzalez and Zengin 2016).

Collaborating with the sovereignty-free and sovereignty-bound actors (SFA-SBA) has led Turkey to '[move] beyond conventional state-to-state dealings in implementing its foreign policy' (İpek and Biltekin 2013). Therefore, it is sound to suggest that combining statist foreign policy tools with sub-state and non-state actors is a characteristic of AKP-led foreign policy vision, which differentiates the AKP from its predecessors. The advent of a cultural kinship and relative closeness with Latin America, sub-Saharan Africa is more suitable for cooperative, complementary, and supplementary interactions among Turkish state and other SFA-SBAs. On the other hand, the kinship bonds and cultural affinity have created a benevolent discourse which has been assumed to enhance Turkey's 'soft-power-generating capacity' (Bacık and Afacan 2013).

In contrast with Latin America and sub-Saharan Africa, regions such as Central Asia, the Middle East, and the Balkans have always been at the centre of Turkey's foreign policy since the end of the Cold War despite state elites' oscillating emphasis on these regions. What the AKP offers in the case of Central Asia is the emergence of a new geographic imagination in which Central Asia is not only a geographic region in the concrete, cartographic sense, but also offers a conceptual and imaginary geography providing Turkey with a chance to appear as an influential player (Aras et al. 2009). Efforts to revitalize Turkey's influence in regions like the Middle East and the Balkans gained the attention of both regional and global circles, some of whom find Davutoglu's Ottomanist discourses obsolete, exaggerated (Türbedar 2011; Ongur 2015), and, perhaps, expansionist. However, long-term outcomes of re-engagement with the Balkans have so far ended up increasing business ties and social interaction, with no visible problem in bilateral relations. Finally, pro-activism was most clearly seen in the cases of the Arab uprisings during which the AKP used shuttle diplomacy to reinforce its regional power status that would, presumably, also enhance its role as a global player within the ideological framework of 'Strategic Depth', featuring cultural-historical and ideational ties (Özpek and Demirağ 2014, 332).

In such an international atmosphere, where the AKP ambitiously has taken risks to energize a vision which foresees Turkey as a game-changer in the global scale (or at least in an extended regional scale), foreign aid plays an important role because of its functionality on promulgating Turkey within a humanitarian/benevolent narrative, enhancing bilateral ties, and urging business associations and NGOs to act in parallel with the state policy (Ongur and Zengin 2016). Speaking of AKP's philosophy of political economy, therefore, focusing on the acts of emerging conservative business associations and think tanks as well as firms, whose long-term aims are in line with those of Turkish state, would help to understand Turkish foreign aid behaviour and the motivations behind it.

Controlled Neo-populism and the Redistribution in the Age of Roll-Out Neoliberalization

Like pro-activism, explaining the very essence of new Turkish foreign policy, controlled neo-populism, coined by Ziya Öniş, captures the totality of the political economy of Turkey under AKP rule in the context of 'the triumph of conservative globalism' led by a successful redistributive economic strategy (Öniş 2012). Although regulatory neoliberalism, which has been used as a cure to the 2001 economic crisis of Turkey, has been followed by the AKP, the novelties brought by the AKP revolve around the creation of a new upper class within a conservative electorate through privatization and public contracts. The abundance of monetary liquidity coming from internal and external sources of privatization and, more importantly, expansionary monetary policies in the world allowed the AKP to pursue mass spending on education and healthcare. The bust cycle in the economy and praises from Western media outlets gave the AKP confidence to entrench both its and Turkey's image in international arenas. Additionally, the high growth rates and broad optimism about the general situation of the economy affected the foreign policy behaviour of consecutive AKP governments in a way in which AKP elites gathered the courage to have a globalist vision. New consulates were opened, many foreign students were given scholarship, business associations were encouraged to diversify their aimed market geography, and the TIKA has been strengthened financially and institutionally.

Özatalay (2011) suggests a two-step neoliberalization process for Turkey, namely a roll-back (abandoning Keynesian collectivist institutions) and roll-out (building a market-friendly state managing economy directly via the rules of neoliberalism). Roll-out neoliberalism in Turkey was concretized by the collaboration among the conservative AKP governments and small- and medium-sized entrepreneurs with Islamist leanings, called the Anatolian Tigers (Özatalay 2011). Öniş suggests that 'the problem with [redistribution] approach is that it is a particularistic form of redistribution that by definition favours insiders close to the party's informal networks' (Öniş 2012, 141). In such an atmosphere, Müsiad comes to the forefront, with the largest conservative business network in Turkey, aspiring to realize beyond-Turkey leaps based on an export-oriented development strategy (Özatalay 2011). Müsiad, IHH, and Deniz Feneri alike aim to focus on the humanitarian and development aid of NGOs and associations and the ways in which they are complementing and supplementing the Turkish state policies abroad as foreign policy agents whose role and behaviour are in parallel with that of Turkish state, which makes them the main tenet of public diplomacy (Çevik 2016).

Foreign aid, as an effective foreign policy tool, which also has implications for strengthening economic ties between the donor and the recipient, was among the key cooperation mechanism used by AKP governments not only to enhance Turkey's image in the international arena but also to entrench the state–society–business triangular relations under a benevolent narrative stemming from Islamist and Ottomanist ideologies (for a discussion on Ottomanism in Turkish foreign policy, see: Uzer 2018; Murinson 2018; Sozen 2010). Bacik and Afacan (2013) argue that opening up to regions other than Turkey with the incentives from the state was an inevitable consequence of traditional secular business tycoons' competitive existence in the local markets. To this end, as the 'major economic and political basis' of AKP, Müsiad had to find a lucrative venue, such as Africa, to kick off its own business ventures (Bacık and Afacan 2013).

Considering the AKP's long-term success in bringing the excluded social and economic segments of Turkey to the core of society and securing the rights of conservative capital owners and the masses, who were once excluded by the Kemalist modernization project (Öniş 2006), we can encapsulate foreign aid behaviour of Turkey in the last decade to better conceptualize the extent to which the AKP has been transforming foreign aid strategy into a multi-level beneficial state diplomacy which is in parallel with controlled neo-populism. On the one hand, electorates with an Islamist background are satisfied with a humanitarian narrative pointing to an Islamist and Ottomanist brotherhood and non-state actors becoming more enthusiastic and devout in investing, experiencing, and even academically studying in regions like Latin America; on the other, the tremendous amount of foreign aid Turkey has been disbursing during the AKP era undertakes the catalyser role of boosting Turkey's image in the international community. The next sections directly delve into the AKP's foreign aid policy in the context of aid strategy's implications for the political economy of Turkey, business–state relations, the strategic depth, and the Turkish foreign policy.

AID-BENEVOLENCE-EXPORT TRIANGLE

A Professionalized Negotiator: TIKA

The international development community has been getting more crowded in recent decades with the newly emerged donor countries'

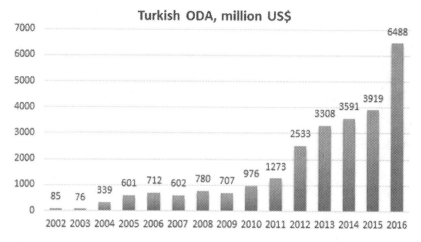

Fig. 6.1 Turkish official development assistance, million US$

willing to take the benevolent role in the humanitarian crises and development-related projects. TIKA is a version of established development agencies like the United States Agency for Development (USAID) and Japan International Cooperation Agency (JICA), to name just a few. In parallel with Turkey's GDP, TIKA's disbursements have increased to more than six billion US dollars in 2016 from only 85 million US dollars in 2002 and it became an assertive state aid institution on a global scale (TIKA 2016, 15). Figure 6.1 illustrates how exponentially Turkish ODA increased in the AKP era and foreign aid emerged as the main pillar of the foreign policy of Turkey.

As the humanitarian crises occur around the world, specifically in the Middle East, Turkey's visibility in the donor world has also become more apparent. The protracted Arab uprisings and civilian deaths caused by the conflicts between the states and the rioter groups posed a great threat for Turkey near its borders and consequently forced Turkey to take a role into disburse tremendous amounts of financial resources. In this respect, we see Syria as an outlier case because in recent years Turkey has given more aid to Syria than all other countries combined (Zengin and Korkmaz 2019). In Figs. 6.2 and 6.3, the top 10 aid recipients are illustrated, which ultimately shows that in spite of increasing monetary flows to Africa from NGOs, associations, and the state, sub-Saharan Africa's existence on the list could not exceed that of Asia where Syria,

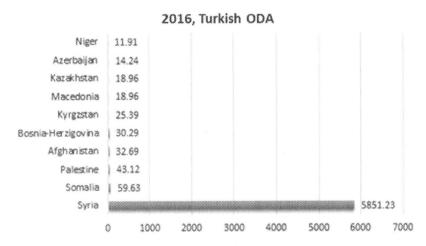

Fig. 6.2 Top 10 Turkish aid receivers in 2016, million US$

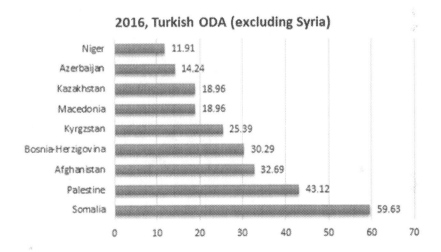

Fig. 6.3 Top 10 Turkish aid receivers in 2016, excluding Syria, million US$

142 A. KORKMAZ AND H. ZENGIN

Afghanistan, Kyrgyzstan, Kazakhstan, Azerbaijan, and Palestine attract Turkish ODA. Second, the figure is important in the sense that it also reveals Syria's vital importance for Turkish state and society, considering the fact that even Palestine could only get less than one-hundredth of what Syria received in 2016.

The Non-state Stakeholders: Islamic NGOs and Müsiad

Pro-activism by the Turkish state in the last decade has also led humanitarian and faith-based NGOs to take courageous actions abroad. After the 1980 coup d'état, Islamic civil society organizations gained new momentum, through which some faith-based NGOs became more visible in society during the 1990s despite the state's reluctance to collaborate with these religion-focused NGOs (Aras and Akpınar 2015). With the freedom wave originating from the AKP's resolution on EU accession, both humanitarian and faith-based NGOs entrenched their existence in Turkish society, which then led the state to include these mostly conservative NGOs in its globalist foreign policy vision, embracing not only the Former Ottoman territory but also more distant geographies, such as sub-Saharan Africa.

The main advantages of NGOs over state activities mostly stem from NGOs' flexible agenda and ability to advocate cultural and religious susceptibility of both their own and their recipients. In addition, in an environment where some recipients are building a viable self-sustaining economy, the policymakers are becoming more sceptical of the motivations of donor countries and do not prefer foreign aid as one of the main resources of their governments. However, these states might be more welcoming if these NGOs collaborated with the donor state and/or act themselves in the recipient countries. With these pros and thanks to the encouraging globalist vision of the AKP, disbursements of Turkish NGOs experienced an upward trend for the period 2005–2016 as seen in Fig. 6.4. These faith-based NGOs have also been funded by donations mainly from conservative business organizations in order to strengthen both the economic and non-economic ties within the Islamic network (Binder and Erten 2013, 6; Buğra and Savaşkan 2014, s. 45).

Emergency assistance, medical relief, building infrastructure, and investing in social and human capital are among the most prominent activities that humanitarian NGOs, such as IHH, Kimse Yok mu,

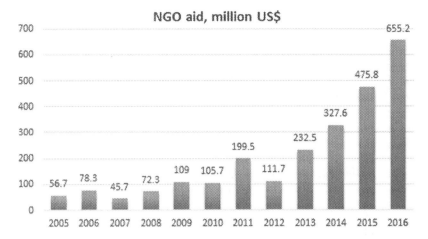

Fig. 6.4 Amount of aid disbursed by Turkish NGOs, 2005–2016, million US$

Doctors Worldwide, Deniz Feneri, and Diyanet Foundation, carry out (Aras and Akpınar 2015). The Turkish NGOs are mostly known for their religiously motivated structure which was precipitated by the AKP's extolment of these NGOs and Erdogan's globalist discourse based on a brotherhood of understanding vitalized around religion. 'From Mogadishu to Sarajevo,…, from Pristina to the Turkish Republic of Northern Cyprus - wherever there is a victim in the world, AKP is at his side'. Seibert (2011) is a clear example of how the AKP tries to locate Turkey in the world order, considering itself as an unyielding humanitarian actor which recognizes no boundary and distance.

The AKP's rise as the key political player in Turkey has not only led to the emergence of NGOs with deep networks abroad, but also on the economic side, it caused entrenchment of new conservative business associations like the Müsiad. Establishing the Müsiad in 1990, the founding conservative elites were able to recruit 3000 businessmen in the mid-1990s, which, indeed, can be seen as a reflection of Turkey's national politics in the 1990s during which Refah Partisi (RP) won the Istanbul mayor election in 1994 and rose to power in 1996. From that date forward, Müsiad has been an economic ally of conservative governments, having a privileged partner position, especially during waves of privatization (Yankaya 2017, 6), i.e. the times of redistributive controlled neo-populism in the words of Öniş.

The pro-activism of the AKP has overlapped the transnational activism (or semi-peripheral expansion) of Müsiad in the last decade. The peak of the relations between the state and this Islamic businessmen community corresponds to the increasing engagement efforts of the AKP and Müsiad to Tunisia and Egypt. While Turkey dramatically increased the amount of foreign aid given to these countries through this process, Müsiad helped Islamist businessmen in Egypt and Tunisia establish their own business association, the Egyptian Business and Development Association and Tunisian Namaa (Rise) (Yankaya 2017, 1). The complementary interaction between the state and civil society abroad has been strengthened through TIKA's efforts in terms of amelioration infrastructure, transportation, and law enforcement in Tunisia, which were severely damaged during the revolution (TIKA, TIKA Kalkınma Raporu 2013, 39) and vital conditions for a safe haven for entrepreneurs.

What Is Attractive in the Turkish Case?

As an emerging donor, Turkey differentiates itself from the established donors in the sense that it has no conditionality (no strings attached aid); in-kind aid (if necessary) makes up all of Turkish aid, and aid is predominantly given in bilateral forms instead of multilateral. Unconditionality and in-kind aid fasten and ease the aid process in case of emergency situations. These two aspects of Turkish foreign aid also built warmer and more direct relations between the recipients and Turkey. The mayor of Mogadishu praised Turkey's in-kind and non-bureaucratic aid while criticizing the conditional and centralized structure of UN agencies:

> [The Turks] are creating modern hospitals and establishing the education system. This cannot be delivered through NGOs and through UN agencies. Bilateral aid is what Somalia needs. If I request computers from the UN, they will take months and require a number of assessments. They will spend $50,000 to give me $7,000 of equipment. If I request computers from Turkey, they will show up next week. (Westaway 2013)

The then-Turkish ambassador to Somalia also pointed out the fact that the method adopted by Turkish foreign aid authorities is distinct in the way in which the Turkish agencies use the money to deal with the problem directly while avoiding administration costs and bureaucracy (Westaway 2013). To this end, bilateral aid strikingly exceeds

6 THE POLITICAL ECONOMY OF TURKISH FOREIGN AID 145

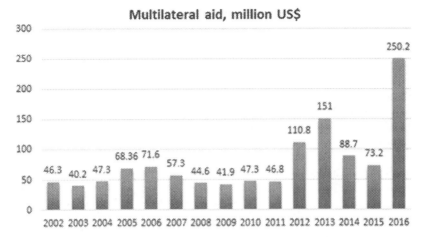

Fig. 6.5 Turkish multilateral aid, 2002–2016, million US$

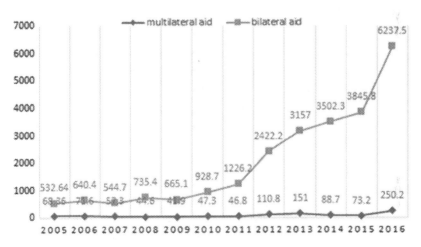

Fig. 6.6 Turkish bilateral-multilateral aid, 2002–2016, million US$

the aid allocated to recipients via international agencies in the Turkish case. Figures 6.5 and 6.6 show Turkey's aid disbursement through multilateral organizations and both bilateral and multilateral aid during the AKP era.

Another idiosyncrasy of foreign aid in Turkey is foreign aid's characterization as a niche aspect of Turkish foreign policy. Having an incremental trend in the last decade, the amount of foreign aid exceeds the aid of almost all prior years. Considering Turkey's endless efforts to alleviate the migration crisis stemming from the Syrian quagmire and the humanitarian emergency in Somalia, alongside the Islamist discourses adopted by AKP elites, we can come up with the idea that foreign aid is an undeniable and indispensable foreign/domestic policy tool through which Turkey, the AKP, and numerous NGOs and business associations gain international recognition, benevolent status, and accession to new markets.

However, one arresting outcome of the tremendous increase in Turkish foreign aid is that the aid is strictly dependent on humanitarian crises in neighbour regions like the Middle East and the Horn of Africa. That is to say that excluding (or ending) the deadliest humanitarian crisis, the Syria war, would cause quite a drop in the amount of foreign aid, which implies the susceptibility of Turkish foreign aid to extraordinary international humanitarian incidents. Syria's weight on the Turkish aid receiver list is indicated by the fact that nine of the top receivers other than Syria got about 250 million US dollars in 2016 while Syria got about 5800 million US dollars.

Foreign aid has sub-categories, and each category has different meanings implicating different policy tools and actors. The point behind this categorization is to make donor countries' efforts evident and make the quantification process more comprehensible. However, due to the public's understanding of what humanitarian could mean is reflected in aid literature and aid discussions where humanitarian assistance and development assistance are intermingled (Binder and Erten 2013, 7).

The non-state thrusts of foreign policy in the AKP era Turkey concretely indicate the existence of a multi-driven foreign policy decision-making process. With the ascent of religion in the public sphere towards 1990 (Habermas 2006), the actors mobilized around religious motivations have had a chance to influence state apparatuses, especially if the incumbent government has religious/conservative leanings. As a conservative democrat political party, the AKP's foreign policy paradigm has been in parallel to that of Islamic associations who were presenting/demanding alternative Western-outlook Turkish foreign policy. Buğra and Savaşkan (2014, 50) put forth the grass roots of Islamic associations to indicate the attraction of opening non-OECD countries through politics-driven capital accumulation mechanisms.

A Brief Analysis on Path Dependency of Donors in a Historical Context

Hypotheses

From the extant aid literature, we know that colony relations matter for donor–recipient relations (e.g. Alesina and Dollar 1998; Kavaklı 2018; Mascarenhas and Sandler 2006). In addition, some researchers place importance on the Ottomanism while discussing Turkish foreign policy (e.g. Uzer 2018; Murinson 2018; Sozen 2010). Therefore, we include some major ex-empire powers, which also represent the established donors in the empirical analysis. We consider France, Spain, and the UK, along with Turkey, as donor countries. The donor countries have some common features: (i) they have strong historical ties with some of the aid recipients at hand, (ii) their languages are spoken beyond their territories, and (iii) they want to deepen their relations with far-away regions. The main purpose of the empirical analysis to be performed in this section is to discuss how Turkey behaves while disbursing foreign aid and how Turkey differs from the above-mentioned ex-empire powers during the AKP era. Based on the extant aid literature and our discussions in the previous parts, we hypothesize our claims as follows[1]:

H1: The recipient countries receive more foreign aid as they import from the donor countries.

H2: The donor countries disburse more foreign aid as they grow.

H3: Poor countries receive more foreign aid.

H4: The donor countries attach a lot of importance to cultural kinship, which is proxied by the religion, the language, and the colonial indicators implying a recipient country had been ruled by a donor country in the past.

---

[1] The definitions of the variables are presented in the following section.

The first three hypotheses above stress the importance of economic factors. The first tests for the aid-benevolence-aid triangle discussed in section "Aid-Benevolence-Export Triangle". As is well known, the main or traditional purpose of disbursing foreign aid is to support the sustainable development and welfare in the developing countries. For instance, Rosenstein-Rodan (1961, 107) states the main purpose of foreign aid is:

> The purpose of an international program of aid to underdeveloped countries is to accelerate their economic development up to a point where a satisfactory rate of growth can be achieved on a self-sustaining basis.

In addition, the OECD–DAC committee set a target that economically advanced countries should spend 0.7% of their gross national income on official development assistance to support the sustainable development and welfare in developing countries. As of 2015 circa, Sweden, Norway, Luxembourg, Belgium, Denmark, the UK, and The Netherlands achieved the target among the twenty-nine members of the OECD–DAC committee. Therefore, it seems plausible to assume that the donor countries disburse more foreign aid as they get richer and that the poorer recipient countries receive more foreign aid. The second and third hypotheses test for the validity of these implications. In addition, we know that the first target of foreign aid was set up by the World Council of Churches.[2] Therefore, it is important to hypothesize the cultural kinship among the recipient and the donor countries. Hence, the fourth hypothesis controls for cultural kinship. We expect that cultural kinship is an important determinant in explaining the amount of foreign aid that a recipient country receives. Also, there are some political factors in the model. The first political factor we consider is the U.N. vote similarity index measuring political proximity between the recipient and donor countries. We expect that a recipient country gets a greater amount of foreign aid from a donor country if their voting behaviour is similar to each other. In addition, we also include the political terror scale indexes of the recipient countries and the cabinet ideology indexes of the donor countries as political factors. The political terror scale index measures whether the foreign aid disbursed by the donor countries is distributed to the recipient countries experiencing political violence

---

[2]For a detailed discussion, see: http://www.oecd.org/dac/stats/the07odagnitarget-ahistory.htm.

6 THE POLITICAL ECONOMY OF TURKISH FOREIGN AID 149

and terror incidence while the cabinet ideology index measures the traditional left-right dimension of the governments in the donor countries (Gibney et al. 2018). We expect that the countries with more political terror incidents will get less foreign aid. Finally, as the donor's cabinet ideology leans towards leftism, it is our prior expectation that increased amount of aid to the poor countries will be highly likely.

Data

To test for our hypotheses, we draw a sample from Kavaklı (2018) dataset for foreign aid for the period from 2005 to 2013. Our donor world consists of France, Spain, the UK, and Turkey. As for the cluster of recipient countries, we draw most favoured seventy-five countries for each of the donor countries in the context of foreign aid. A recipient country in the sample receives a minimum of 0.1% of the foreign aid disbursed by any of the donor countries.

As described above, we attempt to show how some major donors, who also have strong historical ties with aid recipients, act and, more importantly, in what way Turkey is differentiated from them. In Table 6.1, we present some descriptive statistics of the data.

Model

The model is specified in a dynamic nature so as to capture the additional, unobservable, or unmeasurable motives for disbursing foreign aid. The economic, political, and cultural motives are also incorporated into the model:

$$LFA_{ij,t} = \alpha LFA_{ij,t-1} + \beta_1 LX_{ij,t-1} + \beta_2 LYD_{i,t-1} + \beta_3 LYR_{j,t-1} + \beta_4 Colony_{ij}$$
$$+ \beta_5 Religion_{ij} + \beta_6 Language_{ij} + \beta_7 UN\_VS_{ij,t} + \beta_8 Pol\_Ter_{i,t}$$
$$+ \beta_9 Cab\_Ide_{j,t} + \varepsilon_{ij,t}$$

$$(6.1)$$

where $(i = 1, ..., N1)$, $(j = 1, ..., N2)$, $(t = 1, ..., T)$, $(i \neq j)$, $(\varepsilon_{ij,t} = \omega_{ij} + \varphi_i + \gamma_j + \theta_t + \epsilon_{ij,t})$, and $(|\alpha| < 1)$. $(FA_{ij,t})$ is the foreign aid provided by donor country (j) to recipient country (i) at time (t), and therefore $(FA_{ij,t-1})$ is the one period lagged value of the dependent variable. Economic block of the independent variables consists of the following: one period lagged export to the recipient country from the donor country $(X_{ij,t-1})$, and one period lagged per capita gross

150 A. KORKMAZ AND H. ZENGIN

Table 6.1 Descriptive statistics

Variables	Abbreviations	Mean	Std. Dev.	Min	Max
Foreign aid—million US$	FA	40.93	127.38	0	3183.85
Per capita gross domestic products in the recipient country	YR	7.11	1.08	4.95	10.18
Per capita gross domestic products in the donor country	YD	10.05	0.65	8.87	10.64
Export to the recipient country from the donor country	X	18.49	2.06	7.66	23.70
UN vote similarity between the recipient and the donor	UN_VS	0.37	0.20	−0.375	1
Political terror index of the recipient country	Pol_Ter	3.05	1.01	1	5
Cabinet ideology index of the donor country	Cab_Ide	−5.33	11.02	−33.63	15.52
Colony dummy	Colony	0.27	0.45	0	1
Percent of recipient from donor's largest religious group	Religion	0.48	0.38	0	0.992
Percent of recipient from donor's largest religious group	Language	0.13	0.30	0	1

domestic products in the donor country ($YD_{i,t-1}$) and in the recipient country ($YD_{j,t-1}$). The dependent variable and the economic indicators are expressed in real terms, and (L) denotes variables in natural logarithms. The cultural block contains information related to the followings: ($Colony_{ij}$) is a dummy variable that takes the value of one if the recipient country had been ruled by the donor country while ($Religion_{ij}$) and ($Language_{ij}$) are the ratios of population in the recipient country from the largest religious and language groups in the donor country to overall population of the recipient country, respectively. In addition, the political block includes the UN vote similarity index ($UN\_VS_{ij,t}$) between the recipient country and the donor country at time (t), the political terror scale index ($Pol\_Ter_{i,t}$) of the recipient country at time (t), and the cabinet ideology index ($Cab\_Ide_{j,t}$) of the donor country at time (t). Finally ($\varepsilon_{ij,t}$) is the error term consisting of some specific effects to control for omitted variables associated with each bilateral aid flow (ω_{ij}), with the recipient country (φ_i), with the donor country (γ_j), and with time (θ_t), respectively. The remaining component of the error term contains the idiosyncratic shocks ($\epsilon_{ij,t}$). The parameter (α) represents the persistence of adjustment towards an equilibrium, and hence ($1 - \alpha$) is the speed of adjustment. The parameters (β_i's) reflect the short-run effects of the relevant independent variables on the dependent variable. The long-run effects are also calculated as ($\beta_i^{longrun} = \frac{\beta_i}{1-\alpha}$).

Estimation Method

As demonstrated by Nickell (1981), if the sample size (T) is not sufficiently large, the ordinary least squares estimator (OLS) of the dynamic panel data models yields biased and inconsistent estimates because the time-invariant specific (fixed) effects (e.g. $\omega_{ij}, \varphi_i, \gamma_j$) are correlated with the lagged dependent variable (e.g. $LFA_{ij,t-1}$). Transforming the model in first differences (or in orthogonal deviations) to expunge the specific effects, Arellano and Bond (1991) propose a generalized method of moments estimator (GMM), which is entitled difference GMM:

$$\Delta LFA_{ij,t} = \alpha \Delta LFA_{ij,t-1} + \beta_1 \Delta LX_{ij,t-1} + \beta_2 \Delta LYD_{i,t-1} + \beta_3 \Delta LYR_{j,t-1}$$
$$+ \beta_7 \Delta UN\_VS_{ij,t} + \beta_8 \Delta Pol\_Ter_{i,t} + \beta_9 \Delta Cab\_Ide_{j,t} + \Delta \varepsilon_{ij,t} \quad (6.2)$$

where (Δ) is the first difference operator. As discussed in detail by Roodman (2009), the lagged dependent variable is still potentially endogenous because the differenced lagged dependent variable ($\Delta LFA_{ij,t-1} = LFA_{ij,t-1} - LFA_{ij,t-2}$) is still correlated with the differenced disturbance ($\Delta \varepsilon_{ij,t} = \varepsilon_{ij,t} - \varepsilon_{ij,t-1}$) process, even though the specific effects ($\omega_{ij}, \varphi_i, \gamma_j$) are purged after transformations. However, the second and higher lags of the dependent variable in levels are appropriate instruments for the differenced dependent variable because the instruments are no longer correlated with the error terms that are assumed to be not serially correlated. As noticed, the cultural variables are also expunged from the model as well as the specific effects as a result of the transformation procedure. Blundell and Bond (1998) modify the approach of Arellano and Bond (1991) by supplementing Eq. 6.2 in first differences with Eq. 6.1 in levels. The appropriate instruments for the dependent variable in the level equation are the lagged differences while the appropriate instruments for the dependent variable in the differenced equation

152   A. KORKMAZ AND H. ZENGIN

are the lagged levels. The procedure suggested by Blundell and Bond (1998) is so-called the system GMM estimator.[3] Generally speaking, the system GMM estimator is preferable to the difference GMM estimator if the data are persistent and cover a short time span and if the lagged levels are weak instruments for the first differences. In addition, the system GMM estimator is the most appropriate method for the model proposed here because it permits the inclusion of time-invariant variables (e.g. cultural variables) which should not be purged.

Moreover, to test whether Turkey's donor behaviour is different from those of France, Spain, and the UK, we modify Eq. 6.1 so as to yield Eq. 6.2 below:

$$
\begin{aligned}
LFA_{ij,t} = {} & \alpha LFA_{ij,t-1} + \beta_1 LX_{ij,t-1} + \beta_2 LYD_{i,t-1} + \beta_3 LYR_{j,t-1} + \beta_4 Colony_{ij} \\
& + \beta_5 Religion_{ij} + \beta_6 Language_{ij} + \beta_7 UN\_VS_{ij,t} + \beta_8 Pol\_Ter_{i,t} \\
& + \beta_9 Cab\_Ide_{j,t} + +\vartheta_1 D_{TR} * LX_{ij,t-1} + \vartheta_2 D_{TR} * LYD_{i,t-1} \\
& + \vartheta_3 D_{TR} * LYR_{j,t-1} + \vartheta_4 D_{TR} * Colony_{ij} + \vartheta_5 D_{TR} * Religion_{ij} \\
& + \vartheta_6 D_{TR} * Language_{ij} + \vartheta_7 D_{TR} * UN\_VS_{ij,t} \\
& + \vartheta_8 D_{TR} * Pol\_Ter_{i,t} + \vartheta_9 D_{TR} * Cab\_Ide_{j,t} + \varepsilon_{ij,t}
\end{aligned}
\tag{6.3}
$$

where (D_{TR}) is a dummy variable that takes the value of one if the donor country is Turkey and zero otherwise. The interacted terms test that Turkey attaches different levels of importance to the related indicator.

In this chapter, we use a model estimated by two-step version of the system GMM estimator via STATA using xtabond2 routine of Roodman (2009). Windmeijer's (2005) procedure is also implemented so that standard errors are corrected after controlling for the small sample size of the dataset. For the possible weaknesses of the estimation results, such as unobserved heterogeneity, endogeneity, autocorrelation, and weak instruments, we present the Arellano–Bond AR test for autocorrelation, Sargan and Hansen-J tests for over-identifying restrictions and thus the instrument exogeneity, and finally the conventional F test.

---

[3]For a detailed review of the methodologies, see: Arellano and Bond (1991), Arellano and Bover (1995), Blundell and Bond (1998), and Roodman (2009).

Estimation Results

Estimation results of the model are presented in Table 6.2.[4]

The second column of Table 6.2 indicates the estimation results of the model while the third column introduces the estimation results of the augmented version of the model. The estimation results reveal that the model fulfils the stability criteria because the effect of the lagged dependent variable is estimated to be smaller than unity. In addition, the positive estimation of the coefficient belonging to the lagged dependent variable means that the short-run effects of the explanatory variables are the same in the sign but more severe in the magnitude in the long run.[5] Moreover, the models pass all of the diagnostic checks.

According to the empirical results, it is clear that the economic variables have an influential impact on donors' behaviours. It is determined that the donor countries give more foreign aid to recipient countries where they export more. A one-point increase in the donors' exports to the recipient countries stimulates foreign aid (by 0.277%). Also, it is revealed that the donor countries in the sample disburse more foreign aid as they get richer. A one-point increase in the real per capita income in the donor countries leads to a 0.764% increase in the amount of foreign aid they disburse. As discussed previously, the OECD–DAC committee aims that economically advanced countries should spend 0.7% of their gross national income on the official development assistance to support the sustainable development and welfare in the developing countries. So, this finding indicates that countries will hit that target. In addition, we find that the smaller the per capita real income the recipient countries have, the greater foreign aid they receive from the donor countries. A 1% decrease in the per capita real income in the recipient

---

[4] The model is also estimated, but not reported, by ordinary least squares (OLS) estimator and least square dummy variables (LSDV) estimator following by Bond (2002), who suggests that OLS estimator is biased upwards while LSDV estimator is biased downwards for a model of dynamic panel data and that a consistent estimator should lie between the OLS and LSDV estimators. The estimated coefficients of the lagged dependent variable by OLS and LSDV estimators are 0.618 and 0.190, respectively. We therefore conclude that the system GMM estimator is consistent for our model.

[5] For instance, the short-run effect of the per capita real income in the recipient country is -0.585 while the long-run effect of the relevant variable is -0.854 which is calculated as follows: $(-0.585/(1 - 0.315))$.

154 A. KORKMAZ AND H. ZENGIN

Table 6.2 Estimation results

	Model 1	Model 2
LFA_{t-1}	0.274*	0.286*
	(0.052)	(0.052)
LYR_{t-1}	−0.617*	−0.517*
	(0.103)	(0.121)
LYD_{t-1}	0.807*	1.064**
	(0.145)	(0.545)
LX_{t-1}	0.288*	0.201*
	(0.053)	(0.067)
UN_VS_t	0.460	0.251
	(0.339)	(0.347)
Pol_Ter_t	0.063	0.069
	(0.056)	(0.063)
Cab_Ide_t	−0.009	−0.013
	(0.006)	(0.009)
Colony	1.017*	1.091*
	(0.178)	(0.187)
Religion	−0.090	−0.248
	(0.204)	(0.245)
Language	1.298*	1.074*
	(0.268)	(0.285)
$TR*LYR_{t-1}$		−0.029
		(0.240)
$TR*LYD_{t-1}$		−0.309
		(0.205)
$TR*LX_{t-1}$		0.132
		(0.118)
$TR*UN\_VS_t$		1.109
		(0.813)
$TR*Pol\_Ter_t$		0.050
		(0.121)
$TR*Cab\_Ide_t$		0.004
		(0.022)
$TR*Colony$		−0.471
		(0.717)
$TR*Religion$		0.378
		(0.447)
$TR*Language$		1.537**
		(0.658)
F-test	667.64	502.94
	[0.00]	[0.00]
AR(1)	−6.14	−6.18
	[0.00]	[0.00]

(continued)

6 THE POLITICAL ECONOMY OF TURKISH FOREIGN AID   155

Table 6.2 (continued)

	Model 1	Model 2
AR(2)	0.30	0.25
	[0.77]	[0.80]
Sargan	5.66	6.33
	[0.23]	[0.18]
Hansen-J	3.48	3.88
	[0.48]	[0.42]
Num. of Grps.	246	245
Num. of Inst.	23	32
Obs.	1656	1654

Parentheses stand for corrected standard errors. Estimation results written in bold imply statistical significance of the relevant independent variables. *, ** and *** refer to significance levels of 1%, 5%, and 10%, respectively. Numbers in the square brackets are the probability values of the relevant test statistics. The models above also include time dummies, but their estimated coefficients are not reported.

countries increases foreign aid from the donors (by 0.585%). Overall, the donors give more foreign aid to the recipient countries with less per capita real income.

As seen in Table 6.2, it is determined that the cultural variables, except for religion, have statistically significant impacts on the donors' behaviours for the period from 2005 to 2013.[6] The donor countries in the sample disburse more foreign aid (by 153.95%[7]) to the recipient countries they ruled and to the recipient countries that speak the same language (by 240.42%[8]). As for the political variables, they all turned out to be insignificant, except for the political terror scale index. Interestingly, the effect of the political terror scale index, which measures whether a recipient violates human rights, on the amount of foreign aid that the recipient country receives is estimated positively which implies that quantity alone is not enough when evaluating the effectiveness of foreign aid and that the quality is also considered. Finally, the behaviour of Turkey, an emerging donor country, is not different from that of

---

[6] In a more detailed analysis, we found that although overall Islam has impact on Turkish aid, the impact disappears in the Former Ottoman lands and Turkic Republics. For further inquiry, see: Zengin, H., & Korkmaz, A. (2019). Determinants of Turkey's Foreign Aid Behaviour. *New Perspectives on Turkey, 60.*

[7] $(e^{0.932} - 1)*100.$

[8] $(e^{1.225} - 1)*100.$

France, Spain, and the UK except for language. As seen in the third column of Table 6.2, Turkey places more importance (by 307.55%[9]) on the language than the other donors do.

FUTURE CHALLENGES AHEAD

Every foreign policy comes with a price, especially foreign policy strategies that strictly depend on monetary outflow like foreign aid, which requires a robust economy. Regardless of how and to what extent identity and culture matter in the decision-making process, as long as this process is not supported financially, the sustainability of this endeavour would be fragile. In this sense, political and economic motivations are intermingled, affecting and getting affected by each other.

Turkey's prominence as a global aid donor has coincided with its economic success, which was applauded domestically and internationally. The continuous cash inflows and foreign investment, robustness in the banking sector, and a growing construction sector have kept the Turkish economy alive until the summer of 2018 when the lira's value against international currencies like the euro and the dollar decreased dramatically. Despite domestic mobilization among the constituency and decisive discourses adopted by governmental/presidential elites, the lira could not save itself from losing about 40% of its value. Reasons behind this economic problem are out of the scope of this chapter, but it has some implications for Turkey's endeavours to be a major economic actor and donor. First, due to the depreciation in the lira, TIKA's annual budget might decrease in dollar terms. In 2016, Turkey spent over six billion US$ in 2016, but in order to keep up with the past year's disbursements, Turkey would have to spend about 40% more in Turkish liras (if the lira would not gain momentum against the dollar in the near future). Considering the fact that Turkey builds deep relations with some economically underdeveloped countries via the foreign aid it disburses to these countries, we might come to the conclusion that Turkey should, at least try, to enhance relations through activities not solely dependent on monetary flows. Second, the AKP's one important success was to create a new image for Turkey in the international area, especially in its first years in the office, which has also aided by the support of international

[9]$(e^{1.405} - 1)*100.$

media outlets. Turkey's emergence as an aid giver is also used as a way to promote Turkey's new international image. However, the current economic distress might also affect Turkey's marketing as well as create a sense that TIKA might not be able to put forth Turkey's outstanding rankings in terms of donor activities in the world.

Considering the fact that although there is an accrued debate on Ottomanism and on opening towards Turkic states of Central Asia, the extent to which these states regard themselves as either a Former Ottoman state or a Turkic state has not been thoroughly analysed. Ayşe Zarakol argues that even if in Turkey, there is an undeniable emphasis on Ottomanism, in some of Former Ottoman nations, the Ottoman state is not well remembered (Zarakol 2012). In addition to this point, the degree to which Kyrgyzstan, Uzbekistan, Kazakhstan, Turkmenistan, and Azerbaijan define themselves as Turkic is questionable (Dinçerler 2011, 120). This is to say that if Turkey aims at strengthening relations with the recipient countries through providing foreign aid and some related discourse, it needs to add some other policy tools next to foreign aid in order to not depend solely on the monetary outflow.

CONCLUSION

At the onset of the new millennium, emerging powers take firm steps in the donor world and start adopting foreign aid as leverage to benefit in building or strengthening already existing relations with far-off regions. In this realm, thanks to Turkey's Central Asia and Africa openings and subsequently to the AKP's then-economic successes, foreign aid has been employed incessantly by consecutive AKP governments.

So-called pro-activist foreign policy paradigms of the AKP has coincided with a redistributive national economic policy for which we borrow the term 'controlled neo-populism' in the age of multi-stakeholder diplomacy. This applies not only to some humanitarian NGOs and voluntary-based entities, but also to Turkish firms and business associations who were emerging in an environment of relatively continuous and high economic growth rates, optimism around the globe around Turkey's democratization/demilitarization, and a fractured political opposition front. This favourable climate also led the AKP to be more activist in its foreign policy. Therefore, a cooperative interaction has been constituted among AKP and non-state stakeholders to have more lucrative, coordinative, and perennial deals and engagements with foreign countries, and foreign aid is currently an indispensable buttress of this policy.

Turkey adopts an unconditional and in-kind aid sometimes to bypass bureaucratic curbs within which established donors have been criticized by some local officials. And unlike established donors, Turkey mostly adopts a bilateral aid flow through which it can operationalize aid flows by its own and can seek a benevolent image in international platforms.

We also perform an econometric analysis to find out the main motivations behind the foreign aid behaviour of some ex-empire donors. We reveal that Turkey and other ex-empire donors disburse more foreign aid on the countries with low levels of per capita income, and on the countries, they export more to. It is also determined that the donor countries distribute more foreign aid as they get richer. As for the left-right dimension of the government and the UN vote affinity, the empirical findings indicate that there is no statistical significance of cabinet ideology on the allocation of foreign aid. In addition, it should be emphasized that the donor countries attach special importance to the cultural kinship, and Turkey distinguishes with respect to language, a factor that Turkey values more than the other donor countries.

Finally, we discuss challenges ahead for Turkey in the way of sustaining its position as a major donor in two steps. First, the recent Turkish lira depreciation against major international currencies might cause a drop in the total amount of aid Turkey would disburse over the course of the next year(s). Second, counting on historical/ethnic bonds with recipients, Turkish policymakers might not find a commensurate return from recipients in these senses. As Zarakol puts it, some Former Ottoman states do not consider themselves as a Former Ottoman, unlike Turkey, which is, in itself, a notice for Turkey to develop a more inclusive and globalist foreign policy paradigm based on universal values free of strict historical/ethnic bonds.

REFERENCES

Alesina, A., & Dollar, D. (1998). *Who Gives Foreign Aid to Whom and Why?* Cambridge, MA: National Bureau of Economic Research.

Aras, B., & Akpınar, P. (2015). The Role of Humanitarian NGOs in Turkey's Peacebuilding. *International Peacebuilding, 22*(3), 230–247.

Aras, B., Dağcı, K., & Çaman, M. E. (2009). Turkey's New Activism in Asia. *Alternatives, 8*(2), 24–39.

6 THE POLITICAL ECONOMY OF TURKISH FOREIGN AID   159

Arellano, M., & Bond, S. (1991). Some Tests of Specification for Panel Data: Monte Carlo Evidence and an Application to Employment Equations. *The Review of Economic Studies, 58*(2), 277–297.

Arellano, M., & Bover, O. (1995). Another Look at the Instrumental Variable Estimation of Error-Components Models. *Journal of Econometrics, 68*(1), 29–51.

Baba, G. (2018). Turkey's Multistakeholder Diplomacy: From a Middle Power Angle. In E. P. Dal (Ed.), *Middle Powers in Global Governance the Rise of Turkey* (pp. 75–95). Cham: Palgrave Macmillan.

Bacık, G., & Afacan, I. (2013). Turkey Discovers Sub-Saharan Africa: The Critical Role of Agents in the Construction of Turkish Foreign-Policy Discourse. *Turkish Studies, 14*(3), 483–512.

Binder, A., & Erten, C. (2013). From Dwarf to Giant—Turkey's Contemporary Humanitarian Assistance. *World Conference on Humanitarian Studies* (pp. 1–14). Istanbul: Global Public Policy Institute.

Blundell, R., & Bond, S. (1998). Initial Conditions and Moment Restrictions in Dynamic Panel Data Model. *Journal of Econometrics, 87*(1), 115–143.

Bond, S. R. (2002). Dynamic Panel Data Models: A Guide to Micro Data Methods and Practice. *Portuguese Economic Journal, 1*(2), 141–162.

Buğra, A., & Savaşkan, O. (2014). *Türkiye'de Yeni Kapitalizm - Siyaset, Din ve İş Dünyası.* İstanbul: İletişim.

Çevik, S. (2016). *The Rise of NGOs: Islamic Faith Diplomacy.* Los Angeles: USC Center on Public Diplomacy.

Dincer, O. B., & Mehmet, H. (2016). Turkey's Changing Syria Policy: From Desired Proactivism to Reactivism. In A. Kudurs & A. Pabriks (Eds.), *The War in Syria: Lessons for the West* (pp. 147–167). Riga: University of Latvia Press.

Dinçerler, V. (2011). Dış Politikayı Millet Tayin Etmeli. In H. Özdal, O. B. Dinçer, & M. Yegin (Eds.), *Mülakatlarla Türk Dış Politikası.* Ankara: USAK.

Gibney, M., Cornett, L., Wood, R., Haschke, P., Arnon, D., & Pisano, A. (2018, December 27). Retrieved from Political Terror Scale http://www.politicalterrorscale.org/About/FAQ/.

Gonzalez, A., & Zengin, H. (2016). A Decade of Opening: Turkey's New International Role in Sub-Saharan Africa and Latin America. *Tiempo Devorado, 3*(2), 262–285.

Habermas, J. (2006). Religion in the Public Sphere. *European Journal of Philosophy, 14*(1), 1–25.

Hocking, B. (2006). Multistakeholder Diplomacy: Forms, Functions, and Frustrations. In J. Kurbalija & K. Valentin (Eds.), *Multistakeholder Diplomacy: Challenges and Opportunities.* Geneva: DiploFoundation.

İpek, V., & Biltekin, G. (2013). Turkey's Foreign Policy Implementation in sub-Saharan Africa: A Post-international Approach. *New Perspectives on Turkey, 49*, 121–156.

Kavaklı, K. C. (2018). Domestic Politics and Motives of Emerging Donors: Evidence from Turkish Foreign Aid. *Political Research Quarterly, 71*(3), 614–627.

Keyman, F., & Gümüşçü, Ş. (2014). Turkey's Proactive Foreign Policy Under the AKP. In F. Keyman & Ş. Gümüşçü (Eds.), *Democracy, Identity, and Foreign Policy in Turkey* (pp. 70–83). London: Palgrave Macmillan.

Mascarenhas, R., & Sandler, T. (2006). Do Donors Cooperatively Fund Foreign Aid? *The Review of International Organizations, 1*(4), 337–357.

Murinson, A. (2018). *Turkish Foreign Policy in the 21st Century: Neo-Ottomanism and the Strategic Depth Doctrine*. London: I.B. Tauris.

Nickell, S. (1981). Biases in Dynamic Models with Fixed Effects. *Econometrica, 49*(6), 1417–1426.

Ongur, H. O. (2015). Identifying Ottomanisms: The Discursive Evolution of Ottoman Pasts in the Turkish Presents. *Middle Eastern Studies, 51*(3), 416–432.

Ongur, H. O., & Zengin, H. (2016). Transforming Habitus of the Foreign Policy: A Bourdieusian Analysis of Turkey as an Emerging Middle Power. *Rising Powers Quarterly, 1*(2), 117–133.

Öniş, Z. (2006). The Political Economy of Islam and Democracy in Turkey: From the Welfare Party to the AKP. In D. Jung (Ed.), *Democratization and Development New Political Strategies for the Middle East* (pp. 103–128). New York: Palgrave Macmillan.

Öniş, Z. (2012). The Triumph of Conservative Globalism: The Political Economy of the AKP Era. *Turkish Studies, 13*(2), 135–152.

Özatalay, C. (2011). How to Make the Economy "Embedded" in Turkey? One Question, Two Contradictory Answers. *Institution Building Under Neoliberal Globalization* (pp. 1–13). Madrid: Universidad Autónoma de Madrid.

Özpek, B. B., & Demirağ, Y. (2014). Turkish Foreign Policy After the 'Arab Spring': From Agenda-Setter State to Agenda-Entrepreneur State. *Israel Affairs, 20*(3), 328–346.

Roodman, D. (2009). How to Do Xtabond2: An Introduction to Difference and System GMM in Stata. *Stata Journal, 9*(1), 86–136.

Rosenstein-Rodan, P. N. (1961). International Aid for Underdeveloped Countries. *The Review of Economics and Statistics, 43*(2), 107–138.

Seibert, T. (2011, October 19). Turkey Moves Ahead with New Constitution. *The National.* Retrieved May 12, 2018, from https://www.thenational.ae/world/europe/turkey-moves-ahead-with-new-constitution-1.607453.

Sozen, A. (2010). A Paradigm Shift in Turkish Foreign Policy: Transition and Challenges. *Turkish Studies, 11*(1), 103–123.

TIKA. (2013). *TIKA Kalkınma Raporu.* Ankara: Türk İşbirliği ve Kalkınma Ajansı.

TIKA. (2016). *Türkiye Kalkınma Yardımları.* Ankara: Turkish Cooperation and Coordination Agency.

6 THE POLITICAL ECONOMY OF TURKISH FOREIGN AID 161

Türbedar, E. (2011). Turkey's New Activism in the Western Balkans: Ambitions and Obstacles. *Insight Turkey, 13*(3), 139–158.

Ünay, S. (2017, May 6). Domestic Consolidation, International Pro-activism. *Daily Sabah.*

Uzer, U. (2018). The Revival of Ottomanism in Turkish Foreign Policy: "The World Is Bigger Than Five". *Turkish Policy Quarterly, 16*(4), 29–36.

Westaway, K. (2013, September 17). *Turkey Is Poised to Cash in on a Stable Somalia.* Retrieved May 13, 2018, from https://qz.com/124918/turkey-is-poised-to-cash-in-on-a-stable-somalia/.

Windmeijer, F. (2005). A Finite Sample Correction for the Variance of Linear Efficient Two-Step GMM Estimators. *Journal of Econometrics, 126*(1), 25–51.

Yankaya, D. (2017). Crafting a Business Umma? Transnational Networks of 'Islamic Businessmen' After the Arab Spring. *Mediterranean Politics, 24*(3), 1–21.

Zarakol, A. (2012). *Yenilgiden Sonra: Doğu Batı ile Yaşamayı Nasıl Öğrendi.* Koç Üniversitesi Yayınları.

Zengin, H., & Korkmaz, A. (2019). Determinants of Turkey's Foreign Aid Behaviour. *New Perspectives on Turkey, 60*(1), 109–135.

CHAPTER 7

Emerging Middle Powers (MIKTA) in Global Political Economy: Preferences, Capabilities, and Their Limitations

Gonca Oğuz Gök and Radiye Funda Karadeniz

INTRODUCTION

Since the 2008 global financial crisis and the decline in the US's hegemonic dominance, the rise of emerging powers can be seen in "of economic competition, capital accumulation, political and economic influence as well as technical and material capacities" (Xing 2016). Developed economies' share of global GDP declined from 54 to 43% between 2004 and 2014 (Onis and Kutlay 2016) and today the G20 economies produce approximately 80% of global GDP (Diez and O'Donnel 2017). Nye and Acharya claim that in terms of military and economic power the USA maintains its primacy in the world system despite the decline of US hegemony in economic and political

---

G. Oğuz Gök (✉)
Department of International Relations, Marmara University,
Istanbul, Turkey

R. F. Karadeniz
Department of Economics in Islahiye, Gaziantep University,
Gaziantep, Turkey

© The Author(s) 2020
E. Parlar Dal (ed.), *Turkey's Political Economy in the 21st Century*, International Political Economy Series,
https://doi.org/10.1007/978-3-030-27632-4_7

163

governance (Acharya 2017; Nye 2017). Narlikar and Kumar also underline the eroding US hegemony in global economic governance and the current transition from *Pax Americana* to *Pax Mosaica* or toward a more inclusive and multipolar world economic governance (Narlikar and Kumar 2012). Ziya Onis discusses the challenges to established norms such as the post-Washington Consensus from the emerging Beijing Consensus (Onis 2017). Vezirgiannidou argues that in this transition period "informal diplomacy is becoming more important than formalized institutions" (Vezirgiannidou 2013, 636).

This fragmentation has provided middle powers with opportunities of room to maneuver and new roles at regional and global levels described with the concepts such as multi-multilateralism, minilateralism, and the rise of the informals (Fukuyama 2006; Patrick and Feng 2018). Emerging middle powers has utilized their upward mobility capabilities to realize their diplomatic agendas by establishing minilateral (Naim 2009) and informal gatherings. Ikenberry asserts that "today's struggle is about voice" or the willingness of others to increase their say and presence in global governance, not to replace the neoliberal economic order (Ikenberry 2016). By accommodating new actors and approaches in a "G-Plus World" (Acharya 2017), it can be asserted that middle power diplomacy through informal venues presents a new road for cooperation under the posthegemonic world order.

In this regard, the new middle power grouping established by Mexico, Indonesia, Korea, Turkey, and Australia (MIKTA) at the 68th session of the UN General Assembly in September 2013 is one example of such informal gatherings witnessed on the world stage after the 2008 crisis (Engin and Baba 2015, 2). Most scholars have accepted a definition of MIKTA countries as emerging middle powers based not only on their material (positional) power, but also on behavioral and ideational aspects (Chapnick 1999, 73; Carr 2014; Robertson 2017; Dal and Kurşun 2016). Some critics point out their heterogeneity and diversity in terms of domestic political and economic structures as their main source of weakness while others credit the merits of a heterogenous group which could push the creative multilateralism most needed in times of rising fragmentation arising from the crises of established norms (Jordaan 2017; Haug 2017). However, scholars largely agree that although MIKTA is in the early stage of development, this formation provides a significant test of the meaning and modalities of middle power role in changing dynamics of global order (Cooper 2016, 529).

Against this background and drawing on the emerging middle power concept this paper attempts to analyze MIKTA states' capabilities and preferences in the changing global political economy dynamics in order to determine whether there is enough evidence to talk about an enhanced cooperation under MIKTA initiative. What are the material capabilities of MIKTA countries in the current global economic order? Do they share the same or similar ideational preferences and historical attachments toward neoliberal institutions? Are there any common niche areas in political economy that can push for a common constructive MIKTA identity? Is there an increasing or decreasing willingness to push for an enhanced role of MIKTA since 2013 among these countries? In order to answer those questions, the paper will compare and contrast the (1) material capabilities, (2) ideational roles, and (3) MIKTA perceptions of each member countries in the 2010s in a time of clashing norms of global political economy.

To do so, the first part of this paper will depict the changing dynamics of the global political economy from the 2000s to the 2010s in order to better understand the clash between Western-based democratic norms of neoliberalism versus the emerging Chinese development model. The second part will attempt to specifically analyze the role of MIKTA in the changing global political economy dynamics by assessing each state's (1) material capabilities, (2) ideational preferences, and (3) behavioral limitations in a time of clashing norms of global political economy. Accordingly, the political economy dynamics of Mexico, Indonesia, Republic of Korea, Turkey, and Australia will be comparatively discussed with respect to the above-mentioned factors in order to the depict their converging and diverging dynamics. The paper will conclude by discussing the prospects and limitations of informal minilateralism in global governance with reference to MIKTA's future role as a group in the political economy.

Changing Dynamics of the Global Political Economy from the 2000s to the 2010s: The Rise of MIKTA

Today's emerging order encompasses a fundamental clash of norms of political economy in the sense that the key elements of the so-called Beijing Consensus seem to challenge the liberal developmental and democratic norms associated with Western-based norms of the Washington or post-Washington Consensus. In other words, the Chinese development model and authoritarian system defined as strategic capitalism based on the principles of flexibility, and sovereignty is emerging as a serious rival to the established models of the free market model of the USA and the social market model of Europe (Onis 2017, 4).

The rise of the BRICS in the 2000s was the main denominator shaping the political economy of the decade. In the aftermath of the 2008 crisis, the main institutions of the Bretton Woods system such as the International Monetary Fund (IMF), World Bank and WTO began to lose power while the move from multilateralism toward minilateralism was indicated by the strengthening of weakly institutionalized networks of informal groupings such as the G20, IBSA, and MIKTA. As asserted by Higgott, the shifts in global institutions pose risks to global economic stability as a result of decline in the predictability of the great powers' behavior (Higgott 2018, 3). MIKTA, in this regard, represents a vehicle for middle power aspirations at a time of global uncertainty about the intentions of the world's most powerful nations.

MIKTA states are characterized by their exclusion from major groupings within the G20, such as the G7 and BRICS due to the lack of capacity to compete for global leadership (Çolakoğlu 2016, 267–268). However, in response to the uncertainty in the global governance, they show common interest in "strengthening multilateralism by supporting worldwide efforts for stability and prosperity, facilitating pragmatic and creative solutions to regional and international challenges and implementing the needed reforms in global governance structures" in the 2013 UN Session (Heenam 2015, 72). MIKTA countries are generally regarded as bridges between the North and South or the developed and developing world.[1] These states generally have historical links to established powers and have socialized in a US-led liberal international order. However, MIKTA encompasses Turkey, Australia, and Korea, all of which have close links to the Western alliances; Mexico which has avoided formal alliances; and Indonesia with a long legacy as a member of the non-aligned movement. In terms of their trade, the share of China is noteworthy, while Mexico still continues to be highly dependent on the USA (see Table 7.8).

Although all MIKTA states accomplished tremendous economic growth rates in the 2000s, they also differ in terms of their development trajectories (Cooper 2015, 101). As Table 7.1 illustrates MIKTA both

[1] http://oecdobserver.org/news/fullstory.php/aid/6025/Creative_multilateralism:_Stronger_collaboration_for_all.html.

Table 7.1 Comparative economic outlook of MIKTA countries (2000–2017)

	Population		GNI		HDI		GDP		Inflation		Unemployment		Military exp. (% GDP)		FDI	
	2000	2017	2000	2017	2000	2017	2000	2017	2000	2017	2000	2017	2000	2017	2000	2017
Mexico	101.72 (2)	129.16 (2)	592.89 (1)	1047.31 (3)	55 (3)	74 (4)	707.91 (1)	1149.92 (3)	11.2 (3)	6.1 (4)	2.56 (1)	3.42 (1)	0.6 (5)	0.5 (5)	18,382 (1)	32,127 (2)
Indonesia	211.54 (1)	263.99 (1)	122.45 (5)	934.37 (4)	109 (5)	116 (5)	165.02 (5)	1015.54 (4)	20 (4)	4.2 (3)	6.08 (3)	4.18 (3)	0.7 (4)	0.8 (4)	−4550 (5)	21,465 (3)
Korea	47.01 (4)	51 (4)	504.94 (2)	1460.49 (1)	31 (2)	22 (2)	561.63 (2)	1530.75 (1)	1.1 (1)	2.3 (1)	4.42 (2)	3.73 (2)	2.5 (2)	2.6 (1)	11,509 (3)	17,053 (4)
Australia	19.15 (5)	24.6 (5)	404.3 (3)	1263.49 (2)	4 (1)	3 (1)	415.03 (3)	1323.42 (2)	2.6 (2)	3.7 (2)	6.28 (4)	5.59 (4)	1.8 (3)	2 (3)	14,893 (2)	45,100 (1)
Turkey	63.24 (3)	80.75 (3)	271.62 (4)	882.85 (5)	85 (4)	64 (3)	272.98 (4)	851.1 (5)	49.3 (5)	10.8 (5)	6.49 (5)	11.26 (5)	3.7 (1)	2.2 (2)	982 (4)	10,889 (5)

Table 7.2   Comparative economic outlook of MIKTA countries as of % change (2000–2017)

	Population		GNI		HDI		GDP		Inflation		Unemployment		Military Exp.		FDI	
	Rank	% Change	Rank	% Change	Rank	% Change	Rank	% Change	Rank	% Change	Rank	% Change	Rank	% Change	Rank	% Change
Mexico	3	27	5	77	5	35	5	62	3	−46	4	34	1	48	4	75
Indonesia	4	25	1	663	4	6	1	515	1	−79	1	−31	2	14	2	572
Korea	5	8	4	189	1	−29	4	173	5	109	2	−16	4	4	5	48
Australia	2	28	3	213	3	−25	3	219	4	42	3	−11	3	11	3	203
Turkey	1	28	2	225	2	−25	2	212	2	−78	5	73	5	−41	1	1009

GNI: Gross National Income; HDI: Human Development Index; GDP: Gross Domestic Product; FDI: Foreign Direct Investment
Source World Development Indicators database, World Bank; UN Human Development reports 2000 and 2017

encompasses Australia and Indonesia which differ remarkably in terms of UN Human Development index rankings-3rd and 116th—in the world. They are also different from BRICS grouping which encompasses both democratic and authoritarian states such as China and Russia (Jordaan 2003, 167; Nolte 2010, 890). Additionally, MIKTA states' democratization records are disparate and could be regarded as hybrid regimes, with the exception of Australia. Therefore, MIKTA members together represent an intermediate position, bridging or deconstructing the traditional divides between the West-versus-the-Rest (Weiss 2016, 10). It relies heavily on its potential in acting as a transregional governance group and takes as its starting point the concept of democratic governance. It is claimed that "MIKTA has injected cross-regionalism as an innovative format of multi-state cooperation" (Ruddyard 2018) (Table 7.2).

Comparative Political Economy of MIKTA as Emerging Middle Powers in the 2000s

Mexico

Poor Mexico, so far from God and so close to the United States.[2]

Since its independence from Spain in 1821, the Mexico's geo-strategic location at the southern border of the USA has been one of the most significant international factors affecting its political economy. Hence, most of its political economy has been directly or indirectly related to its main bilateral relations with the USA throughout its history (Schiavon 2018, 41). Some scholars have argued that Mexico "belongs to the North," not solely in terms of geographic location, but also in terms of its foreign relations (Pellicer 2006, 4). However, Mexico is culturally a Latin American country. Beginning in the early 1990s, Latin American countries concluded that Mexico had changed sides and chose the North at the expense of the South with the inception of NAFTA and Organization for Economic Cooperation and Development (OECD) membership (Gök and Karadeniz 2018). Therefore, Mexico's role within

---

[2]A famous quote attributed to Porfirio Diaz, A General and President of Mexico (1877–1911).

170   G. OĞUZ GÖK AND R. F. KARADENIZ

the global political economy should be conceived in terms of the duality of this "bi-regional" identity (Pellicer 2006, 4).

Material Capabilities

In his book *The Growth Map: Economic Opportunities in BRICS and Beyond*, economist Jim O'Neill, coiner of the BRICS acronym, conceptualized Mexico among the Next 11 (N11) countries which he argues will be the newly emerging economies after BRICS (O'Neill 2011).

Mexico's economy experienced tremendous growth rates in the 2000s (Table 7.3). Although Mexico City has become the 15th largest economy in the world, its economy continues to rely heavily on trade with the USA and minimally on Latin America (Flake and Wang 2017, 8). One striking facet of the Mexican economy is that it carries out more than 80% of its total foreign trade with the USA (see Table 7.8). Mexico is to a large extent located in the middle of the MIKTA grouping in terms of its economic outlook in the 2000s, 2nd in Population, 3rd in GDP, 4th in HDI, and 5th in Military Expenditures as of share of its total GDP (Table 7.1).

Table 7.3   Mexico's economic outlook (2000–2017)

	2000	2017	% Change
Population total (millions)	101.72	129.16	27
GNI, Atlas method (current US dollar, billions)	592.89	1047.31	77
GNI per capita Atlas method (current US Dollar)	5830	8930	53
Human Development Index (World Rank)	55	74	−35
GDP (current US dollar, billions)	707.91	1149.92	62
GDP growth (annual %)	4.9	2	−59
Inflation GDP deflator (annual %)	11.2	6.1	−46
Unemployment (% labor force)	2.56	3.42	34
Exports of goods and services (% of GDP)	25	38	52
Imports of goods and services (% of GDP)	27	40	48
Military expenditure (% of GDP)	0.6	0.5	−17
High technology export (% of manufactured exports)	22	15	−32
Foreign Direct Investments (millions)	18,382	32,127	75
Official development assistance received (US dollar millions)	−45.3	809.3	1887

Source World Development Indicators database, World Bank; UN Human Development reports 2000; 2017 (https://databank.worldbank.org/data/views/reports/)

Ideational Preferences

Mexico City initiated a "return to Latin America" as one of its main foreign policy objectives following the election of President Nieto in 2012 and initiated the establishment of the Community of Latin American and Caribbean States (CELAC) in 2011 (Maihold 2016, 546–551). In fact, as a country almost absent from Latin America until the 2000s, this new regional initiative was very much interlinked with the confidence of a growing economy widely regarded as the "Mexican Moment." Under Nieto (2012–2018), Mexico has positioned itself as an emerging economic power and an actor with global responsibility in the international community (Maihold 2016, 549).

President Nieto declared that Mexico City will participate in UN peacekeeping operations in 2014, a remarkable departure from its previous practice of caution and distance for a leading role in the UN (Pellicer 2006, 2). In a single decade, Mexico has twice been a non-permanent member of the UN Security Council, a significant outcome after its two terms of non-permanent seats in 1946 and 1980–1981.[3] Furthermore, heads of major international financial institutions came from Mexico, including Agustin Carstens at the IMF in 2009 and Herminio Blanco Mendoza as director general of the WTO in 2013. Mexico chaired the G20 summit and sought to broaden its agenda, which included hosting the first ever meeting of G20 foreign ministers meeting in 2012 in which the first MIKTA foreign ministers meeting was held (Wright 2015, 24–28).

MIKTA for Mexico: Remedy for Behavioral Limitations?

The MIKTA initiative coincided with a time period in which Mexico has begun to strive for more status in international relations and attempted to expand its foreign policy reach with a value-creating rationale. Mexico's preferences historically have been for looser formats and terms, avoiding binding commitments that could endanger possible obligations in other partnerships (Maihold 2016, 558). Hence, following

---

[3] http://www.providingforpeacekeeping.org/2014/04/03/contributor-profile-mexico/.

Granovetter's (1973) conceptualization of "the strength of weak ties,"[4] for Mexico MIKTA has become an opportunity to launch the multiple presence of the country in global politics. In other words, MIKTA has so far offered Mexico City an opportunity to overcome the limitations of a "rising Brazil" in BRICS on the one hand and economic overdependence on a declining hegemon on the other (Maihold 2016, 546).

One should note here that internal security problems like crime and violence as well as government corruptions continue to be serious problems in Mexico which in turn further complicate Mexico's preferences. Considering the increasing appeal of the Chinese authoritarian development model and decreasing faith in democracy and human rights among hybrid regimes (Onis 2017). MIKTA's future role in Mexico will be highly dependent on the willingness of Mexican leaders to push for a middle power role in the MIKTA platform.

INDONESIA

After recovering from the 1997 Asian Financial Crisis Indonesia's GDP increased 37% between 2010 and 2016 (Diez and O'Donnel 2017, 15), launching it into one of the top 20 economies in the world. In addition to its growing material capabilities, after the Suharto era, by promoting itself also as a normative actor (Acharya 2014 in Santikajaya 2016, 565), Jakarta became a middle power "punching above its weight" in global governance (Darmosumarto 2013).

Material Capabilities

With a population of more than 250 million, Indonesia is the world's fourth-largest country and the largest in Southeast Asia in terms of area and the size of its economy. Its huge domestic market, abundant natural resources, and economic growth (Brooks 2014) encourage predictions that the Indonesian economy will become the 7th largest in the world by 2030 (Oberman et al. 2012). Its economic growth increased around 5%

---

[4] In his article entitled "Strength of the Weak Ties," Granovetter argues that in social relationships relatively weak ties can actually be quite valuable because they are more likely to provide new opportunities than a strongly embedded tie.

7 EMERGING MIDDLE POWERS (MIKTA) IN GLOBAL POLITICAL ECONOMY ... 173

Table 7.4 Indonesia's economic outlook (2000–2017)

	2000	2017	% Change
Population total (Millions)	211.54	263.99	25
GNI (current US dollar, billions)	122.45	934.37	663
GNI per capita (current US dollar)	580	3540	510
Human Development Index (World Rank)	109	116	6
GDP (current US dollar, billions)	165.02	1015.54	515
GDP growth (annual %)	4.9	5.1	4
Inflation GDP deflator (annual %)	20	4.2	−79
Unemployment (% labor force)	6.08	4.18	−31
Exports of goods and services (% of GDP)	41	20	−51
Imports of goods and services (% of GDP)	30	19	−37
Military expenditure (% of GDP)	0.7	0.8	14
High technology export (% of manufactured exports)	16	6	−63
Foreign Direct Investments (Millions)	−4550	21.465	572
Official development assistance received (US dollar millions)	1663.4	−112.1	−107

Source World Development Indicators database, World Bank; UN Human Development reports 2000; 2017

on average since the last decade (see Table 7.4). Today, Indonesia is the 16th biggest economy in the world. Indonesia's exports and imports are largely dependent on China (see Table 7.8). However, despite its economic growth, its place on the Human Development Index has declined (Table 7.4) and income inequality, corruption, and infrastructure problems not only destabilize its economic growth trajectory but also deter foreign investment from coming into the country.

As Table 7.1 shows, among MIKTA countries Indonesia holds the weakest material capabilities (see also Gök and Karadeniz 2018).

Ideational Preferences

Under the leadership of President Susilo Bambang Yudhoyono (2004–2014) and President Joko Widodo (2014–present), Indonesia has shown its willingness to become a more influential player in the world as a middle power. Indonesian policymakers began officially using the term middle power during Yudhoyono's second term (2009–2014) and incorporated it into the official mid-term development plan during Joko

174   G. OĞUZ GÖK AND R. F. KARADENIZ

Widodo's presidency (2014–2019) (Faysal 2018, 11).[5] Jakarta consolidated its place as a middle power in the global governance through four main role conceptions: "regional leadership, a voice for developing countries, an advocate of democracy, and bridge-builder" (Faysal 2018, 11) and increased its voice on issues such as sustainable development, disarmament, climate change, poverty, financial assistance for less developed countries, and peacekeeping.[6]

Indonesia has acted as an agenda-setter and bridge builder between developed and developing nations by proposing a global partnership for development (A/61/PV.18) in the fields of agricultural and rural infrastructure reform (A/61/PV.14). It is declared that Indonesia vowed to no longer "depend on just a few industrialized nations to solve the world's economic problems" (A/64/PV.13) and proposed a Global Expenditure Support Fund (GESF) at the G-20 platform, placing infrastructure financing as a top G-20 agenda item (Santikajaya 2016, 573–574).

Indonesia underlines the importance of multilateralism and good governance in the economic and security order and presents itself as a "contributor to global partnership, global peace and security, and global prosperity" (A/72/PV.13). For instance, it has increased its contribution to UN Peacekeeping Operations throughout the 2000s (Hutabarat 2014, 186) aimed during Joko Widodo's presidency among the top ten contributing countries (Wiharta 2016) and took its seat as a non-permanent member of the United Nations Security Council for the fifth time in the 2019–2020 period (Gnanasagaran 2018).

Under Yudhoyono's presidency, Indonesia used its regional leadership role in ASEAN to pursue its middle power status at the global level (Fealy and White 2016). It wanted to establish an institutionalized connection between its neighbors and various global platforms and has pursued a regional leadership style of "accommodative leadership"

---

[5] With Faysal's words, "*according to the strategic plan for the Ministry of Foreign Affairs, Indonesia's foreign policy will be directed to enhance Indonesia's global role as a middle power and to position Indonesia as a regional power with selective global involvement by giving priority to issues directly related to Indonesia's national interests.*" Moch Kerim Faysal, "Middle Power, Status-Seeking, and Role Conceptions: The Cases of Indonesia and South Korea," *Australian Journal of International Affairs*, Vol. 78, No. 4, 2018, p. 11.

[6] Please refer to various Statements by Indonesian Officials in the UN General Assembly between 2000 and 2017.

(Santikajaya 2016, 569, 571, and 586). However, recent years have seen debate over whether ASEAN will continue being a cornerstone in Indonesia's foreign policy (Sukma 2009). Newly established informal forums such as the G-20 and MIKTA therefore provide new institutionalized connections venues for Jakarta.

MIKTA for Indonesia: Remedy for Behavioral Limitations?

The emergence of MIKTA became an opportunity for Jakarta to "intensify its economic diplomacy and financial cooperation" (Çolakoğlu 2016, 279). President Joko Widodo devoted its government's energy more to the domestic issues of endemic corruption and sustainable economic growth to deal with both poverty and unemployment ("Opening Indonesia", 2014) and hence gave priority to "economic diplomacy" to increase Indonesian exports and attract investment (Fealy and White 2016, 98) in line with his aims to improve infrastructure and make fiscal reforms (Rajah 2018). At this point, Jakarta's relations with China become important due to its trade dependency on China. Jakarta joined the Asian Investment Bank in 2016 (Parameswaran 2016) and since the introduction of the Chinese Belt and Road Initiative in 2013, its investments to Indonesia increased significantly, with five contracts worth $23.3 billion signed as part of the initiative (Aisyah 2018). In order to balance its trade and investment dependency on China, MIKTA also offers Jakarta unique opportunities.

Today policymakers place greater value to the MIKTA platform due to the country's increasingly apparent financial insecurity (Bharat 2018) and inclusion among the fragile five economies (Kuepper 2018).[7] Therefore, under Indonesia's MIKTA leadership in 2018, Jakarta gave priority to the economy and declared its chairmanship theme to be counterterrorism, peacekeeping, and creative economy. Indonesia views MIKTA as an innovative platform for a mutual partnership between MIKTA member states and external members and thus defined MIKTA's agenda as

---

[7] "The 'Fragile Five' is a term developed by a Morgan Stanley financial analyst in 2013 to describe emerging market economies that are too dependent on unreliable foreign investment to finance their growths and are chosen according to six factors: current account balance, FX reserves to external debt ratio, foreign holdings of government bonds, U.S. dollar debt, inflation, and real rate differential." Justin Kuepper, "Five Emerging Markets Overly Dependent on Foreign Investment," *The Balance*, September 30, 2018.

176 G. OĞUZ GÖK AND R. F. KARADENIZ

"Fostering Creative Economy and Contributing to Global Peace" (Xinhuanet 2017). With the term creative economy, Jakarta underlines the importance of the value of start-ups, innovation, and creativity and envisages the potential of MIKTA in enhancing the creative economy with its total population of 500 million, GDP of more than 5.9 trillion USD, economic growth averaging 4%, and large youth population (*The President Post* 2018). How MIKTA will be effective in providing tools to realize its changing perceptions of itself and world order remains to be seen. In light of weak institutionalized capacity of MIKTA, for the time being, the platform provides a status for Indonesia rather than remedy for its middle power limitations.

SOUTH KOREA

South Korea is accepted in the literature as a middle power in terms of its material factors. Today it is 12th largest economy in the G-20. Yet despite its powerful material capabilities as seen in Table 7.5, South Korean officials' narratives also support the view that South Korea is pressured by the imperatives of its regional security concerns and military

Table 7.5 South Korea's economic outlook (2000–2017)

	2000	2017	% Change
Population total (Millions)	47.01	51	8
GNI (current US dollar, billions)	504.94	1460.49	189
GNI per capita (current US dollar)	10,740	28,380	164
Human Development Index (World Rank)	31	22	−29
GDP (current US dollar, billions)	561.63	1530.75	173
GDP growth (annual %)	8.9	3.1	−65
Inflation GDP deflator (annual %)	1.1	2.3	109
Unemployment (% labour force)	4.42	3.73	−16
Exports of goods and services (% of GDP)	35	43	23
Imports of goods and services (% of GDP)	33	38	15
Military expenditure (% of GDP)	2.5	2.6	4
High technology export (% of manufactured exports)	35	27	−23
Foreign Direct Investments (Millions)	11,509	17,053	48
Official development assistance received (US dollar millions)	−55	0	100

Source World Development Indicators database, World Bank; UN Human Development reports 2000; 2017

alliance with the USA in formulating its diplomatic posture and identifying itself as a middle power.[8]

Material Capabilities

South Korea's economic development is described as the Miracle on the Han River, symbolizing its development success story as the transformation of one of the poorest countries in the world with a GDP per capita of $158 in 1960 to one of $29,742 in four decades.[9] South Korea's economy has grown by an average of 7% annually (Noland 2014). The country became a member of the OECD in 1996 and its membership has been described as its "successful graduation from the Third World" (Pirie 1998, 1). In 2010, South Korea became a Development Assistance Committee member and changed its international status from aid recipient country to donor country. In the same year, it became the first Asian country and the first non-G-7 member to host a G-20 summit (Noland 2014). Chaebols,[10] or large family-owned conglomerates, play

---

[8] South Korea operates in a complex geopolitical situation due to the division of the Korean peninsula, North Korean's nuclear weapons program, and the unstable East Asian security context involving three permanent members of the UN Security Council (China, the US, and Russia) and four nuclear powers. In addition, relations with the USA are the main determinant of defining South Korea's international identity. Sung-Mi Kim, *South Korea's Middle Power Diplomacy: Changes and Challenges*, Chatham House Asia Programme, June 2016, Research Paper, p. 11 and Yul Sohn, *Searching For a New Identity: South Korea's Middle Power Diplomacy*, Policy Brief No: 212, December 2015, p. 3.

[9] The World Bank Data, https://data.worldbank.org/indicator/NY.GDP.PCAP.CD?end=1960&locations=KR-GH-JP&start=1960&view=bar (current US dollars).

[10] After the Korean war, export-led economic growth became a postwar national strategy of authoritarian developmentalism. South Korea's initial rapid growth was created by both political authoritarianism and extensive state intervention in the economy. The governments were in control of economic development process and acted together with major family owned mega conglomerates called as *chaebols*. These favored firms enjoyed trade preferences and monopoly rights, among other favors like massive amounts of capital through subsidies and low-interest-rate loans extended by the government. The privileged status of chaebols continues today as firms like Hyundai, Samsung, and Lotte dominate the most profitable industries without any real restrictions. Marcus Noland, "Six Markets to Watch: South Korea," *Foreign Affairs*, January/February 2014; Andrew O'Neil, "South Korea as a Middle Power: Global Ambitions and Looming Challenges," in Scott Synder (Ed.), *Middle-Power Korea: Contributions to the Global Agenda*. New York: Council on Foreign Relations, 2015; and Liberty Smith, "Antitrust Activism for a More Inclusive Economy," *The Peninsula*, January 16, 2019, http://blog.keia.org/2019/01/9491/.

an important role in the country's economy (Smith 2019).[11] China and USA are the major trading partners (see Table 7.8). In terms of material capabilities, it ranks second within MIKTA countries (Table 7.1).

Ideational Preferences

The middle power rhetoric of Seoul policymakers was officially first adopted to Korean foreign policy during the Lee Myung-bak presidency (2008–2013) (John 2015, 39 in Watson 2016, 11) and the diplomatic discourse was based on the concept of a Global Korea (Watson 2011), signaling the will of the country to increase its international influence through its "networking capacity" (Sohn 2015, 4). South Korea has described its position in the system "as a balancer, a hub, a middle power" (Kim 2016, 2) and, took on "convener, conciliator and agenda-setter roles in international negotiations and multilateral platforms such as the G20, Nuclear Security Summit and OECD" (Kim 2016, 5). In the wake of its G20 presidency, then President Lee openly declared that "the world can be split into two groups. One group sets global rules, the other follows" and that South Korea had "successfully transformed itself from a passive follower into an active agenda-setter" (Oliver and Pilling 2010).

South Korea's middle power diplomacy gave priority to issues of international development, environment, and economic cooperation. In the aftermath of the 2008 global financial crisis, a financial development model was proposed for developing countries "as a country transferred from aid recipient to a donor country" (A/64/PV.3). Seoul showed its willingness to act as a bridge between developed and developing countries in development issues by sharing its experiences of economic transformation (A/70/PV.13) and with its growing economic capacity.[12] Korea took the lead in adopting the Seoul Development Consensus for Shared Growth, which is now one of the G20's top priorities (Flake and Wang 2017, 32).

---

[11] Today top ten chaebols control 67.8% of Korean GDP and 62% of its exports. Liberty Smith, "Antitrust Activism for a More Inclusive Economy," *The Peninsula*, January 16, 2019, http://blog.keia.org/2019/01/9491/.

[12] In 2015, Korea provided USD 1.9 billion in net Official Development Assistance (ODA) and within MIKTA comes second after Australia in 2015 with its 3.2 billion spending based on OECD Data. http://www.oecd.org/dac/korea.htm.

During Park Geun-hye's presidency (2013–2018), the diplomatic rhetoric was less focused on the middle power narrative so as not to provoke any misunderstanding on the part of the USA and China that it was dissociating itself from the US alliance (Kim 2016, 7). The diplomatic discourse also refrained from directly referring to middle power terminology in the UN platform. It only used the term in MIKTA-related activities and international development programs (Kim 2016, 5). Therefore, in the mid-2000s while developing a Global Korea concept, Korea's freedom of action in the region is limited because of its security concerns.

MIKTA for South Korea: Remedy for Behavioral Limitations?

MIKTA's emergence as a platform of cooperation of middle powers provided South Korea with the opportunity to "guarantee its middle power role" (Çolakoğlu 2016, 280) on an ideational level. The alliance emerged as the Global Korea initiative was launched and became an effective tool to enhance the perception of South Korea as a middle power. Yet, South Korea faces two main challenges in sustaining its middle power ambitions: uncertain relations with its northern neighbor North Korea and the challenge of balancing the influence of great powers, the USA and China in particular (O'Neil 2015, 87). The shrimp among the whales perception reflects the idea of South Korea as wedged between larger powers due to its geopolitical situation throughout history (O'Neil 2015, 78). This creates limitations on acting with its middle power capacity.

In addressing these issues, Korea has actively sought to utilize its diplomatic options, from its security alliance with the USA and its increasingly close economic relationship with China, to its leadership in the UN and a range of other venues such as the ASEAN Regional Forum (Flake and Wang 2017, 23). In this context, Korea has welcomed the articulation of middle power diplomacy and determined that MIKTA can provide it with new opportunities in its foreign policy. It is asserted that Seoul needs to attract significant international support to deal with the continuing challenges from North Korea and that MIKTA will be a useful platform for this aim (O'Neil 2015, 76). Korea hosted a very active chairmanship year of MIKTA in 2015 and expanded the scope of both official and related MIKTA meetings (Flake and Wang 2017, 23).

180   G. OĞUZ GÖK AND R. F. KARADENIZ

It remains to be seen how Seoul decides the ways in which MIKTA matches with President Moon's main foreign policy aims of reconciliation with North Korea, diversification of diplomatic interaction, and promotion of democracy at home (Robertson 2018).

TURKEY

Until the 2000s, the Turkish economy was largely identified with recurring crises, low economic growth rates, high government debts, and a controversial relationship with international institutions, such as the IMF. Turkey was defined as a developing country. In fact, Turkey experienced two major economic transformations until the 2000s. First, Turkey rearranged its economic policy framework and reform agenda according to economic liberalization principles under Prime Minister Turgut Ozal during the 1980s. Secondly, after the financial crisis in 2001, Turkey developed a robust regulatory state compatible with the fundamental principles of the post-Washington Consensus (Eken and Schadler 2012). In the 2000s, economic factors started to occupy an increasingly important place in the making of Turkey's foreign policy (Kutlay 2011, 71). It has also resorted to a variety of economic instruments. The business world has become a primary driver of foreign policy by underlying the importance of economic interdependence conceptualized by Kemal Kirisci as "trading state" (Kirişçi 2009, 43).

After the 2010s Turkey began to formulate a proactive industrial strategy, which embodies what Onis asserts the elements of a "neo-developmentalist" turn. Development cooperation activities emerged as one of the most active foreign policy instruments to facilitate Turkey's involvement in various regions (Gök and Dal 2017). In the 2017 Global Humanitarian Assistance Report, with respect to the international contributions of government donors, Turkey was the second-largest donor of humanitarian assistance following the USA.[13] Turkey has also been an active supporter of the Least Developed Countries (LDCs) at the UN during the 2000s. Ankara hosted the fourth LDC conference in Istanbul 2011. Most recently, Ankara supported the establishment of the UN Technology Bank for LDCs in Turkey in cooperation with the Scientific and Technological Research Council of Turkey (TUBITAK). Turkey

---

[13]2017 Humanitarian Assistance Report. Available at http://devinit.org/wp-content/uploads/2017/06/GHA-Report-2017-Full-report.pdf.

7 EMERGING MIDDLE POWERS (MIKTA) IN GLOBAL POLITICAL ECONOMY ... 181

Table 7.6 Turkey's economic outlook (2000–2017)

	2000	2017	% Change
Population total (millions)	63.24	80.75	28
GNI (current US dollar, billions)	271.62	882.85	225
GNI per capita (current US dollar)	4300	10,930	154
Human Development Index (World Rank)	85	64	−25
GDP (current US dollar, billions)	272.98	851.1	212
GDP growth (annual %)	6.6	7.4	12
Inflation GDP deflator (annual %)	49.3	10.8	−78
Unemployment (% labor force)	6.49	11.26	73
Exports of goods and services (% of GDP)	19	25	32
Imports of goods and services (% of GDP)	23	29	26
Military expenditure (% of GDP)	3.7	2.2	−41
High technology export (% of manufactured exports)	5	2	−60
Foreign Direct Investments (Millions)	982	10,889	1009
Official development assistance received (US dollar millions)	328.6	3613	1000

is thus likely to continue its support for LDC issues for the foreseeable future and MIKTA could support one strand of LDC support under Turkish leadership (Haug 2017, 133).

Material Capabilities

According to OECD economic survey analyses, relative to other OECD countries, Turkey has achieved substantial gains in well-being in the 2000s. These improvements were largely generated by the employment and income gains from strong growth, thanks to the effective macroeconomic stabilization and EU-convergence reforms of the 2000s, which benefitted all social groups.[14] Turkey has become the 17th largest economy in the last two decades (see Table 7.6).

Among MIKTA countries, Turkey ranks 5th in GDP analysis, 2nd in terms of military spending, 3rd in terms of HDI, and again 3rd in terms of population size. However, with respect to the percentage change between the years of 2000–2017, Turkey ranks 2nd in terms of GDP (Table 7.2). These indicators put Turkey into a "middle position"

[14] http://www.oecd.org/eco/surveys/Turkey-2018-OECD-economic-survey-overview.pdf.

in terms of material factors among other MIKTA countries. As yet, the Turkish economy has been confronted with serious challenges especially in the 2010s accompanied with a relative decreasing faith in the rule of law and democratization. Onis and Kutlay (2016) assert that these factors in the political sphere spilled over and had negative repercussions in the economic realm in the 2010s. In this regard, unemployment and inflation rates of Turkey continue to be the highest among other MIKTA countries (Table 7.1). Yet, Ankara's increasing material prosperity and economic growth, especially in the first half of 2000s, have provided favorable domestic conditions for Turkey to adopt new roles in regional and global politics.

Ideational Preferences

Turkish rulers usually refrained from using "middle power" to describe Turkey's status and identity in international arena in the 2000s, yet Ankara began to act as an efficient and responsible actor in global governance and follow niche diplomacy, especially in the field of humanitarian issues such as development cooperation in the 2000s (Dal and Kurşun 2016, 618). Ankara took every opportunity to emphasize the crucial role of an effective UN in the preservation of international order as well as Turkey's commitment to strengthening multilateralism in its own foreign policy. Accordingly, one of the defining aspects of Turkish foreign policy has become the increased role of development cooperation programs as evidenced by an expanding international aid budget in the 2000s (Gök and Karadeniz 2018).

Although the core narrative of Turkey's agenda in the global governance institutions like the UN focused on the reform issue, its quest for institutional design and equal representation was also reflected in its World Bank and IMF (IMF) policies where Turkey sought a greater voting power (Dal and Kurşun 2018). Yet, Turkey's democratic middle power identity could be argued to have challenged by the rise of authoritarian Russia–China axis as a new developmental model in a time of decreasing appeal of the liberal "West" in general. In other words, as a country whose democracy is still a "work in progress," Turkey could be conceptualized among what Onis calls "hybrid regimes" (Onis 2017) in which increasing attractiveness of China–Russia axis could pose a challenge toward the future of Turkey's middle powermanship.

MIKTA for Turkey: A Remedy for Behavioral Limitations?

MIKTA offers significant opportunities in rebranding Turkey's global status by defining itself as a democratic emerging middle power state fully committed to the multilateralism in international relations (Çolakoğlu 2015). Today there is a growing consciousness among Turkish scholars' of analyzing Turkey's middle power role, but there is still lack of comprehensive strategy for the operationalization of its MIKTA strategy as well as middle power identity among MIKTA. One should note here that it is not only Turkey that faces substantial constraints on the thickening of MIKTA identity, other MIKTA countries also face a wide number of distractions, internal instabilities, and conflicting identities (Cooper 2016, 529–530).

In fact, there are some concrete signs demonstrating an increasing willingness on the side of Turkey to further push MIKTA in global governance in the last couple of years. Most recently, on October 25, 2018, Turkey talked on behalf of MIKTA countries at United Nations Security Council open debate on Women, Peace, and Security (WPS). Turkey underlined the importance of the fulfillment of the 2030 Agenda for Sustainable Development emphasizing that all MIKTA countries are members of the Group of Friends of Gender Parity (S/PV.8382).[15] Most recently the establishment of the UN Technology Bank for LDCs once again illustrates Turkey's adopted niche area as well as willingness to support for LDC and development issues. Thus, MIKTA could also be a creative partnership that might support the wider title of "sustainable development" under Turkish leadership.

AUSTRALIA

"We come to the relationship with China as a dependable economic partner, a constructive participant in regional affairs, one of the world's oldest democracies, a good international citizen, and a close ally of the United States. None of these dimensions will change."

(The Asian Century White Paper, 2012, 229)[16]

---

[15] https://digitallibrary.un.org/record/1651125/files/S_PV-8382-EN.pdf.

[16] *The Asian Century White Paper.* Available at https://espas.secure.europarl.europa.eu/orbis/sites/default/files/generated/document/en/Australia%20in%20the%20Asian%20century_White%20Paper.pdf.

184   G. OĞUZ GÖK AND R. F. KARADENIZ

Australia stands apart from the other MIKTA states as a traditional middle power in terms of its economic development and long-lasting commitment to liberal democratic norms (Onis and Kutlay 2016). Australia actively identifies and aligns its economic policies with the neoliberal market-oriented norms of global governance since 1945. The emergence of alternatives such as the Chinese model or the so-called Beijing Consensus in the last two decades poses challenges to the capabilities, preferences, and limitations of Australia's role in global governance (Beeson 2013, 197).

Material Capabilities

Australia sits aside from other MIKTA states in the sense that it is considered an advanced economy, enjoying relatively high living standards, represents almost the entirety of a continent and does not share any territorial boundary, giving Canberra a sense of isolation and strength. Yet, the country itself is thinly populated with approximately 21.5 million people (Scott 2013, 115) (Table 7.7).

Among MIKTA states, Australia ranks 5th in Population, 2nd in GDP, 1st in GNP, 1st in HDI, and 2nd in the share of Military Expenditures

Table 7.7   Australia's economic outlook (2000–2017)

	2000	2017	% Change
Population total (millions)	19.15	24.6	28
GNI (current US dollar, billions)	404.3	1263.49	213
GNI per capita (current US dollar)	21,110	51,360	143
Human Development Index (World Rank)	4	3	−25
GDP (current US dollar, billions)	415.03	1323.42	219
GDP growth (annual %)	3.9	2	−49
Inflation GDP deflator (annual %)	2.6	3.7	42
Unemployment (% labor force)	6.28	5.59	−11
Exports of goods and services (% of GDP)	19	21	11
Imports of goods and services (% of GDP)	22	21	−5
Military expenditure (% of GDP)	1.8	2	11
High technology export (% of manufactured exports)	15	15	0
Foreign Direct Investments (millions)	14,893	45,100	203
Official development assistance received (US dollar millions)	0	0	0

Source World Development Indicators database, World Bank; UN Human Development reports 2000 and 2017 (https://databank.worldbank.org/data/views/reports)

(Table 7.1). Australia's economic ties to China has been one of the main denominators of its political economy in the 2000s. China accounted for approximately 33% of Australia's main merchandise exports and 22% of import destinations in 2017 (Table 7.8).

Ideational Preferences

Australia is a traditional middle power by virtue of its demonstrated capabilities, distinctive middle power behavior, and long-standing identity as a middle power since the end of the World War II (Wilkins 2014, 163). Australia is a significant contributor to the UN at both financial and personnel levels. The key purpose of this contribution is presented by Canberra to strengthen the liberal global and regional order.[17] However, Australia faces certain limitations toward its middle power diplomacy at both the regional and the global levels as a result of the crises of neoliberalism (Scott 2013, 119).

In fact, Australia is quite sensitive to the changing global order and norms of international governance. Declining US hegemony accompanied with the eroding status of the Washington Consensus could affect the future of the Australia-backed neoliberal paradigm in East Asia (Beeson 2013, 201). Talk of an emerging Asian century in the last decade points away from Australia (White 2010, 68). Australia and the USA share common neoliberal political economy norms and have been allies since the 1950s, allowing Canberra to maintain low levels of defense spending. In a long-awaited Foreign Policy White Paper in late November 2017, Canberra announced that it will maintain an open economy.[18] However, Australia has yet to develop a clear strategy on how it will deal with transformations in the global political economy.

MIKTA for Australia: Remedy for Behavioral Limitations?

Australia faces certain behavioral limitations as a middle power on both the regional and the global level. In the Asia-Pacific, it faces an

---

[17] Speech by Foreign Minister Kevin Rudd, "Australia's Foreign Policy Interests in the Middle East." Available at https://foreignminister.gov.au/speeches/Pages/2011/kr_sp_110222.aspx?ministerid=2.

[18] *2017 Foreign Policy White Paper*, Australia. https://www.fpwhitepaper.gov.au/file/2651/download?token=Q5CYuX29.

Table 7.8   MIKTA countries trade statistics

Mexico		Indonesia		Korea		Australia		Turkey	
	Import (%)		Import (%)		Import (%)		Import (%)		Import (%)
USA	46.39	China	21.93	China	20.45	China	21.87	China	10
China	17.64	Singapore	10.8	Japan	11.52	USA	10.34	Germany	9.11
Japan	4.33	Japan	8.98	USA	10.64	Japan	7.23	Russia	8.35
	Export (%)		Export (%)		Export (%)		Export (%)		Export (%)
USA	79.95	China	13.65	China	24.78	China	29.59	Germany	9.63
Canada	2.78	US	10.55	USA	12	Unspecified	15.04	UK	6.12
Germany	1.7	Japan	10.54	Vietnam	8.32	Japan	10.43	UAE	5.85

Source Australian Government, Department of Foreign Affairs and Trade

7 EMERGING MIDDLE POWERS (MIKTA) IN GLOBAL POLITICAL ECONOMY ...

uncomfortable situation where it has both strong economic links with China and equally close security links with the USA (Scott 2013, 119). It may have more in common with other middle powers and more to gain from acting collaboratively in platforms like MIKTA (Beeson 2013, 205).

Canberra has already put considerable weight on promoting MIKTA as a new middle power partnership since its inception. Yet, the future of Australia's middle power role through MIKTA appears problematic. In the 2017 White Paper, MIKTA was mentioned in only one line in the Global Cooperation section and was not referred to in active terms (Rimmer 2018, 166). Whether or not Australia continues to push for MIKTA will be crucial for the future of this minilateral partnership in the global political economy.

CONCLUSION

As an informal middle power grouping established after the 2008 financial crisis, MIKTA with its members' having different material capabilities and ideational roles became a new interregional platform for cooperation. Yet, despite its members' willingness to increase their common voices as "middle powers" on niche diplomacy areas such as "health governance, infrastructure promotion, disaster risk management and humanitarian assistance" (MIKTA Vision 2015), MIKTA, for the time being, is far from providing remedies for its members' behavioral limitations. This is both from its organizational weaknesses and member countries' focusing on their domestic problems in recent years.

The main weakness of MIKTA relates to its organizational structure. Unlike BRICS which has its own development bank, independent financial capacity, MIKTA has difficulty in coordinating policies of member countries and paving way for concrete results in defined niche areas. Among others, so far, "sustainable development" issues have played a relatively prominent role in MIKTA's general rhetoric; however, it is suggested that in order MIKTA to develop an influential and more effective model of global governance for middle powers, it needs to focus on three possible modes of action, "creative regionalism, problem solver and bridge builder" as in line with their potential niche diplomacy areas (Çolakoğlu 2018).

In order to do this, in other words, to be more effective model of global governance for middle powers, the members should devote more energy to MIKTA. Yet, since 2016, all MIKTA members have experienced various domestic political problems and diverted their attention away from the institutional empowerment of cooperation within the MIKTA partnership. For instance, South Korea struggled with corruption cases and a change in the presidency while Turkey dealt with difficulties in its Middle East foreign policy and the domestic political repercussions of the failed July 2016 coup d'état. Federal elections in Australia in 2016 and regional and upcoming state elections in Indonesia, together with the impacts of US President Trump's anti-Mexico campaigns in Mexico, forced policymakers in these nations to devote their energy to domestic politics (Çolakoğlu 2017). The domestic developments and the "willingness" in forming effective coalition-buildings around MIKTA platform will determine member states' capacity to turn this new initiative to a "role model" of a more constructive minilateral emerging middle power collaboration.

REFERENCES

Official Documents

Statement by Mr. Hassan Wirajuda, Minister for Foreign Affairs of the Republic of Indonesia, UN General Assembly, 14th Plenary Session, 27 September 2008. Available at http://www.un.org/ga/search/view_doc.asp?symbol=A/63/PV.14.

Statement by Mr. Susilo Bambang Yudhoyono, President of the Republic of Indonesia, UN General Assembly, 3rd Plenary Meeting, High-level Plenary Meeting of the General Assembly: separate meeting on Financing for Development, 14 September 2005. Available at http://www.un.org/ga/search/view_doc.asp?symbol=A/60/PV.3.

Statement by Mr. Hassan Wirajuda, Minister for Foreign Affairs of the Republic of Indonesia, UN General Assembly, 13th Plenary Session (p. 12), 29 September 2009. Available at: http://www.un.org/ga/search/view_doc.asp?symbol=A/64/PV.13.

Statement by Mr. Lee Myung-bak, President of the Republic of Korea, UN General Assembly, 3rd Plenary Session, 23 September 2009. Available at http://www.un.org/ga/search/view_doc.asp?symbol=A/64/PV.3.

Statement by Mr. Lee Myung-bak, President of the Republic of Korea, UN General Assembly, 13th Plenary Meeting (p. 28), 28 September 2015. Available at http://www.un.org/ga/search/view_doc.asp?symbol=A/70/PV.13.

Statement by Mr. Hassan Wirajuda, Minister for Foreign Affairs, UN General Assembly, 18th Plenary Session (pp. 17–18), 25 September 2006. Available at http://www.un.org/ga/search/view_doc.asp?symbol=A/61/PV.18.

Australian Government, Department of Foreign Affairs and Trade. Available at https://dfat.gov.au/trade/resources/Documents/.

The World Bank Data. https://data.worldbank.org/indicator/NY.GDP.PCAP.CD?end=1960&locations=KR-GH-JP&start=1960&view=bar (current US dollars).

Books and Articles

Acharya, A. (2014). *Indonesia Matters: Asia's Emerging Democratic Power*. Singapore: World Scientific.

Acharya, A. (2017). After Liberal Hegemony: The Advent of a Multiplex World Order. *Ethics and International Affairs, 31*(3), 278–282.

Aisyah, R. (2018, May 2). Chinese Investments Trending in Indonesia. *The Jakarta Post*.

Beeson, M. (2013). Symposium: Australia–US Economic Relations and the Regional Balance of Power: The Decline of US Economic Power and Influence: Implications for Australian Foreign Policy. *Australian Journal of Political Science, 48*(2), 197–207.

Bharat, S. S. (2018). China's Belt and Road Initiative and Indonesia's Financial Security. *The Jakarta Post*. Available at https://www.thejakartapost.com/academia/2018/10/01/chinas-belt-and-road-initiative-and-indonesias-financial-security.html.

Brooks, K. (2014, January/February). Six Markets to Watch: Indonesia and the Philippines. *Foreign Affairs*.

Carr, A. (2014). Is Australia a Middle Power? A Systemic Impact Approach. *Australian Journal of International Affairs, 68*(1), 70–84.

Chapnick, A. (1999). The Middle Power. *Canadian Foreign Policy Journal, 7*(2), 73–82. https://doi.org/10.1080/11926422.1999.9673212.

Çolakoğlu, S. (2015). MIKTA: A Global Vision of Middle Powers. *Expert Opinion*. Available at https://scolakoglu.blogspot.com/2015/03/?view=classic.

Çolakoğlu, S. (2016). The Role of MIKTA in Global Governance: Assessments & Shortcomings. *Korea Observer, 47*(2), 267–268.

Çolakoğlu, S. (2017, July 11). Is MIKTA Sustainable as a Middle Power Grouping in Global Governance? *Diplo*. Available at https://www.diplomacy.edu/blog/mikta-sustainable-middle-power-grouping-global-governance.

Çolakoğlu, S. (2018). Has MIKTA Augmented the Global Governance Role of Middle Powers? *The Global*. Available at https://theglobal.blog/2018/05/29/has-mikta-augmented-the-global-governance-role-of-middle-powers/.

Cooper, A. (2015). MIKTA and the Global Projection of Middle Powers: Toward a Summit of Their Own? *Global Summitry, 1*(1), 95–114.

Cooper, A. (2016). Testing Middle Power's Collective Action in a World of Diffuse Power. *International Journal, 71*(4), 529–544.

190 G. OĞUZ GÖK AND R. F. KARADENIZ

Creative Multilateralism: Stronger Collaboration for All. (2018, March). *OECD Observer*. Available at http://oecdobserver.org/news/fullstory.php/aid/6025/Creative_multilateralism:_Stronger_collaboration_for_all.html.

Dal, E. P., & Kurşun, A. M. (2016). Assessing Turkey's Middle Power Foreign Policy in MIKTA: Goals, Means, and Impact. *International Journal, 71*(4), 608–629.

Dal, E. P., & Kurşun, A. M. (2018). Turkey's Global Governance Strategies at the UN Compared to the BRICS (2008–2014): Clarifying the Motivation—Contribution Nexus. *Third World Quarterly, 39*(9), 1770–1790.

Darmosumarto, S. (2013). *Indonesia and the Asia-Pacific: Opportunities and Challenges for Middle Power Diplomacy* (German Marshall Fund Policy Brief). Available at http://www.gmfus.org/publications/indonesia-and-asia-pacific-opportunities-and-challenges-middle-power-diplomacy.

Diez, S. G., & O'Donnel, D. (2017). *G-20 in Figures, Summit of the G-20 States in Hamburg 2017*. Federal Statistics Office of Germany. Available at https://www.destatis.de/EN/Publications/Specialized/InternationalData/G20/G20InFigures0000168179004.pdf?__blob=publicationFile.

Eken, S., & Schadler, S. (2012). *Turkey 2000–2010: A Decade of Transition Discussions Among Experts*. Foreign Economic Relations Board of Turkey (DEIK) Turkey in Global Economy Series. Available at https://www.tepav.org.tr/upload/mce/haberler/2013/_a_decade_of_transitiondiscussions_among_experts.pdf.

Engin, B., & Baba, G. (2015). MIKTA: A Functioning Product of "New" Middle Power-Ism. *Uluslararası Hukuk ve Politika*, Cilt 11, Sayı, *42*, 1–40.

Faysal, M. K. (2018). Middle Power, Status-Seeking, and Role Conceptions: The Cases of Indonesia and South Korea. *Australian Journal of International Affairs, 78*(4), 1–22. Available at http://www.mochfaisalkarim.com/uploads/1/0/2/9/102975644/middle_power_status_seeking_and_role_conceptions_the_cases_of_indonesia_and_south_korea.pdf.

Fealy, G., & White, H. (2016). Indonesia's 'Great Power' Aspirations: A Critical View. *Asia & the Pacific Policy Studies, 3*(1), 92–100.

Flake, G., & Wang, X. (2017). *MIKTA: The Search for a Strategic Rationale*. Perth USAsia Center. Available at http://perthusasia.edu.au/getattachment/2e8754a3-8e76-4e16-ade3-18bcf9f6131e/PUAC-MIKTA-Flake-Xu-Jan2017.pdf.aspx?lang=en-AU.

Fukuyama, F. (2006). The Paradox of International Action. *The American Interest, 1*(3). Available at https://www.the-americaninterest.com/v/francisfukuyama/.

Gnanasagaran, A. (2018). What Would Indonesia Bring to the UN Security Council? *The ASEAN Post*. Available at https://theaseanpost.com/article/what-would-indonesia-bring-un-security-council.

Gök, G. O., & Dal, E. P. (2017). Understanding Turkey's Emerging 'Civilian' Foreign Policy Role in the 2000s Through Development Cooperation in the Africa Region. *Perceptions: Journal of International Affairs, 2*, 67–100.

Gök, G. O., & Karadeniz, R. F. (2018). Analyzing 'T' in MIKTA: Turkey's Changing Middle Power Role in the United Nations. In *Middle Powers in Global Governance* (pp. 133–163). New York: Palgrave.

Granovetter, M. S. (1973). The Strength of Weak Ties. *American Journal of Sociology, 78*(6), 1360–1380.

Haug, S. (2017). Exploring 'Constructive Engagement': MIKTA and Global Development. *Rising Powers Quarterly, 2*(4), 61–68.

Heenam, C. (2015). Middle Power Cooperation and Related Issues in the G20. In M. Jongryn (Ed.), *MIKTA, Middle Powers, and New Dynamics of Global Governance* (pp. 69–85). New York: Palgrave Macmillan.

Higgott, R. (2018). Globalism, Populism, and the Limits of Global Economic Governance. *Journal of Inter-regional Studies: Regional and Global Perspectives, 1*. Available at https://www.waseda.jp/inst/oris/assets/uploads/2018/03/JIRS-Vol.1_Invited-Article_Higgott.pdf.

Hutabarat, L. F. (2014). Indonesian Participation in the UN Peacekeeping as an Instrument of Foreign Policy: Challenges and Opportunities. *Global & Strategis, 8*(2), 183–199.

Ikenberry, J. (2016). American Leadership May Be in Crisis, But the World Order Is Not. *Foreign Affairs*.

Indonesia Launches Theme of MIKTA Group for 2018. Xinhuanet, December 19, 2017.

Indonesia Promotes Startup as a Motor of Creative Economy in MIKTA. *The President Post*, September 21, 2018. Available at http://en.presidentpost.id/2018/09/21/indonesia-promotes-startup-as-a-motor-of-creative-economy-in-mikta/.

John, J. V. (2015). Globalization, National Identity and Foreign Policy: Understanding Global Korea. *Copenhagen Journal of Asian Studies, 33*(2), 38–57.

Joint Communique of the 5th MIKTA Foreign Ministers' Meeting. (2015, May 22). South Korea Republic, Department of Ministry of Foreign Affairs Web Site, Seoul. http://www.mofa.go.kr/eng/brd/m_5676/view.do?seq=315255&srchFr=&srchTo=&srchWord=Foreign&srchTp=0&multi_itm_seq=0&itm_seq_1=0&itm_seq_2=0&company_cd=&company_nm=&page=89&titleNm=.

Jordaan, E. (2003). The Concept of a Middle Power in International Relations: Distinguishing Between Emerging and Traditional Middle Powers. *Politikon, 30*(1), 165–181.

Jordaan, E. (2017). The Emerging Middle Power Concept: Time to Say Goodbye? *South African Journal of International Affairs, 24*(3), 395–412.

Kim, S.-M. (2016). *South Korea's Middle Power Diplomacy: Changes and Challenges, Chatham House Asia Programme*. Available at https://www.chathamhouse.org/publication/south-koreas-middle-power-diplomacy-changes-and-challenges.

Kirişçi, K. (2009). The Transformation of Turkish Foreign Policy: The Rise of the Trading State. *New Perspectives on Turkey, 40*, 29–56.

Kuepper, J. (2018). *Five Emerging Markets Overly Dependent on Foreign Investment*. The Balance. Available at https://www.thebalance.com/what-are-the-fragile-five-1978880.

Kutlay, M. (2011). Economy as the 'Practical Hand' of 'New Turkish Foreign Policy': A Political Economy Explanation. *Insight Turkey, 13*(1), 67–88.

Maihold, G. (2016). Mexico: A Leader in Search of Like-Minded Peers. *International Journal, 71*(4), 545–562.

Naim, M. (2009). Minilateralism. *Foreign Policy*. Available at http://foreignpolicy.com/2009/06/21/minilateralism/.

Narlikar, A., & Kumar, R. (2012). From *Pax Americana* to *Pax Mosaica*: Bargaining Over a New Economic Order. *The Political Quarterly, 83*(2). https://doi.org/10.1111/j.1467-923X.2012.02294.x.

Noland, Marcus. (2014, January/February). Six Markets to Watch: South Korea. *Foreign Affairs*.

Nolte, D. (2010). How to Compare Regional Powers: Analytical Concepts and Research Topics. *Review of International Studies, 36*(4), 881–890.

Nye, J. S. (2017, January/February). 'Will the Liberal Order Survive?' The History of an Idea. *Foreign Affairs*.

Oberman, R., Dobbs, R., Budiman, A., Thompson, F., & Rossé, M. (2012). *The Archipelago Economy: Unleashing Indonesia's Potential*. McKinsey Global Institute. Available at https://www.mckinsey.com/featured-insights/asia-pacific/the-archipelago-economy.

Oliver, C., & Pilling, D. (2010). Into Position. *Financial Times*. Available at http://www.petracm.com/pdf/Into_Position_-_FT.pdf.

O'Neil, A. (2015). South Korea as a Middle Power: Global Ambitions and Looming Challenges. In S. Synder (Ed.), *Middle-Power Korea: Contributions to the Global Agenda* (pp. 75–89). New York: Council on Foreign Relations.

O'Neill, J. (2011). *The Growth Map: Economic Opportunities in BRICS and Beyond*. New York: Penguin Groups.

Onis, Z. (2017). The Age of Anxiety: The Crisis of Liberal Democracy in a Post-hegemonic Global Order. *The International Spectator, 52*(3), 18–35.

Onis, Z., & Kutlay, M. (2016). The Dynamics of Emerging Middle-Power Influence in Regional and Global Governance: The Paradoxical Case of Turkey. *Australian Journal of International Affairs, 71*(2), 164–183.

Opening Indonesia: A Conversation with Joko Widodo. *Foreign Affairs*, November/December 2014.

Parameswaran, P. (2016). *Indonesia and China's AIIB, The Diplomat*. Available Online at https://thediplomat.com/2016/07/indonesia-and-chinas-aiib/.

Patrick, S. M., & Feng, A. (2018). *MIKTA in the Middle: A Little-Known Multilateral Group Turns Five*. Council on Foreign Relations. Available at https://www.cfr.org/blog/mikta-middle-little-known-multilateral-group-turns-five.

Pellicer, O. (2006). *New Powers for Global Change? Mexico—A Reluctant Middle Power?* (Friedrich-Ebert-Stiftung, Briefing Paper, 2006). Available at https://library.fes.de/pdf-files/iez/global/50417.pdf.

Pirie, I. (1998). *The Korean Developmental State from Dirigisme to Neo-liberalism.* New York: Routledge.

Rajah, R. (2018). *Indonesia's Economy: Between Growth and Stability.* Lowy Institute Report. Available at https://www.lowyinstitute.org/publications/indonesia-economy-between-growth-and-stability.

Rimmer, S. H. (2018). What Does the New Australian Foreign Policy White Paper Mean for MIKTA? In S. Pramono et al. *MIKTA: Current Situation and the Way Forward* (pp. 163–176). Jakarta: Policy Analysis and Development Agency, Ministry of Foreign Affairs, Republic of Indonesia.

Robertson, J. (2017). Middle-Power Definitions: Confusion Reigns Supreme. *Australian Journal of International Affairs, 71*(4), 355–370.

Robertson, J. (2018). South Korea's Quandary: What to Do About MIKTA? *The Interpreter.* https://www.lowyinstitute.org/the-interpreter/south-korea-quandary-what-do-about-mikta.

Ruddyard, F. A. (2018). Navigating MIKTA Under Indonesia's Coordinatorship and Beyond. In S. Pramono et al. *MIKTA: Current Situation and The Way Forward* (pp. 11–17). Jakarta: Policy Analysis and Development Agency, Ministry of Foreign Affairs, Republic of Indonesia.

Santikajaya, A. (2016). Walking the Middle Path: The Characteristics of Indonesia's Rise. *International Journal, 71*(4), 563–586.

Schiavon, J. A. (2018). Mexico and MIKTA: Behaving as Entrepreneurial Powers. In S. Pramono et al. *MIKTA: Current Situation and the Way Forward* (pp. 35–51). Jakarta: Policy Analysis and Development Agency, Ministry of Foreign Affairs, Republic of Indonesia.

Scott, D. (2013). Australia as a Middle Power: Ambiguities of Role and Identity. *Seton Hall Journal of Diplomacy and International Relations, 14*(2), 111–122.

Smith, L. (2019). Antitrust Activism for a More Inclusive Economy. *The Peninsula.* Available at http://blog.keia.org/2019/01/9491/.

Sohn, Y. (2015). *Searching for a New Identity: South Korea's Middle Power Diplomacy* (Policy Brief, No. 212).

Sukma, R. (2009). Indonesia Needs a Post-ASEAN Foreign Policy. *The Jakarta Post.* http://www.thejakartapost.com/news/2009/06/30/indonesia-needs-a-postasean-foreign-policy.html.

Vezirgiannidou, S.-E. (2013). The United States and Rising Powers in a Post-hegemonic Global Order. *International Affairs, 89*(3), 635–651.

Watson, I. (2011). Global Korea: Foreign Aid and National Interests in an Age of Globalization. *Contemporary Politics, 17*(1), 53–69.

Watson, I. (2016). From Middle Power to Pivot Power? Korea's Strategic Shifts. *Asian International Studies Review, 17*(2). https://doi.org/10.1111/pafo.12079.

Weiss, T. (2016). Rising Powers, Global Governance, and the United Nations. *Rising Powers Quarterly, 1*(2), 7–19.

White, H. (2010). Power Shift: Australia's Future Between Washington and Beijing. *Quarterly Essay, 39*, 68. In Scott, D. 2013. Australia as a Middle Power: Ambiguities of Role and Identity. *Seton Hall Journal of Diplomacy and International Relations, 14*(2), 111–122.

Wiharta, S. (2016). *Peacekeeping Contributor Profile: Indonesia, Providing for Peacekeeping.* Available at http://providingforpeacekeeping.org/2016/02/05/peacekeeping-contributor-profile-indonesia.

Wilkins, T. S. (2014). Australia: A Traditional Middle Power Faces the Asian Century. In B. Gilley and A. O'Neill (Eds.), *Middle Powers and the Rise of China.* Georgetown University Press.

Wright, T. (2015). Middle Powers and the Multilateral Pivot. In M. Jongryn (Ed.), *MIKTA, Middle Powers, and New Dynamics of Global Governance: The G20's Evolving Agenda.* Asan-Palgrave Macmillan Series. New York: Palgrave.

Xing, L. (2016). The Nexus Between the Emerging Powers and the Existing World Order: Interdependent Hegemony. Op-Ed, *Rising Powers in Global Governance.* Available at http://risingpowersproject.com/nexus-emerging-powers-existing-world-order-interdependent-hegemony/.

CHAPTER 8

The Determinants of Turkish Foreign Aid: An Empirical Analysis

Hakan Mehmetcik and Sercan Pekel

INTRODUCTION

The main research question of this chapter is to understand the political economy of Turkish foreign aid program and interests/ motivations in the formulation and implementation of Turkish foreign aid policies in order to synthesize Turkish humanitarian and development assistance. In this chapter, we analyze the bilateral aid allocation of Turkey between 2004 and 2013 upon the data from Turkish Cooperation and Coordination Agency (TIKA). We chose the period between 2004 and 2013 because that decade serves as a unique period where we can both left out the effect of the Syrian crisis and bring in all other meaningful determinants in Turkish foreign aid allocation. Since the mid-1980s, Turkey has been providing humanitarian and

H. Mehmetcik (✉)
Department of International Relations, Marmara University,
Istanbul, Turkey

S. Pekel
Department of Political Science and International Relations,
Marmara University, Istanbul, Turkey

© The Author(s) 2020
E. Parlar Dal (ed.), *Turkey's Political Economy
in the 21st Century*, International Political Economy Series,
https://doi.org/10.1007/978-3-030-27632-4_8

195

development assistance, but it was quite minimal before 2004. From 2004 to 2013, aid volumes rose from \$190.16 million to \$3.04 billion with a nearly 16-fold increase. That increase fundamentally stems from a growing economy, a more international outlook, but particularly a series of disasters on its doorstep, the gravest of which is the Syrian crisis. In this sense, 2013 is important because since then the Syrian crisis creates a situation where Turkey's humanitarian and development assistance aid is even boosted more with the unfolding civil war in Syria. According to UNCHR, as of August 2017, there are 3,622,366 Syrian refugees in Turkey ('Situation Syria Regional Refugee Response' 2018). Under the Organization for Economic Cooperation and Development (OECD)'s Development Assistance Committee (DAC) criteria, countries receiving refugees may only report assistance to refugees as humanitarian assistance during the first 12 months of the refugees' stay. As refugee inflow from Syria has continued incessantly, Turkey's reported humanitarian assistance volume has sharply increased since 2013. The overall amount might drop in the future depending on the course of the civil war in Syria. In this sense, leaving out the time frame after 2013 helps us to provide a dataset with adjusted figures in terms of taking out the effects of the Syrian crisis on the interests and motivations behind Turkish foreign aid policies.

Nevertheless, the Turkish case is important and worth to analyze for several reasons. First, some foreign aid recipients have become a major donor by undertaking their own aid programs over the last decades. One such country is Turkey. From humble beginnings, Turkey has made its way to becoming a major player in the field. Turkey is now the largest donor of humanitarian and development aid in terms of GDP per capita and the largest non-Western and non-DAC donor. In addition, Turkey has initiated numerous global activities such as hosting the first-ever World Humanitarian Summit in Istanbul on 23–24 May 2016, which is another indicator that shows Turkey's high profile in the field. It is also clear that foreign aid has become an essential foreign policy tool in Turkey's toolbox along with other soft-power instruments.

Second, as an emerging donor, studying Turkey would inform us about many cross-national trends among emerging donors and fast-changing foreign aid regimes. Retrospectively, foreign aid and development assistance are always important foreign policy tools (Black 1968). Yet, it has been dominated by a group of wealthy Western countries like the US, Sweden, Germany, Canada, France, Belgium and so forth. That profile has been changing as rising/emerging powers gain more weight in the world economy and politics since the early third-millenniums. Nevertheless, many of the emerging donors have been transformed from a recipient to a donor country over the last decade as their economic capacities have increased. Countries such as China, India, Brazil and Turkey have become important actors operating in the field, which also has led to significant changes in the institutional and political frameworks of traditional foreign aid structures and practices. What is important here is that although there are a large number of scientific studies already done in this area for Western countries (traditional donors), such comparative studies on development aid for and among emerging powers (emerging donors) are limited. There are also a number of studies that deal with the recipient side of the story by focusing on various issues like welfare effects, the effects on economic growth, the level of corruption, etc. Contrary to the large literature mentioned, this paper deals with the donor side of the equation by studying the motivating factors behind Turkey's aid policies.

As such, the paper informs us about the many potential self-interests at play in the execution of Turkish aid policy by identifying different independent variables. In the existing literature, there are several explanations stemming from the logic of economics, politics and humanitarianism behind the motivation of Turkey's increasing humanitarian and development assistance. Many of these studies are descriptive. Thus, Turkey's rapidly increasing humanitarian and development assistance merits further study. Departing from this lacuna, in this chapter, we provide an empirical analysis on the interests and motivations in formulation and implementation of Turkish foreign aid policies. To this end, we survey through the volume of aid flows from Turkey to 143 countries around the world. In addition, we use five sets of independent variables drawing upon 19 different interval and nominal type of vectors. The determinant factors we use here are the following: (i) Economic grounds; (ii) Humanitarian grounds; (iii) Political grounds; (iv) Cultural/religious grounds; and (v) Regional outlook.

BACKGROUND: FOREIGN AID PUZZLE

Many countries conduct their foreign aid policies with different means and purposes. It is sometimes a tool and sometimes a goal in the foreign policy agendas (Brautigam 1992; Eberstadt 1989).

There are several reasons that incentivize foreign aids at social/humanitarian, economic/trade and political/security domains. At social and humanitarian level, most of the countries have direct external assistance in order to reduce the effects of wars, tragedies and crises. In many places, there exist a large number of people largely depending on foreign aids for basic humanitarian needs. Many different types of aids are designed to address urgent humanitarian needs of the people. Developed countries also contribute to developing economies through development assistance programs to ease/solve technical and institutional problems that have significant ramifications at the local level such as poor governance and accountability. Transfer of technical skills and manpower is one of the most needed types of help in many parts of the underdeveloped world. Foreign aid may also be an important driver of institutional and political reforms in recipient countries as aids are generally attached to certain conditions. In the economic/trade dimension, it appears that many countries opt for foreign aid and development assistance programs as an initiator of stronger economic/trade relations with the recipient countries. There are studies analyzing the relationship between aid and trade flows from donors to recipients to address if donors use aid to increase their trade with recipients (Osei et al. 2004). On the political/security domain, throughout much of the Cold War, foreign aid was one of the strategic imperative that was inherent in the containment of communism (Omoruyi 2017, 1) whereas in the post-Cold War period, foreign aid has often been justified in terms of assisting development and economic growth to reduce the possibility that the poor and uneducated in the recipient countries could easily be drafted into terrorist organizations (Pevehouse and Goldstein 2016, 208). Developed countries also try to contribute to developing economies through foreign aid to solve problems that have negative externalities toward them such as immigration (Clements 2016). However, foreign aid decision emerges as an amalgam of economic, political and altruistic intents at social/humanitarian, economic/trade and political/security domains, and it is not always easy to apprehend why and how a country or a group of country provide aid and development assistance (Mehmetcik 2018, 255).

At the theoretical front, the differences are in parallel with the practice of foreign aid. Realists assume that aid policies are fundamentally driven by the economic-political-military strategic importance of recipient states (Black 1968). Idealists, on the other hand, argue that aid policies are driven by altruistic approaches in order to find solutions for Third-World economic and development problems and as such humanitarian needs are the cornerstone of many foreign aid programs (Lumsdaine 1993). Neo-Marxists underline that donor states' economic calculation and interests play the major role in implementation of foreign aid programs. Accordingly, foreign aid programs are just a tool of the capitalist exploitation in widening the economic disparities between North and South (Wood 1986, 18).

These broad theoretical and practical assumptions oversimplify the general foreign aid puzzle, yet they are illustrative for us to understand the merits of a particular foreign aid program. However, the scarcity of reliable data on new donors remains a major obstacle to studying their motives systematically. Foreign aid puzzle is also not explained properly by quantitative and case study-oriented literature that seeks to scrutinize the motivations behind many foreign aid programs. Departing from here, this study tries to explain the Turkish foreign aid motivations with empirically rich and data-based analyses.

TURKEY AS A RISING DONOR

Turkey launched its first foreign aid program on June 5, 1985, with an aid package of 10 billion dollar to Sahel countries. In the mid- and late 1980s and 1990s, Turkey operationalized its foreign aid policies to support its foreign policy objectives in Caucasus and Central Asia at the height of the collapse of the Soviet Union when then-president Turgut Özal attempted to form a cultural and political unification of all Turkic-speaking people (Kulaklikaya and Nurdun 2010). Even Turkey's humanitarian and development assistance coordination office, TIKA, was established at that time (Fidan and Nurdun 2008; Kardaş and Erdağ 2012). Even though this aspiration failed, Turkey has continued its engagement with the region through development assistance and conflict mediation (Aras and Fidan 2009). However, Turkey stayed as an aid recipient country. As a matter of fact, the process of transforming from an aid recipient to a major donor country in Turkish case is a very recent happening. Turkey's growing contributions are in line with the broader global trends which reflect the transformation of world economy as well. As the share of the emerging powers has increased in global governance, foreign aid structure has been changing accordingly. Turkey's growing visibility in this field, first and foremost, is another indicator of the emerging donors phenomenon (Kardaş 2013).

The emerging donors such as China, India, Brazil and Turkey have turned foreign aid concept into a complex and contested area (Woods 2005, 2008). Among these emerging donors, Turkey is an important one for several reasons. First, Turkey merits study as one of the major emerging donors. According to recent reports on the foreign aids, Turkey is the largest emerging aid donor in 2018 ('Global Humanitarian Assistance Report 2018' 2018), and the most charitable nation in 2017 ('Humanitarian Aid Spending Makes Turkey Most Charitable Country' 2018). Turkey's emergency and humanitarian aid fund were around $3.2 billion in 2015, $6.4 billion in 2016 and surpassed $8 billion in 2017, corresponding to 0.85% of the country's national dividend. With these numbers, Turkey is leading the world in humanitarian aid (Erbay 2018). For Turkey, humanitarian aid and development assistance are an instrument of expanding its influence and position as a global actor (Tol 2015). Recently, Turkey's instruments such as public diplomacy, peace operations, economic interdependence, mediation, cultural diplomacy and foreign aid to support its foreign policy have dramatically expanded. This paved the way for more institutionalized Turkish foreign aid structure, which makes it more sustainable and more reliable. Second, Turkey offers a new model of foreign aid bringing a multi-track approach that promotes involvement of non-state actors and resolute and fast implementation (Aras 2018; Dal et al. 2018; Osman 2018; Inanc 2017). Even though it is sometimes criticized as a collaborative relationship between the government and like-minded civil society representing a division in the larger Turkish society (Binder 2014), it is important to note that Turkey's foreign aid practice with its capacity to create tangible results merits scientific analysis.

As a rising power, Turkey has been clearly seeking to use foreign aid in its quest for becoming a regional power by establishing linkages beyond its immediate geography (Bayer and Keyman 2012). In many regions of interest, Turkey's counterparts are developing societies or countries that are undergoing major social, economic or political transformation, and Turkey's provision of development assistance in various forms has facilitated the deepening of ties to different countries. As such, foreign aid is generally characterized as an entry ticket to Africa or a tool to expand Turkish influence in Balkans and Caucasus. It is also argued that Turkey's foreign aid program is humanitarian in its essence. Turkey as a middle power willingly makes the humanitarian and development aid a niche diplomacy area by branding itself as a humanitarian/virtuous power

('Virtuous Power New Defense Doctrine: Turkish President' 2012). In line with this fact, Turkey has been conducting a "humanitarian foreign policy" in which a group of governmental bodies such as TIKA, AFAD, Kızılay, YTB and Turkish Airlines along with civilian humanitarian NGOs cooperates and coordinates a "humanitarian approach" through a targeted foreign aid program. Therefore, Turkey characterizes its foreign aid policies as principally driven by humanitarian purposes while many regards that the ideational and economic expansions are the backbone of Turkey's growing influence in regional and global affairs (Binder 2014). Turkey provides humanitarian and development aid to expand its "humanitarian/virtuous power" brand. Indeed, in some cases, Turkey's assistance is motivated by purely global humanitarian considerations. Yet, like many other middle powers, Turkey also tries to find a niche diplomacy area (Cooper 1997; Solomon 1999) in its foreign aid programs by focusing on carefully selected individual countries and regions (Sucuoglu and Stearns 2016). Turkey's contributions to development aid is also a form of ethical criticism to the international order on the grounds that it fails to distribute justice. It is also reflecting the globalist emphasis on Turkey's foreign policy. There are studies indicating that domestic politics has had a large impact on Turkey's priorities in giving aid (Kavakli 2018) while some other studies refer to Turkish ethnicity in the allocation of the Turkish aid. The literature also suggests that Turkey's religious affinities and cultural, historical roots are important drivers of its foreign aid program (Antonopoulos et al. 2017; Piccio 2014). As such, Turkey's foreign aid policies are generally characterized as ideologically (solidarity among Muslim or solidarity with Turks or solidarity with past-Ottoman geographies) driven. Indeed, Turkey pursues projects and works toward the goal of reconnecting with the Ottoman-Turkish cultural zone (Kardaş 2013). Turkey also began to give more economic aid to trade partners and more humanitarian aid to Muslim nations. Therefore, it is sometimes referred as Turkey substituted "Islamic solidarity first" in the 2000s instead of the former "Turkic ethnic solidarity" in 1990s as the main motto of its foreign aid scheme. The logic of economics has an important explanatory power in any foreign aid program. In this sense, economic interests are also integral beside the motivations of humanitarian needs, ideology and politics. So, it is often argued that Turkey seeks new markets for its growing economy and foreign aid serves an entry ticket in this respect. While this new focus on trade ties makes Turkey more similar to traditional donors, the growing role of cultural ties sets Turkey apart (Kavakli 2018). Kulaklikaya and Nurdun (2010) put forward a different dimension against the above-mentioned literature and argue that policy performance of the recipient states is also a determinant factor in Turkish foreign aid (Kulaklikaya and Nurdun 2010).

Given the lack of empirical evidence, this highly confusing set of explanations needs to be revised/resolved by empirical research. Based on a statistical analysis derived from numbers of empirical data, this study addresses this issue in decrypting the motivations behind Turkey's foreign aid policies focusing on the political economy of the Turkish state.

Research Design

Which motivation has been the greatest important in the foreign aid allocation decision in Turkish case? What is the role of economy? These are the main research questions of these chapters. In parallel with the research questions, our dependent variable is Turkey's foreign aid program. For these purposes, we use TIKA statistics on Turkey's foreign aid flows (including both private and official aid flows) to 143 countries between 2004 and 2013. We draw upon five sets of independent variables: (i) Economic grounds; (ii) Humanitarian grounds; (iii) Political grounds; (iv) Cultural/religious grounds; and (v) Regional outlook. Our conclusion is that the Turkish foreign aid is a function of these five individual motivations. These independent variables are constructed from both interval and nominal data to test for the possible determinants of Turkish foreign aid policies. These interval and nominal data are the following:

1. **Economic grounds**: Serve as the first independent variables set. Foreign aid is generally acknowledged for its positive effect on economic relations promoting trade and well-being between donor and recipient. Investigating the link between foreign aid and donor's exports is the first-hand approach here. According to Zarzoso et al. in the long term, there is a positive effect between the donor's exports and every aid dollar spent on bilateral aid (Martínez-Zarzoso et al. 2010). Our aim is here similar, to measure the linkage between Turkish aid and increase in the trade relations between Turkey and aid receiving countries. Thus, the economic ground as an independent determinant is operationalized by utilizing three measures:

I. The recipient GDP per capita[1] (GDP),
II. The level of Turkish export[2] to the recipient country (EXP).
III. Existence of Free Trade Agreement (FTA).

In short, if the economic motivations drive the foreign aid program, the coefficients of these variables should be significant. If the economic potential of the recipient country is operative, one should expect to find foreign aid directed disproportionately toward those countries.

2. **Humanitarian grounds**: Foreign aid is most often rhetorically portrayed by policymakers as humanitarian efforts to alleviate the sufferings of those in distress. Turkey is not an exception in this regard. In many studies and political rhetoric, Turkey's foreign aid program is characterized as one that is principally driven by humanitarian grounds. If it is the case, foreign aid has to address the vital needs of the underdeveloped regions in the world. To find out whether Turkey's aid program motivated by humanitarian need, i.e., altruistic, we use two widely adopted measures:
I. the daily food supply measured as kcal/capita (DFS),
II. the average life expectancy[3] of the recipient country (LE).

In brief, if the humanitarian needs of the recipient country are operative, one should expect to find foreign aid directed toward those countries with highest humanitarian needs which means that the countries in question have populations with an inability to access the required food (energy) to sustain their lives. The other measure is also relevant to the first one. Combined with other factors inhibiting a decent life, the average lifecycle span in a country diminishes as the humanitarian problems deepen.

3. **Political grounds**: In the relevant literature, it is widely accepted that foreign aid is also used as a tool to enhance the national interests of donor. Especially realist approaches argue that foreign aid plays an important bargaining chip in the hands of the great

---

[1] Derived World Bank National Accounts Data.

[2] Derived from Turkish Statistical Institute Data.

[3] Derived from WHO Data (Life Expectancy of both sexes at birth).

powers. For instance, there are studies that link the UN-voting cohesion and foreign aid (*The Economist* 2016; Rose 2018) or support to a major foreign policy initiative such as US war on terror (Moss et al. 2005). When it comes to Turkey, its foreign policy strategizes different countries for different reasons. To find out whether Turkey's foreign aid plays such a role, we operationalize four measures:

   I. Existence of formal defense and military agreements (DMA),
   II. The number of visits made by Turkish leaders (NOV),
   III. The number of agreements between the countries (NOA),
   IV. Existence of TIKA Office (EOT).

In brief, the existence of such relations would be an indication of political (security) thinking behind foreign aid program. If the strategic importance of the recipient country on political grounds is operative, one should expect to find foreign aid directed disproportionately toward those countries.

4. **Cultural/religious grounds**: Cultural/religious factors are generally acknowledged as significant in foreign aid allocation. Former colonies, religious sensitivities, historical roots, and ethnic affinities are such variables. In order to carve this out for Turkey, we look at three measures:

   I. The number of Muslims as a percentage of recipient population (POM),
   II. Whether or not it is former Ottoman territory as a dummy variable (OT),
   III. Turkish origin as a dummy variable (TR).

If the cultural/political similarities of the recipient country are operative, one should expect to find foreign aid flows leaning more on those countries with Muslim identity, Turkish ethnicity or former Ottoman territories.

5. **Regional outlook**: Regional identification (REG) plays a potential role as a determinant of aid flows. This regional division has been taken from TIKA's own categories. Therefore, the question of regional favoritism is interrogated by applying a regional code with the following labels:

I. South and Central Asia (reference variable),
II. Europe,
III. North Sahara,
IV. South Sahara,
V. North and Central America,
VI. South America,
VII. Far East,
VIII. Oceania,
IX. Middle East.

STATISTICAL ANALYSIS AND DISCUSSION

A Panel data has been compiled based on the variables discussed above and analyzed in R. 143 countries with a ten-year span ($N>T$) allowed us to observe the determinants of Turkish foreign aid in a linear regression model. The diagnostics tests directed us for a random effects model which takes into account time-invariant variables like existence of TIKA Office and individual random effects on error terms. Hence, the equation with all the variables involved is;

$$TFA_{it} = lnGDP_{it} + lnEXP_{it} + lnDFS_{it} + LE_{it} + FTA_i + NOA_{it} + NOV_{it} + EOT_i + DMA_i + TR_{it} + POM_i + OT_i + REG_i + v_{it}$$

The output of the regression model indicates the results of the analysis in a nutshell (Table 8.1).

Our statistical analysis reveals that different combinations of motivations influence Turkish foreign aid policies. The findings reinforce some of the existing assumptions while some are challenged. The first and foremost insight to be gained from the statistical inquiry is the importance of economic potential/relations vis-a-vis the recipient country. Both of the regressors under the set of economic independent variables—except free trade agreements—have positive coefficients with a decent level of significance. Turkish foreign aid seems to flow toward the countries that are more active and stronger in terms of their GDP and toward the countries that Turkey seeks to export its goods/services. The two-track approach toward economic potential determinant set is solidified based on these results. Not only the ability to export and accumulate surplus is important for Turkey, but also the prospective economic potential of the recipient country to strengthen economic ties is accounted for in the foreign aid decision-making process. That finding

Table 8.1 The determinants of Turkish foreign aid

	b	p
(Intercept)	−2.5504	0.9764
Economic ground		
GDP (log)	2.1415	0.0470**
Level of Turkish Export (log)	0.6312	0.0830***
Free Trade Agreement	−1.3394	0.5305
Humanitarian ground		
Daily food supply/log (kcal/capita)	2.2371	0.8578
Life expectancy at birth	−0.4002	0.0196**
Political ground		
Number of total agreements	0.0136	0.9547
Number of visits	4.0173	0.0246**
TIKA Office	6.2070	0.0010***
Defense and military agreement	−3.3656	0.3393
Cultural/religious ground		
Percentage of Muslims	0.0496	0.0217**
Former Ottoman Territory	−5.3383	0.3465
Regional outlook		
Europe	−11.1041	0.0198**
North Sahara	−7.1076	0.7497
South Sahara	−20.7859	< 0.0001***
North and Central America	−14.3667	< 0.0001***
South America	−16.3124	< 0.0001***
Far East	−15.1031	< 0.0001***
Oceania	−10.7497	0.0016***
Middle East	−16.3611	0.0012***

***$p < .01$, **$p < .05$, *$p < .1$
F-statistics: 4.22 ($p < 0.01$), $N = 1137$
Note Random Effects Panel Data Regression allows for individual variances and time-invariant regressors. Robust coefficient estimators are presented

confirms the suggestion that Turkey seeks to expand its trade by finding new markets to its goods and services and the foreign aid functions as an entry ticket. The negative coefficient of the existence of free trade agreement between Turkey and the recipient country is understandable given the fact that these agreements are relatively small and do not have trade creation features.

The second set of regressors lean on the critical essence of foreign aid literature and practice. In a normative world order, *aid* naturally should be directed to those in need and the countries should allocate their donations/assistance under humanitarian concerns. Among the well-known indicators regressed here, only the life expectancy variable seems significant. The negative coefficient and strong significance of the variable suggest that Turkey also extends its foreign aid to the countries where the life conditions are relatively worse. As the life expectancy at birth decreases, the amount of Turkish foreign aid increases. That is affirmative for the rhetoric that Turkey's humanitarian and development assistance are inclined on humanitarian grounds. The other argument that should be mentioned, however, is that the countries with critical levels of food supply per capita such as Zambia, Ethiopia or Haiti are ignored while Afghanistan is the exception here and receives substantial amounts of Turkish aid.

Based on the literature presented above, the strategic importance of the aid recipient countries on political grounds is analyzed based on different independent variables. The regression output puts forth an indifference of agreements between Turkey and the recipient country whether it be on security, trade or another subject. Elaborating on this result, one can assume that the recipient countries may be readily involved in a free trade agreement or in a similarly structured trade regime with their past-time colonizers. Similarly, the major powers, extending a security umbrella, would be considered as a safer and traditional bet to bandwagon against the option to opt for Turkey, an emerging but still a middle power in terms of security commitments. These issues may effect the total number of agreements that could be concluded between Turkey and the recipient country. The significant and positively correlated regressors are the number of official high-level visits from Turkey and the existence of TIKA Office in the recipient country in question. As the number of visits between the countries implies the strength and intensity of the relations, this indicator may naturally be considered to vary in accordance with the amount of aid allocated to that specific country. The existence of a TIKA Office within a recipient country is the most significant regressor in our analysis and again the relationship may be argued to be expected in advance. The a priori decision to set up a TIKA base in a country means that Turkey is eager to send remarkable amount of aid to the recipient country and to utilize that aid in an organized way. TIKA Office means more institutionalization in every phase of the aid program which means more systemized utilization, organizational benefits and most importantly more institutionalized procedure to request and allocate funds from Turkey.

Another set of determinants of Turkish aid is cultural and religious similarity between Turkey and the recipient countries. The independent variables employed here are generally indigenous to Turkey; however, they capture the factors to be measured in a sensible way. The only significant variable is the percentage of Muslims living in the recipient country which should be interpreted with caution. While it obviously adds to the assumption that Turkey extends its hand to the Muslim-populated countries more, this finding should be accompanied by the fact that the countries, especially the ones in focus of Turkish aid which will be elaborated below under the regional concerns, are populated with significant numbers of Muslims who are deprived of humanitarian needs with varying degrees. Being a former Ottoman territory is not a significant factor within Turkish aid allocation according to the regression model. This may stem from the fact that the Ottoman frontiers were inconstant and shifting spatially and temporally, especially for specific regions like African territories and for the late periods of its reign.

The linkage between foreign aid amounts and possessing a Turkic origin is another issue that has been tested in a renewed model. As, all the Turkic Republics are also listed in the *South & Central Asia* subregion, these correlated dummy variables (TR vs. REG) were integrated to the model interchangeably. Being a Turkic Republic is not a significant determinant within the overall Turkish foreign aid scheme. This may be explained by the fact that the Turkic Republics have been and are more closely in cooperation with Russia, a historical watchdog in the region on both security and economic terms.

The last independent variable is the region-based categorization of the recipient countries by TIKA. The countries are represented in yearly reports under continental and sub-continental level, if applicable. *Region* variable is the only multi-level factor variable in our regression, and multiple regression models have been computed in order to get a grasp of its effect on the dependent variable. The continent-level models have not provided any meaningful effect; so, sub-continental regions are tested. Each region has been integrated as the reference variable and one of them has stood out as significant in majority of the models.

8 THE DETERMINANTS OF TURKISH FOREIGN AID ...   209

Table 8.2   Top Turkish foreign aid total flows by country (2004–2013)

Country	Aid ($, mil)	Economic	Humanitarian	Political	Cultural religious	Regional
Syrian Arab Republic	1991.09	x	x	x	x	x
Pakistan	922.92			x	x	
Afghanistan	848.46		x	x	x	
Kyrgyzstan	756.35		x	x	x	x
Egypt, Arab Rep.	551.37	x	x	x	x	x
Kazakhstan	489.98	x	x	x	x	x
Somalia	325.08		x	x	x	
Iraq	302.75	x	x	x	x	x
Azerbaijan	287.42	x	x	x	x	x
Palestine	263.65		x	x	x	

The South & Central Asia[4] region, thus, has been selected as the reference level in the model whose output is presented above. As it can be observed, the other regions' significant coefficients are negative which implies a region-based pattern functioning as a subtle determinant for Turkish foreign aid. The top recipients in terms of aid flows from Turkey within the study time period are listed in Table 8.2. It is clear from the table that Afghanistan, Pakistan as well as Kyrgyzstan and Kazakhstan— the Syrian case is different as discussed above and may be ignored for a general overview—are consistently the top benefactors of Turkish foreign aid while distant countries located in Americas or Far East are left out disproportionate of their economic potential or humanitarian needs.

Table 8.2 shows the 10 largest Turkish aid recipient country between 2004 and 2013. From the raw data, we can intuitively suggest that humanitarian, political, cultural and religious interests and motivations drive Turkish aid decision more than economic interests at first glance. However, as our panel data analysis reveals, when you look at the overall picture, Turkish aid decision is also driven by the economic potential of the recipient country for Turkey as well as regional positioning. Overall, Turkish foreign aid allocation depends on a multi-track approach embodying distinct interests and motivations.

[4]The countries in this region are Afghanistan, Armenia, Azerbaijan, Bangladesh, Bhutan, Georgia, India, Kazakhstan, Kyrgyz Republic, Maldives, Myanmar, Nepal, Pakistan, Sri Lanka, Tajikistan, Turkmenistan and Uzbekistan.

Conclusion

With a growing economy, a more international outlook and numerous crisis looming in its immediate geography, Turkey—as one of the major emerging donors—has become an important player in the foreign aid field in the last decade. Even though there are pilings of theoretical and practical assumptions, existing literature is still elusive in understanding the interests and motivations behind emerging donors' foreign aid programs. When it comes to Turkey, due to the lack of empirical analysis, our knowledge is limited. Departing from this fact, the chapter tries to explain the determinants of Turkish foreign aid policies by analyzing the aid allocation of Turkey between 2004 and 2013. To do that, we survey through the aid flows from Turkey to 143 countries in the given time period and statistically analyze it with respect to five sets of independent variables, namely economic, humanitarian, political, cultural/religious grounds and regional outlooks. These independent variables are constructed from both interval and nominal data to test for the determinants of the allocation and implementation of Turkish humanitarian and development assistance.

The main findings of the chapter can be summarized along the dimensions of economic pragmatism, altruism or different types of affinity the part of Turkey. The results signify a conflux of all these grounds argued extensively above with varying degrees and distinct insights. The economic potential of the recipient country for Turkey seems an important factor to extend Turkey's economic interests. That is an expected outcome when the literature on foreign aid on various other donors also puts forward similar findings. The institutional capacity-building of aid management via TIKA Offices in recipient countries and the number of official high-level visits are significant variables determining Turkish foreign aid. The effects of the existence of free trade agreements as well as defense and military agreements are negligible stemming from the emerging power status of Turkey versus a major power in both strands and from the idiosyncratic features of the countries with which Turkey has such ties. The altruistic side of Turkish foreign aid scheme is not undermined as aid flows more to countries with lower life expectancy despite the lack of sufficient aid toward countries with critical food shortage in distant regions. The religious similarity and regional positioning are the last significant determinants of Turkish foreign aid according to our model and this pair holds up the assumption of foreign aid as a function of affinity with Turkey. The insignificance effects of Middle East as a sub-region or reigning over former Ottoman territories are interesting findings which should be tested with more fine-grained hypotheses and analysis in future research.

REFERENCES

Antonopoulos, P., Villar, O., Cottle, D., & Ahmed, A. (2017). Somalia: Turkey's Pivot to Africa in the Context of Growing Inter-Imperialist Rivalries. *Journal of Comparative Politics, 10*(2), 4–18.

Aras, B. (2018, February). Medical Humanitarianism of Turkey's NGOS: A "Turkish Way?" *Alternatives: Global, Local, Political*, 030437541875440. https://doi.org/10.1177/0304375418754404.

Aras, B., & Fidan, H. (2009). Turkey and Eurasia: Frontiers of a New Geographic Imagination. *New Perspectives on Turkey, 40*, 193–215. https://doi.org/10.1017/S0896634600005276.

Bayer, R., & Fuat Keyman, E. (2012). Turkey: An Emerging Hub of Globalization and Internationalist Humanitarian Actor? *Globalizations, 9*(1), 73–90. https://doi.org/10.1080/14747731.2012.627721.

Binder, A. (2014). The Shape and Sustainability of Turkey's Booming Humanitarian Assistance. *International Development Policy | Revue internationale de politique de développement, 5*(5.2). https://doi.org/10.4000/poldev.1741.

Black, L. D. (1968). *Strategy of Foreign Aid* (1st ed.). Princeton, NJ: Van Nostrand Reinhold Inc.

Brautigam, D. (1992). Governance, Economy, and Foreign Aid. *Studies in Comparative International Development, 27*(3), 3–25. https://doi.org/10.1007/BF02687132.

Clements, M. (2016, October 31). Development Aid to Deter Migration Will Do Nothing of the Kind. *Refugees Deeply*. https://www.newsdeeply.com/refugees/community/2016/10/31/development-aid-to-deter-migration-will-do-nothing-of-the-kind.

Cooper, A. F. (1997). *Niche Diplomacy: Middle Powers After the Cold War* (1st ed.). New York, NY: Macmillan.

Dal, E. P., Kurşun, A. M., & Mehmetcik, H. (2018). Decoding Turkey's Institutional Accommodation in the Changing International Order: The UN and G20 Cases. *International Politics*. https://doi.org/10.1057/s41311-018-0153-1.

Eberstadt, N. (1989). *Foreign Aid and American Purpose*. Washington, DC; Lanham, MD: Aei Pr.

Erbay, N. Ö. (2018, December 9). TIKA President Serdar Çam: Turkey Keeps Breaking Records in Humanitarian Aid and Development Assistance. *Daily Sabah.* https://www.dailysabah.com/politics/2018/12/10/tika-president-serdar-cam-turkey-keeps-breaking-records-in-humanitarian-aid-and-development-assistance.

Fidan, H., & Nurdun, R. (2008). Turkey's Role in the Global Development Assistance Community: The Case of TIKA (Turkish International Cooperation and Development Agency). *Journal of Southern Europe and the Balkans, 10*(1), 93–111. https://doi.org/10.1080/14613190801895888.

'Global Humanitarian Assistance Report 2018'. (2018, June 19). *Development Initiatives* (Blog). http://devinit.org/post/global-humanitarian-assistance-report-2018/.

'Humanitarian Aid Spending Makes Turkey Most Charitable Country'. (2018, June 20). *Daily Sabah.* https://www.dailysabah.com/turkey/2018/06/21/humanitarian-aid-spending-makes-turkey-most-charitable-country.

Inanc, B. (2017, November 27). Turkish Aid Model Combines Humanitarian Relief with Development Aid. *Hürriyet Daily News.* http://www.hurriyetdailynews.com/turkish-aid-model-combines-humanitarian-relief-with-development-aid-123073.

Kardaş, Ş. (2013, February 4). *Turkey's Development Assistance Policy: How to Make Sense of the New Guy on the Block.* Ankara: The German Marshall Fund of the United States.

Kardaş, T., & Erdağ, R. (2012). Bir Dış Politika Aracı Olarak TİKA. *Akademik İncelemeler Dergisi, 7*(1). https://doi.org/10.17550/aid.93873.

Kavakli, K. C. (2018). Domestic Politics and the Motives of Emerging Donors: Evidence from Turkish Foreign Aid. *Political Research Quarterly, 71*(3), 614–627, 1065912917750783.

Kulaklikaya, M., & Nurdun, R. (2010). Turkey as a New Player in Development Cooperation. *Insight Turkey Ankara, 12*(4), 131–145.

Lumsdaine, D. H. (1993). *Moral Vision in International Politics: The Foreign Aid Regime, 1949–1989 by David Halloran Lumsdaine.* Princeton: Princeton University Press.

Martínez-Zarzoso, I., Nowak-Lehmann, F. D., & Klasen, S. (2010). *The Economic Benefits of Giving Aid in Terms of Donors Exports.* 28 Proceedings of the German Development Economics Conference, Hannover 2010. Verein für Socialpolitik, Research Committee Development Economics. https://ideas.repec.org/p/zbw/gdec10/28.html.

Mehmetcik, H. (2018). Turkey and India in the Context of Foreign Aid to Africa. In E. P. Dal (Ed.), *Middle Powers in Global Governance: The Rise of Turkey.* Cham: Palgrave Macmillan. www.palgrave.com/la/book/9783319723648.

Moss, T. J., Roodman, D., & Standley, S. (2005, July 18). *The Global War on Terror and US Development Assistance: USAID Allocation by Country, 1998–2005.* https://doi.org/10.2139/ssrn.1114154.

Omoruyi, L. O. (2017). *Contending Theories on Development Aid: Post-Cold War Evidence from Africa*. London and New York: Routledge.

Osei, R., Morrissey, O., & Lloyd, T. (2004). The Nature of Aid and Trade Relationships. *The European Journal of Development Research, 16*(2), 354–374. https://doi.org/10.1080/0957881042000220859.

Osman, J. (2018, April 2). How Turkey Is Winning Hearts and Minds in Somalia. *New Internationalist*. https://newint.org/features/2018/04/01/turkey-somalia-humanitarian-aid.

Pevehouse, J. C. W., & Goldstein, J. S. (2016). *International Relations* (11th ed.). Boston: Pearson.

Piccio, L. (2014, February 17). Post-Arab Spring, Turkey Flexes Its Foreign Aid Muscle. *Devex*. https://www.devex.com/news/sponsored/post-arab-spring-turkey-flexes-its-foreign-aid-muscle-82871.

Rose, S. (2018, May 4). *Linking US Foreign Aid to UN Votes: What Are the Implications?* Center For Global Development. https://www.cgdev.org/publication/linking-us-foreign-aid-un-votes-what-are-implications.

'Situation Syria Regional Refugee Response'. (2018, December 31). *UNHCR: Syria Regional Refugee Response*. https://data2.unhcr.org/en/situations/syria.

Solomon, R. (1999). Niche Diplomacy: Middle Powers After the Cold War. *Political Science, 50*(2), 312–314.

Sucuoglu, G., & Stearns, J. (2016). *Turkey in Somalia: Shifting Paradigms of Aid*. South African Institute of International Affairs. http://cic.nyu.edu/sites/default/files/publication_turkey_somalia_shifting_paradigms_aid_sucouglu_stearns_final_web.pdf.

The Economist. (2016, April 16). *A Despot's Guide to Foreign Aid*. https://www.economist.com/middle-east-and-africa/2016/04/16/a-despots-guide-to-foreign-aid.

Tol, G. (2015, September 30). 'The Rise of Turkish Foreign Aid'. *News. Middle East Institute*. https://www.mei.edu/publications/rise-turkish-foreign-aid.

'Virtuous Power New Defense Doctrine: Turkish President'. (2012, April 6). *Hürriyet Daily News*. http://www.hurriyetdailynews.com/virtuous-power-new-defense-doctrine-turkish-president.aspx?pageID=238&nID=17784&NewsCatID=338.

Wood, R. E. (1986). *From Marshall Plan to Debt Crisis: Foreign Aid and Development Choices in the World Economy*. Complete Numbers Starting with 1 (1st ed.). Berkeley: University of California Press.

Woods, N. (2005). The Shifting Politics of Foreign Aid. *International Affairs (Royal Institute of International Affairs 1944–), 81*(2), 393–409.

Woods, N. (2008). Whose Aid? Whose Influence? China, Emerging Donors and the Silent Revolution in Development Assistance. *International Affairs, 84*(6), 1205–1221. https://doi.org/10.1111/j.1468-2346.2008.00765.x.

PART III

Geographical Diversification of Turkey's Political Economy

CHAPTER 9

The Political Economy of Turkey's Integration into the MENA Economy

Imad El-Anis

Introduction

In the early post-Cold War era, space opened-up for renewed Turkish interest in the Middle East and North Africa (MENA) and Central Asia—regions in which the Ottoman Empire, as the predecessor to the modern Turkish Republic, had played a pivotal role. Through the 1990s and early 2000s, Turkey's political, economic and sociocultural links with the MENA, in particular, rapidly expanded. Whereas through the 1900s Ankara had looked westwards to Europe and did not pay significant attention to its neighbours to the south and east (outside of security interests), Turkey has 'rediscovered' the MENA and now plays a very significant role in the region's political and economic affairs. A body of literature has emerged that explores the emergence of these expanding ties and the policy interests driving them (see, e.g.: Öniş 2010; Kardas 2010; Kirişci and Kaptanoğlu 2011; Hürsoy 2013). It is time to deepen our understanding of the ways in which Turkey has not only reengaged with the MENA but has more fully *integrated* with it. Turkey now plays

I. El-Anis (✉)
Nottingham Trent University, Nottingham, UK
e-mail: imad.el-anis@ntu.ac.uk

© The Author(s) 2020   217
E. Parlar Dal (ed.), *Turkey's Political Economy*
in the 21st Century, International Political Economy Series,
https://doi.org/10.1007/978-3-030-27632-4_9

an important role in the region's political and economic system in a number of ways. This chapter explores this new reality by analysing the political economy of Turkey's relations with MENA partners.

According to Ziya Öniş and Mustafa Kutlay (2013, 1412), '[t]he current proactivism in Turkish foreign policy [...] increasingly relies on two pillars: economic interdependence, and explicit pro-democracy rhetoric'. It is the first of these two pillars that is the focus of this chapter. Levent Aydin and Mustafa Acar (2013, 42) highlight that there is '[n]o doubt that the greater Middle East [...] capture[s] more attention now in the new Turkish foreign policy as opposed to the past'. And that '[c]hanging patterns or direction in Turkey's foreign trade could be taken as one of the indicators' of this shift in Turkey's foreign economic policy. Understanding these changing patterns in its economic interactions with the MENA will allow us to better understand the extent to which Turkey is integrating with its neighbours to the south and east, and whether this integration is symmetrical or asymmetrical—which will largely determine whether Turkey is an emerging regional hegemon or simply a key part of a broader regional market. This chapter explores these issues by analysing several aspects of Turkey's economic interactions with states in the broader MENA in terms of commercial institutions, trade volumes and balance, foreign direct investment (FDI) and the role of Turkish corporations.

This chapter employs a mixed-method approach that favours quantitative analysis of macroeconomic linkages between Turkey and the MENA, and qualitative analysis of the interests and discourse informing institutional interactions. We will first consider the ways in which the political economy of Turkey's integration into the MENA regional economy has been framed. Then we will explore Turkey-MENA trade and FDI patterns and structures. The importance of Turkish corporations will be highlighted before conclusions are drawn about the importance and longevity of Turkey's integration with the region.

Conceptualising Turkey-MENA Economic Integration

There is some validity to the claim that in the historical context, the abolishment of the Caliphate and Ottoman dynasty cut ties and 'breached the "social contract" between Kurds, Arabs and Turks' (Ehteshami and Elik 2011, 644). The leading view now is that '[a] major structural transformation in Turkish central-periphery relations occurred when the Justice and Development Party [...] won parliamentary elections in November 2002. The nature of Turkey's policy towards the Middle East changed under the banner of new activism in Turkish foreign policy' (ibid., 645–646). However, it can also be argued that '[t]his characterization is an injustice to the continuation in Turkey's relations with the region' (ibid.). Nevertheless, as will be discussed below, Turkey's economic relations with the MENA (in particular, trade and FDI, and the roles that Turkish corporations play) have deepened since the early 2000s and in many ways have repositioned Turkey in the broader MENA market. Some scholars (see: Pollack 2005; Cagaptay 2009) state that Turkey's supposed 'Eastern Turn' has been driven by the AKP's Islamist agenda, while others (see: Kirişci 2009, 2011; Logan 2009) claim that changes in Turkey's domestic and foreign economic relations have transformed Turkey into a 'trading state' and there is nothing unique about Turkey's economic integration with the MENA. Thus, Turkey's 'foreign policy is guided to a greater extent by economic considerations such as trade, export markets, [FDI], and energy security' (Ekmekci and Yildirim 2013, 53). Kirişci (2011, 33–34) claims that 'economic considerations such as the need to trade, expand exports, and attract and export [FDI]' have replaced narrow security considerations as the main drivers behind Turkey's foreign policymaking. While Ekmekci and Yildirim (2013, 58) find that Turkey's economics-first approach has in some ways necessitated the 'maintenance of good neighbourly relations with countries in the [MENA]'. In other words, Turkey's economic interests now heavily influence its broader foreign interests rather than the other way around as in the past. Furthermore, Turkey has largely followed a neo-functionalist framework in order to maximise gains from both the economic opportunities that the MENA market represents and the interdependence that accompanies greater levels of trade and FDI. This has allowed Turkey to institutionalise its relations with MENA states by 'downgrading military power in favor of economic interactions' (Kutlay 2011, 71).

Ageliki and Ioannis (2016, 285) find that 'Turkey's trade integration in the world system is [...] balanced while, at the same time, Turkey seems to develop intensive trade relations with specific subsystems in [the] Eurasian region based on geographical (in a broader geopolitical sense), cultural and historical proximities'. This is in contrast to the Interwar and Cold War eras when Turkey's political and economic strategies towards the MENA were perceived by its neighbours, in particular Arab states, as founded on the need to balance extra-regional and regional actors and not as a sign that Turkey sought to become the regional hegemon (Ehteshami and Elik 2011, 646). This perception of Turkey as a balancing rather than aggressive actor in the region has merit when considering the changes taking place within Turkey's domestic political economy. In the early 2000s, a 'power shift in domestic finance capital underpinned an active foreign policy engagement' (Kutlay 2011, 75). The increased power and influence of the Anatolian Tigers in this period helped to change the economic structures informing power relations within Turkey which 'inevitably spilled-over into foreign policy' (ibid.). The rise of the Anatolian Tigers allowed the emergent Anatolian bourgeoisie to have a greater say in where Turkey *looked* for both inspiration and opportunities to exploit. Thanks to 'geographical proximity and cultural factors' Turkish policymakers were encouraged to reformulate their policies towards both the MENA and Central Asia (ibid., 76). In effect, Turkey began to look east and south, finding economic, political and sociocultural opportunities to expand its role in the global political economy.

We can identify three sets of structures that have informed the manner in which this deepening of Turkey's role in the MENA (what we can term its *reintegration* into the region—at least in terms of its economic relations) has taken place. Firstly, we can consider *material interests*. 'The material interests established between Turkish firms and neighbouring countries' are a clear demonstration of the integrative relationships that underpin Turkey's foreign policy activism since the AKP assumed power in 2002. Mustafa Kutlay refers to the economic and personal interactions between Turkish businesspersons and their counterparts from other MENA states as one of the *practical hands* of Turkey's diplomacy (ibid., 77–78). The second key structure is the *multiple dialogue channels* that originate in the business realm, but which have spilled-over (in the rather classical functionalist sense) into other areas of Turkey's state and market interactions with MENA actors. 'The increasing intensity of commercial relationships between Anatolian businessmen and [MENA] markets has created spill-over effects and facilitated the establishing of new dialogue and cooperation mechanisms' (ibid., 80). Furthermore, the deepening of economic links between Turkey and its MENA neighbours has a significant impact on the broader relationship between Turkey and the region, as 'relationships are not restricted to bureaucratic state-state relations anymore. The interaction between non-state actors at different levels and on different issue areas has multiplied the ways in which parties gather information about each other' (ibid., 81). The third way in which Turkey's reintegration into the MENA market has been shaped is the *perceptions* of Turkey's roles and interests by other MENA actors. Kutlay concludes that 'the spill-over effects of commercial interests and the institutionalization of multiple dialogue channels in new relationships [have] gradually change[d] perceptions' (ibid.). In particular, Arab perceptions of Turkey have changed since the early 2000s, with surveys finding that a majority (approximately 75%) of the Arab population now view Turkey either *very positively* or *positively*. We should not underestimate the role of Turkey's economic interactions with the region here. Increasing economic interdependence has encouraged more intense 'interaction and human mobility that [has] changed the historically and ideologically loaded (mis)perceptions' (ibid., 81–82) of communities in Turkey and the Arab world.

Economic interactions between Turkey and the MENA should also be considered in the broader context of Turkey's position on the world stage. Anoushiravan Ehteshami and Suleyman Elik (2011, 646) argue that Turkey has aspirations in the global political economy that extend well beyond its roles in the MENA and Central Asia. 'Turkey sees the Middle East as a key strategic region in the global power struggle, in addition to its concerns over access to the region's gas and oil resources'. Specifically, they suggest that Turkey's reintegration with the MENA as a whole, and with Iran and the larger Arab states in particular, has become 'a function of Ankara's application of its soft power, which includes broad economic engagement and deepening ties in the energy sector' (ibid., 657–658). Although Turkey remains economically connected to Europe, North America, and South and East Asia, by integrating with the MENA, it has been able to increase its relative economic power and political importance on the world stage (Kirişci et al. 2010) and offset some of its reliance on Western markets—which come with political considerations that hinder Turkey's ability to pursue its broader foreign policy goals (Sorhun 2013, 22). This reorientation of Turkey's overarching foreign policy strategy and its involvement in the MENA, in particular, date back to at least the 2002 electoral success of the AKP (Öniş and Yilmaz 2009). Englin Sorhun (2013, 22) highlights, however, that the MENA does not represent a panacea for Turkey's weaknesses. 'The Arab Spring has been jeopardizing Turkish export market[s] and this has a possibility of breaking down the recent development in trade flows. Moreover, political instability, the risk of war, worsened economic situation, [and] slowing reform process resulting from awakening movements seem to be the signs that the impacts of the Arab Spring on trade flows can last longer'.

The limitations of relying on economic integration with the MENA to help Turkey develop greater leverage in its broader international relations also informs the move away from its long-standing strategic policy of 'zero problems with neighbours' (ZPN) that was dominant in the early 2000s. Turkey attempted to 'develop relations with [the] Arab world as a trade partner at the beginning of the 1990s [but] it did not last long. Trade volume with Arab countries remained below [their] potential level until the implementation of the [ZPN] policy' in 2002 (ibid., 23). The most obvious macroeconomic impact of the ZPN was that Turkey 'diversified its export markets especially with the members of the Organisation for Islamic Cooperation (OIC) [and this] market diversification alleviated the dependence of Turkey on [the] European export market' (ibid., 25) and made it less vulnerable to the global economic recession that followed the 2008–2009 financial crisis. Yet, while economic interactions between Turkey and the MENA have dramatically increased (as demonstrated below) since 2002, Turkey has been unable to insulate itself from the upheavals of the Arab Spring in 2010–2011 (note that Turkey was very active in the region prior to 2010 [Kardas 2010]) and the post-Arab Spring instability experienced by many states in the region. It has been one of the most actively engaged external actors in Syria's civil war, for example, and this has undermined its relations with leading international powers as well as the Syrian regime of Bashar al-Assad. Some now argue that the ZPN policy was drastically undermined or even purposefully changed post-2011 into a 'zero friends policy' (Subasat 2017, 1). Regardless of the post-2011 changes in Turkey's security relations with the MENA, previous work to institutionalise its political and economic relations with Iran and the Arab states has embedded and formed a framework that may facilitate greater economic interdependence over the coming years. We now turn to an overview of the main institutional mechanisms and Turkey's trade relations with the region.

Turkey's Bilateral Trade with MENA States

The post-2002 expansion of Turkey's foreign trade and its integration with the regional economy in the MENA is part of a longer-term and somewhat deep-rooted restructuring of the Turkish economy along neoliberal lines that dates back to the 1980s (see: Donmez and Zemandl 2019; Öniş and Senses 2009). Europe remains the most important single regional market for Turkey (both in terms of imports and exports) and the Turkey-EU Customs Union Agreement (in force since 1995) reflects this fact. Turkey has also pursued (with some vigour) greater institutionalisation of its trade relations with the global economy (Turkey was a member of GATT since 1951 and a subsequent founding member of the World Trade Organisation [WTO] in 1995) and the MENA. Turkey is a member of a number of commercial institutions, including: a free trade agreement (FTA) with the Economic Cooperation Organization (Afghanistan, Azerbaijan, Iran, Kazakhstan, Kyrgyzstan, Pakistan, Tajikistan, Turkmenistan and Uzbekistan); the European Free Trade Area (Iceland, Liechtenstein, Norway and Switzerland); and bilateral FTAs with: Albania, Bosnia and Herzegovina, Chile, Croatia, Egypt, Georgia, Israel, Jordan (at the time of writing this FTA was being re-negotiated), Macedonia, Malaysia, Mauritius, Moldova, Montenegro, Morocco, Palestine, Serbia, Singapore, South Korea, Syria (suspended at the time of writing) and Tunisia. While the effectiveness of commercial institutions on creating trade and promoting political cooperation (read: peace and stability in international relations) is still debated (see: Oneal and Russett 1999; Polachek et al. 1999; Aydin 2010; Barbieri 1996; El-Anis 2018), it is clear that the Turkish government has sought to institutionalise its economic integration with the global economy. Ankara wants either to facilitate trade and deepen economic integration or to promote channels for political dialogue (or both) and the MENA and Central Asia feature quite prominently here with 16 of Turkey's 35 FTA partners being in these regions.

Turkey's overarching foreign economic policies appear to have significantly influenced both the country's position in the global economy and its economic integration with states both near and far. Turkey has now become deeply integrated into the world economy as its 14th largest national market by purchasing power ($2.173 trillion [World Bank 2018]) and an outward-oriented trading state—albeit one with significant imports too. A survey of Turkey's trading partners demonstrates the deepening level of global integration that the Turkish economy has achieved in the past two decades or so, and the increasing importance of the MENA market for Turkey. Its leading trade partners are located across different regions (see Table 9.1). Perhaps unsurprisingly, given their historical and contemporary political and sociocultural connections,

224   I. EL-ANIS

Table 9.1   Turkey's trade with leading partners, 2016 (US$billions)

State	Exports	Exports (% of total)	Imports	Imports (% of total)	Trade balance	Total trade volume
Germany	13.999	9.82	21.475	10.8	−7.476	35.474
China	2.328	1.63	25.441	12.8	−23.113	27.77
Italy	7.581	5.32	10.218	5.14	−2.638	17.799
USA	6.624	4.65	10.868	5.47	−4.244	17.492
UK	11.686	8.2	5.320	2.68	6.366	17.006
Russia	1.733	1.22	15.162	7.63	−13.429	16.895
France	6.026	4.23	7.365	3.71	−1.339	13.391
Spain	4.989	3.5	5.679	2.86	−0.690	10.668
Iran	4.966	3.48	4.7	2.37	0.267	9.666
UAE	5.407	3.79	3.701	1.86	1.706	9.108
Iraq	7.637	5.36	0.836	0.421	6.8	8.473
South Korea	0.519	0.364	6.384	3.21	−5.866	6.903
Netherlands	3.589	2.52	3	1.51	0.589	6.59
India	0.652	0.457	5.757	2.9	−5.106	6.409
Poland	2.651	1.86	3.244	1.63	−0.594	5.895
Belgium	2.548	1.79	3.2	1.61	−0.653	5.749
Switzerland	2.681	1.88	2.506	1.26	0.175	5.187
Saudi Arabia	3.172	2.23	1.835	0.924	1.337	5.007
Romania	2.671	1.87	2.196	1.11	0.476	4.867
Bulgaria	2.384	1.67	2.143	1.08	0.241	4.526

Source World Bank (2018)

Turkey's leading trade partner remains Germany with bilateral trade totalling $35.474 billion in 2016. Turkey exports more goods and services to Germany than anywhere else ($13.999 billion in 2016, equivalent to 9.82% of all Turkish exports), but it also imports more from Germany ($21.475 billion, 10.8% of all imports) than anywhere else except China. This means that the 2016 balance of trade favoured Germany by $7.476 billion (this is Turkey's third-largest trade deficit with any individual trade partner). As is the case for many states, China is also a key trading partner for Turkey and bilateral trade in 2016 totalled $27.77 billion, with imports from China amounting to $25.441 billion, equivalent to 12.8% of Turkey's total imports that year, which is good enough to be Turkey's largest source of imports. At the same time, however, Turkish exports to China are quite limited, totalling only $2.328 billion in 2016, equivalent to 1.63% of Turkey's exports and leading to Turkey's largest trade deficit with any single state ($23.113 billion

9 THE POLITICAL ECONOMY OF TURKEY'S INTEGRATION ... 225

in 2016). The rest of Turkey's top 20 trading partners demonstrate Turkey's advanced trading links with Europe,[1] North America,[2] Asia[3] and the MENA.[4]

Interestingly, out of Turkey's top trading partners, only four are from the MENA. However, Iran, the UAE, Iraq and Saudi Arabia together did represent over $32 billion in total trade for Turkey in 2016, and importantly Turkey has trade surpluses with each of them. Turkey's total trade with Iran is larger than with any other MENA state at $9.665 billion in 2016, and while it had a trade surplus of only $266.4 million, Iran represents Turkey's largest imports market in the region ($4.7 billion in imports in 2016, equivalent to 2.37% of total imports that year). Turkey exports more to Iraq ($7.637 billion in 2016, equivalent to 5.36% of total exports) than to any other MENA state, yet it only imported $836.3 million of goods and services in that year (0.4% of imports), leading to a trade surplus of $6.8 billion, its largest with a MENA state in 2016. Turkish-Emirati bilateral trade is the second largest for Turkey in the region at $9.1 billion in 2016 and with $5.41 billion accounted for by Turkish exports (3.79% of all exports) and $3.7 billion in imports (1.86% of all imports) leading to a Turkish trade surplus of $1.7 billion that year. Turkish-Saudi trade expresses a similar structure but albeit of lower monetary values. Turkey exported $2.68 billion in goods and services to Saudi Arabia in 2016 (2.23% of total exports) and imported a further $1.835 billion (0.92% of total imports) leading to a trade surplus of $1.337 billion.

Turkey's MENA trade structure is relatively unique in terms of the trade surpluses it generates. Out of its top 20 trading partners, Turkey has a trade deficit with 11 (all but one of which are more advanced economies in Europe, Asia and North America). The MENA allows Turkey to offset some of these deficits. In fact, in 2016 Turkey did not have a single trade deficit with any state in the MENA. While some trade surpluses were not large in comparison with some of Turkey's other trading partners in Europe, North America and Asia, Turkey's combined trade surplus with MENA states meant that a balance of $20.5 billion flowed

---

[1] Italy, 3rd; the UK, 5th; Russia, 6th; France, 7th; Spain, 8th; the Netherlands, 13th; Poland, 15th; Belgium, 16th; Switzerland, 17th; Romania, 19th; and Bulgaria, 20th.

[2] The USA, 4th.

[3] India, 14th.

[4] Iran, 9th; the UAE, 10th; Iraq, 11th; Saudi Arabia, 18th.

226   I. EL-ANIS

Table 9.2   Turkey's trade with MENA partners, 2016 (US$billions)

State	Exports	Exports (% of total)	Imports	Imports (% of total)	Trade balance	Total trade volume
Iran	4.966	3.48	4.67	2.37	0.266	9.666
UAE	5.407	3.79	3.701	1.86	1.706	9.108
Iraq	7.637	5.36	0.836	0.421	6.8	8.473
Saudi Arabia	3.172	2.23	1.835	0.924	1.337	5.007
Israel	2.956	2.07	1.386	0.698	1.57	4.341
Egypt	2.733	1.92	1.443	0.727	1.29	4.176
Morocco	1.469	1.03	0.918	0.462	0.551	2.387
Algeria	1.736	1.22	0.461	0.234	1.273	2.2
Syria	1.322	0.928	0.65	0.0329	1.257	1.387
Tunisia	0.911	0.639	0.214	0.108	0.696	1.125
Libya	0.906	0.636	0.161	0.0811	0.745	1.067
Lebanon	0.735	0.515	0.82	0.0412	0.653	0.817
Jordan	0.711	0.499	0.102	0.0515	0.609	0.813
Qatar	0.439	0.308	0.271	0.136	0.168	0.71
Kuwait	0.431	0.303	0.11	0.0557	0.321	0.542
Yemen	0.536	0.376	0	0	0.536	0.536
Sudan	0.461	0.323	0.05	0.025	0.411	0.51
Bahrain	0.193	0.136	0.128	0.0643	0.066	0.321
Oman	0.244	0.171	0.049	0.0247	0.195	0.293
Mauritania	0.073	0.0514	0.015	0.00762	0.058	0.088

Source World Bank (2018)

into Turkey from the rest of the MENA (see Table 9.2). This is a significant annual surplus and is all the more important given that Turkey-MENA exports accounted for almost 26% of Turkey's total exports in 2016. At the same time, though, one can question the depth of Turkish-MENA economic integration because of this trade imbalance and the limited amount of Turkish imports from the region which accounted for only 8.3% of total Turkish imports in 2016 (or perhaps it is more a case of Turkish consumers lacking interest in MENA products and services). However, a consideration of the changes witnessed in Turkey-MENA trade over the past two decades or so does offer some relevant insights into how important this trade is becoming for Turkey.

Through the mid- to late 1990s, Turkey's total trade with the MENA remained limited, generally around $8 billion a year and never exceeding $10 billion (see Table 9.3). This trade also remained largely constant with little sign of increasing interaction even though the MENA market did expand quite significantly during this decade. There was a clear economic transformation, however, after 2002 when there was a dramatic and rapid increase in Turkey's bilateral trade with MENA states. We cannot be entirely certain about whether or not this increase resulted from the AKP coming into power, and its subsequent policies aimed at institutionalised economic integration with the region as discussed above, but the coincidence is significant. It is possible that the AKP decision-makers at the time had identified emerging patterns of economic interaction with MENA states and sort to facilitate these. Either way, Turkey-MENA trade through the 2000s grew exponentially, reaching almost $45 billion in 2008 until declining to $33.6 billion in 2009, which was largely caused by the global financial crisis and recession of 2008–2009, which negatively affected Turkey's overall foreign trade and not just that with the MENA. By 2010, Turkey's trade with the region once again began to grow rapidly reaching $71.8 billion in 2012 until a slowdown and decline from 2013 ($66.9 billion) to 2016 ($53.7 billion). This latter period coincides with significant regional turmoil that has negatively affected the region's market as a whole. This turmoil includes the following: the worsening of the Syrian civil war and its internationalisation, with Russian, USA, Saudi Arabian, Iranian and Turkish involvement, in particular, deepening; the rise of ISIS in Syria and Iraq and the subsequent conflict to defeat it; increased tension between Iran and its Arab neighbours; the Saudi-led coalition's involvement in Yemen's civil war; and deteriorating relations between Qatar and its GCC and broader Arab neighbours. Regardless of these periods of decline in 2009 and 2013–2015, Turkey-MENA trade has grown by approximately 900% since 2002, a very dramatic increase given the lack of growth in the pre-2002 era (Table 9.3).

Interestingly, Turkey's economic relationships with MENA states are not heavily affected by geographical proximity except for with Iran and Iraq, Turkey's first- and third-largest trading partners. Syria ranks ninth out of the 20 MENA states considered here in terms of total trade with Turkey, although, of course, trade between these two states has been negatively impacted by Syria's civil war. Beyond Turkey's immediate neighbours, the mix of key trading partners in the region becomes varied with the UAE (2nd), Saudi Arabia (4th), Israel (5th) and Egypt (6th) being somewhat close to Turkey. However, Turkey's other main regional trade partners are not nearby: Morocco (7th), Algeria (8th), Tunisia (10th) and Libya (11th) account for the majority of Turkey's remaining

Table 9.3 Turkey's total trade with the MENA, 1996–2017 (US$billions)

	Algeria	Bahrain	Egypt	Iran	Iraq	Israel	Jordan	Kuwait	Lebanon	Libya	Mauri-tania	Morocco	Oman	Qatar	Saudi Arabia	Sudan	Syria	Tunisia	UAE	Yemen	Total
1996	1.015	0.015	0.589	1.104	0.22	0.447	0.180	0.211	0.21	0.72	0	0.134	0.02	0.014	2.138	0.028	0.619	0.145	0.235	0.074	8.12
1997	1.085	0.032	0.704	0.953	0	0.625	0.137	0.297	0.235	0.72	0	0.105	0.02	0.024	1.553	0.035	0.725	0.18	0.29	0.087	7.806
1998	1.13	0.047	0.867	0.628	0	0.762	0.149	0.17	0.185	0.438	0.000	0.146	0.22	0.074	1.144	0.046	0.617	0.414	0.272	0.062	7.175
1999	1.09	0.023	0.576	0.794	0	0.884	0.105	0.167	0.173	0.642	0.002	0.135	0.029	0.022	0.946	0.041	0.539	0.305	0.419	0.089	6.979
2000	1.576	0.058	0.516	1.052	0	1.156	0.127	0.235	0.151	0.882	0.003	0.143	0.025	0.021	1.348	0.042	0.73	0.227	0.356	0.07	8.717
2001	1.486	0.026	0.513	1.2	0	1.335	0.132	0.228	0.21	0.915	0.004	0.136	0.031	0.014	1.23	0.056	0.745	0.214	0.445	0.100	9.022
2002	1.072	0.036	0.445	1.255	0	1.406	0.135	0.166	0.229	0.207	0.012	0.207	0.032	0.026	0.676	0.072	0.582	0.193	0.558	0.12	7.427
2003	1.074	0.044	0.535	2.395	0.871	1.543	0.167	0.182	0.22	0.288	0.006	0.258	0.024	0.024	0.95	0.071	0.672	0.318	0.817	0.156	10.612
2004	1.432	0.073	0.728	2.775	1.966	2.029	0.244	0.292	0.382	0.42	0.010	0.436	0.031	0.053	1.123	0.101	0.642	0.357	1.327	0.205	14.624
2005	1.669	0.061	0.955	4.383	2.817	2.272	0.317	0.252	0.341	0.579	0.011	0.514	0.044	0.133	1.549	0.153	0.694	0.412	1.881	0.200	19.235
2006	1.739	0.080	1.102	6.694	2.711	2.311	0.331	0.275	0.367	0.731	0.009	0.725	0.073	0.409	1.606	0.225	0.609	0.475	2.338	0.198	23.009
2007	2.176	0.196	1.556	8.057	2.964	2.74	0.401	0.312	0.509	0.26	0.019	0.920	0.116	0.48	2.223	0.188	1.057	0.76	3.711	0.275	28.918
2008	3.201	0.402	2.313	10.23	4.05	3.383	0.486	0.574	0.844	1.411	0.023	1.318	0.226	1.233	3.111	0.243	1.439	1.144	8.667	0.354	44.652
2009	2.546	0.138	3.241	5.431	5.244	2.597	0.476	0.396	0.798	2.153	0.024	0.833	0.122	0.375	2.544	0.255	1.643	0.881	3.564	0.34	33.638
2010	2.573	0.244	3.177	10.689	6.19	3.44	0.614	0.61	0.847	2.358	0.039	1.021	0.169	0.34	3.598	0.233	2.297	0.994	4.031	0.331	43.794
2011	2.621	0.272	4.142	16.051	8.397	4.449	0.507	0.568	1.001	0.887	0.091	1.341	0.271	0.669	4.765	0.253	1.947	1.052	5.356	0.273	54.912
2012	2.738	0.367	5.021	21.886	10.972	4.04	0.867	0.569	0.176	2.556	0.115	1.444	0.321	0.724	5.848	0.291	0.565	0.992	11.771	0.486	71.751
2013	2.717	0.372	4.829	14.576	12.095	5.068	0.815	0.626	1.006	3.057	0.107	1.765	0.524	0.618	5.206	0.295	1.109	1.181	10.35	0.605	66.922
2014	3	0.498	4.732	13.72	11.156	5.832	1.033	0.569	0.923	2.304	0.108	2.046	0.592	0.739	5.39	0.32	1.917	1.112	7.909	0.649	64.548
2015	2.566	0.33	4.341	9.76	8.847	4.371	0.963	0.624	0.790	1.616	0.110	2.048	0.385	0.784	5.59	0.449	1.574	0.963	6.69	0.407	53.205
2016	2.2	0.321	4.176	9.666	8.473	4.341	0.813	0.542	0.817	1.067	0.088	2.387	0.293	0.71	5.007	0.51	1.387	1.125	9.108	0.536	53.568
2017	2.48	0.414	4.358	10.751	10.582	4.913	0.795	0.609	1.021	1.129	0.0132	2.582	0.317	0.913	4.845	0.481	1.434	1.119	14.731	0.572	64.177

Source Turkstat (2018)

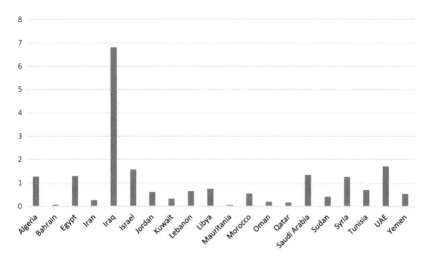

Fig. 9.1 Turkey's trade balance with MENA Partners, 2016 (US$billions) (*Source* World Bank 2018)

trade with the MENA. Proximity is less important in determining Turkey's MENA trade than other variables including, the overall size of partners' markets, trading partners' levels of economic development, and the success of private sector actors (especially Turkish corporations operating in the region) in foreign markets. Turkey exports 'finished goods to and imports raw materials and energy commodities from [Arab countries]. Raw materials and energy commodities are the only goods [...] leading to production complementarity' (Sorhun 2013, 26). Turkey trades more with the larger economies of the region and those that are more advanced (Fig. 9.1).

Overall, the past decade and a half or so has seen Turkey's economic interaction with the rest of the MENA expand rapidly and deepen. Total trade volume has increased so rapidly that economic integration has deepened drastically between Turkey and the region as a whole, even though Turkey has maintained an overall trade surplus. The make-up of Turkey's trade with the region, however, has not led to Turkey's economy becoming the central market in the region (the GCC states collectively still hold the most economically influential position) yet it has developed significant trade with all states considered here—something which other MENA states cannot claim to have managed to achieve (Fig. 9.2).

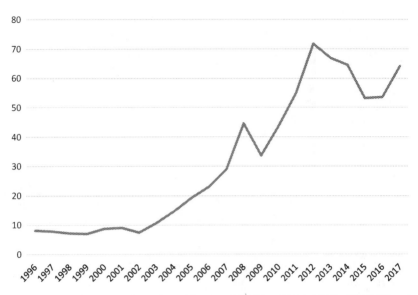

Fig. 9.2 Turkey's total trade with the MENA, 1996–2017 (US$billions) (*Source* Turkstat [www.turkstat.gov.tr] 2018)

Foreign Direct Investment

The second pillar of economic integration is FDI. While trade in goods and services demonstrates economic integration in the form of production, exchange and consumption (important features that speak to the health and stability of national economies), perhaps more important in terms of signalling *deep* economic integration between states is FDI. Producers of goods and services will always seek to increase sales and profits and will do so by exploiting opportunities in any market where it is profitable to do so. Turkey's trade with the MENA as discussed above, therefore, does not demonstrate significant *trust* and *interest* as much as it does profiteering. Investing capital (whether liquid or fixed) in foreign markets, on the other hand, does signal trust and interest—which are central to reinforcing economic integration and interdependence (see: Bearce 2003; Bearce and Omori 2005)—and can tie markets together.

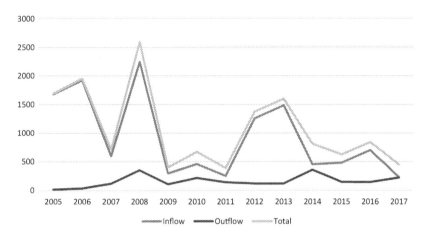

Fig. 9.3 Turkey's FDI flows with the MENA 2005–2017 (US$millions) (*Source* Central Bank of the Republic of Turkey [CBRT]: Statistical Data [EVDS] 2018)

Capital flows in the form of FDI between Turkey and the MENA in the past two decades or so have been important but somewhat limited (totalling just over $14 billion). Interestingly, change in FDI flows does not mirror the overall trends in Turkey-MENA trade in goods and services since the turn of the millennium. Prior to 2005, total FDI levels were insignificant and certainly far below what one might expect, although this began to change with overall growth in FDI levels. However, after 2005, a period of notable annual increases followed by equally notable annual declines in bilateral FDI emerged (see Fig. 9.3). The growth seen may have been linked to the rise of the AKP in 2002 and subsequent macroeconomic policy changes, although further research is needed to verify this hypothesis. Total FDI stood at $1.7 billion in 2005, increased slightly the following year to just under $2 billion, but then declined rapidly in 2007 to $713 million. Even as the global financial crisis began to bite in 2008 FDI rapidly increased to $2.6 billion but then dropped to $397 million in 2009 (the second lowest level since 2005). The impact of the global downturn lingered in the MENA as a whole, as it did elsewhere around the world, and negatively impacted the Turkish economy more than most other large economies in the region. This may help explain the poor performance of Turkey-MENA FDI between 2009 and 2011. The Arab Spring did not hinder FDI in 2012 ($1.4 billion) and 2013 ($1.6 billion) but the intensification of the regional instability best demonstrated by the Syrian civil war, as well as the increasing centralisation of power in Ankara, suppressed FDI since 2014 with 2017 seeing only $448 million in bilateral FDI between Turkey and the MENA states.

Even though total FDI levels have not been high or even constant over the past decade, importantly, Turkey has maintained an overall FDI surplus with the region in each year as FDI inflows to Turkey outstripped net outflows. Furthermore, these surpluses were significant in 2005 ($1.7 billion), 2006 ($1.9 billion), 2008 ($1.9 billion), 2012 ($1.1 billion) and 2013 ($1.6 billion) representing a source of external income that has helped to slightly offset Turkey's unfavourable terms of trade with its main economic partners in Europe, North America and Asia. Turkey's smallest surplus came in 2017 with a mostly insignificant $10 million. This overall surplus demonstrates the relative attractiveness of the Turkish market for MENA investors and the relative lack of trust and interest that Turkish investors have in MENA markets. It is also an indicator of the inward orientation of Turkish investors who have had success at home during a period of solid economic growth since 2002. Yet, while trade levels recovered and continued the high annual growth rates seen before the 2008–2009 global financial crisis, the stagnation of FDI levels suggests there are structural limitations to Turkey's economic integration with the region. This could signal that both state and non-state actors in the MENA have struggled to raise capital for investment abroad, or that Turkey's economy offers limited incentives for foreign capital (or both). Of course, the aftermath of the 2016 coup attempt in Turkey has led to a stiffening of AKP policies, including greater scrutiny of foreign capital ventures and this could well discourage FDI inflows from the MENA and elsewhere.

Undoubtedly, Turkey-MENA FDI flows since the turn of the millennium have favoured the former and the long-term trend, despite the limitations witnessed in the past few years and the inconsistent annual FDI levels, demonstrates this. Turkey has had FDI surpluses with 10 states, with its largest unsurprisingly being with hydrocarbon-rich GCC states with large amounts of petrodollars to invest. Since 2005, Turkey's largest surplus is with the UAE (approximately $3.8 billion: $4.2 billion inflow and $381 million outflow), its second is with Saudi Arabia (just over $1.9 billion: $2 billion inflow and only $68 million outflow), its third is with Kuwait (approximately $1.592 billion: $1.7 billion inflow and only $32 million outflow) and its fourth is with Qatar ($1.589 billion: $1.621 billion inflow and only $32 million outflow). Meanwhile, Turkey's largest FDI deficit is with Iraq (-$422 million) which is unsurprising given the lack of Iraqi investor power and the investment opportunities for reconstruction in Iraq since 2003. Turkey also has significant deficits with Egypt (-$225 million) and Tunisia ($-223 million) which have received modest Turkish FDI ($227 million and $223 million, respectively) but have sent virtually no FDI to Turkey over this period (Egyptian FDI totalled only $2 million and Tunisian FDI $0). Furthermore, the geographical spread of FDI inflows is relatively broad with states across the region investing in Turkey, however, FDI flows are largely limited to the more prosperous (hydrocarbon rich and/or more industrialised) states and immediate neighbours. Turkey has been perhaps the most attractive MENA market for FDI from across the region

Table 9.4 Turkey's total FDI flows with MENA states, 1990–2016 (US$millions)

	FDI inflows	FDI outflows	FDI total	FDI balance
Algeria	0	105	105	−105
Bahrain	484	183	667	301
Egypt	2	227	229	−225
Iran	103	155	258	−52
Iraq	11	433	444	−422
Israel	395	12	407	383
Jordan	216	7	223	209
Kuwait	1648	56	1704	1592
Lebanon	1280	28	1308	1252
Libya	98	36	134	62
Mauritania	0	0	0	0
Morocco	0	87	87	−87
Oman	0	0	0	0
Qatar	1621	32	1653	1589
Saudi Arabia	1964	68	2032	1896
Sudan	0	12	12	−12
Syria	11	17	28	−6
Tunisia	0	223	223	−223
UAE	4206	381	4587	3825
Yemen	0	0	0	0

Source Central Bank of the Republic of Turkey (CBRT): Statistical Data (EVDS) (2018)

234   I. EL-ANIS

over the past twenty years or so, which has helped to slightly re-position it as a key market in the broader regional economy. However, political uncertainty within Turkey and other MENA states, as well as structural economic vulnerabilities inherent within the regional economic system (chief among them: reliance on the export of hydrocarbons and the rentierism that is prevalent in most states [whether resource rich or poor]) may restrict further economic integration. Turkey's integration into regional capital flows appears to have reached its ceiling (Table 9.4).

MARKET INTEGRATION AND TURKISH CORPORATIONS

Multi-national corporations (MNCs) play important roles in promoting and deepening economic integration between markets. They not only take part in processes of production, exchange and consumption, but also increase the opportunity costs of defection from cooperative relations at the same time as they increase the rewards of continued engagement for both state and non-state actors. As discussed above, businesspersons engage in international projects, play significant roles in developing and maintaining interpersonal relationships and can help connect political decision-makers together through both formal and informal channels as part of their transboundary activities. Trust can be built in the private sector perhaps more easily than in the governmental sector, and on a regular basis (perhaps even we could say daily) corporate actors engage with each other. Furthermore, corporations based in one state but operating in others reinforce shared interests that are best-served by cooperative and stable political relationships. Turkish corporations have been among the most active and successful of any MNCs in the MENA and a large number operate in numerous sectors across the region. Turkey's 'active political role [in the MENA has] encouraged Turkish private enterprise to invest in construction, oil, natural gas and telecommunication systems' (Ehteshami and Elik 2011, 656–657) in a large number of states in the region. The roles MNCs play are not easily captured by macroeconomic measure such as trade and FDI, so we will now turn to some specific examples.

Turkish corporations working in the construction sector have been highly successful since the early 2000s. Much of this work has been commissioned by national governments, has involved large-scale infrastructure projects and has been related to important and politically sensitive issues such as energy security, resource security, social welfare and defence. In Algeria, for example, KAYI Construction and its subsidiary Bilyap Construction, ENKA Insaat, Rönesans Holding (Rönesans 2018) and Yapi Merkezi have been very active. KAYI Construction and Bilyap Construction have completed a large number of projects including residential complexes, hotels, official administrative buildings, container terminals, retail centres, power plants, military infrastructure and educational institutions (Kayi 2018). ENKA Insaat (ENKA 2018) has been involved in the building of dams and water treatment infrastructure, while Yapi Merkzei (Yapi 2018) constructed the Bir Touta-Zeralda Railway and Sidi Bel Abbes tramway. In Iraq, KAYI Construction has been involved in building and restoring power generation infrastructure, hydrocarbons processing and transport facilities and healthcare centres among other projects. ENKA Insaat has also been involved in building power plants and hydrocarbon pumping infrastructure in Iraq as well as marine works (mostly in Basra). As a measure of their competitiveness, many Turkish corporations not only operate in neighbouring countries but across the region. For example, TAV Construction (TAV 2018) has been involved in numerous airport and aviation infrastructure projects in Bahrain, Egypt, Libya, Oman, Qatar, Saudi Arabia, Tunisia and the UAE since it was founded in 1997.

Conclusions

Regardless of the internal processes shaping its domestic politics, Turkey's economic integration with the MENA looks set to deepen, largely due to the increasing levels of trade in goods and services, and the agency of Turkey's private sector actors and the links they have established with the broader MENA market. Coupled with the structural changes most clearly manifest in commercial institutions, Turkey has become a more central component of the MENA system than at any time in the post-First World War era. The MENA has become an important market for Turkish exports and imports, and a source of FDI, which have combined to further strengthen growth in the Turkish economy. The overall trade and FDI surpluses that Turkey has experienced vis-à-vis the MENA since the early 2000s have helped to offset some of the less advantageous economic relationships it has experienced with European, North American and Asian states. Growth in bilateral trade with MENA states, in particular, has been very strong and although there have been some negative effects of the instability felt in some post-Arab Spring states and within Turkey itself, growth looks set to continue in the coming decade. Turkey is a trading state and the neoliberal economic reforms begun in the 1980s have become entrenched (even though political liberalisation has taken steps backwards) leading to Turkey's economic growth relying on Ankara diversifying its foreign markets and developing economic relations with MENA states as well as other countries around the world.

Economic integration with the MENA and its potential spill-over effects into political, security and sociocultural relationships may face some limitations, however. The rather mixed record of Turkey-MENA FDI and the apparent limitations on the expansion of capital flows across the region suggest that investors in Turkey and other MENA states do not have absolute trust and interest in each other's markets. Political instability and the lack of profitable opportunities to invest, and political restrictions will continue to hinder this important aspect of economic integration in the coming years. Without expanding economic links through FDI, Turkey's role in the MENA market can continue to grow, but this role will be limited to processes of production, exchange and consumption. These processes, ultimately, will integrate Turkey further into the region but will not likely allow Turkey to become the centre of the MENA economy. Furthermore, increased trade will most likely go some way to promoting political cooperation between Turkey and other MENA states over time but is unlikely to lead to the type of economic interdependence that promotes regional security. If Ankara aspires to greater regional leadership, or even hegemony, then it will have to facilitate FDI further and promote Turkish private sector actors as they engage more in the regional market.

References

Ageliki, A., & Panteladis I. (2016). Eurasian Orientation and Global Trade Integration: The Case of Turkey. *Eurasian Economic Review, 6*(2, Summer), 275–287.

Aydin, A. (2010). The Deterrent Effects of Economic Integration. *Journal of Peace Research, 47*(5, Summer), 523–533.

Aydin, L., & Acar, M. (2013). Economic Implications of Turkey's Regional Integration with Its Neighbourhood. *Bilig, 66*(Summer), 42–58.

Barbieri, K. (1996). Economic Interdependence: A Path to Peace or a Source of Interstate Conflict? *Journal of Peace Research, 33*(1, Winter), 29–49.

9 THE POLITICAL ECONOMY OF TURKEY'S INTEGRATION ... 237

Bearce, D. H. (2003). Grasping the Commercial Institutional Peace. *International Studies Quarterly, 47*(3, Autumn), 347–370.

Bearce, D. H., & Omori, S. (2005). How Do Commercial Institutions Promote Peace? *Journal of Peace Research, 42*(6, Autumn), 659–678.

Cagaptay, S. (2009, October 26). Is Turkey Leaving the West? *Foreign Affairs.*

Central Bank of the Republic of Turkey (CBRT). (2018). *EVDS (Electronic Data Distribution System).* Accessed October 12, 2018. http://evds.tcmb.gov.tr/cbt.html.

Donmez, P., & Zemandl, E. (2019). Crisis of Capitalism and (De-)Politicisation of Monetary Policymaking: Reflections From Hungary and Turkey. *New Political Economy, 24*(1, Spring), 125–143.

Ehteshami, A., & Elik, S. (2011). Turkey's Growing Relations with Iran and the Arab Middle East. *Turkish Studies, 12*(4, Winter), 643–662.

Ekmekci, F., & Yildirim, A. (2013). The Political Economy of Turkey's Eastern Turn: An Empirical Analysis of Erdogan's State Visits (2003–2010). *Romanian Journal of Political Science Papers, 13*(1, Summer), 52–75.

El-Anis, I. (2018). Economic Integration and Security in the Middle East and North Africa: What Prospects for a 'Liberal' Peace? *Journal of Developing Societies, 34*(3, Autumn), 233–263.

ENKA. (2018). *Our Projects.* Accessed October 13, 2018. https://www.enka.com/our-projects/.

Hürsoy, S. (2013). Turkey's Foreign Policy and Economic Interests in the Gulf. *Turkish Studies, 14*(3, Autumn), 503–519.

Kardas, S. (2010). Turkey: Redrawing the Middle East Map or Building Sandcastles? *Middle East Policy, 17*(1, Spring), 115–136.

Kayi. (2018). *Projects in Algeria.* Accessed October 13, 2018. http://www.kayi.com.tr/projects/country/algeria.

Kirişci, K. (2009). The Transformation of Turkish Foreign Policy: The Rise of the Trading State. *New Perspectives on Turkey, 40*(Spring), 29–56.

Kirişci, K. (2011). Turkey's 'Demonstrative Effect' and the Transformation of the Middle East. *Insight Turkey, 13*(2, Summer), 33–55.

Kirişci, K., & Kaptanoğlu, N. (2011). The Politics of Trade and Turkish Foreign Policy. *Middle Eastern Studies, 47*(5, Autumn), 705–724.

Kirişci, K., Tocci, N., & Walker, J. (2010). *A Neighbourhood Rediscovered: Turkey's Transatlantic Value in the Middle East.* Washington, DC: German Marshall Fund for the United States.

Kutlay, M. (2011). Economy as the 'Practical Hand' of 'New Turkish Foreign Policy': A Political Economy Explanation. *Insight Turkey, 13*(1, December), 67–88.

Logan, D. (2009). Turkey and Its Middle Eastern Neighbours: Threat or Opportunity for the European Union? *Asian Affairs, 15*(1, Spring), 34–43.

Oneal, J. R., & Russett, B. (1999). The Kantian Peace: The Pacific Benefits of Democracy, Interdependence and International Organizations, 1885–1992. *World Politics, 52*(1, Autumn), 1–37.

Öniş, Z. (2010). Crises and Transformations in Turkish Political Economy. *Turkish Policy Quarterly, 34*(2, Winter), 251–286.

Öniş, Z., & Kutlay, M. (2013). Rising Powers in a Changing Global Order: The Political Economy of Turkey in the Age of BRICS. *Third World Quarterly, 34*(8, May), 1409–1426.

Öniş, Z., & Senses, F. (Eds.). (2009). *Turkey and the Global Economy: Neo-liberal Restructuring and Integration in the Post-crisis Era.* Abingdon: Routledge.

Öniş, Z., & Yilmaz, S. (2009). Between Europeanization and Euro-Asianism: Foreign Policy Activism in Turkey During the AKP Era. *Turkish Studies, 10*(1, Spring), 7–24.

Polachek, S. W., Robst, J., & Chang, Y.-C. (1999). Liberalism and Interdependence: Extending the Trade-Conflict Model. *Journal of Peace Research, 36*(4, July): 405–422.

Pollack, R. (2005, February 16). The Sick Man of Europe—Again? *Wall Street Journal.*

Rönesans. (2018). *About Us.* Accessed October 13, 2018. http://ronesans.com/en/about/about-us.

Sorhun, E. (2013). Arab Spring vs. Zero Problems Policy: Impact of the Arab Spring on the Trade Expansion of Turkey. *International Journal of Research in Business and Social Science, 2*(4, October), 21–36.

Subasat, T. (2017). Turkey at the Crossroads: The Political Economy of Turkey's Transformation. *Markets, Globalization and Development Review, 2*(2, Spring), 1–32.

TAV. (2018). *About Us—Overview.* Accessed October 13, 2018. http://tavcon-struction.com/about-us#overview.

Turkstat. (2018). *Foreign Trade Statistics.* Accessed October 10, 2018. www.turkstat.gov.tr.

World Bank. (2018). *Databank—World Development Indicators.* Accessed October 10, 2018. http://databank.worldbank.org/data/source/world-development-indicators.

Yapi. (2018). *Project Archive.* Accessed October 9, 2018. http://www.ym.com.tr/en/project-archieve/.

CHAPTER 10

Assessing the Turkish "Trading State" in Sub-Saharan Africa

Emel Parlar Dal and Samiratou Dipama

INTRODUCTION

Trade is one of the most preferred instruments of soft power through which states attempt to reinforce their international cooperation on both economic and diplomatic levels. This preference is mostly explained by the increasing interdependency among states in the current globalized era. The concept of the "trading state" was introduced by Richard Rosecrance in 1987 in his seminal book "The Rise of the Trading State: Commerce and Conquest in the Modern World" and refers to the increasing role that trade has occupied in international relations. Rosecrance argues an increasing shift from the Westphalia politico-military international system to a trading system, especially due to the increasing interdependence among states. Unlike the politico-military system in which states are homogeneous in their functions and aim to conquer territorial pace using military means, in the trading world states are differentiated in terms of their functions and are more likely to form alliances to protect themselves against military-political states. In doing so, trading states attempt to improve their welfare by pursuing a trade

E. Parlar Dal (✉) · S. Dipama
Marmara University, Istanbul, Turkey

© The Author(s) 2020   239
E. Parlar Dal (ed.), *Turkey's Political Economy*
in the 21st Century, International Political Economy Series,
https://doi.org/10.1007/978-3-030-27632-4_10

strategy that aims to pacify their relations with other countries and to minimize conflicts among themselves.

The current study aims to investigate whether Rosecrance's concept of trading states applies to Turkey in the context of its relations with sub-Saharan Africa. This question is also timely given recent changes in the dynamics of both Turkey's political economy and in trade wars between the USA and China on one hand and the USA and its Western partners on the other. The few studies that have examined the transformation of Turkey's foreign policy from the "trading state" approach have been somehow limited to Turkey's relations with its Middle Eastern and Central Asian neighbours. This article also aims to fill this gap in the existing literature by expanding its empirical framework.

Against the conceptual background employed by Rosecrance, this study scrutinizes Turkey as a trading state in sub-Saharan Africa by taking into consideration the benefits and limitations of this role. Given the linkage between trade and foreign policy, this study will also examine how Turkey's foreign policy achievements in Africa have impacted its trading state in terms of motivations, strategies, and practices. The paper then first outlines the conceptual framework of Rosecrance's trading state. It then delves into the current shifts occurring in a world trade system marked by trade wars between the USA and China and the rise of protectionism. The impact of the fragmented nature of multilateralism and uncertainties of the post-Washington consensus on trading states will also be analysed. Secondly, the paper reviews the Turkish trading state since 2005 and showcases the strengths and the weaknesses of Turkey's trading state strategy. Finally, it attempts to assess whether Turkey shows the characteristics of a real trading state in the context of sub-Saharan Africa. Here, Turkey's achievements and challenges in terms of trade relations with the sub-Saharan countries will be detailed based on comparative statistical data.

The Concept of the "Trading State" Versus Military State: Rosecrance's Views

Richard Rosecrance was the first scholar to introduce the concept of the "Trading State" in his 1986 book "The Rise of the Trading State: Commerce and Conquest in the Modern World". More than thirty years ago, Rosecrance used this concept to highlight the increasing importance given to economic factors in states' foreign policy making and implementation. According to Rosecrance, since the end of the Second World War the international structure has progressively shifted from a politico-military systemic structure to one that is more focused on economics and trade. This basically means that states have gradually become less interested in territorial conquest and expansion. In this view, trading strategy is seen as an appropriate instrument for increasing state welfare. Conquest strategy, the alternative to trading strategy, has been impacted by dramatic changes in technology and military technology in particular leading to a significant reduction in the benefits gained from its implementation. Rosecrance also investigated whether a balance can be established between a trade and military strategy. His cost-benefit analysis is quite clear: "the greater the restraints on trade and the fewer its likely benefits, the more willing nations have been to seek to improve their position through military force. The higher the cost of war and the more uncertain its benefits, the more nations have sought trade as livelihood" (Rosecrance 1986, 31; Ozdemir and Serin 2016).

Arguing that the trading state has supplanted the military-territorial state, Rosecrance suggested that the benefit of trade and cooperation surpasses that of territorial expansion, and he refers to Japan as a good example of a trading state which preferred a trade strategy based on economic development over a military strategy based on intervention. In an evaluation of the international dynamics of the mid-1980s marked by the rise of liberalism in world economics, Rosecrance argued that trading strategy is more likely to generate influence than the military-political strategy and that "if war provides one means of national advancement peace offers another" (Rosecrance 1986, 9). However, it must also be remembered that Rosecrance's argument on the trading state was also cautious in asserting that each state has different trajectories and strategies on their path towards becoming a trading state. The rising interdependency among states does not necessarily bring peace. Greater economic contact between states could increase the costs of going to war, but they could also lead to conflicts of interest among these states.

Despite these reservations, Rosecrance underlined that those states that do not follow the trend of prioritizing soft economic factors over hard military ones are likely to become the greatest losers of the international system. This would primarily result from their failure to establish one of the important requirements of becoming a trading state, namely "setting free the productive and trading energies of people and merchants who would find markets for their goods overseas" (Rosecrance 1986). However, Rosecrance also took the transformations occurring on the other side of the calculus into account by referring to the costs and benefits of territorial expansion. For him, this means that the advantages of the trading strategy are high and can increase but that there is always a risk of losing these benefits as a result of the changes on the other side of the calculus (Brawley 2005, 69).

One of Rosecrance's central arguments is the impact of advances in technology on trade. Changes in technology decrease the costs of engaging in trade. This perspective may also lead to the conclusion that greater economic interdependence may generate benefits for all states (Rosecrance 1986, 68). Another key feature of the trading state is the increasing involvement of a wide range of non-state actors, namely business and interest groups in the making of states' foreign policy to the extent that the interests and priorities of these actors influence the content and direction of states' foreign policies.

Trading states share the following common features: they are interdependent, differentiated based on functions, seek internal economic development and trade, prefer to create worldwide market for their products instead of conquest, have goals that do not require preventing other states from achieving similar goals, and have no incentive to wage war because it disrupts the economic system. Rosecrance further highlighted that the establishment of peaceful relations with neighbouring countries is crucial for trading states to promote and deepen trade and economic relations (Rosecrance 1999). For trading states, "national interest does not mean security concern; trade, economic priorities, such as the expansion of export markets and foreign direct investment are equally important" (Kirişçi 2009).

Emre Işeri and Oguz Dilek summarized the difference between the Westphalia politico-military state and Rosecrance's trading state:

> a security state in its classical definition is one that gives priority to political considerations ahead of potential economic gains. A trading state, on the other hand, seldom pays heed to ensuring an identity/space/benefit overlap to conduct its economic affairs. The proximity and identity are still mattering of substance to managing a trading state's economic relations, but only when an impending deal with another state offers negligible economic returns, or when such cooperation inescapably runs incompatible with a trading state's security perceptions. (Iseri and Dilek 2013, 48)

In today's changing global politics landscape, the trading state remains the dominant model for an important number of countries depending on the existence of high benefits associated with the trading strategy. However, as a result of the rising security threats emanating most specifically from international terrorism, some states have increasingly embraced military state strategies together with trading ones. Despite the fact that high costs associated with the military strategy, they prefer pursuing a hybrid policy of both trading and conquest strategies mainly due to their domestic/national and regional priorities. In some cases, each strategy can dominate the other at some points in the past. Today, the coexistence of trading and military state strategies is much more common than in the past. States seek to reinforce their statehood in two realms: military-security and trade. For developing countries such as Turkey, trading statehood is as important as military statehood due to changing domestic conditions and the regional impasses from the ongoing Syrian civil war.

States prefer to adopt a two-layered strategy encompassing both trading and military state strategies. Compared to the Washington consensus and the post-Washington consensus era in which states engaged in reinforcing their trading state status, in the current age of uncertainties states utilize both strategies to increase their status at the international level. In this "non-consensus" or "hybrid" era, leading trading states like China continue to enact their trading state role even more vocally than in the past and simultaneously pursue conquest/military strategies in their own regions. This embedded strategy seems to provide much more flexibility in domestic and international politics.

Review of Turkey's Regional and Global Trading State: Quo Vadis?

According to Kemal Kirisci, until the end of the 1990s Turkey was considered a politico-military or "post-cold war warrior" and was increasingly seen as a "soft power" in the beginning of the 2000s. This transformation of Turkey's foreign policy was mainly attributed to the increasing importance attached to economic factors in Turkey's foreign policy making through normalization of relations with neighbouring countries (Kirişçi 2009).

Kirisci's categorization of Turkey as a "trading state" was particularly relevant from 1980 to 2011, despite the fact that PKK problem and domestic instabilities weakened the importance of economic objectives in the 1990s (The Conversation 2016). Former PM Davutoglu's zero problems with neighbours policy was coined to highlight the necessity for Turkey to pacify its relations with neighbouring countries through intensification of economic ties and diversification of trading partners. The rapprochement with Greece, steps taken towards normalization of its relations with Armenia, and the reviving of ties with its Middle Eastern and Eurasian neighbouring countries all showed Turkey's increasing status as a trading state (The Conversation 2016).

The importance attached to trade in Turkey's foreign policy making and implementation during this period is corroborated by the sharp increase in trade volume with the world from 190.25 billion USD in 2005 to 389.006 billion USD in 2012 (see Tables 10.1 and 10.2). The decline in trade volume from 333.09 billion USD in 2008 to 243.07 billion USD in 2009 (Tables 10.1 and 10.2) is particularly due to the global economic crisis negatively impacted the European market most specifically.

While Kirisci's arguments were relevant in the pre-Arab spring era, current domestic, regional, and international dynamics have undermined Turkey's trading state status as security issues have remerged at the centre of Turkey's foreign policy making, more resembling a typical Westphalia politico-security state. Regarding the regional dynamics, Mustafa Kutlay argues that "state capacity problems in Turkey's neighbourhood largely invalidate previous assumptions regarding Turkey's role because the economy-driven integration theses, which relied on a functionalist logic of bilateral cooperation, took a certain level of stateness for granted" (Kutlay 2016, 2). Indeed, the decreasing stateness of Turkey's key trading partners in the MENA region has significantly challenged Turkey's trading status potential because the increasing insecurity of neighbouring countries has undermined traditional trade routes, which in turn has considerably reduced the volume of trade exchange between Turkey and its former key regional economic partners (Kutlay 2016).

The ongoing Syrian civil war and its ramifications on Middle Eastern regional security constitute a real challenge for Turkey in its use of trade as an effective foreign policy instrument. As we can see from Table 10.1, Turkey's exports to the MENA region began a sharp decline in 2012,

Table 10.1 2005–2016 exports of Turkey by regions (billion USD)

Partner Name	2005	2006	2007	2008	2009	2010	2011	2012	2013	2014	2015	2016
World	73.476	85.534	107.271	132.027	102.142	113.883	134.906	152.461	151.802	157.610	143.850	142.529
Europe and Central Asia	48.628	57.891	74.110	82.997	61.786	68.330	80.558	79.865	84.686	90.164	83.194	82.240
MENA	12.205	13.524	18.061	29.591	25.121	28.401	32.375	49.001	42.287	41.806	37.118	36.819
North America	5.275	5.488	4.547	4.846	3.589	4.246	5.461	6.665	6.581	7.293	7.067	7.353
East Asia and Pacific	1.744	2.357	3.026	4.491	3.942	5.088	6.076	5.933	7.001	6.501	5.886	6.042
Sub-Saharan Africa	1.079	1.458	1.900	3.168	2.639	2.224	3.584	3.540	3.761	3.625	3.393	3.108
South Asia	0.671	0.576	0.724	0.941	0.984	1.331	1.442	1.619	1.342	1.262	1.417	1.505
Latin America and Caribbean	0.639	0.798	0.986	1.599	1.089	1.737	2.420	2.918	3.026	2.764	2.140	1.899

Source WITS, Turkey all products export US$ thousand, https://wits.worldbank.org/CountryProfile/en/Country/TUR/StartYear/2005/EndYear/2016/TradeFlow/Export/Indicator/XPRT-TRD-VL/Partner/BY-REGION/Product/Total

Table 10.2 2005–2016 imports of Turkey by Regions (in Billion USD)

Partner name	2005	2006	2007	2008	2009	2010	2011	2012	2013	2014	2015	2016
World	116.774	139.576	170.062	201.963	140.928	185.544	240.841	236.545	251.661	242.177	207.206	198.618
Europe and Central Asia	74.653	87.506	105.863	122.352	84.516	105.796	131.064	128.731	137.868	128.405	109.791	102.277
MENA	16.619	20.483	26.817	30.175	23.067	30.863	39.808	37.589	42.465	43.427	42.345	43.795
North America	11.649	14.781	15.736	15.959	9.080	15.758	23.528	24.413	25.260	23.445	16.149	16.506
East Asia and Pacific	5.822	6.935	9.033	13.405	9.513	13.238	17.353	15.084	13.966	13.835	12.061	11.930
Sub-Saharan Africa	2.030	2.465	3.116	3.818	2.752	3.560	5.394	5.143	5.009	5.055	4.689	5.041
South Asia	1.834	2.525	3.167	2.059	1.698	1.724	3.424	2.602	2.493	2.489	2.067	2.104
Latin America and Caribbean	1.731	2.179	3.149	3.606	3.151	5.174	8.411	7.267	7.923	8.495	7.037	7.048

Source WITS, Turkey all products import US$ THOUSAND, https://wits.worldbank.org/CountryProfile/en/Country/TUR/StartYear/2005/EndYear/2016/TradeFlow/Import/Indicator/MPRT-TRD-VL/Partner/BY-REGION/Product/Total

moving from 49.001 billion USD in 2012 to 36.819 billion USD in 2016. Turkey's total trade volume with the MENA region declined from 86.59 billion USD in 2012 to 80.614 billion USD in 2016. Turkey's trade volume with the world has also fallen from 399.787 billion USD in 2014 to 341.147 billion USD in 2016 (Tables 10.1 and 10.2). In the same vein, Turkey's response to the Syrian and Egyptian uprisings by breaking with the Assad regime in Syria and by siding with the Muslim brotherhood in Egypt demonstrates the increasing decline in the importance of economic factors in Turkey's post-Arab Spring foreign policy making. These moves undermined considerably the trading state status Turkey developed during its zero problems foreign policy era, which recommended the use of foreign policy to serve the country's economic interests by preferring cooperation over confrontation.

Furthermore, the rise of chaos in the MENA region pushed Turkey to further adopt military/security-based strategies in order to prevent and counteract the spillover effects of the deepening Syrian civil war into its territory. This resulted in several military interventions into Syrian territory to combat against terrorist groups like ISIS and the YPG-PYD which threatened the territorial security of Turkey. In the same manner, the worsening of Turkey–Russia relations following an incident in which Turkey shot down a Russian fighter in November 2015 suggests that Turkey adopted a different trading state strategy compared to the past by confronting one of its major economic partners over a border violation issue (The Conversation 2016).

Turkey's trading state status further declined due to domestic factors. 2016 saw significant unrest, including several deadly terrorist attacks and culminating in the failed military intervention of July 2016. In this context, security issues, more than trade, gained prominence in the setting of Turkish foreign policy. Turkey's increasing suspicions of its NATO allies following the July 2016 coup resulted in a growing belief that the country could not count on its Western allies for the protection of its borders and that it should diversify its partners as much as possible. The acquisition of sophisticated military equipment by the Turkish military is one sign of a resurgence of the traditional politico-military state in recent years.

On the other hand, Turkey's current economic difficulties appear to have further reduced its financial capacity to conduct a comprehensive and effective trading state policy. Turkey has also adopted some protectionist measures in order to encourage domestic production and consumption, which contrasts with Rosecrance's conception of a trading state pursuing free economic and trade policies. Measures to protect its domestic economy, especially in the current Trump era of trade wars in which trade is used as an instrument of coercion by the current US president, have been undertaken by Ankara. The USA doubled steel and aluminium tariffs on Turkey following political tension between both countries on American Pastor, Andrew Brunson, who was jailed in Turkey on terrorism charges and Turkey in turn retaliated by imposing sanctions on US goods. The security interdependency between Turkey and the USA did not prevent the leaders of both countries from engaging in a fierce trade war. This demonstrates that the world has become less and less a "trading" place where security and politics weight more heavily than states' economy/trade in the making of their foreign policies.

However, with respect to its relations with Europe, economic factors still appear to be one of the most important factors that tie the EU and Turkey together. Statistically, the EU remains Turkey's top trading partner, and Turkey ranks among the top five trading partners of the EU. This economic interdependency, combined with some security interdependency (migration deals for instance), explains why the EU cannot totally turn its back to Turkey and vice versa, despite increasing political tensions over normative issues in the last two years. As the table showcases, Europe and Central Asia hold the largest share of Turkey's total trade, in terms of both imports and exports.

The prevalence of economic factors in EU–Turkey relations is further demonstrated by recent positive discussions on the modernization and widening of the Customs Union to include agricultural products, services, and public procurement, despite increasing value and normative gap between the EU and Turkey, especially since the declaration of the state of emergency in Turkey in 2016 (Council of the EU 2016). While in the past Turkey was reluctant to engage in such discussion fearing that the modernization of the Customs Union might be a "hidden" alternative of its accession to the EU, it recently showed some enthusiasm to go ahead with this modernization project. This can be explained by the fact that, faced with decreasing hopes of accession to the EU and with the increasing number of FTAs concluded by the EU in recent years with third countries (such as TTIP and CETA), a modernized Customs Union seems to be the most rational alternative to economically benefit both Turkey and the EU. In this sense, Turkey acted as a trading state, which attaches higher consideration to economic factors over ideological or political ones.

10 ASSESSING THE TURKISH "TRADING STATE" IN SUB-SAHARAN AFRICA 249

Table 10.3 Share of Turkey's exports, imports, and total trade by regional groupings

	Import in % (2016)	Export in % (2016)	Total Trade in % (2016)	Change in total trade in a 10-year period (2006–2016)
World	100	100	100	51.54
Europe and central Asia	51.49	57.70	54.08	26.90
MENA	22.04	25.83	23.63	137.05
North America	8.31	5.15	6.99	17.71
East Asia and Pacific	6.00	4.23	5.26	93.62
Sub-Saharan Africa	2.53	2.18	2.38	107.72
South Asia	1.05	1.05	3.81	16.38
Latin America and Caribbean	3.54	1.33	2.62	200.53

Source Self prepare based on WITS, Turkey All Products Import US$ Thousand, https://wits.world-bank.org/CountryProfile/en/Country/TUR/StartYear/2005/EndYear/2016/TradeFlow/Import/Indicator/MPRT-TRD-VL/Partner/BY-REGION/Product/Total

Recent developments, namely the tightening of the relations between the USA and Turkey on one hand and between the USA and Europe on the other, which resulted in the rapprochement of Turkey and the EU to face President Trump's "uncertain" trade and multilateral policies, corroborates our view that Turkey is a trading state with respect to its relations with the EU (Table 10.3).

IS TURKEY A TRADING STATE IN AFRICA? OPPORTUNITIES AND LIMITATIONS

Although Turkey's orientation towards Africa began at the end of the 1990s and was largely based on diplomatic purposes aiming to increase Turkey's soft power and attraction, it certainly included a number of reasons shaping the benefits of pursuing a trade strategy in the continent. The 1990s and the first decade of the 2000s witnessed Turkey's increasing share in world trade as a result of significant increases in exports. The strengthening of its ties with its Middle Eastern neighbours largely contributed to the construction of its trading state actorness in both its own region and other extra-regional geographies, including Africa. The need of Turkish SMEs to find new markets to sell their products and to invest in has also played a significant role in Turkey's reinvention of Africa during the first decade of the 2000s. The following sections will first attempt to grasp the foreign policy-trade linkage in Turkey's African policy towards SSA. Second, it will delve into an assessment of Turkey's trade strategy towards the region with a special focus on its instruments, its geographical focus, and the sectors in which it is engaged. Third, it will discuss the benefits and limitations of the Turkish trading state in the SSA region.

Decrypting Turkey's Foreign Policy-Trade Linkage in SSA

Trade was historically been a secondary concern in the formulation of Turkish foreign policy since the Republican era. Although this changed progressively starting in the early 1980s with the launch of liberal economic reforms pushing for economic liberalization and the opening of markets to the rest of the world, the political instability that hit Turkey in the 1990s reduced the importance of economic factors in the formulation and implementation of Turkish foreign policy. While trade occupied 9% of Turkey's GDP in 1975, it increased to respectively 23% in 1995, 39% in 2005, 42% in 2007, and 54% in 2017. These percentages clearly show how Turkey has progressively become a trading country in the last forty years. The Customs Union and the start of Turkey's accession talks with the EU have also contributed to the rise of the role of trade in Turkish foreign policy. Added to this, the power shift observed in the changing international order which was characterized by the rise of emerging powers and informal groupings like the G20 and BRICS in the world economy. Turkey also profited from the rise of the rest and has progressively become a pole of attraction in terms of trade and investment in the eyes of both its Western allies and rising peers.

The changing domestic environment in Turkey with the arrival of the AKP in 2002 offered new trading options for Turkey as a consequence of its shifting neighbourhood policy which led to the diversification of its trade partners, the lifting of visa requirements with some of its neighbours, and the increasing of FDI and money flows from oil-rich Arab countries most specifically. Here, it must be remembered that Turkey's changing trade trends observed during the first decade of the 2000s led to the diminishment of the EU's share in Turkey's trade in the face of Turkey's decreasing trade with its Middle Eastern and other extra-regional countries.

The first decade of the 2000s in Turkey, in this sense, can be considered a shift from a politico-security state to Rosecrance's trading state. From this perspective, the 2000s can be seen as a period witnessing Turkey's increasing attention towards economic diplomacy and trade policies.

Turkey's opening to the SSA region in the early years of the 2000s should be considered as part and parcel of its evolving "trading state" status. Although Turkey has been associated with the SSA region since the early years of the Ottoman era, a quasi-absence of the African continent from Turkey's foreign policy priorities from the decline of the Ottoman Empire to the Ataturk era until the 1990s can be observed. While Turkey launched its Africa's opening policy in 1998 under Ismail Cem's leadership, the effective beginning of Turkey's foreign policy towards Africa is generally traced back to the 2000s where "initial assessments of Africa's potential were made and lower-level meetings were held between Turkish officials and their African counterparts" (Özkan 2016, 1–14). A strategy on the Development of the Economic Relations with African countries was prepared in 2003 by the Under-secretariat for Foreign Trade (Kizilarslan 2009, 20–21), and Turkey has since begun to adopt a high-profile picture in the sub-Saharan African regions in the areas of politics, economics, and development assistance. The fact that this strategy has exclusively focused on increasing trade and investment ties between the EU and Africa constitutes another clear indication of the predominant role played by trade as one of the main motivations behind Turkey's opening to SSA. Indeed, the strategy enumerated the following aims:

> to increase the share of Turkey in the total trade volume of African countries up to 3% in three years (The share of Turkey in the total trade volume of Africa which is 567 billion dollars in 2005 is 2.1%), To open way for our small and medium sized enterprises so that they can penetrate into the region countries, To make either joint investments or direct Turkish investments with the relevant countries in Africa in order to increase the competitive power of Turkey in certain sectors, To transfer technology from Turkey to the region countries, To raise the share of Turkish construction, consultancy and engineering firms in the African markets, To diminish the poverty by investing in African countries through increasing the economic activities and creating more value added in those domestic economies. (Kızılarslan 2009, 20–21)

Following the declaration of 2005 as the year of Africa, Turkey-SSA relations intensified to an unprecedented rate. With respect to Turkey's

252   E. PARLAR DAL AND S. DIPAMA

relations with African regional communities, it must be remembered that some Turkish embassies were accredited to some regional communities.[1] In terms of economic cooperation between Turkey and sub-Saharan African countries, trade relations between both partners have been flourishing since the 2000s. According to the Turkish Ministry of Foreign Affairs, Turkey's bilateral trade volume with Africa has reached 17.5 billion USD in 2015, which represents a threefold increase in volume compared to the accounts of 2013. Trade volume with SSA amounted to 6 billion USD in 2015 (Turkish Ministry of Foreign Affairs). The expansion of Turkish Airlines direct flights to 33 sub-Saharan African countries has contributed tremendously to further intensify commercial interconnection between Turkey and SSA (Turkish Airlines Website).

In this context, some have argued that economic factors were the real motivations behind Turkey's engagement in SSA and that non-economic means such as development aid and diplomacy were used only as the point of contact that will ease the penetration of Turkey's business groups in SSA. Another clear indication of Turkey's trading state posture in Africa is the signature of several free trade agreements with some African countries and the conclusion of economic, commercial, and technical cooperation agreements with some African countries (Tepebas 2015, 18).[2] This also explains why trade volume between Turkey and SSA countries has exponentially increased since the beginning of Turkey's opening to Africa with Turkish total trade volume (export and imports) reaching $19.5 billion in 2015, up from 810 million USD in 2002 (Turkish Ministry of Foreign Affairs).

In this vein, we can argue that economic factors were the top pushing factors behind Turkey's opening to SSA, although non-economic means such as the provision of development and humanitarian aid and

---

[1] For instance, the Turkish Embassy in Addis Ababa is accredited to the Intergovernmental Authority on Development Partners Forum (IGAD) (2012); Turkish Embassy in Abuja is accredited to the Economic Community of West African States (ECOWAS) (2005); Turkish Embassy in Dar-es-Salaam is accredited to the East African Community (EAC) (2010); Turkish Embassy in Lusaka is accredited to Common Market for Eastern and Southern Africa (COMESA) (2012); and Turkish Embassy in Libreville is accredited to Economic Community of Central African States (ECCAS) (2013).

[2] These countries include Angola, Benin, Botswana, Burkina Faso, Burundi, Capo Verde, Djibouti, Chad, Eritrea, Ethiopia, Ivory Coast, Gabon, Gambia, Guinea, Ghana, South Africa, DRC, Lesotho, Liberia, Madagascar, Malawi, Mali, Mauritania, Namibia, Nigeria, RCA, Sao Tome and Principe, Senegal, Seychelles, Sierra Leone, Somalia, Tanzania, Cameroon, Kenya, and Uganda.

strengthening of diplomatic ties were used to achieve this goal of intensifying economic relations between Turkey and SSA. One scholar stressed that in this sense "Turkey wants to legitimize its role on the world stage and make out that it is not interested in just trade and economics, but humanitarian issues too" (Christie-Miller 2012). In this sense, some contend that "the current Turkish government has therefore been using humanitarian assistance as an initial point of contact with African countries" (Tepeciklioglu et al. 2017). Similarly, another scholar, Brendon Cannon, also underscores the prevalence of politico-economic interests behind Turkey's engagement in Somalia by arguing that the main reason behind Turkey's engagement is to "gain political and diplomatic capital outside of Somalia as well as the locating of another market for Turkish goods" (Cannon 2016, 103).

Turkey's Trade Strategy Towards Africa: Instruments, Geographical Focus, Sectors

Given this background, this section will turn to the ground, with a special focus on the instruments used by the Turkish trading state in the SSA context and its geographical and sector-related priorities in this region. Finally, it will evaluate the opportunities and challenges of Turkish trading state in the SSA.

Instruments

Development Aid

In the field of development aid, Turkey has acquired a pivotal role as a development aid provider in Africa over the last decade. Multiple actors intervene in the field of Turkish development aid to SSA. These actors include governmental institutions, namely the Turkish Cooperation and Coordination Agency (TIKA), the Disaster and Emergency Management Presidency (AFAD), and other non-governmental organizations such as the Humanitarian Relief Foundation (IHH) and *Kimse Yok MU*. According to OECD statistics, Turkey's official development assistance's disbursement to sub-Saharan Africa increased from 23.6 million USD in 2007 to 152.31 million USD in 2017. TIKA currently has coordination offices in 16 countries in SSA: Cameroon, Chad, Comoros, Djibouti, Ethiopia, Guinea Conakry, Kenya, Mozambique, Namibia, Niger, Senegal, Somalia, South Africa, South Sudan, Sudan, and Tanzania. The pursuit of economic benefits does not fall outside of Turkey's development aid agenda towards SSA. There is no need to say that Turkey is in quest for new markets to export its low-valued manufactured goods as well as for new economic partners. Some observers argue in this line that foreign aid "has been the main tool for Turkey to gain a foothold in African countries" (Kucuk 2015, 24) and to open pace for the "Anatolian tigers" to promote and expand trade and investment activities in Africa. In this respect, an anonymous interviewee from TIKA underlines that although the pursuit of humanitarian goals is of outmost importance, Turkey also looks at the strategic importance and commercial relations with recipient countries while designing its foreign policy (Interviewee 1). As a consequence of this strategy, trade volume between Turkey and SSA countries has exponentially increased since the beginning of Turkey's opening to Africa with Turkish total trade volume (exports and imports) reaching $19.5 billion in 2015, up from $810 million in 2002.

In Somalia, for instance, some observers argue that Turkey's development and humanitarian aid policy has played an important role in the preference given to Turkish companies for the implementation of some infrastructure projects in the country by the Somali government. In illustration, the Turkish company Favori received a 20-year Somali government contract in September 2013 to manage Mogadishu's airport, which was renovated by Kozuva, another Turkish company. Under the terms of the agreement, Favori receives half of all revenues, while it provides the other half to the government during the 20 years (*The Somali Investor* 2016).

Similarly, another Turkish company, Al Bayrak, was offered a 20-year contract in October 2013 for the management of the seaport of Mogadishu (Achilles et al. 2015, 20). Under this agreement, 55% of revenue generated at the port will be earmarked for the government while the Turkish company receives 45%. According to statistics, the share of economic infrastructure in TIKA's budget allocation for the implementation of aid projects in Somalia increased from 16% in 2012 to 70% in 2014 (Achilles et al. 2015, 24).

Based on the above examples, one could easily argue that Turkey's increasing focus on the physical infrastructure sector in Somalia, such as repaving roads and renovating the airport in Mogadishu, is also due to the need to create a smooth and adequate space for the development of business activities between Somalia and Turkey. Underscoring the prevalence of politico-economic interests behind Turkey's engagement in Somalia, Brendon Cannon argues that,

Turkey's interest in Somalia is driven not by Turkey's and Somalia's common Sunni Muslim heritage, or its Muslim Brotherhood ties, or because of some greater appeal to charity and development. Rather, Turkey's main aim in engaging Somalia is to gain political and diplomatic capital outside of Somalia as well as the locating of another market for Turkish goods. (Cannon 2016, 103)

Free Trade Agreements and Other Economic Facilitations

Free trade agreements and other trade exchange facilitations have also been used by Turkey as an instrument of its trading state strategy towards the SSA countries. According to sources, Turkey signed FTAs with Morocco (2004), Tunisia (2004), Egypt (2005), and Mauritius (2011) (Bacchi 2016, 16). An additional FTA concluded by Ghana has not yet been signed (allAfrica 2014). In addition, it must be noted that four new FTA negotiations are still ongoing with the Democratic Republic of Congo, Cameroon, Seychelles, and Libya, whereas the possibility of the opening of new FTA negotiations with Algeria and South Africa remain on the table. The number of the countries with which Turkey has signed Trade and Economic Cooperation Agreement and established a bilateral regular follow-up mechanism covering several topics such as trade, investment, SMEs, health, and technology increased from 23 in 2003 to 45 in 2017. The number of SSA countries with which Turkey signed Reciprocal Protection of Investment Agreements rose from 4 in 2003 to 24 in 2018 (Investment Policy Hub). Finally, Turkey has signed 11 Prevention of Double Taxation Agreements with African countries, up from only 4 in 2003 (Website of Turkey–Africa Forum).

FDI

In terms of FDI, it is important to note that Turkish business groups have established various frameworks to encourage Turkish companies to invest in SSA and to further increase commercial ties between Turkey and the countries of this region. In this context, regular meetings and business trips are organized with African business partners in Turkey by several Turkish businessmen associations such as the Foreign Economic Relations Board (DEIK), Independent Industrialists' and Businessmen's Association (MUSIAD), and the Turkish Industry and Business

Association (TUSIAD), to encourage its members to invest in Africa. In this line, the Foreign Economic Relations Board (DEIK) has established business councils in many African countries (see Table 10.4), whose purpose is "to help increase and diversify Turkey's exports to African countries, and to encourage host countries to engage in joint investments" (DEIK website). The Business Councils organize joint meetings in their respective countries and support Turkish Export Fairs to promote products made in Turkey. With investments in African countries, Turkish companies have the long-term opportunity to tap into the potential of this continent" (DEIK website). The sending of business consultants to the newly opened Turkish embassies in SSA is another measure adopted to promote and increase Turkish trade with Africa.

According to official data, "Turkish contractors so far have undertaken in Africa over 1,150 projects which worth $55 billion. In this regard, total Turkish investment in Africa is estimated to be around 46.2 billion" (Turkish Ministry of Foreign Affairs), while it was less than $100 million in 2003. Here, it must be underlined that it is difficult to obtain comprehensive and detailed data about FDI inflow into SSA. However, some sources indicate that in terms of FDI, Turkish companies contributed up to US$6 billion in direct investments in Africa, with the Horn of Africa keeping the largest share to date (*Hurriyet Daily News* 2016).

Geographical and Sectoral Focus
In terms of geographical distribution, Table 10.5 indicates that four out of the top ten trading partners of Turkey in SSA are in West Africa (Nigeria, Senegal, Cote d'Ivoire, and Ghana), two in South Africa (Angola and South Africa), three in East Africa (Sudan, Ethiopia, and Tanzania), and one in Central Africa (Cameroon). This geographical distribution clearly shows that Turkey has managed to diversify during the last decade its largest trading partners across all the sub-regions of SSA as much as possible.

Among its top 10 trading partners, three are notable. Turkey has concluded but not yet signed an FTA with Ghana and is in the process of discussing the opening of FTA negotiations with South Africa while negotiations are ongoing with Cameroon. Table 10.5 also illustrates Turkey's difficulties in signing an FTA with its largest trading partners. This may also emanate from the reluctance of these SSA countries to open their own markets to Turkish products due to competition.

Table 10.4 List of business councils created in the bottom of DEIK between Turkey and SSA countries

Turkey–South Africa Business council	1997
Turkey–Ethiopia Business council	2008
Turkey–Sudan business council	2008
Turkey–Kenya business council	2010
Turkey–Angola business council	2011
Turkey–Ghana business council	2011
Turkey–Mauritania business council	2011
Turkey–Nigeria business council	2011
Turkey–Tanzania business council	2011
Turkey–Uganda business council	2011
Turkey–Gambia business council	2012
Turkey–Rwanda business council	2012
Turkey–Equatorial Guinea business council	2014
Turkey–Ivory Coast business council	2014
Turkey–Cameroon business council	2014
Turkey–Mauritius business council	2014
Turkey–Benin business council	2015
Turkey–Djibouti business council	2015
Turkey–Chad business council	2015
Turkey–Republic of Congo business council	2015
Turkey–Mali business council	2015
Turkey–Mozambique business council	2015
Turkey–Niger business council	2015
Turkey–Senegal business council	2015
Turkey–Somalia business council	2015
Turkey–DRC Business council	2016
Turkey–Guinea business council	2016
Turkey–Cape Verde business council	2017
Turkey–Zimbabwe business council	2017
Turkey–Burundi business council	2017
Turkey–Malawi business council	2017
Turkey–Namibia business council	2017
Turkey–Zambia business council	2017
Turkey–Burkina Faso business council	2018
Turkey–Togo business council	2018

Source DEIK website

Turkey also signed agreements on avoiding double taxation and on investment protection with Ethiopia, Sudan, and South Africa. Some sources further indicate that Ethiopia received $3.2 billion of Turkey's total FDI to Africa while other significant recipients have been Sudan, South Africa, and Nigeria. On the other hand, the leading sectors for Turkish investment in SSA are construction, textiles, manufacturing, and agricultural vehicles (Shinn 2016).

Table 10.5 Trading partners of Turkey in SSA, in 2018

Country	Ranking
South Africa	1st
Nigeria	2nd
Sudan	3rd
Senegal	4th
Cote d'Ivoire	5th
Ethiopia	6th
Ghana	7th
Tanzania	8th
Angola	9th
Cameroon	10th

In terms of sectors, Table 10.6 showcases that consumer products made up the largest group (around 42.86%) of Turkey's export products to SSA in 2016, followed by intermediate goods (34.47%) and capital goods (20.48%). An analysis of the above table further indicates that in terms of Turkey's imports from SSA, raw materials (44.12%) constitutes the largest import product in 2016. Given that Turkey only exports 1.38% of raw material to SSA, it can be concluded that Turkey ran a raw material trade deficit with SSA because of the large gap existing between Turkey's raw material exports to and imports from SSA.

Benefits and Limitations

Opportunities

Turkey's opening to the African continent has gone hand in hand with the increase in trade relations with the African continent. Together with the development of Turkey's diplomatic and political relations with the region since 2005, the volume of trade exchange with SSA countries has also showed a significant rise. Table 10.7 further corroborates the prevalence of economic factors in Turkey's approach towards SSA. As can be seen from the table, SSA's imports from Turkey increased by 192% between 2006 and 2016 and SSA's exports to Turkey increased by 61% in the same period. In a 10 years period, the Turkey-SSA trade volume increased by almost 253%, far above the change in trade volume of SSA with the world (74%).

An examination of Table 10.8 indicates that Turkey's trade volume with almost every African country has significantly increased between

10 ASSESSING THE TURKISH "TRADING STATE" IN SUB-SAHARAN AFRICA 259

Table 10.6 Share of products imports and exports by turkey with SSA in 2016

	Export product to SSA Share (%)	Import products from SSA Share (%)
All products	100	100
Capital goods	20.48	8.37
Consumer goods	42.86	20.85
Intermediate goods	34.47	26.65
Raw materials	1.38	44.12
Animal	0.70	0.56
Chemicals	9.02	1.83
Food products	13.23	34.93
Footwear	0.41	0.00
Fuels	2.91	9.66
Hides and skins	0.05	0.51
Ores and metals	2.96	9.93
Minerals	4.29	2.24
Miscellaneous	5.23	0.16
Plastic and rubber	7.01	0.55
Stone and glass	1.90	4.77
Transportation	4.70	21.55
Vegetables	7.43	9.97
Woods	4.27	2.19

Source https://wits.worldbank.org/CountryProfile/en/Country/TUR/StartYear/2016/EndYer/2016/TradeFlow/Export/Indicator/XPRT-PRDCT-SHR/Partner/SSF/Product/86-89_Transport

Table 10.7 SSA's trade with Turkey and the world

	Change in imports (2006–2016) (%)	Total value of imports in million USD	Share of total import (%)	Change in exports (2006–2016) (%)	Total value of exports in million USD	Share of total exports (%)
Turkey	192	26.139	0.8	61	10.023	0.3
World	56	3432.539	100	18	3573.221	100

Source Retrieved from: REASSESSING AFRICA'S GLOBAL PARTNERSHIPS: Approaches for engaging the new world order, p. 110, https://www.brookings.edu/wp-content/uploads/2018/01/foresight-2018_chapter-6_web_final.pdf

2005 and 2018. In this sense, it can be argued that behind this significant increase in Turkey's trade volume with SSA lays both economic necessities and strategic engagement of Turkey with the continent which is also a clear sign of the rising Turkish trading state in SSA (Dal et al. 2018).

Trade clearly appears as one of the main pushing factors behind Turkey's opening to Africa policy. Indeed, the global financial crisis that hit Europe in 2008 and had negative spillover effects on Turkey's economy pushed Turkey to increasingly look for strategies to diversify its markets and commercial partners. Africa in this context constitutes the most dynamic market where Turkey can export its low-valued and medium-quality products and at the same time import raw materials and oil (Dal et al. 2018). In addition, Turkey feels the necessity of diversifying its economic partners as much as possible in order not to be too much dependent on a small group of countries. In face of the current economic crisis in Turkey, Turkish authorities have even called on African partners to trade in the local currency in order to counteract the currency diplomacy increasingly used by the Trump administration against its detractors. In this context, during the recent Turkey–Africa Economy and Business Forum in Istanbul, President Erdogan underlined the necessity to trade in local currencies as the country faced speculative attacks. He further added that Turkey is ready to strengthen its trade relations using local currencies with both its main trade partners and African partners (Anadolu Agency 2018).

The prevalence of economic considerations is particularly remarkable in the cases of some SSA countries such as Ethiopia, Nigeria, and South Africa since Turkey's relations with these countries are more based on trade and investment than on development and humanitarian assistance. In Ethiopia, for instance, Turkey appears as the leading country with US$2.5 billion direct investment, and Turkish companies located in this country are the single largest foreign employer in the country (Dal et al. 2018). This is explainable by the fact that Turkey hails its development aid based on recipient needs, which means that priority is given to poor countries (Table 10.9).

Furthermore, the increasing involvement of Turkish civil society organizations in the field of humanitarian aid in SSA is another indication of the prevalence of economic considerations in Turkey's foreign policy towards SSA. Here, it must be underlined that in recent years, public institutions in Turkey started to work more intensively with Turkish civil society organizations (Tepeciklioglu et al. 2017) in the formulation and implementation of development and humanitarian projects in SSA. Since most of the activities of these humanitarian NGOs are financed by Turkish business groups having economic interests in SSA, humanitarian assistance conducted by CSOs constitutes another channel

Table 10.8 Change in Turkey's trade with SSA countries between 2005 and 2018

Country	Trade 2005(USD)	Trade 2010(USD)	Trade 2016 (USD)	Trade 2018 (USD)	Change in a 13 Year period (%)
Angola	35.93	109.39	134.8	184.89	414.58
Benin	7.30	119.91	87.14	121.2	1560.27
Botswana	0.26	0.62	2.90	1.07	311.53
Burkina Faso	4.17	55.17	69.42	40.86	879.85
Burundi	2.03	4.39	0.14	2.13	4.92
Cameroon	52.39	88.52	111.83	166.80	218.38
Chad	1.14	39.07	42.18	45.01	3848.24
Congo	29.50	56.66	111.09	47.53	61.11
Cote d'Ivoire	59.66	115.14	361.17	325.3	445.25
DRC	2.24	17.04	60.2	33.31	1387.02
Djibouti	7.23	31.17	78.03	150.81	1985.89
Equatorial Guinea	10.77	32.80	24.21	22.68	110.58
Eritrea	12.23	6.84	18.03	7.19	−41.21
Ethiopia	139.67	215.78	439.71	293.53	110.15
Gabon	27.45	23.87	25.66	29.27	6.63
Gambia	10.53	20.71	18.19	40.01	279.86
Ghana	104.81	290.84	478.93	284.73	171.66
Guinea	12.34	30.34	68.65	153.84	1145.67
Guinea-Bissau	0.18	2.51	5.7	4.33	2035.55
Kenya	52.32	99.74	140.92	148.34	183.52
Lesotho	0.54	0.70	0.37	2.40	344.44
Liberia	58.75	75.06	73.57	124.31	111.59
Madagascar	9.46	28.93	64.2	66.98	608.03
Malawi	18.56	23.62	18.39	19.07	2.74
Mali	12.89	11.32	73.83	69.92	442.43
Mauritania	11.05	38.88	88.33	132.8	1101.80
Mauritius	15.67	29.07	40.52	59.52	279.83
Mozambique	18.73	89.38	115.03	135.28	622.26
Namibia	0.93	3.70	41.7	24.37	2520.43
Niger	4.01	14.75	24	40.4	907.48
Nigeria	129.98	471.15	399.414	404.35	211.08
Rwanda	0.36	7.99	29.64	17.21	2768.33
Senegal	35.41	84.76	160.13	326.51	822.08
Seychelles	5.90	4.69	11.52	18.75	217.79
Sierra Leone	5.42	35.07	43.76	48.26	790.40
Somalia	3.05	6.17	118.04	149.79	4811.14
South Africa	1575.72	1258.87	1463	1613.46	2.39
Sudan	153.19	232.96	510.10	352.35	130

(continued)

262   E. PARLAR DAL AND S. DIPAMA

Table 10.8 (continued)

Country	Trade 2005(USD)	Trade 2010(USD)	Trade 2016 (USD)	Trade 2018 (USD)	Change in a 13 Year period (%)
Tanzania	33.05	103.65	118.64	211.74	540.66
Togo	7.60	37.51	39.91	72.18	849.73

Source Turkish Ministry of Trade statistics, available at https://biruni.tuik.gov.tr/disticaretapp/disticaret_ing.zul?param1=4&param2=9&sitcrev=0&isicrev=0&sayac=5911

through which Turkish business groups enter the African markets and acquire stronger legitimacy vis-à-vis their African partners.

Moreover, the increasing involvement of non-state actors in Turkey's foreign policy towards SSA is another signal of Turkey's rise as a trading state in the region. In this vein, Turkish non-state actors, mainly business and interest groups, attempt to influence Turkish trade policies in Africa thanks to lobbying and agenda setting and Turkish public authorities set the background for the achievement of their objectives by the help of diplomatic and logistic support, trade deals, and Turkish Airlines direct flights (Dal et al. 2018). In this sense, the significant involvement of non-state actors in Turkey's opening policy towards SSA is often considered as increasing evidence of a "smooth convergence of both governmental and business policies" (Özkan 2012, 129). For some authors, Turkey is not different from other "imperial" powers acting in the African continent, but rather constitutes "one more player" for African markets (Langan 2016, 1409).

In addition, several recent developments seem to further confirm the fact that Turkey is still a trading state, prioritizing trade relations over political considerations. Following the attempted coup d'état of July 2016, Turkey extracted pledges from African countries to either close schools in Africa belonging to the Fethullah Gulen movement or facilitate their take over by the Maarif Foundation, established after the 2016 coup attempt (Anadolu Agency 2017). To date, nineteen African countries have handed over Gulen schools to Maarif or closed them at Ankara's request (Niger, Chad, Djibouti, Equatorial Guinea, Mali, Tanzania, Congo, DRC, Senegal, Somalia, Sudan, Mauritania, Cameroon, Gabon, Guinea, Gambia, Cote d'Ivoire, Burundi, and Sierra Leone) (Anadolu Agency 2017).

Table 10.9 Turkey's trade with Nigeria, Ethiopia, and South Africa (in USD)

	2005	2010	2016	2018	Rank as Turkey's trading partner in SSA in 2018
South Africa	1.57572	1.25887	1463	1613.46	1st
Ethiopia	139.67	215.78	439.71	293.53	6th
Nigeria	129.98	471.15	399.414	404.35	2nd

Source Turkish Trade Ministry

Three of Turkey's top 10 trading partners in SSA, respectively, South Africa, Nigeria, and Ethiopia (Table 10.9), have not yet agreed to Turkey's request to either take control or close schools linked to the Gulen movement (Angey 2018, 53–68). As one scholar argued,

> dissymmetrical relations with several African states would make it easier for Turkey to make pression on these governments about passing the administration of FETO-linked schools under the Maarif Foundation. Conversely, other countries whose political and economic strength are comparable to Turkey's (such as South Africa) have been notably reluctant to comply with Turkish demands. (Angey 2018, 60).

However, the stalemate in the closing or handing over of schools does not seem to have negatively impacted trade relations between Turkey and each of these countries. As can be seen in the table above, with the exception of Ethiopia, Turkey's trade with Nigeria and South Africa has increased from 399.414 USD in 2016 to 404.35 USD and from 1463 USD in 2016 to 1613.46 USD in 2018, respectively. Table 10.9 furthermore indicates that South Africa (1st), Nigeria (2nd), and Ethiopia (6th) remained among Turkey's top ten largest trading partners in SSA in 2018.

In this context, Turkey continues to use soft diplomatic and economic means to get the governing authorities to respond positively to its request. In the case of South Africa, Birol Akgün, the head of Turkey's Maarif Foundation, told Anadolu Agency that they had "signed an education cooperation deal with South Africa's National Education Ministry…{and} are planning to open a school there in the 2018–2019 term" (*Daily Sabah* 2018). Turkey also signed a memorandum of understanding with the Ethiopian Foreign Ministry which gives it the right to run schools in this country, initially in the cities of Addis Ababa, Harar, and Mekele (*Yeni Safak* 2018).

Challenges

Despite this sharp increase in trade relations between Turkey in SSA and the increasing importance of economic factors in Turkey's transformative foreign policy towards SSA, several factors considerably undermine and limit Turkey's trading status in SSA. First, it remains difficult to qualify Turkey as a successful trading state in Africa because the economic interdependence between Turkey and African countries is not as pronounced as one may expect. Africa still lags far behind in terms of potential economic partners of Turkey and a restricted number of Turkish companies intervening in Africa are mostly small and medium-sized firms. Despite the fact that Turkey aims to reach US$50 billion in trade with Africa as of 2023, its trade with African countries remains imbalanced, and this asymmetry in their bilateral relations refrains the latter from further developing their economic relations with Turkey (Dal et al. 2018).

As seen in Table 10.7 above on SSA's trade with Turkey and the world, there is a non-negligible trade imbalance between Turkey and SSA because Turkey exports more to SSA than it imports from SSA. Table 10.7 also showcases that, although Turkey's share of SSA total exports increased to around 63% between 2006 and 2016, its share of SSA's total exports in 2016 (0.3%) was largely below its share of SSA's total imports (0.8%) in the same year. This further stems from the fact that Turkey's rank among SSA's import partners positively changed from 34th in 2005 to 22nd in 2015 (Table 10.10). Although this is a clear sign of increasing trade exchange between Turkey and SSA, Turkey is still not a key trading partner of SSA compared to other EU, Arab, and Asian countries (see Table 10.10). The same trend is observed about the ranking of Turkey among SSA export partners, as shown in Table 10.11.

In addition, there are some existing obstacles that considerably limit the intensity and sustainability of Turkey's trade with SSA and cast doubts on Turkey ability to be a successful "trading state". One of these obstacles is the lack of sufficient access to finance in Turkey for Turkish companies willing to operate in SSA (*Daily Sabah* 2015). In this vein, some observers claim that bank credits and insurance services offered to Turkish companies are far from sufficient. Other challenges facing Turkish companies include among others double taxation and transportation-related problems, which further limits intensification of its trade relations in SSA (Aybar 2018).

Furthermore, whether Turkey's African policy towards SSA is based on a comprehensive and long-projected strategy constitutes another

10 ASSESSING THE TURKISH "TRADING STATE" IN SUB-SAHARAN AFRICA   265

Table 10.10   Rankings of Import Partners of sub-Saharan Africa

Partner name	2005 ($Billion)	Rank	2015 ($Billion)	Rank
South Africa	11.151	1	20.195	2
Germany	9.891	2	11.945	4
China	9.650	3	37.120	1
France	8.407	4	8.306	7
USA	7.207	5	10.277	5
Japan	6.013	6	6.611	10
UK	5.990	7	5.209	11
Saudi Arabia	5.107	8	9.425	6
Nigeria	3.813	9	7.444	8
India	3.561	10	12.450	3
Turkey	0.813	34	2.264	22

Source WITS, Sub-Saharan All Products Import US$ Thousand, https://wits.worldbank.org/
CountryProfile/en/Country/SSF/StartYear/2005/EndYear/2015/TradeFlow/Import/Indicator/
MPRT-TRD-VL/Partner/BY-COUNTRY/Product/Total

Table 10.11   Rankings of export partners of sub-Saharan Africa

Partner name	2005 ($Billion)	Rank	2015 ($Billion)	Rank
UK	11.276	1	5.370	9
USA	10.899	2	9.057	3
Japan	6.007	3	4.446	14
China	5.736	4	23.477	1
Netherlands	5.467	5	7.120	6
France	4.631	6	4.882	10
South Africa	4.613	7	7.845	4
Germany	4.362	8	6.063	7
Switzerland	3.180	9	7.461	5
Spain	3.063	10	4.504	13
India	1.953	14	10.344	2
Turkey	0.366	42	2.264	22

Source WITS, Sub-Saharan all products export US$ thousand https://wits.worldbank.org/
CountryProfile/en/Country/SSF/StartYear/2005/EndYear/2015/TradeFlow/Export/Indicator/
XPRT-TRD-VL/Partner/BY-COUNTRY/Product/Total

preoccupation for the future development of Turkey–SSA relations. Given the foreign policy-trade linkage, any change in Turkey's foreign policy activism might harm Turkey's trading state posture in Africa. Another factor that might limit Turkey's trading power in the region is the deterioration of Turkish economics as a result of the ongoing implications of the recent economic crisis on Turkey–Africa trade relations. In this regard, the sustainability of Turkey's African activism is very much dependant on the combination of multiple factors including the amelioration of Turkey's current economic indicators, the continuity of Turkey's willingness to be an active partner of Africa in trade, security, and other global governance-related areas, and other major and rising powers' policies towards the region.

Lastly, aside from its pursuit of a trading state strategy, Turkey has recently engaged in adopting a security-based/military strategy towards SSA. However, it must be noted that this military strategy is still weak in content and practice given that, compared to traditional and emerging powers with larger military presences in SSA (USA, France, India, and UAE), Turkey's military presence in the region is still minimal. Like China, Japan, Saudi Arabia, Germany, and the UK, Turkey only has one official military base in Somalia (Table 10.12). On the other hand, some claims (not yet verified by Turkish authorities) have been made about the possibility of the opening of a military unofficial hotspot of Turkey in Suakin/Sudan and a new military base in Djibouti in the upcoming years. However, despite this limited "military/security" turn in Turkey's African strategy, it is still too early to claim that Turkey's military/security state strategy towards SSA weighs heavily on its trading state posture in this region. On the other hand, Turkey's emerging security-based approach to Africa is a clear sign of its willingness to extend its geopolitical influence in the Horn of Africa and to rival with other

Table 10.12 Number of official foreign military bases in SSA by owner

Turkey	1 (Somalia)
China	1 (Djibouti)
Japan	1 (Djibouti)
France	8 (Chad, Mali, Gabon, Burkina Faso, Cote d'Ivoire, Djibouti, Niger)
UK	1 (Kenya)
UAE	2 (Eritrea, Somaliland)
India	2 (Madagascar, the Seychelles)
Saudi Arabia	1 (Djibouti)
Germany	1 (Niger)
USA	13 (Burkina Faso, Cameroon, Chad, CAR, DRC, Djibouti, Ethiopia, Kenya, Niger, Somalia, the Seychelles, Uganda, South Sudan)

Source IRIN News

foreign powers intervening in this region. The increasing use of hardcore military capabilities by Turkey in the Horn of Africa may also be seen as a manoeuvre undermining its trading state in one of the strategic locations of international trade (Telci and Horoz 2018, 144).

CONCLUSION

This article argues that Turkey is undoubtedly playing the role of a trading state in SSA. However, yet this trading status needs to be further consolidated through overcoming some domestic challenges. Indeed, economic factors have been the most important factors pushing Turkey's opening to SSA policy, although it has predominantly used diplomatic, development, and humanitarian assistance policies to achieve its primary objective of increasing economic ties with SSA countries. This is evidenced by the fact that the growing relations between Turkey and SSA in terms of diplomacy and development have gone hand in hand with an exponential rise of trade and investment relations between them. From 2006 to 2016, Turkey's trade with individual African countries increased at an unprecedented rate (Turkey–SSA trade volume has increased by almost 253% during this period). In some SSA countries such as Nigeria, Ethiopia, and South Africa, trade relations outweighed humanitarian and to some extent diplomatic relations, although humanitarian aid and diplomatic relations were initially used as the first point of contact.

Humanitarian and development aid, especially that implemented by Turkish humanitarian NGOs in SSA and mostly financed by Turkish business groups, has been the most effective instrument to enhance economic relations with SSA countries. The growing involvement of these non-state actors in Turkey's African policy follows one of the preconditions of trading states as defined by Rosecrance, which is the influence of a wide range of non-state actors in the making of a state's foreign policy.

While underscoring the prevalence of economic factors in Turkey's foreign policy towards SSA, some even argue that Turkey's business and interest groups have pushed the hardest for Turkey to formulate and implement its African opening policy since they see it as an opportunity to enter the African market.

Recent development in Turkey's domestic politics, especially the failed military intervention of July 2016, is another factor impacting Turkey's trading state in SSA. The fact that Turkey has continued to increase economic relations with South Africa, Nigeria, and Ethiopia, the three main trading partners in SSA that have not yet responded positively to Turkey's demands for the closing of Gulen-linked schools in SSA or the handing over of these schools to the newly established Maarif Foundation confirms the country's pursuit of a trading state strategy. The existing stalemate with these countries seems to have not negatively impacted their economic relations with Turkey. In this respect, Turkey seems to have been acting as a trading state which prioritizes, in Rosecrance's terms, economic factors over political ones in the making of its foreign policy.

Last but not least, Turkey is undoubtedly a trading state in SSA with limited impact mainly due to its weaknesses in overcoming the challenges relevant to its domestic politics and its asymmetrical trade relations with its SSA partners. Indeed, the existing transportation and double taxation problems and the limited source of finance for Turkish companies willing to settle their business in SSA are among other factors which considerably weaken and limit Turkey's trading state status and its sustainability in SSA. It is imperative for Turkey to overcome all these challenges and to intensify symmetric trade relations with SSA countries if it wants to be an efficient trading state in this region in line with Rosecrance's conception.

REFERENCES

Achilles, K., et al. (2015, March). *Turkish Aid Agencies in Somalia: Risks and Opportunities for Building Peace.* Saferworld and Istanbul Policy Center.

Angey, G. (2018). The Gülen Movement and the Transfer of a Political Conflict from Turkey to Senegal. *Politics Religion and Ideology, 19*(1), 53–68.

Aybar, S. (2018, January 15). *Turkey Is in Africa to Stay as an Equal Partner.* Turkish and African Civil Society Organizations (TASAM).

Bacchi, E. (2016, April). *The Strategic Guidelines of Turkey's Foreign Policy According to Ahmet Davutoglu—Turkey's Opening to Africa Policy: The Case of Ethiopia.* Università Degli Studi Di Perugia.

Brawley, M. R. (2005). The Rise of the Trading State Revisited. In E. Aydinli & J. Rosenau (Eds.), *Globalization, Security and the Nation-State* (pp. 67–80). Albany: SUNY Press.

Cannon, B. 2016. Deconstructing Turkey's Efforts in Somalia. *Bildhaan: An International Journal of Somali Studies, 16*(14), 98–123. Available at: https://digitalcommons.macalester.edu/bildhaan/vol16/iss1/14.

Christie-Miller, A. (2012, June 5). Turkey Takes Lead in Rebuilding Somalia. *The Christian Science Monitor.* http://www.csmonitor.com/World/Middle-East/2012/0605/Turkey-takes-lead-in-rebuilding-Somalia. Accessed 20 October 2015.

10 ASSESSING THE TURKISH "TRADING STATE" IN SUB-SAHARAN AFRICA 269

Council of the EU. (2016, March 18). *EU–Turkey Statement* (Para. 7). Brussels: European Council of the European Union. Available At: https://www.consilium. europa.eu/en/press/press-releases/2016/03/18/eu-turkey-statement/pdf.

Dal, E. P., Kurşun, A. M., & Mehmetcik, H. (2018). Assessing the Role of Trade in the Formation of Turkey's Civilian Power in Africa. *Perceptions, 23*(1), 63–94.

Ghana and Turkey Sign Agreement to Mark New Beginning in Ghana/ Turkey Relation. 2014. allAfrica, 17 April. https://allafrica.com/stories/201404170896.html.

Has the Economy Lost Its Influence on Turkey's Foreign Policy? 2016. The Conversation, 25 January. https://theconversation.com/has-the-economy-lost-its-influence-on-turkeys-foreign-policy-53203.

Inside the New Aden Adde Airport Terminal. 2016. *The Somali Investor*, 7 April.

Interviewee by Email with an Official at TIKA who prefers to remain anonymous. Response Received On 24 July 2018 (Interviewee 1).

Investment Policy Hub. *Turkey-Bilateral Investment Treaties.* https://investmentpolicyhub.unctad.org/IIA/CountryBits/214.

Işeri, E., & Dilek, O. (2013). Trading with a Virtual Neighbor: Mongolia in Turkey's New Foreign Economic Policy in a Polycentric World [Sanal Komşuyla Ticaret: Çok Merkezli Dünyada Türkiye'nin Yeni Dış Ekonomi Politikasında Moğolistan]. *Bilge Strateji, 5*(9), 45–59.

Kirişçi, K. (2009). The Transformation of Turkish Foreign Policy: The Rise of the Trading State. *New Perspectives on Turkey, 40*, 29–56.

Kizilarslan, A. G. (2009). Economic Relations Between Turkey and African Countries. In U. Tepebas (Ed.), *Turkish and African Civil Society Organizations (CSOs): Cooperation and Development* (pp. 19–27). Istanbul: Tasam Publications.

Kucuk, Y. K. (2015, June 5). *Ten Years of Turkish Engagement with Africa: Discourse, Implementation and Perception in Somalia.* M.Sc. thesis in African Studies, University of Oxford.

Kutlay, M. (2016, February). *Whither the Turkish Trading State? A Question of State Capacity?* German Marshall Fund.

Langan, M. (2016). Virtuous Power Turkey in Sub-Saharan Africa: The 'Neo-Ottoman' Challenge to the European Union. *Third World Quarterly, 38*(8), 1399–1414. https://doi.org/10.1080/01436597.2016.1229569.

'No Going Back' for Turkey-Africa Trade. 2015. *Daily Sabah*, 21 January. https://www.dailysabah.com/business/2015/01/21/no-going-back-for-turkeyafrica-trade.

Ozdemir, E., & Serin, Z. V. (2016). Trading States and Reflections of Foreign Policy: Evidence from Turkish Foreign Policy. *Procedia Economics and Finance, 38*, 468–475.

Özkan, M. (2012). A New Actor or Passer-By? The Political Economy of Turkey's Engagement with Africa. *Journal of Balkan and Near Eastern Studies, 14*(1), 113–133. https://doi.org/10.1080/19448953.2012.656968.

Özkan, M. (2016). Turkey's African Experience: From Venture to Normalisation. *IAI Istituto Affari Internazionali Working Paper, 16*(20), 1–14.

Rosecrance, R. N. (1986). *The Rise of the Trading State: Commerce and Conquest in the Modern World*. New York: Basic Books.

Rosecrance, R. N. (1999). *The Rise of the Virtual State: Wealth and Power in the Coming State*. New York: Basic Books.

Shinn, D. (2016, March 3). *Turkey–Africa Relations*. Madison, WI: Turkish-American Cultural Center Madison.

Telci, I. N., & Horoz, T. Ö. (2018). Military Bases in the Foreign Policy of the United Arab Emirates. *Insight Turkey, 20*(2), 143–165.

Tepebas, U. (2015). Turkey's Foreign Policy Towards Africa. In U. Tepebas (Ed.), *Sectoral and Financial Transformation in Africa: Opportunities and Risks*. Istanbul: TASAM Publications, International Relations Series.

Tepeciklioglu, E. E., Tok, M. E., & Basher, S. A. (2017, March 15). *Turkish and BRICS Engagement in Africa: Between Humanitarian and Economic Interests*. Munich Personal RePEc Archive.

Turkey–Africa Relations. Turkey-Africa Forum. http://www.turkeyafricaforum.org/about-tabef/turkey-africa-relations.

Turkey Urges Africa to Close Down FETO Schools. 2017. Anadolu Agency, 19 October. https://www.aa.com.tr/en/africa/turkey-urges-africa-to-close-down-feto-schools/942192.

Turkey's Erdoğan Urges African Countries to Trade in Local Currencies. 2018. Anadolu Agency, 10 October. http://www.anews.com.tr/economy/2018/10/10/turkeys-erdogan-urges-african-countries-to-trade-in-local-currencies.

Turkey's Maarif Foundation Expands Network, Opens New School in South Africa. 2018. *Daily Sabah*, 27 July. https://www.dailysabah.com/politics/2018/07/28/turkeys-maarif-foundation-expands-network-opens-new-school-in-south-africa.

Turkey's Foundation Begins Activities in Ethiopia. 2018. *Yeni Safak*, 25 September. https://www.yenisafak.com/en/world/turkeys-foundation-begins-activities-in-ethiopia-3441901.

Turkish Envoy Foresees Vibrant Cooperation with Africa. 2016. *Hürriyet Daily News*, 26 March. http://www.hurriyetdailynews.com/turkish-envoy-foresees-vibrant-cooperation-with-africa---96933.

Turkish Ministry of Foreign Affairs. *Turkey–Africa Relations*. http://www.mfa.gov.tr/turkey-africa-relations.en.mfa.

CHAPTER 11

The Political Economy of Turkey's Relations with the Asia-Pacific

Altay Atlı

INTRODUCTION

Addressing a group of international investors and entrepreneurs on November 24, 2018, in Istanbul, Turkey's minister of trade, Ruhsar Pekcan, a former businesswoman herself, said that one cannot interpret the global economy correctly without understanding the developments in the Asia-Pacific[1] first. "The Asia-Pacific region has become the world's new focal point with respect to global production and trade," she said, "in the following decades the Asia-Pacific region will bear strategic importance for the Turkish economy and Turkey's exporters.

---

[1] In this chapter, the term "Asia-Pacific" refers to the 38 countries classified by the World Bank under "East Asia and Pacific" in its list of country and lending groups. These countries belong to the subgroupings commonly called as North, East, and Southeast Asia as well as Oceania, and they include neither South Asia nor those countries in the Americas littoral to the Pacific Ocean. For a full list of the countries included, see World Bank, n.d.

A. Atlı (✉)
Department of International Relations, Koç University, Istanbul, Turkey
e-mail: aatli@ku.edu.tr

© The Author(s) 2020
E. Parlar Dal (ed.), *Turkey's Political Economy in the 21st Century*, International Political Economy Series,
https://doi.org/10.1007/978-3-030-27632-4_11

As Turkey, we are implementing policies in accordance with this global megatrend" (BloombergHT 2018).

The Turkish government, in collaboration with the representative institutions of the country's business community, has indeed taken substantial steps over the past few years with the purpose of improving economic ties with the Asia-Pacific. Two of the four countries that were designated in 2018 by the Ministry of Trade as "priority markets" for Turkish exporters, China and India, are in the Asia-Pacific.[2] Other ministries are following suit; for the Ministry of Foreign Affairs, the Asia-Pacific is of great importance "for the diversification of our export markets, attracting foreign direct investment to our country and securing international support for our political positions" (MFA, n.d). China, being the second largest economy of the world, is very much at the center of Ankara's attention, and several Turkish ministries have included specific objectives with regard to the rising economic powerhouse of the Asian continent in their action plans and policy papers (Atlı 2018a), yet in the meantime, other parts of the Asia-Pacific are not neglected either, as evidenced by the fact that in 2017, after years of diplomatic efforts, Turkey has commenced "sectoral dialogue partnership for stronger cooperation" with the Association of Southeast Asian Nations (ASEAN) (Anadolu Agency 2017).

Turkey's interest in improving economic relations with the countries of the Asia-Pacific is real and profound, and it is in line not only with the conjunctural realities of the global economy today but also with Ankara's efforts for greater foreign policy proactivism, which "did not detach Turkey from its historical and strategic ties but aimed to develop a more multi-faceted and global outlook via increasing Turkey's outreach to the Middle East, Africa, Asia-Pacific and Latin America" (Baba 2017, 574). Moreover, as the Turkish economy continues to sail through turbulent waters, with a chronic current account deficit,[3] excessive dependence on external funding, and industrial productivity levels much lower than the potential,[4] the country has to make a breakthrough toward long-term

---

[2] The other two "priority markets" are Russia and Mexico (Aydınlık 2018).

[3] As of November 2018, the 12-month current account deficit of Turkey was $33.9 billion. In year 2001, Turkey had a current account surplus of $3.8 billion (TCMB 2018).

[4] Turkey has one of the lowest labor productivity rates among OECD countries, with $28.3 of GDP per hour worked, compared to $56.8 in the United States, $54.3 in Germany, $38.3 in Japan, and $34.4 in Greece, as of 2017 (OECD, n.d.).

sustained growth, a process during which constructive interaction with a rising Asia-Pacific can be beneficial. However, Turkey's economic relations with these countries, including the economic behemoth that is China, are at the moment far from producing the desired effect. As will be discussed in the following section in greater detail, merchandise trade with the Asia-Pacific is one of the largest sources of Turkey's deficit, whereas foreign direct investment (FDI) from the economic powerhouses of Asia into the Turkish economy is still much lower compared to investment from European countries. Turkey has expectations from the Asia-Pacific, but the Asia-Pacific is not yet a major contributor to Turkey's economic development, although there is enough reason to be realistically optimistic for the future.

This chapter will commence with an overview of the actual state of Turkey's economic relations with the Asia-Pacific, focusing on bilateral merchandise trade and flows of FDI. The argument brought forward is that while in the short term Turkey aims to increase its exports to the region and improve the value added obtain from imports, in the long term what matters for the Turkish economy is to establish a sustainable relationship with the Asia-Pacific, not necessarily with equilibrium in bilateral trade figures, but one where Turkey makes the best of its export potential while at the same time securing increased amounts of FDI from the Asia-Pacific that will contribute to the economy not only through its effect on the balance of payments, but also, and more importantly, by facilitating the flows of technology, know-how, and infrastructure into the Turkish economy. As an early case to illustrate this argument, Japanese and Korean FDI into the Turkish economy in the 1980s and 1990s will be examined, after which Turkey's position with regard to, and its expectations from, China's Belt and Road Initiative (BRI) will be discussed in detail as a current example.

Overview of Turkey's Economic Relations with the Asia-Pacific

In 2018, Turkey had the nineteenth largest economy in the world as measured by nominal gross domestic product (GDP). Turkey's GDP of $713.5 billion placed it right after the oil-rich Saudi Arabia and just before Switzerland in the ranking (IMF 2018). The year has been a difficult one for the country, with a currency crisis taking a toll on the economy, including high inflation and deteriorating levels of investment and consumption. After having registered a 7.4% GDP growth in 2017, Turkey's economy is expected to have grown by 3.3% in 2018 and to contract by 0.4% in 2019 (OECD 2018). This is not a rosy picture; however, despite the slowing domestic demand an increase in exports can be expected to offset the adverse effects and pave the way toward recovery as early as 2020 as long as and to the extent business, household and investor confidence in monetary and fiscal policies are restored (ibid.). Turkey's merchandise exports have actually increased in 2018, rising to $168.0 billion in annual volume, compared with $157.0 billion in the previous year,[5] a trend that is aimed to be further developed by the government and the business community through initiatives such as the "e-Export Mobilization" launched by the Ministry of Trade and Turkish Union of Chambers and Commodity Exchanges (TOBB) in June 2018, and the establishment of Turkey Trade Centers around the globe, of which the current number of 5 is planned to be increased to 35 in the near future as stated in the action plan released by the President's Office (TCCB 2018).

As mentioned above, two of the Turkish government's designated "priority markets" for exports are in the Asia-Pacific region. However, while this appears to be a rational objective given the current structure of the global economy, the question remains where exactly the Asia-Pacific located today in Turkey's current bilateral trade with the rest of the world (Fig. 11.1).

The figure above illustrates the geographical composition of Turkey's merchandise trade with various regions of the world comparing the most recent data, year 2018, with year 2001. Besides the overall increase in trading volumes, the most significant feature observed here is that the European Union (EU) has been the main partner of Turkey, both as an export destination and source of imports. This is a fact that is not surprising given the geographical proximity, a strong Turkish diaspora in Europe with business links with their ancestral land, and, perhaps more importantly, a customs union in effect between Turkey and the EU since 1996, allowing free movement of goods between the two entities

---

[5] All figures related to Turkey's total bilateral merchandise trade with other countries are either directly taken or calculated by the author using the data from the website of the Turkish Statistical Institute (TUIK, n.d.) unless stated otherwise.

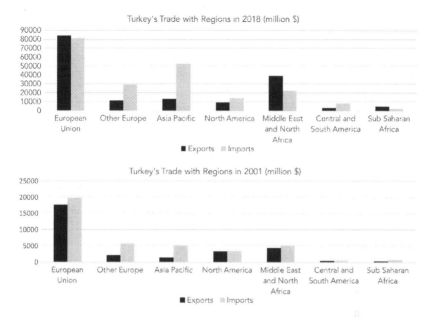

Fig. 11.1 Turkey's Bilateral Trade with the Regions of the World (*Source* TUIK)

(i.e., tariff-free), although this free movement does not cover individuals.[6] In 2018, Turkey's exports to the 28 countries of the EU amounted to $54.0 billion, corresponding to exactly 50.0% of Turkey's total exports to the world.[7] The share of the non-EU countries of Europe was 7.0%. As for imports, in the same year, EU was the source of

---

[6] The customs union between Turkey and the EU covers all industrial goods but not agriculture (with the exception of processed agricultural products), services, and public procurement. Bilateral trade concessions do apply to agricultural goods, coal and steel products. Turkey and the EU aim to modernize the customs union and to further extend economic relations to areas currently not included in the deal as well as sustainable development.

[7] In 2018, Turkey's largest export market in the world as a whole was Germany with a total volume of $16.1 billion, followed by Britain, Italy, Iraq, and the United States. Among the ten top export destinations for Turkey, there were seven entries from the EU.

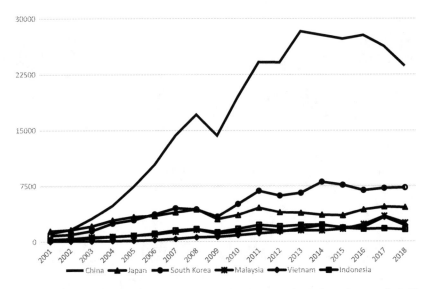

Fig. 11.2 Turkey's Bilateral Trade with the Asia-Pacific (selected countries) ($ million) (*Source* Calculated by the author using TUIK data)

$80.8 billion worth imports made by Turkey, corresponding to 36.2% in the total portfolio.[8] The share of non-EU Europe was 13.2%.

From 2001 to the current day, the share of the Asia-Pacific in Turkey's bilateral trade increased remarkably, however so did Turkey's trade deficit with this region. In 2018, Turkey's total trade with the countries of the Asia-Pacific amounted to $65.8 billion, corresponding to 16.8% of the country's total foreign trade. In 2001, these numbers were $6.6 billion and 9.0%, respectively. As seen in Fig. 11.2, despite a relative decline in the past few years, China is by far the largest trading partner of Turkey in the Asia-Pacific, with a bilateral trade volume of $23.7 billion as of 2018. This figure had reached a peak in 2013 with $28.3 billion. In 2018, Japan has surpassed South Korea as the second largest trading partner for Turkey in the Asia-Pacific with a total

---

[8] In the list of top import sources for Turkey in 2018, Russian Federation ranked first with $22.0 billion, a figure that includes Turkey's purchases of hydrocarbons from the said country. Russia was followed by China, Germany, the United States, and Italy. Among the ten top import sources for Turkey, there were four entries from the EU.

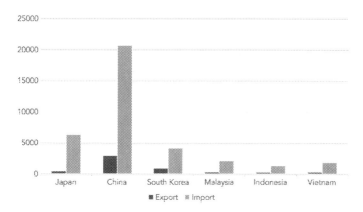

Fig. 11.3 Turkey's Exports to and Imports from the Asia-Pacific in 2018 (selected countries) ($ million) (*Source* Calculated by the author using TUIK data)

bilateral trade volume of $6.8 billion, compared to $5.1 billion worth of trade between Turkey and South Korea in the same year. In Southeast Asia, Turkey's largest trading partner is Malaysia, followed by Vietnam, Indonesia, Thailand, and Singapore.

On the other side of the coin, there is an ever-growing trade deficit for Turkey in its merchandise trade with the countries of the Asia-Pacific. In 2018, Turkey had a trade deficit with every single Asia-Pacific country with which it has an annual trade volume larger than $300 million, the only two exceptions being Singapore and Hong Kong, which are transit hubs rather than final destinations or original sources of products anyway. As seen in Fig. 11.3, Turkey's largest trade deficit in the Asia-Pacific stems from its trade with China with a massive deficit of $17.8 billion in 2018, followed by Japan with a deficit for Turkey amounting to $5.9 billion and South Korea with $3.2 billion. In 2018, 71.7% of Turkey's total bilateral trade deficit originated from the Asia-Pacific, whereas this figure was merely 36.6% in 2001.

As another metric which adequately illustrates the situation, the export-to-import ratio in Turkey's trade with the Asia-Pacific was 25.0% in 2018, representing not only a much weaker performance compared to the same ratio in Turkey's overall trade, which is three times higher at 75.3%, but also a slight deterioration since 2001 when it was 27.9%. Taken together, all these parameters suggest that since 2001, Turkey managed to establish some kind of a balance in its trade with the rest of the world, but not with the Asia-Pacific, despite the fact that that the Asia-Pacific is not a source of hydrocarbons for Turkey's energy-hungry and import-dependent economy. Although Turkey has already signed free trade agreements with three countries of the Asia-Pacific, namely South Korea (entered into effect in 2013), Malaysia (2015), and Singapore (2017), these deals appear to have done little in terms of reversing the trend for Turkey.[9]

While the numbers paint a bleak picture from a Turkish perspective, it is necessary to investigate the product-wise composition of Turkey's trade with the Asia-Pacific countries in order to gain a fuller understanding of the economic relations between Turkey and the region. Turkey's export to the Asia-Pacific countries is not only lower in volume compared with imports from the same region, but they are also less diversified in terms of the number of products subject to trade.

Turkey's trade with China provides a good illustration of this point. In 2018, the biggest item in Turkey's export portfolio to China was marble, with Turkey supplying 3.9 million tons of marble for China's total purchases of 8.3 million tons throughout the year, for a revenue of $776.9 million.[10] Marble alone contributed to 26.5% of all the exports Turkey made to China in one year, followed by chromium ores (7.6%), borates (4.8%), lead ores (4.4%), and precious metal ores (4.3%). The top ten items exported by Turkey make up a massive 67.3% of the country's export portfolio to China. In other words, Turkey has a relative limited range of products to sell to China, and it is mostly made of primary commodities such as precious stones and ores, which are low value-added products.[11]

---

[9] In additions to the agreements already in effect, Turkey is undertaking free trade negotiations with Japan, which are planned to be concluded by the end of the first half of 2019 (*Daily Sabah* 2018).

[10] All figures related to Turkey's bilateral merchandise trade with other countries at the commodity level are either directly taken from or calculated by the author using the data from Trade Map (ITC, n.d) unless stated otherwise.

[11] The low value-added nature of Turkey's exports to China is a concern particularly for the representatives of the industry that supplies the largest volume among all products exported, i.e., marble. Turkey sells the marble to China in raw form at lower prices, and buys back processed marble at higher prices, which remains a major concern. Moreover, currently around hundred marble quarries in Turkey are now Chinese-owned.

11 THE POLITICAL ECONOMY OF TURKEY'S RELATIONS ...   279

What Turkey buys from China in return is more diversified and higher in value added. In 2017, the largest import item in this respect was telephone sets with a price tag of $2.8 billion, followed by automatic data-processing machines and units thereof valued at $1.3 billion, and both items related to Turkey's purchases of the products of international mobile phone handset makers that are "assembled in China" as well as products that are related to the supply chains of large Chinese telecommunication companies like Huawei and ZTE that are active in the Turkish market for almost two decades now. These products are followed by synthetic filament yarn, parts of transmission devices and motor vehicles, and electrical transformers, with the top ten items in the list making up 31.2% of Turkey's whole import portfolio from China, which indicated a greater diversity at the product level compared with exports.

Turkey's trade with Japan exhibits a similar pattern albeit with divergences in certain areas. In 2017, Turkey's largest export item to Japan was parts and accessories for tractors and motor vehicles for the transport of ten or more persons, with 8946 tons sold during the year for a revenue of $49.3 billion. This item, which corresponded to 12.0% of Turkey's total exports to Japan, can apparently be associated with the activities of the Turkish-Japanese joint ventures that dominate the Turkish automotive sector. The rest of the list of exported products, however, demonstrate a similar patent to Turkey's exports to China, as automotive parts mentioned above are followed by fish (10.9% of all exports), pasta (10.0%), zinc ores (6.3%), ferro-alloys (2.7%), tomatoes (2.5%), engine parts (2.1%), and dates and figs (1.9%). What Turkey sells to Japan are foodstuff, metals and ores, again products with limited value added. The top ten items in the list make up 51.8 of all exports from Turkey to Japan.

As could be expected, Turkey's imports from Japan are much higher in value added; they are technology intensive rather than labor intensive in production. At the top of the list are tractor and motor vehicle parts, motor vehicles themselves, bulldozers, piston engines, electrical accumulators and transformers, and pumps. The top ten items in the list make up 46.8% of all the imports made by Turkey from Japan. In other

Turkish industry representatives argue that if the processing can be done in Turkey instead of China, more local value added will be provided on the final product, and the Turkish economy would benefit more from the whole process (*Yeniçağ* 2014).

words, Turkey's trade with Japan is more balanced in terms of commodity diversity compared with Turkey's trade with China.

Turkey's exports to South Korea are led by blood products (both human and animal), of which 24 tons were exported in 2017, making up less than 1% of Korea's total purchases of the product during the year, which amounted to 2488 tons. This product, which is extraordinary in every sense, made up 23.1% of all of Turkey's exports to this country, followed by lead ores (8.5%), engine parts (4.8%), molybdenum ores, tractor and motor vehicle parts (2.5%), and zinc ores (2.3%). In return, Turkey imports from Korea automotive parts, steel products, polymers, cruise ships, motor vehicles themselves, and certain chemicals. Turkey's trade with Korea is similar to its trade with Japan in terms of both volume and the range of products traded.

Turkey's trade with Southeast Asian countries is different than the trade with the economic powerhouses of Northeast Asia. Basically, Turkey sells to these countries low value-added products in areas such as textile, metals, ores, and agricultural produce and buys back similar items. In 2017, Turkey's leading export items to Indonesia were steel, tobacco, carpets, and carbonates, while Turkey's imports from this country were led by natural rubber, yarns, palm oil, and paper. In the same year, Turkey exported iron and steel and carpets to Malaysia and ginger, saffron, animal parts, medicaments, and fabrics to Vietnam, while buying back diodes, aluminum, textiles, and coconuts from the former and telephone sets (produced by multinational companies), shoes, cotton, and natural rubber from the latter.

This difference in the product range between Northeast Asia and Southeast Asia as a source of imports for Turkey reveals an important point from the Turkish vintage point. While increasing imports lead to an ever-widening trade deficit for Turkey, imports of sophisticated, higher value added, high-technology content products can actually be beneficial for Turkey's economy, as long as they come with relatively low price and high quality. Considering that Turkey is still highly dependent on imported intermediary products for its own production, high-technology high-value added imports of such products from these countries can and do provide significant benefits for Turkey's producers. Intermediary products with lower levels of technology are already imported by Turkey from both Northeast and Southeast Asian countries; for example, in diodes, transistors, and semiconductor devices, for which Turkey spent $3.8 billion in imports in 2017, Turkey's top suppliers are Vietnam, Malaysia, Thailand, Germany, and China. Asia offers a clear cost advantage here, as a kilogram of these products costs Turkey $34.9 when imported from Vietnam and $54.5 when purchased from Germany; however, when it comes to higher levels of sophistication and technology content, Northeast Asian countries offer advantages for Turkey here in terms of quality well. Japan and South Korea are technologically developed countries, and China is currently making efforts for a breakthrough in indigenous technological capacity through state-led initiatives like "Made in China 2025," which aims to turn China into a world leader in ten different industries by incorporating more sophisticated technology at every stage of production. This is precisely why two recent reports published by the Foreign Economic Relations Board of Turkey (DEIK), one on China the other on South Korea, recommend in both of them "focusing on the imports of those intermediary products that can add value to local production in our country" (DEIK 2016, 47; 2017, 41).

In brief, Turkey makes significant efforts to increase its exports to the Asia-Pacific, while at the same coming to terms with its relatively higher volumes of imports, as it is not so much the monetary value of the imports but the value they can provide for the Turkish economy that matters more.

Economists argue that Turkey is facing a middle-income trap, a case where after achieving high growth through capital accumulation and increases in employment in early stages of development, an economy that has reached the middle-income level fails to sustain its growth rate if higher productivity gains that are needed to further fuel growth cannot be realized. In order to avoid this trap and proceed toward the high-income status, an economy needs greater value added in production and higher labor productivity, which can be possible through high technology investment, increases in human capital, and increases in efficiency through better economic governance and institutions (Gürsel and Soybilgen 2014, 2). Improving human capital and the quality of governance and institutions is a process domestically pursued in Turkey; however, when it comes to high technology investment, relations with other countries, particularly those who invent, develop, and own the technology, are crucial.

Rising states acquire new technology through three distinct pathways: "making," wherein domestic producers are supported in the development of new technologies; "transacting," which entails commercial transactions with foreign entities that result in technology transfer; and "taking," which implies the acquisition of technology from the outside world through non-transactional means, such as learning from open sources or foreign experts (Kennedy and Lim 2018, 556–557). As mentioned above, Turkey's economy is at a stage where it needs to improve its own technological capabilities and reduce its dependence on the outside world in this realm. Importing technological intermediary products certainly do help the producers and provide them with a competitive edge; however, when it comes to acquiring new technology, it can only be hoped to have a certain degree of contribution in what Kennedy and Lim call "taking" of technology. For a country like Turkey, "transacting" with the owners of technology can help make significant leaps in technological progress, which in time may lead the way toward the "making" of technology indigenously. The question is whether and to what extent transacting with the countries of the Asia-Pacific is helping to serve this purpose. Efficient ways of "transacting" include purchasing or licensing technology and utilizing cross-border investment, in the form of purchasing foreign companies with technological assets or ensuring foreign companies investing in a country are sharing technology with domestic actors (ibid., 557).

Turkish companies in the countries of the Asia-Pacific are minimal in number and limited to low value-added sectors such as retail trade, foodstuff, low-end machinery, and basic services. According to data released by the Turkish Central Bank, out of the $38.0 billion worth of total Turkish outward FDI stock as of the end of 2017, only $766 million was invested in the Asia-Pacific, China being the most favorite destination for Turkish outward FDI with $231 million.[12] Therefore, for the time being it is not possible to talk about Turkish companies purchasing technological corporate assets in the countries of the Asia-Pacific. When it comes to companies from the Asia-Pacific investing in Turkey and enabling some form of technology transfer, a proper starting point would be examining the distribution of FDI in Turkey's economy.

As seen in Fig. 11.4, the EU is by far the largest investor in the Turkish economy with a total stock of $124.8 billion as of the end of 2017. The Netherlands is the leading source of FDI from the EU in

---

[12] All figures related to foreign direct investment are either directly taken from or calculated by the author using the data from Turkish Central Bank (TCMB, n.d) unless stated otherwise.

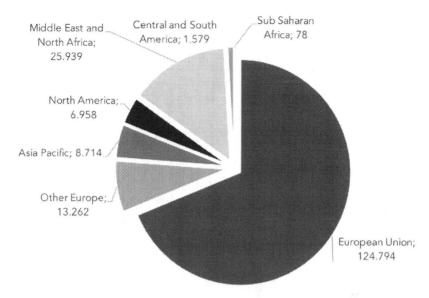

Fig. 11.4 Regional sources of FDI into the Turkish economy as of 2017 ($ million) (*Source* Turkish Central Bank [TCMB, n.d.])

Turkey with a stock of $40.7 billion, followed by Germany ($18.3 billion) and Spain ($11.7 billion). The largest source of non-EU European FDI is Russia with $12.7 billion, whereas the largest sources of FDI into from outside Europe are Azerbaijan ($9.4 billion), the United States ($6.9 billion), and Qatar ($5.5 billion). FDI from the Asia-Pacific amounts to $8.7 billion. The largest investor here is Japan with a total FDI stock of $3.2 billion, followed by China ($1.6 billion), Malaysia ($1.4 billion), Singapore ($1.1 billion), and South Korea ($1.0 billion).

European FDI has so far been a facilitator of technology flows into Turkey, supported by funding opportunities provided through European agencies such as the research and development support loans offered by the European Investment Bank (EIB) and the Technology Transfer Accelerator Turkey (TTA Turkey) initiative managed by the European Investment Fund (EIF) with the aim to commercialize applied research and scale up the technology transfer market in Turkey. However, Turkey needs to diversify its sources in order to avoid being excessively dependent on one party. The crucial point here is to ensure that the technology imported into the economy helps to improve local technological capabilities and productivity, and this is not necessarily always the case. In most instances, developed countries sell the other party the technology, or the joint venture established through FDI from these countries bring in the technology; however, they do not supply the local party with the information related to the technology. In this way, competitive advantage always remains with the country that has developed and owns the technology, who can be hesitant in sharing their technologies in a way that the receiving side would be enabled to improve its own capabilities. This was best illustrated in a case back in 2002, when the Turkish–American joint defense projects were troubled by the disagreement between the two sides over the technology transfer, an American bureaucrat in charge of the project reported to have said that "they were spending billions of dollars on research and development studies every year, so it was not easy for them to transfer technology to other countries" (*Hürriyet Daily News* 2002). This is why diversification of partners is of vital importance, and while Asia-Pacific investment into Turkey is so far limited in terms of total value compared with European investment, it nevertheless offers a channel for such diversification, and there are early examples for this, as observed in Japanese and South Korean investment entering Turkey since the 1980s.

Japanese and South Korean FDI in Turkey

Turkey's industrial cooperation with Japan dates back to the 1980s. Japanese corporations have been operating in Turkey since 1987, and several Japanese household names, such as Toyota, Honda, Isuzu, Bridgestone, Mitsui, Sumitomo, and Marubeni, have established production facilities in Turkey through the joint ventures they formed with Turkish partners, and these facilities have not only exported a large portion of their output to third countries, particularly to the EU, with which Turkey has a customs union, but they have played a key role in utilizing Japanese technology in Turkey, particularly in the automotive industry. This had a positive effect on Turkey exports as well. In 2017, Turkey exported $17.4 billion worth of motor vehicles to the entire world, and an overwhelming majority of the vehicles exported were produced by joint ventures with foreign participation, including Japanese one, as Turkey itself is yet to manufacture its first homegrown automobile brand.

Starting with early 2000s, the flow of investment capital from Japan to Turkey lost its pace, due to the adverse economic conditions Japan has been experiencing, the failure of the business environment in Turkey to offer favorable conditions for Japanese business decision makers (Esenbel and Atlı 2013), and the image of Turkey in Japan as "an ossified Middle Eastern country rather than an EU customs union country" (Pehlivantürk 2011, 111). However, this trend soon began to reverse as greater incentives emerged for Turkey and Japan to undertake joint projects, which in most cases had a significant technology transfer component. The *Türksat-4A* satellite has been a milestone in this respect. It was produced by a Japanese company with the participation of Turkish engineers trained in Japan. According to the then Minister of Transport, Maritime Affairs and Communications, Binali Yıldırım, *Türksat-4A* was "not only a satellite procurement project," but also "a project that enables Turkey to build its own satellite" and "opens the way (for Turkey and Japan) to establish a strategic partnership in space policies" (*Hürriyet* 2011). The satellite was successfully launched from the Baykonur base in Kazakhstan on February 14, 2014, and in 2016, Turkey and Japan signed a deal regarding satellite and space technologies, under which related institutions from the two countries are building an infrastructure of space technologies in Turkey (*Yeni Şafak* 2016).

The Turkish government's decision in May 2013 to appoint a Japanese-led consortium including Mitsubishi Heavy Industries and the Itochu Corporation, as well as the French company GDF Suez, to build the second nuclear plant in Turkey (in the Black Sea town of Sinop) represents another key stage in relations. Despite protests by anti-nuclear groups, Ankara has been pursuing nuclear energy due to plans for growth in the next decade that will necessitate high energy use. As is the case with the project for the first nuclear plant (in Akkuyu, built by the Russian company Rosatom) the contract requires the contracting party to train Turkish personnel, an efficient way for the transfer of technology and skills. While within the Akkuyu project Russia is training Turkish nuclear energy experts, the contract with Japan implies the establishment of a Turkish-Japanese Technology University that will include a nuclear physics program to train experts for the Sinop plant. The decree for the establishment of the university was published in Turkey's Official Gazette on June 24, 2017. In late 2018, reports circulating in the Japanese media claimed that the Japanese side is dropping the project due to rising costs; however, no official announcement has been made to that effect (*Asahi Shimbun* 2018).

Japanese companies have also actively taken part in several large infra-structure projects in Turkey including the Fatih Sultan Mehmet Bridge over the Bosphorus, the Golden Horn Bridge, the Marmaray subway system crossing underneath the Bosphorus, and the Osmangazi Bridge spanning the Izmit Bay, which brought to Turkey Japanese technology and know-how as well as Japanese finance through institutions such as the Japan International Cooperation Agency (JICA) (Pehlivantürk 2011, 112).

South Korean companies followed a similar pattern with their Japanese counterparts when entering the Turkish market. Starting with the early 1990s, companies like Hyundai, Daewoo, LG, Samsung, and Korea Tobacco formed joint ventures with Turkish partners in industries such as the automotive sector, electrical appliances, electronics, and energy, producing in Turkey and selling not only in the domestic market, but also exporting to the EU and Turkey's near neighborhood, while at the same bringing in technology, know-how and expertise into Turkey. Korean companies have also participated in large infrastructure projects such as the Eurasia Tunnel connecting the European and Asian sides of Istanbul and Yavuz Sultan Selim Bridge over the Bosphorus, while new projects such as the 1915 Çanakkale Bridge connecting the two sides of the Dardanelles strait and Turkey's largest solar power facility are on the pipeline.

The scale and influence of Japanese and Korean joint ventures in Turkey are best illustrated in the ranking of the 500 largest industrial enterprises of Turkey as compiled by the Istanbul Chamber of Commerce (ISO).

CHINESE INVESTMENT IN TURKEY AND THE BELT AND ROAD INITIATIVE

If Chinese companies were to be included in Table 11.1 above, the only entry would have been CSUN Eurasia, a producer of solar energy cells, which ranked 418th with annual sales of TL 376.6 million. Energy is a significant sector for joint projects by Turkey and China, and in addition to projects in solar energy, hydro-energy, coal, and renewables, nuclear energy is emerging as an area of cooperation between the two countries. Following the two nuclear plants mentioned above, one currently under construction by a Russian company and the other planned to be built by a Japanese-French consortium, a third nuclear plant will

Table 11.1 Japanese and Korean companies in Istanbul Chamber of Commerce 500 rankings

2017 rank	2016 rank	Name of enterprise	Number of employees	Production-based sales (million TL)	Exports (million $)
3	6	Toyota	5339	17,830.5	4593.8
10	8	Hyundai Assan	n/a	8361	1986.4
56	57	Brisa Bridgestone Sabancı	2726	2088.1	184.3
60	103	Honda	1239	1909.7	n/a
92	64	Japan Tobacco International	481	1380.4	120.0
101	113	Yazaki Automotive	n/a	1259.3	n/a
143	149	Federal Mogul Powertrain	1880	992.3	229.9
157	194	Toyota Boshoku Automotive	1221	917.5	12.8
170	150	Anadolu Isuzu	875	862.0	60.6
254	283	Kansai Altan Paint	808	616.3	8.3
265	311	İnci GS Yuasa Batteries	n/a	594.7	n/a
301	317	Polisan Kansai Paint	n/a	528.7	n/a
398	367	Panasonic Eco Solutions	1030	396.1	42.1
489	442	Yazaki Wiring	n/a	319.2	n/a

Source ISO500 website (ISO, n.d.)

be constructed in Kırklareli, west of Istanbul, for which the Turkish government has already signed an agreement of exclusivity with China's State Nuclear Power Technology Corporation (SNPTC) in 2014. Turkey aims to achieve greater self-sufficiency in terms of energy security, and this requires, in addition to indigenous energy generation, technological capabilities and know-how that will ensure sustainability in the long run. The Chinese option ensures diversification of partners for Turkey as well as transfer of technology and know-how in this field. In the meantime, the Turkish–Chinese Agreement for Cooperation in Peaceful Uses of Nuclear Energy that has entered into effect in June 2016 covers a whole range of activities where the two countries will cooperate, including designing, constructing, and operating nuclear plants, joint research and development, mining, and waste management.

Telecommunication is another field where Turkey attracts significant levels of investment from China. Huawei, the global information and communication technologies provider, is active in Turkey since 2002, and despite being excluded from projects in Western countries due to "national security" reasons, the company has been expanding its activities in Turkey recently. It has started with a representative office Ankara, eventually moving to Istanbul and turning Turkey into a base for operations in Central Asia, the Caucasus, Ukraine, and Belarus. Besides supplying telecommunication infrastructure equipment and services for Turkish landline and GSM operators, Huawei opened a research and development center in Istanbul in 2010, its largest center of this kind outside China. With the participation of Turkish engineers, this center designs and implements new technologies, while the laboratory the company has launched in cooperation with Istanbul Technical University is also serving the purpose of joint technological development between Turkey and China. Another Chinese telecommunications company, ZTE, has purchased a 48% stake in Turkey's Netaş and is actively pursuing projects including those in research and development.

In the realm of military technologies, Turkey has been cooperating with China since the early 1990s. In 1997, Turkey signed a contract with China for the procurement of rockets for licensed assembly in Turkey, which were produced under the Turkish designation *Kasırga*. One year later, Turkey began to cooperate with China on advanced short-range surface-to-surface missiles, and the first of these armaments, named *Yıldırım*, was deployed in 2001. A different variant of this missile as well as the guided air-to-surface missile, *Cirit*, was subsequently developed in cooperation by the Scientific and Technological Research Council of Turkey (TUBITAK), Mechanical and Chemical Industry Corporation (MKEK), and the state-owned China Aerospace Science and Industry Corporation, to be produced by the Turkish company Roketsan.

In September 2013, the Turkish government decided to open negotiations with China Precision Machinery Export-Import Corporation (CPMIEC) to jointly develop a long-range air and missile defense system. This was a controversial decision, which drew swift and severe reaction from Turkey's Western allies, because the Chinese company in question was under American sanctions for violating the Iran, North Korea, and Syria Nonproliferation Act, and also because the particular missile defense system proposed by the Chinese company was incompatible with the NATO missile defense shield already installed on Turkish territory. What mattered for Turkey's policy makers was that not only that the Chinese offer came with the lowest price tag, but also that the Chinese side was the only one offering joint production with Turkey, in contrast with all the other bidders who simply proposed to sell the final product to Turkey, without providing access to the technology itself. In this case, Turkey was primarily aiming to "gain know-how to develop its own long-range missile system and to expand the indigenous capabilities" in a move that "astounded (Turkey's) transatlantic allies, (yet) cohered perfectly with Turkey's broader defence industrial strategy" (Kibaroğlu and Sazak 2016). After more than two years of negotiations, Ankara decided to annul the tender and to focus on local development instead; however, the whole event showed that China is seriously regarded as a partner that can help Turkey to improve its technological capabilities.

A major area of Chinese involvement in Turkey's economy refers to large infrastructure projects. As early as the 1980s, the state-owned China Machinery Engineering Corporation (CMEC) entered the Turkish market with a number of small-scale hydro-energy projects, eventually launching larger coal mine infrastructure projects and entering Turkey's thermal energy sector. The technology brought by the company has been a crucial contribution to the development of the relevant industries in Turkey.

Recent infrastructure projects undertaken by Chinese companies in Turkey focus predominantly on the transportation infrastructure, and the BRI is opening up new possibilities and raising expectations in this area. The BRI, which aims to improve connectivity between China, Central Asia, Middle East, and Europe through joint projects by China and countries on the route of the initiative, is welcomed by Turkey's policy makers and businesspeople. Turkey's president Recep Tayyip Erdoğan said "initiatives (like the BRI) provide significant opportunities for both enhancing the integration between the countries of the region and integrating them with the global economy. Due to its geographical position, Turkey is one of the key countries within the BRI. This project matters profoundly for the strategic cooperation between Turkey and China as well" (TCCB 2015). In a similar vein, the chairwoman of Turkey's most influential business organization, Turkish Industry and Business Association (TUSIAD), Cansen Başaran-Symes stated "(The BRI) is a giant project that will profoundly affect the economies of several countries. Turkey has to be in the project, as a connector between China, Central Asia and the Caspian on the one side and Europe on the other, as this is the shortest and most competitive route" (*Fortune Turkey* 2016). The arguments made by Erdoğan and Başaran-Symes are similar: Turkey is located geographically between Europe and Asia; therefore, it has a key position on the BRI, and this is important for both Turkey's connectivity with the neighboring regions and Turkey's relations with China.

So far, the BRI is more about expectations and less about actual results for Turkey. Currently the only investment project that can be classified under the BRI header is the 2015 purchase of a 65% stake at Kumport near Istanbul, Turkey's third largest seaport in terms of container processing capacity, by a consortium of Chinese companies, namely COSCO Pacific, China Merchants Group, and China Investment Corporation, for a sum of $940 million. This is for the time being the largest Chinese investment in Turkey in terms of value, and enabling China to launch a new regional service of container shipping that connects the ports in Northern Europe and those in the Mediterranean (XinhuaNet 2017), it forms a segment of the twenty-first-century Maritime Silk Road, which is the sea route part of the BRI.[13] Chinese companies have already taken part in four different projects related to Turkey's railroad network, including segments of the Istanbul-Ankara high-speed railway line; however, these products predate the BRI which was first mentioned by China's president Xi Jinping in 2013.

Turkey wants to improve its transportation infrastructure, and this idea fits very well with the objectives of the BRI, which offers significant prospects for developing Turkey's domestic transportation network, enhancing Turkish economy's linkages with foreign markets, and consolidating Turkey's position as an economic hub between Europe and Asia. As mentioned above, BRI is so far more about expectations rather than actual outcomes, but it has to be noted that there are certain advantages that can help turn these expectations into concrete results for Turkey as well. First of all, the two governments have

---

[13] As mentioned by President Erdoğan during the BRI International Forum in Beijing on May 14, 2017, Turkey intends to add three more seaports, Çandarlı on the Aegean Sea near Izmir, Mersin on the Mediterranean, and Zonguldak Filyos on the Black Sea, into this framework (TCCB 2017).

signed a number of agreements to define the contents and boundaries of their cooperation. Two agreements concluded by the two governments during the G20 Summit in Antalya on November 14, 2015, the Agreement on Harmonizing the Silk Road Economic Belt and twenty-first Century Maritime Silk Road with the Middle Corridor Initiative and the Rail Transport Cooperation Agreement serve this purpose. Integrating Turkey's Middle Corridor Initiative, which connects Turkey with the Caucasus, Central Asia, and China, with the BRI aims to officially integrate Turkey into China's grand project. The Rail Transport Cooperation Agreement, on the other hand, foresees a total investment of $40 billion, including the proposed Kars-Edirne high-speed railway line that will span the country's entire width connecting Turkey's easternmost point with its border to Europe in the west, and covers an entire range of activities related to railway construction. Moreover, the Land Transportation Agreement signed by Turkey and China in May 2017 makes it possible for TIRs and other land transport vehicles from Turkey and China to carry cargo into each other's territories. All of these agreements provide a roadmap for Turkish-Chinese cooperation in transportation infrastructure.

The second advantage that can help to turn BRI-related expectations into concrete results for Turkey relates to the recently improving political climate and communication between the Turkish and Chinese governments. Since the beginning of 2015, president Erdoğan and Xi met in person five times for various occasions, and two other consultation mechanisms, the Turkish–Chinese Intergovernmental Cooperation Committee, and the Turkish-Chinese Ministers of Foreign Affairs Consultation Mechanism, were launched, both meeting regularly since November 2016 and the former issuing an Action Plan for the Development of Bilateral Trade and Investment Cooperation between Turkey and China.

Thirdly, improving banking and finance relations between Turkey and China can help facilitating joint investments within the framework of the BRI. The Industrial and Commercial Bank of China (ICBC) has been operating in the Turkish market since 2015, and a second Chinese bank, Bank of China, has been granted a license by the Turkish authorities to open branches in Turkey. Activities and funding facilities of these banks, such as the new credit line worth $3.6 billion released by ICBC for financing energy and transportation infrastructure projects in Turkey (*Dünya* 2018), can be expected to be useful in this respect.

In the meantime, two Turkish banks, Garanti and İşbank, are active in China, albeit only at the level of representative offices.

There are also risks and disadvantages involved. Most importantly, despite improving dialogue between the two sides, the issue of the Uyghur, a Muslim-Turkic ethnic minority in the Xinjiang Uyghur Autonomous Region of China with a sizable diaspora in Turkey, remains as a factor still undermining trust and confidence between Turkey and China, although some progress has been made toward a mutual understanding on this issue that would address both sides' concerns (Atlı 2018b).

CONCLUSION

Turkey is making efforts to improve its relations with the countries of the Asia-Pacific, with the motivation being predominantly economic in nature. This a region with which Turkey is running large and growing trade deficits, and facing this situation, Turkey wants to improve its exports as much as possible, to ensure that imports made from these countries add value to Turkey's economy especially in the form of high quality intermediary products and to achieve a more balanced economic relationship by drawing more investment from the countries of the region, which would not only imply inflows of capital into the Turkish economy, but also, and more importantly, help Turkey to close its gaps in technology, know-how, energy sufficiency, and infrastructure. While an overwhelming majority of FDI in the Turkish economy originates from Europe, investment from the Asia-Pacific offers similar prospects as well. Japanese and Korean investment coming into Turkey starting with the 1980s has benefited the Turkish economy in this way, and more recently, Chinese investment is following the same path, with rising expectations on Turkey's behalf due to the newly launched BRI, which promises to contribute significantly to turning Turkey into a transit hub between Europe and Asia. There is a favorable political environment for Turkey's improved economic relations with the Asia-Pacific as well; Turkey's relations with Japan and South Korea have historically been cordial, relations with China are improving despite ups and downs, and in Southeast Asia, Turkey's status of a sectoral dialogue partner of ASEAN provides a firm footing for furthering relations.

This rapprochement of Turkey with the countries of the Asia-Pacific does not, however, represent an attempt for replacing the West as an economic partner. As discussed in detail in the above sections and supported with statistics, Turkey remains deeply tied to the West economically, and it is simply impossible for Turkey's economic relations with the Asia-Pacific to reach the level of relations with the West in the foreseeable future. Moreover, Turkey and the West share mutual economic interests established and institutional linkages that have been developed over decades. Substituting Europe and the United States as economic partners with the countries of the Asia-Pacific, even with the world's new economic superpower China, is not an option, and a wiser choice for Turkey is to diversify the portfolio, to maintain and further develop economic linkages with the established partners in the West, while at the same time exploring opportunities with potential partners in the Asia-Pacific. If Turkey wants to establish itself as a global player in an increasingly interconnected and interdependent world, there is no other option, anyway.

BIBLIOGRAPHY

Albayrak: 3,6 Milyar Dolarlık Kredi Paketi Tamamlandı. (2018, July 26). *Dünya*. https://www.dunya.com/finans/haberler/albayrak-36-milyar-dolarlik-kredi-paketi-tamamlandi-haberi-423604.

Atlı, A. (2018a, August 11). Turkey Sees Long-Term Partner in China. *Asia Times*. http://www.atimes.com/article/turkey-sees-long-term-partner-in-china.

Atlı, A. (2018b). Making Sense of Turkey's Rapprochement with China. *On Turkey*, no. 7, German Marshall Fund of the United States. http://www.gmfus.org/publications/making-sense-turkeys-rapprochement-china.

Baba, G. (2017). The Waves of Turkey's Proactive Foreign Policy Hitting South-Asian Coasts: Turkey-Bangladesh Relations. *Journal of Administrative Sciences*, 15(30), 573–584.

Central Bank of the Republic of Turkey (TCMB). 2018. *Ödemeler Dengesi İstatistikleri*. http://tcmb.gov.tr/wps/wcm/connect/609ef884-3b3c-4bc3-84fe-9254244c3490/odemelerdengesi.pdf.

China's COSCO Shipping Lines Opens New Service for Northern Europe, Mediterranean. XinhuaNet. April 10, 2017. http://news.xinhuanet.com/english/2017-04/10/c_136194731.htm.

Ekonomide Yeni Öncelik: Çin-Meksika-Rusya-Hindistan. *Aydınlık*, August 4, 2018. https://www.aydinlik.com.tr/ekonomide-yeni-oncelik-cin-meksika-rusya-hindistan-ekonomi-agustos-2018.

294 A. ATLI

Esenbel, S., & Atlı, A. (2013). *Turkey's Changing Foreign Policy Stance: Getting Closer to Asia?* Middle East Institute. https://www.mei.edu/publications/turkeys-changing-foreign-policy-stance-getting-closer-asia.

Foreign Economic Relations Board of Turkey (DEIK). (2016). *Asya Yüzyılında Ejder & Hilal: Türkiye-Çin Ekonomik İlişkilerinin Geliştirilmesi için Bir Yol Haritası.* https://www.deik.org.tr/uploads/cin-raporu-2.pdf.

Foreign Economic Relations Board of Turkey (DEIK). (2017). *Türkiye ve Güney Kore: Kan Kardeşliğini Daha Güçlü Bir Ekonomik Ortaklığa Dönüştürmek için Öneriler.* https://www.deik.org.tr/uploads/turkiye_guney_kore_oneriler_eylul_2017.pdf.

Gürsel, S., & Soybilgen, B. (2014). *Turkey is on the Brink of Middle Income Trap.* BETAM Research Brief, no. 13/154.

International Monetary Fund (IMF). (2018). *World Economic Outlook Database, October 2018 Edition.* https://www.imf.org/external/pubs/ft/weo/2018/02/weodata/index.aspx.

International Trade Centre (ITC). *Trade Map.* https://trademap.org.

Istanbul Chamber of Commerce (ISO). (n.d.). *Türkiye'nin 500 Büyük Sanayi Kuruluşu.* http://www.iso500.org.tr.

Japan Dropping Nuclear Plant Export to Turkey over Rising Costs. *Asahi Shimbun,* December 6, 2018. http://www.asahi.com/ajw/articles/AJ201812060029.html.

Kennedy, A. B., & Lim, D. J. (2018). The Innovation Imperative: Technology and US-China Rivalry in the Twenty-First Century. *International Affairs,* 94(3), 553–572.

Kibaroğlu, M., & Sazak, S. C. (2016, February 3). *Why Turkey Chose, and Then Rejected, a Chinese Air-Defense Missile.* Defense One. http://www.defenseone.com/ideas/2016/02/turkey-china-air-defense-missile/125648.

Mermer Ocağı Çinlilere Geçti. (2014, July 10). *Yeniçağ.* https://www.yenicaggazetesi.com.tr/100-mermer-ocagi-cinlilere-gecti-99902h.htm.

Ministry of Foreign Affairs (MFA). (n.d.). *Asya-Pasifik Ülkeleri İle İlişkiler.* http://www.mfa.gov.tr/dogu-asya-ve-pasifik-ulkeleri-ile-iliskiler.tr.mfa.

Office of the President of the Republic of Turkey (TCCB). (2015, July 30). *Cumhurbaşkanı Erdoğan, Türkiye-Çin İş Forumu'na Katıldı.* https://tccb.gov.tr/haberler/410/34000/cumhurbaskani-erdogan-turkiye-cin-is-forumuna-katildi.html.

Office of the President of the Republic of Turkey (TCCB). (2017, May 14). *Bölgemizde İstikrar ve Refah Temelli Yeni Bir Dönemin Kapıları Aralanacak.* https://www.tccb.gov.tr/haberler/410/75192/bolgemizde-istikrar-ve-refah-temelli-yeni-bir-donemin-kapilari-aralanacak.html.

Office of the President of the Republic of Turkey (TCCB). (2018). *100 Günlük İcraat Programı.* https://www.tccb.gov.tr/assets/dosya/100_GUNLUK_ICRAAT_PROGRAMI.pdf.

11 THE POLITICAL ECONOMY OF TURKEY'S RELATIONS ... 295

Organization for Economic Cooperation and Development (OECD). (2018, November). *Turkey—Economic Forecast Summary.* http://www.oecd.org/eco/outlook/turkey-economic-forecast-summary.htm.

Organization for Economic Cooperation and Development (OECD). (n.d.). *Level of GDP per Capita and Productivity.* https://stats.oecd.org/Index.aspx-?DataSetCode=PDB_LV&_ga=2.232652319.1470440593.1549189117-1567909275.1549189117.

Önümüzdeki On Yıllarda Asya Pasifik Bölgesi Stratejik Bir Öneme Sahip. BloombergHT, November 24, 2018. https://www.bloomberght.com/haberler/haber/2175493-onumuzdeki-on-yillarda-asya-pasifik-bolgesi-stratejik-bir-oneme-sahip.

Pehlivantürk, B. (2011). Turkish-Japanese Relations: Turning Romanticism into Rationality. *International Journal, 67*(1), 101–117.

Turkey Becomes Sectoral Dialogue Partner of ASEAN. Anadolu Agency, August 8, 2017. https://www.aa.com.tr/en/asia-pacific/turkey-becomes-sectoral-dialogue-partner-of-asean/877622.

Turkey Hopes to Sign Free Trade Deal with Japan by 2019, Minister Says. *Daily Sabah,* September 19, 2018. https://www.dailysabah.com/economy/2018/09/19/turkey-hopes-to-sign-free-trade-deal-with-japan-by-2019-minister-says.

Turkey's Defense Procurement from US Challenged by Disagreement Over Technology Transfer. *Hürriyet Daily News,* March 28, 2002.

Turkish Statistical Institute (TUIK). *Dış Ticaret İstatistikleri.* http://tuik.gov.tr/PreTablo.do?alt_id=1046.

Türkiye ile Japonya Arasında Uzay İşbirliği. Yeni Şafak, September 8, 2016. https://www.yenisafak.com/teknoloji/turkiye-ile-japonya-arasinda-uzay-isbirligi-2528666.

TÜRKSAT 4A Haberleşme Uydularının İmza Töreni. *Hürriyet,* March 7, 2011. http://www.hurriyet.com.tr/teknoloji/turksat-4a-haberlesme-uydularinin-imza-toreni-17204869.

TÜSİAD 'Çin'i Anlamak & Çin ile İş Yapmak' Konferansını Düzenledi. *Fortune Turkey.* December 16, 2016. http://www.fortuneturkey.com/tusiad-cini-anlamak-cin-ile-is-yapmak-konferansini-duzenledi-41397.

World Bank. (n.d.). *World Bank Country and Lending Groups.* https://datahelpdesk.worldbank.org/knowledgebase/articles/906519-world-bank-country-and-lending-groups.

INDEX

A
African partners, 260, 262
Aid-benevolence-export triangle, 135, 139
Arab Spring, 3, 21, 117, 221, 222, 232, 236
Arab states, 220–222
Asia-Pacific, 4, 23, 24, 185, 271–274, 276–278, 281–284, 292, 293
Association of Southeast Asian Nations (ASEAN), 174, 175, 179, 272, 292
automotive sector, 24, 279, 286

B
banking and finance relations, 291
Beijing Consensus (BJC), 4, 5, 10, 12, 18, 164, 165, 184
Belt and Road Initiative (BRI), 23, 24, 175, 273, 286, 289–292
Brazil, Russia, India, China and South Africa (BRICS), 166, 169, 170, 172, 187, 250

C
Central Asia, 137, 157, 199, 205, 208, 209, 217, 220, 221, 223, 245, 246, 248, 249, 288–291
China, 2, 11, 23, 24, 39, 52, 166, 169, 173, 175, 177–179, 182, 185–187, 197, 200, 224, 240, 243, 265, 266, 272, 273, 276–283, 286, 288–293
China Machinery Engineering Corporation (CMEC), 289
China Precision Machinery Export-Import Corporation (CPMIEC), 288
Civil Society Organizations (CSOs), 25, 142, 260
civil war, 3, 7, 16, 196, 222, 227, 232, 243, 244
Cold War, 134, 137, 198, 219
Common Market for Eastern and Southern Africa (COMESA), 252
Community of Latin American and Caribbean States (CELAC), 171
cooperation, 18, 20–22, 139, 164, 165, 169, 175, 178–180, 182,

---

© The Editor(s) (if applicable) and The Author(s) 2020
E. Parlar Dal (ed.), *Turkey's Political Economy in the 21st Century*, International Political Economy Series,
https://doi.org/10.1007/978-3-030-27632-4

297

298 INDEX

187, 188, 208, 220, 223, 236, 239, 241, 242, 244, 247, 252, 263, 272, 284, 286, 288, 289, 291
corruption, 34, 127, 172, 173, 175, 188, 197
crisis, 2, 4, 5, 7, 9, 13–15, 21, 31–33, 40, 46, 48, 51–53, 55, 56, 58–61, 63–65, 70, 81, 90–92, 116, 146, 164, 166, 172, 180, 187, 210, 222, 273

D
development aid, 2, 19, 133, 197, 201, 252–254, 260
developmentalist state, 10–12
Development Assistance Committee (DAC), 133, 134, 148, 153, 177, 196
Development of the Economic Relations, 251
diplomacy, 134–139, 157, 164, 182, 187, 200, 201, 220, 252, 260, 267
Disaster and Emergency Management Presidency (AFAD), 116, 201, 253
distribution, 13, 14, 20, 65, 67, 68, 70, 72, 74, 81, 82, 95, 100, 121, 256, 282
domestic environment, 250
domestic market, 124, 125, 172, 286
domestic producers, 281
donor countries, 134, 135, 139, 142, 146–153, 155, 158, 177, 178, 197, 199

E
East African Community (EAC), 252
economic actor, 3, 7, 9, 89, 156

Economic Community of Central African States (ECCAS), 252
Economic Community of West African States (ECOWAS), 252
Economic Cooperation Organization, 223
economic crisis, 6–8, 10, 41, 51, 85, 90, 138, 244, 260, 266
economic development, 6, 8, 10, 81, 111, 148, 177, 184, 229, 241, 242, 273
economic diplomacy, 175, 251
economic disparities, 199
economic growth, 4–10, 15, 33, 42, 52, 63, 86, 87, 89, 93, 95, 96, 110, 111, 157, 166, 172, 173, 175–177, 180, 182, 197, 198, 232, 236
economic relations, 4, 20, 21, 23, 24, 202, 219, 220, 222, 236, 242, 253, 264, 267, 268, 272, 278, 292
economy, 2, 3, 8, 11–13, 16, 18, 23, 24, 31–34, 38, 43, 45, 49, 52, 53, 55–61, 70, 73, 74, 85–87, 90–92, 98, 111, 116, 117, 120, 124–126, 138, 142, 156, 170–173, 175–178, 180–182, 184, 185, 196, 201, 202, 210, 218, 222, 223, 229, 231, 232, 234, 235, 248, 260, 271–274, 278–283, 289, 290, 292
emerging donors, 3, 19, 25, 134, 144, 196, 197, 199, 200, 210
Emerging Middle Powers (MIKTA), 2, 3, 18, 19, 25, 164–173, 175, 176, 178–184, 186–188
emerging powers, 2, 4, 19, 157, 163, 197, 199, 210, 250, 266
employment generation, 24
ENKA Insaat, 235
European export market, 222

INDEX 299

European Investment Bank (EIB), 283
European Investment Fund (EIF), 283
European Union (EU), 6, 8, 10, 24, 34, 86, 90, 97, 103–105, 117, 118, 142, 248–251, 264, 274–276, 282, 284–286
export, 11, 21, 24, 32, 33, 42, 51, 52, 116, 120–125, 149, 150, 153, 158, 170, 173, 175, 176, 178, 181, 184–186, 202, 203, 205, 206, 219, 221–226, 229, 234, 235, 242, 244, 245, 248, 249, 252, 254, 256, 258–260, 264, 265, 272–275, 277–281, 284, 286, 287, 292
external funding, 272

F

female, 15, 67, 77, 82, 83, 86, 87, 89, 94, 96–104, 108–111
financial system, 6, 8
flow of investment capital, 285
foreign aid, 2, 3, 17–20, 134, 136, 137, 139, 140, 142, 144, 146–150, 153, 155–158, 196–208, 210, 254
foreign aid decision emerges, 198
foreign direct investment (FDI), 5–9, 20–22, 24, 64, 86, 90, 168, 170, 173, 176, 181, 184, 218, 219, 230–236, 242, 250, 255–257, 272, 273, 282–284, 292
Foreign Economic Relations Board of Turkey (DEIK), 255–257, 281
foreign markets, 229, 230, 236, 290
foreign policy, 1, 4, 7, 9, 17, 20, 22, 135–140, 142, 146, 156–158, 171, 174, 175, 178–180, 182, 185, 188, 196, 197, 199–201, 204, 219–221, 240–244, 247,

251, 254, 260, 262, 264, 265, 267, 268, 272
foreign trade, 119, 120, 170, 218, 222, 227, 251, 276
free trade agreement (FTA), 2, 20, 203, 205–207, 210, 223, 248, 252, 255, 256, 278

G

G20, 16, 18, 163, 166, 171, 178, 250, 291
G7, 166
generalized method of moments (GMM), 18, 151–153
geographical focus, 22, 250, 253
geographical proximity, 220, 227, 274
geopolitical influence, 266
Global Expenditure Support Fund (GESF), 174
global financial crisis, 13, 32, 163, 178, 227, 231, 232, 260
global order, 136, 164, 185
global peace, 174, 176
global political economy, 2, 3, 18, 19, 165, 170, 185, 187, 220, 221
Great Recession, 15, 86, 87, 90, 105, 110
gross domestic product (GDP), 7, 9, 11, 13–15, 19, 31–33, 35–38, 42–54, 58, 64, 86, 87, 89, 90, 92, 93, 95, 103, 110, 111, 140, 149, 150, 163, 167, 168, 170, 172, 173, 176–178, 181, 184, 196, 203, 205, 206, 250, 272–274
gross national income (GNI), 133, 167, 168, 170, 173, 176, 181, 184
growth, 7, 9, 11, 13–15, 32, 33, 36–43, 45, 51–53, 56, 57, 63, 64, 70, 72, 75, 81, 86–90, 92–96,

300 INDEX

98, 99, 101, 107, 109–111, 138,
148, 170, 173, 175–177, 181,
184, 227, 231, 232, 235, 236,
274, 281, 285
Gulf Cooperation Country (GCC),
21, 227, 229, 232

H
high inflation, 34, 58, 63, 274
Horn of Africa, 146, 256, 266, 267
humanitarian and development aid,
19, 138, 196, 200, 201, 267
humanitarian and development assistance, 19, 195–197, 199, 207, 210

I
IBSA, 166
import partners, 264, 265
income inequality, 3, 13, 14, 64, 68,
72, 75, 77, 81, 173
Independent Industrialists' and
Businessmen's Association
(MUSIAD), 136, 255
industrial productivity levels, 272
industry sector, 11
inflation, 6, 8, 10, 32, 36, 43, 56–58,
63, 86, 89, 92, 167, 168, 170,
173, 175, 176, 181, 182, 184
instability, 63, 117, 222, 232, 236,
250
instrumental diversification, 3, 17
integration, 4, 16, 20–22, 119, 127,
218, 219, 222, 223, 226, 227,
229, 230, 234–236, 244, 289
Intergovernmental Authority on
Development Partners Forum
(IGAD), 252
International Monetary Fund (IMF),
5–9, 13, 14, 63, 85, 86, 166,
171, 180, 182, 273

international relations, 134, 171, 183,
222, 223
international trade, 126, 267
investment, 10, 11, 13, 16, 21, 24,
31–33, 35, 36, 50–52, 56–59, 64,
89, 90, 92, 93, 106, 126, 156,
173, 175, 232, 233, 250, 251,
254–257, 260, 267, 273, 274,
281, 282, 284, 288, 290–292
Investment Policy Hub, 255
ISIS, 227, 247
Istanbul Chamber of Commerce
(ISO), 286, 287

J
Japan, 23, 186, 241, 265, 266, 272,
276–281, 283–285, 287, 292
JPD, 89
Justice and Development Party (AKP),
7–10, 12, 13, 32, 34, 38, 40–42,
48, 49, 51, 58–61, 64, 65, 101,
135–140, 142–144, 146, 147,
156, 157, 219–221, 227, 231,
232, 250

K
Know Your Customer (KYC), 126
Korea, 164–168, 174, 176–180, 186,
188, 223, 224, 276–278, 280,
281, 283, 286, 288, 292

L
labor force participation rates (LFPR),
15, 89, 92, 94, 97–103
labor market, 3, 14–16, 65, 66,
86–88, 90, 91, 93–103, 106–111,
117, 119, 127
Latin America, 20, 24, 136, 137, 139,
170, 171, 245, 246, 249, 272

Least Developed Countries (LDCs), 133, 180, 181, 183
liberalization, 5, 6, 8, 32, 180, 250
limitations on the expansion of capital flows, 236
long-term sustained growth, 272–273

M
major structural transformation, 218
material capabilities, 18, 165, 170, 172, 173, 176–178, 181, 184, 187
Mechanical and Chemical Industry Corporation (MKEK), 288
MENA Economy, 4, 20, 236
MENA partners, 218, 226, 229
Middle East, 7, 20, 24, 116, 137, 140, 146, 185, 188, 205, 206, 211, 218, 219, 221, 272, 289
Middle East and North Africa (MENA), 2, 20–22, 217–223, 225–236, 244–247, 249
middle power diplomacy, 164, 177–179, 185
migration, 117, 118, 146, 248
military capabilities, 267
military state, 22, 242, 243
Multi-national corporations (MNCs), 22, 234
Muslim nations, 201

N
neoliberalism, 138, 185
neoliberal paradigm, 185
non-governmental organizations (NGOs), 12, 136–138, 140, 142–144, 146, 157, 201, 253, 260, 267

O
Office of the President of the Republic of Turkey (TCCB), 274, 289, 290
official development assistance (ODA), 134, 140, 142, 148, 153, 170, 173, 176, 178, 181, 184, 253
opportunities, 4, 16, 17, 25, 53, 60, 92, 102, 108, 110, 116, 120, 126, 164, 172, 175, 179, 182, 183, 219, 220, 230, 233, 234, 236, 249, 253, 256, 258, 267, 283, 289, 293
Organisation for Islamic Cooperation (OIC), 222
Organization for Economic Cooperation and Development (OECD), 14, 15, 36, 64, 91, 97, 104, 105, 108, 111, 133, 134, 148, 153, 169, 177, 178, 181, 196, 253, 272, 274
Ottoman Empire, 217, 251
Ottomanism, 137, 139, 147, 157
Ottomanist ideologies, 139
Ottoman territory, 142, 204, 206, 208, 211

P
parliamentary elections, 219
political economy, 1–6, 8, 10, 12, 17–20, 23, 25, 135–139, 165, 166, 169, 185, 195, 202, 218, 220, 240
poor countries, 147, 149, 260
populism, 17, 135
post-Cold War, 198, 217, 243
Post-Washington Consensus (PWC), 2, 5, 6, 8, 10, 18, 164, 165, 180, 240, 243
Presidency for Turks Abroad and Related Communities (YTB), 201

302 INDEX

presidential system, 60
proactivism, 218, 272
PYD, 247

R
Rail Transport Cooperation
  Agreement, the, 291
raw materials, 125, 229, 258–260
reform program, 6, 8
refugees, 16, 17, 115, 116, 124, 196
regional identification (REG), 204,
  208
regional leadership, 174, 236
regional power, 137, 174, 200
revision, 13, 32, 34–38, 49, 51, 52,
  59, 60, 99
rising donors, 199
rising power, 3, 19, 200, 266
rising states, 281

S
Scientific and Technological Research
  Council of Turkey (TUBITAK),
  180, 288
self-determination, 5
Silk Road, 290, 291
social policy, 6, 8
space technologies, 285
stability, 6, 8, 17, 34, 57, 82, 125,
  153, 166, 223, 230
Sub-Saharan Africa (SSA), 2, 4, 22,
  23, 136, 137, 140, 142, 240,
  245, 246, 249–268
sustainable development, 5, 19, 134,
  148, 153, 174, 183, 187, 275
Syria, 116, 120–126, 140–142, 146,
  196, 222, 223, 226–228, 233,
  247, 288
Syrian crisis, 7, 195, 196
Syrian regime, 222

T
technology, 10, 11, 24, 109, 170,
  173, 176, 180, 181, 183, 184,
  241, 242, 251, 255, 273,
  279–289, 292
Technology Transfer Accelerator
  Turkey (TTA Turkey), 283
trade, 5, 6, 8, 10, 11, 20–24, 34, 91,
  119–122, 126, 127, 166, 170,
  175, 177, 186, 198, 201, 202,
  206, 207, 218, 219, 221–232,
  234–236, 239–244, 247–256,
  258–264, 266–268, 271,
  273–280, 282, 292
trade balance, 21, 120, 218, 224, 226,
  229
trade surpluses, 21, 225, 229
trading partners, 21, 178, 223–225,
  227, 229, 244, 248, 256, 258,
  263, 264, 268, 276, 277
trading state, 4, 7, 9, 22, 23, 180,
  219, 223, 236, 239–244, 247–
  253, 255, 259, 262, 264–268
trading strategy, 241–243
traditional donors, 134, 135, 197, 201
transacting, 281, 282
"Transition to the Strong Economy"
  program (TSEP), 6, 8
Turkey, 1–25, 31–34, 36–43, 45–61,
  63–67, 72, 73, 75, 81, 82,
  85, 88–91, 93, 97, 98, 100,
  102–111, 115–117, 120–127,
  133, 134, 136–140, 143, 144,
  146, 147, 149, 152, 155–158,
  164–168, 180–183, 186, 188,
  195–197, 199–211, 217–236,
  240, 243–268, 271–293
Turkey's African strategy, 266
Turkey's bilateral trade, 222, 252,
  275, 276
Turkey's economic relations, 219,
  227, 273, 293

Turkish Airlines, 136, 201, 252, 262
Turkish Cooperation and
    Coordination Agency (TIKA),
    20, 133, 136, 138–140, 144,
    156, 157, 195, 199, 201, 202,
    204–208, 210, 253, 254
Turkish corporations, 218, 219, 229,
    234, 235
Turkish foreign aid, 17, 19, 20, 135,
    137, 144, 146, 195–197, 199,
    200, 202, 205–210
Turkish foreign policy, 2, 5, 18, 135,
    137, 139, 146, 147, 182, 218,
    219, 247, 250
Turkish Industry and Business
    Association (TUSIAD), 255, 289

U
unemployment, 8, 10, 15, 34, 36, 51,
    56, 86–97, 99, 100, 102–111,
    167, 168, 170, 173, 175, 176,
    181, 182, 184
United Arab Emirates (UAE), 21,
    124, 186, 224–228, 232, 233,
    235, 266
United Nations High Commissioner
    for Refugees (UNHCR), 115,
    116
United Nations Security Council, 174,
    183
United States (US), 5, 31, 33, 43,
    123, 140, 141, 143, 145, 146,

150, 156, 163, 164, 166, 169,
    170, 173, 176–179, 181, 184–
    188, 196, 204, 224, 226–231,
    233, 240, 248, 249, 256, 260,
    264, 265, 283, 293
UN Peacekeeping Operations, 171,
    174

W
Washington consensus (WC), 4–6, 8,
    185, 243
Western allies, 247, 250, 288
Westphalia, 239, 242, 244
World Bank (WB), 5, 13, 21, 63, 86,
    166, 177, 182, 203, 271
World Council of Churches, 148
world economy, 4, 164, 197, 199,
    223, 241, 250
World War II, 185, 241
WW I, 22

Y
YPG, 247

Z
zero problems policy, 33
zero problems with neighbours
    (ZPN), 222, 244

Printed in the United States
By Bookmasters